NAVIGATING THE FUTURE

NAVIGATING THE FUTURE

Social Identity, Coping, and Life Tasks

Geraldine Downey
Jacquelynne S. Eccles
Celina M. Chatman
Editors

Russell Sage Foundation
New York

The Russell Sage Foundation

The Russell Sage Foundation, one of the oldest of America's general purpose foundations, was established in 1907 by Mrs. Margaret Olivia Sage for "the improvement of social and living conditions in the United States." The Foundation seeks to fulfill this mandate by fostering the development and dissemination of knowledge about the country's political, social, and economic problems. While the Foundation endeavors to assure the accuracy and objectivity of each book it publishes, the conclusions and interpretations in Russell Sage Foundation publications are those of the authors and not of the Foundation, its Trustees, or its staff. Publication by Russell Sage, therefore, does not imply Foundation endorsement.

Library of Congress Cataloging-in-Publication Data

Navigating the future : social identity, coping, and life tasks / Geraldine Downey, Jacquelynne Eccles, Celina Chatman, editors.
   p. cm.
  "This volume grew out of a shared interest among members of the Social Identity Consortium . . . funded by the Russell Sage Foundation"—Introd.
  Includes bibliographical references and index.
  ISBN 0-87154-282-X
  1. Group identity. 2. Adjustment (Psychology) 3. Social role. 4. Intergroup relations. 5. Interpersonal relations. I. Title: Social identity, coping, and life tasks. II. Downey, Geraldine. III. Eccles, Jacquelynne S. IV. Chatman, Celina.

HM753.N38 2005
305'.01—dc22

2005049001

Text design by Genna Patacsil.

RUSSELL SAGE FOUNDATION
112 East 64th Street, New York, New York 10021
10 9 8 7 6 5 4 3 2 1

CONTENTS

CONTRIBUTORS

GERALDINE DOWNEY is professor of psychology at Columbia University.

JACQUELYNNE S. ECCLES is professor of psychology and education at the University of Michigan.

CELINA M. CHATMAN is program director at the Center for Human Potential and Public Policy at the Harris Graduate School of Public Policy Studies at the University of Chicago.

J. LAWRENCE ABER is professor of applied psychology and public policy at New York University and academic director of its new Institute on Human Development and Contextual Change.

LARUE ALLEN is Raymond A. and Rosalee G. Weiss Professor of Applied Psychology at New York University and visiting scholar at the American University of Paris.

SUSAN M. ANDERSEN is professor of psychology and director of the social psychology program at New York University.

YAEL BAT-CHAVA is assistant professor of psychology at the New York University Child Study Center.

NIALL BOLGER is professor of psychology at Columbia University.

JENNIFER CROCKER is professor of social psychology at the University of Michigan, and research professor at the Institute for Social Research.

WILLIAM E. CROSS JR. is professor of psychology at The Graduate Center of the City University of New York, and is head of the Social-Personality Psychology subprogram.

ANDREA L. DOTTOLO is a doctoral candidate in psychology and women's studies at the University of Michigan.

CAROL S. DWECK is Lewis and Virginia Eaton Professor of Psychology at Stanford University.

ANDREW J. FULIGNI is associate professor in the Department of Psychiatry and Biobehavioral Sciences at the University of California, Los Angeles.

DIANE HUGHES is associate professor of psychology at New York University.

JASON S. LAWRENCE is assistant professor of social psychology at the University of Massachusetts, Lowell.

BONITA LONDON is a doctoral candidate in social psychology at Columbia University.

OKSANA MALANCHUK is senior research associate at the Institute for Research on Women and Gender and the Institute for Social Research at the University of Michigan.

TRACY MCLAUGHLIN-VOLPE is assistant professor of psychology at the University of Vermont.

RODOLFO MENDOZA-DENTON is assistant professor of psychology at the University of California, Berkeley.

ELIZABETH MOJE is associate professor in the School of Education at the University of Michigan.

EDWARD SEIDMAN is senior vice president for program at the William T. Grant Foundation and professor of psychology at New York University.

J. NICOLE SHELTON is assistant professor of psychology at Princeton University.

ABIGAIL J. STEWART is professor of psychology and women's studies at the University of Michigan.

LINDA C. STRAUSS is affiliate faculty member in the Higher Education Program at Penn State University and director of basketball operations for Lady Lion Basketball at Penn State.

TOM R. TYLER is university professor at New York University.

ELIZABETH VELILLA is a doctoral student in social psychology at The Graduate Center of the City University of New York.

NIOBE WAY is associate professor of applied psychology at New York University.

CAROL WONG is assistant professor in the School of Education at the University of Delaware.

TIFFANY YIP is assistant professor of psychology at Fordham University.

CHAPTER 1

INTRODUCTION

Geraldine Downey, Celina M. Chatman, Bonita London,
William E. Cross Jr., Diane Hughes, Elizabeth Moje,
Niobe Way, and Jacquelynne S. Eccles

Because of the increasing diversification of the United States and more frequent intergroup contact through globalization, people confront a greater number of situations that impel them to consider themselves in terms of social categories. In addition, in the United States, issues such as changing immigration patterns, the significant growth of the black middle class, and an increase in dual-career families have widened people's options for self-definition and social categorization. But this widening of options also creates greater potential for role and identity diffusion, identity conflicts, marginalization, and a host of other challenges to individuals' sense of belonging and self-coherence. Therefore, it is perhaps more urgent to conduct research that furthers the understanding of social identity and self-categorization. Toward this end, we have charged the contributors of this volume with addressing several questions concerning people's membership in social groups and their sense of who they are: What is social identity? How and for what does it matter? Which identities matter most?

This volume grew out of an interest in such questions on the part of members of the Social Identity Consortium, a working group funded by the Russell Sage Foundation to advance collaborative research and scholarship on social identity. The contributors, scholars with established expertise in some aspect of social identity, have taken up the challenge of examining people's identification and engagement with institutions such as government, community, educational institutions, work organizations, and families. The central message in the volume is that social identities matter for individuals as they confront societally and personally significant life tasks and transitions. Identities are both a source of stress and a source of strength as people go about their daily lives, especially in contexts where their most important identities are challenged or threatened. In this volume, we highlight the efforts of many scholars to understand how people seek to balance these costs and benefits and to discover ways to most effectively minimize the former and maximize the latter.

WHAT IS A SOCIAL IDENTITY?

There is a growing consensus that identities are best viewed as multidimensional and dynamic, that identity activation is highly context-dependent, and that identity transformation is constantly occurring. Although the contributors generally accept this view, their operationalization of the construct reflects the types of questions being addressed in a particular paper, as well as differences in theoretical orientation. Four main approaches to operationalizing identity are explored in this volume:

1. Identity as a social category

2. Individual differences in subjective meanings of social-category membership

3. Particular dimensions of social identity

4. Qualitative differences in individuals' orientation to social identity

(For a more extensive review of identity operationalization see Ashmore, Deaux, and McLaughlin-Volpe 2004.)

In the first approach, utilizing the most basic definition of social identity, social identity is operationalized as a categorical membership that is shared with others who have some characteristic in common. The assumption is that acknowledging oneself as a category member implicitly encompasses many important aspects of group identity, including beliefs about group stereotypes. The basis of Claude Steele's theory of stereotype threat (Steele and Aronson 1995), reviewed by Jason S. Lawrence, Jennifer Crocker, and Carol S. Dweck in chapter 2, is that the mere acknowledgment of shared category membership in a domain where one's group is negatively stereotyped can give rise to a sense of threat that undermines performance. In a daily-diary study of identity activation, Bonita London, Geraldine Downey, Niall Bolger, and Elizabeth Velilla (chapter 3) show that members of devalued groups report more events where their membership in that group was relevant than members of more privileged groups. The strength of the self-categorization approach to social identity lies in documenting the powerful consequences of simply making salient one's membership in a stereotyped group. The approach does, however, leave unexplained precisely how identifying oneself as a member of a particular category leads to underperformance. Lawrence, Crocker, and Dweck in chapter 2 undertake the task of unpacking this "black box" of social identity and underperformance by exploring differences in belief systems and motivations that can help clarify this phenomenon. Finally, self-categorization does not readily permit assessment of intragroup differences in how people identify with their social groups.

The second approach, one emphasizing individual differences in what membership in a category means, is exemplified in Robert Sellers's Multidimensional Model of Racial Identity (Sellers et al. 1997, described in Shelton et al., chapter 5, this volume).

This approach can be used to identify how specific dimensions combine to influence adaptation and adjustment. There is still no consensus on what dimensions are involved in identity, and different multidimensional theories emphasize different dimensions of identity (Ashmore, Deaux, and McLaughlin-Volpe 2004). Nonetheless, identity scholars generally agree on the significance of the following dimensions of identity (Ashmore, Deaux, and McLaughlin-Volpe 2004):

- Importance of one's group membership
- Personal regard for one's group
- Attachment to one's group
- Ideological stance vis-à-vis one's group and the dominant, or superordinate, group
- Perceptions of how others' view one's group
- Behavioral engagement with one's group members and cultural practices

Although these dimensions tend to be positively correlated, there is ample evidence in several chapters in this volume (see especially chapters 5 and 6) that identity is better understood by examining combinations of these dimensions than by treating them as interchangeable indicators of a single latent construct. For example, Nicole Shelton et al. (chapter 5) propose that viewing one's ethnicity or race positively is protective for those who perceive their ethnicity or race to be an important part of the self, whereas it is not protective for those whose race is not an important aspect of the self.

In the third approach to operationalizing social identity, examining a particular dimension of identity, two broad dimensions are typically the focus: how one sees oneself in relation to the group (the strength and positivity with which one views one's membership in the group, the closeness or attachment to the group, or the level of one's identification with the group) and how others view one's group. Illustrating this emphasis, chapter 9 examines sensitivity to status-based rejection (Mendoza-Denton et al. 2002)—which refers to one's expectations and concerns about how others will treat one because of one's group membership. The chapters in part IV all support the finding that being high on the first dimension, positive identification and regard for one's social group membership, is linked with more adaptive functioning under stress, whereas being high on the second dimension of concern about, expecting, and perceiving rejection or discrimination from others because of one's social-category membership increases vulnerability in situations and contexts where one's group is negatively stereotyped.

The fourth approach is to identify qualitatively different orientations toward identity. William E. Cross Jr.'s black identity theory, described by Linda Strauss and Cross in chapter 4, exemplifies this approach. What Cross calls "nigrescence theory" is rooted in the view that the identity-relevant socialization task of black parents is to teach their children to deal with the mainstream, with oppression, and with relationships with the black community. Three qualitatively different stances have been isolated that reflect different socialization emphases: (1) an assimilationist, or pre-encounter, stance, whereby race and black culture are accorded limited importance; (2) an immersion-emersion stance, whereby oppression and intragroup bonding are emphasized, but from a militantly antiwhite perspective; and (3) an internalization stance, whereby race and black culture are accorded much importance but in the context of a resolved, achieved identity. There are interesting parallels among these orientations and the racial ideologies identified by Robert Sellers et al. (1997).

HOW AND FOR WHAT DO SOCIAL IDENTITIES MATTER?

While contemporary discourse around issues of diversity is generally positive, it is still widely recognized that there are challenges to multiple groups' coexistence within shared spaces. For instance, in this era of "identity politics," multiple factions have formed on the basis of shared social group memberships and compete with each other for political and economic representation. One example is the post–September 11 emergence of an Arab American faction, comprising individuals from nations as diverse as Lebanon, Turkey, and Iraq. This ethnic group, comprising a number of otherwise distinct ethnicities, has emerged partly in response to others' treatment of them as one monolithic group, and perhaps also in part because their cultural and political solidarity affords them greater visibility in such a diverse society as that of the United States. In this volume we explore how people cope with such demands of living in a diverse society, especially as they work toward the accomplishment of important life tasks such as educational attainment and the formation of social relationships.

What Is Coping?

Just as the chapters differ in how they operationalize social identity, they differ in how they operationalize coping. The impact of a stressor on important life outcomes, such as health and achievement, depend on how it is coped with. Effective coping can buffer against the negative effects of stressors, and thus plays a great role in the discussion of life tasks. One important distinction in definitions of coping is between generic ways of coping, such as problem-focused coping, emotion-focused coping, and support seeking (see chapter 3), that are enlisted in the service of identity-relevant challenges, and identity-related ways of coping—called ways of enacting by Strauss and Cross (chapter 4) and negotiating identity by Celina M. Chatman, Jacquelynne Eccles, and Oksana Malanchuk (chapter 6)—that are an inherent aspect of identity development.

A second distinction is whether the emphasis is on tactics or strategies used to deal with a specific challenge or on more global beliefs that guide coping in particular situations. Both London et al. (chapter 3) and Strauss and Cross (chapter 4) identify specific tactics used in challenging situations in daily life. London et al. draw on the stress and coping literature to identify generic tactics for dealing with interpersonal stress (self-silencing, confronting the other person, transforming the situation into something less threatening). By contrast, Cross and Strauss focus on identity-related coping tactics utilized by black individuals to deal with different types of racialized situations. The types of identity-related coping that they must engage in include stigma management (buffering); mainstream management (code switching); intimacy with selected whites (bridging); positive connectivity with blacks (bonding); and experiences with personal self (individualism). Abigail J. Stewart and Andrea L. Dottolo (chapter 8) use a hybrid of these two approaches. Drawing on the stress and coping literature, they identify broad categories of tactics for coping with stress (including emotion- and problem-focused coping, and enlisting social support) but then, drawing on qualitative data, they describe how these generic coping tactics are customized to fit situations where aspects of preexisting core identities are being challenged in the process of forming a new identity.

Global beliefs that guide coping in specific situations are highlighted in chapters 2, 4, and 5. Drawing on Carol Dweck's work (1999), Lawrence, Crocker, and Dweck in chapter 2 discuss the role that implicit beliefs about intelligence, as either a fixed entity or malleable quality, may have in mediating the link between the activation of stereotype threat and performance. The basic idea is that viewing intelligence as a fixed attribute can diminish effort and persistence in the face of difficulty whereas viewing intelligence as malleable can motivate persistence. Shelton et al. (chapter 5) and Strauss and Cross (chapter 4) draw attention to how one's global ideological stance on the relation of one's group with the dominant group—for example, whether one is assimilationist, nationalist, or bicultural or integrated—can guide what specific identity-related coping tactics and identity enactments one uses in specific situations.

Other possible ways in which social identity can aid coping are briefly alluded to in several chapters. For example, a shared group identity can provide access to the support of other group members, and the shared community can also be drawn upon as a source of motivation to deal with the challenge or as a source of perceived support or inspiration. Thus, the community with whom one is identified can act as a source of perceived support that aids coping.

Life Task: Engagement in Educational Institutions

This volume examines not only how social identities matter in people's coping with a variety of circumstances but also where—in what specific aspects of life—they matter. The chapters demonstrate that identities matter for mental and psychological health, for all forms of interpersonal relationships, and for the process of setting valued goals that we are willing to work vigorously and sacrifice much to attain. The particular life task that is the focus of most of the chapters in this volume is obtaining an education. Why education? Irrespective of ethnicity, race, religion, or economic circumstances, all parents want their children to do well educationally. Becoming educated prepares people to be healthy, productive, engaged, and valued members of society, and the extent of success or failure in this task has critical implications for many important life domains. Beyond simply missing out on education, high school dropouts suffer significant psychological, economic, and social costs. Dropouts are two and a half times more likely than high school graduates to be on welfare and four times more likely to be unemployed. Dropouts are more likely to be arrested and make up over 80 percent of the prison population. High school dropouts between the ages of twenty-five and thirty-four earn about two thirds as much as their graduate peers (Bhanpui and Reynolds 2003). These significant personal and societal costs reflect the importance of successful engagement in school. In studying how the individual negotiates the life task of acquiring education, focus must be placed on what factors and experiences hinder or promote successful engagement. Despite the great importance of academic engagement in later-life success, there is evidence that not every demographic group fares equally well. The consensus in this volume is that social identity may be a critical factor that helps both explain and moderate this evidence.

At all academic levels blacks and Latinos fare worse than other groups. The testing program of the National Assessment of Educational Progress (NAEP), in existence for three decades, consistently shows that African American and Hispanic students underperform relative to their white peers in reading, math, and science when tested at the end of middle school (eighth grade) and high school (College Board 1998). NAEP data also show that at the "proficient" and "advanced" levels in all three subjects, African American and Latino students severely lag behind whites and Asian students (College Board 1998). Similar patterns emerge for SAT scores, with the gap actually becoming wider over time (Bennett et al. 2004). These achievement differences appear to not be reducible to socioeconomic status. Data collected since the 1950s show that the achievement gap exists, and remains, across all levels of socioeconomic status, and may in fact be most pronounced at the middle and higher social classes (College Board 1998). These patterns have clear ramifications for college acceptance rates and the fulfillment of life tasks that this volume focuses on.

These differences can not be attributed to a lack of achievement motivation. Black Americans' historical commitment to education is well documented. At the end of the American Civil War, ex-slaves' motivation to be educated reflected their realization that education distinguished the privileged and powerful slave owners from the poor and powerless white peasants (Butchart 1980; Webber 1978). Immediately following the end of slavery, several historically black colleges, including Howard University were established (DuBois 1935). However, in the mainstream of American higher education, reactionary forces won out and from the late 1880s to the late 1960s, blacks were systematically excluded from many institutions of higher education. In addition, blacks' elementary schools were underfunded and the few high schools available to them were trade schools. Such institutionalized economic and political disadvantage and discrimination is the historical context of today's gap between blacks and other groups in the area of education and achievement.

Today, although structural barriers to the entry of black and Latino students into college have been largely removed, at the nation's top institutions these students typically receive lower grades on average than similarly qualified white students (Bowen and Bok 1998). Those who graduate are less likely to pursue doctoral degrees and academic careers, perpetuating the underrepresentation of black students and faculty at these universities and compromising the recruitment and training of future generations of black and Latino Americans for leadership roles in society.

The subject of gender differences in educational success is an interesting counterpoint to racial and ethnic differences. Women's educational success surpasses that of men at all but the highest levels (Eagly and Karau 2002). They are more likely to complete high school and to enter college, where they are also successful. Yet differences emerge favoring men in domains that are male-stereotyped, such as the sciences, especially at the graduate school level. At that stage, women begin to drop out of the pipeline; like academically successful blacks and Latinos, they are less likely to pursue academic careers than equally qualified men. Why are women and blacks and Latinos apparently choosing not to enter some fields and why do they not pursue academic careers? In chapter 8, Stewart and Dottolo propose that the social identity of "graduate student" may conflict more with what it means to be a woman or a member of an ethnic or racial minority than to be a white man. Thus, the issue of compatibility of identities, in this case social and educational identities is of great concern in efforts to understand the enduring legacy of structural barriers to educational attainment.

WHICH IDENTITIES MATTER MOST?

In this volume we focus on identities associated with membership in relatively large, visible, underprivileged groups. Specifically, we highlight three salient organizing forces within U.S. social life, and, indeed, throughout much of the world: Race, ethnicity, and gender. Both race and gender are commonly viewed as master categories because of their perceptual salience and relative immutability. Ethnic group membership is also highly salient but not always as perceptible. Nonetheless, ethnic differences, perhaps especially among racially similar people, are the basis of much conflict and strife worldwide. Ethnicity refers to characteristics of a current or once geographically contiguous set of people that are socially as well as genetically transmitted (Ocampo, Bernal, and Knight 1993). These characteristics include cultural values, language, race, traditions, religion, and behavioral practices. Hispanic ethnic identity receives most attention in this volume.

Because race, ethnicity, and gender continue to reflect differential access to power and privilege, ostensibly similar developmental contexts pose greater challenges to forming a positive self-identity for members of less privileged categories (nonwhite, being of non-European origin, and women) than for those of more privileged categories (white, being of European origin, and men). For the privileged, group membership is less salient and to a certain extent even invisible or unnoticed, whereas for the less privileged, a sense of group membership is omnipresent. The authors focus on ethnic and racial minorities and women as they undertake important life tasks in contexts where their group membership is likely to give rise to threat and challenge.

THE AIMS OF THIS VOLUME

Contributors to this volume were given the task of considering how social identity matters in people's efforts to navigate the accomplishment of important life tasks in a diverse society. The focus is on everyday life where identity becomes vivid and real. The volume is organized along four related themes:

1. Coping challenges that arise because of membership in social groups or participation in social roles

2. Adaptive functions of identity

3. Contextual demands on identity and competing identities

4. The interplay between social identities and social relationships

Several chapters draw on multiple data sets from different research programs to address a particular question or to develop a theoretical integration. Many of the data sets are large and longitudinal and together span the period from adolescence through early adulthood. The chapters showcase the application of different and often new approaches to investigating the workings of identity. These include laboratory experiments, daily diaries, longitudinal and cross-sectional surveys, qualitative interviews, model testing, and grounded theory development. The integration of approaches and methods provides broad and deep insights into the nature of particular contexts and the relationship among contexts, identity enactments, and outcomes of interest. To conduct such integrated work in a single research program is virtually impossible, but the collaborative activities of the social identity research group is a model of how an interdisciplinary team can effectively share theories, data, and methods to make substantial inroads into documenting how social identity matters in daily life.

We now turn to a discussion of the four main themes addressed in the volume.

PART I: IDENTITY AS A SOURCE OF STRESS: CHALLENGES FROM MEMBERSHIP IN STIGMATIZED SOCIAL GROUPS

The two chapters in part I are concerned with how generally successful and engaged members of historically marginalized groups handle stigma-related stress in challenging educational contexts. Lawrence, Crocker, and Dweck take as their starting point the well-documented phenomenon of stereotype threat (ST). They seek to explain why otherwise accomplished and capable black students and women can, under conditions of diagnostic test taking, score far below the range of performance predicted by other intellectual markers found in their academic portfolios. London et al. focus on these same accomplished and capable students as they negotiate the transition to a highly academically selective college. They investigate students' perceived exposure to stigma-related stress, how they cope with such stress, and the effectiveness of the coping strategies they use. Other than to suggest that people of color and women report a generally positive transition to college, there was no evidence of persistent vulnerability of the type evident in the high-stakes testing situations where stereotype threat has been examined. Thus, although the London et al. study adds to the literature showing that many members of stigmatized groups are very adept at negotiating various forms of stigma-related stress, the stereotype threat literature shows that the protective shield–associated stigma management is not perfect. The important message from both chapters, however, is that individual differences in both coping tactics and beliefs are key moderators of the effects of stigma-related stress on academic performance, sense of belonging, and psychological well-being.

The critical contribution of chapter 2, by Lawrence, Crocker, and Dweck, is to highlight how the impact of ST can be alleviated while also documenting the important and ubiquitous nature of the phenomenon. At a point in history when structural explanations for the race gap in educational achievement were being overshadowed by personal-psychological explanations, Steele and Joshua Aronson (1995) introduced the concept of stereotype threat. Their goal was to explain how cues in situations where negative stereotypes about black achievement might trigger normative psychological defenses against threat, could then undermine performance. Lawrence, Crocker, and Dweck's review of the ST literature emphasizes that ST can be experienced by any individual who, because of membership in a social group, is "prone" to compare attributes of the group to attributes of other social groups, especially when a sense of "superiority" and "inferiority" is at stake. ST has been found not only among blacks in academic achievement but also in many performance domains and among white males and white women, Asian Americans, Latinos, the wealthy, and the working class. Evidence of ST effects in groups seldom associated with negative stereotypes demonstrates that every social group has a group image that under some conditions can be threatened. That ST effects are socially constructed rather than an inherent group vulnerability was recently demonstrated in a study of Afro-Caribbean immigrants. Whereas first-generation Afro-Caribbean immigrants are impervious to ST effects, second-generation immigrants who grew up in the United States show the effect, thus resembling the African Americans of earlier studies (Deaux et al. forthcoming).

What psychological processes link being in an identity-threatening situation and underperformance? Lawrence, Crocker, and Dweck posit that pinpointing the psychological processes underlying ST has been so difficult because a spectrum of individual difference factors may be operating, with some people being anxious, others stymied, and others being mildly depressed, in reaction to ST. They even speculate that for any ST episode, there may be a sequence of responses, and different emotions or cognitions may be recorded depending on whether the focus of research is on the onset, zenith, or climax of the ST reaction. They propose that individuals who view their self-worth as contingent on academic performance (Crocker and Wolfe 2001) and who also view their test performance as diagnostic of their ability (Dweck 1999) are particularly vulnerable to experiencing ST. The concepts and variables highlighted in their discussion lead to a certain degree of excitement that perhaps we are drawing closer to a clear view of the contents of the ST "black box." Lawrence, Crocker, and Dweck also note that student beliefs about whether other people view intelligence as fixed or malleable may affect student test-taking performance and may indeed be a particularly powerful moderator of the stereotype threat effect.

In the chapter by London et al., attention shifts from the microdynamics of people's adjustment in the important but narrow world of test taking to the broader identity adjustments and identity shifting that take place in daily life. The key contribution is a methodology for viewing and analyzing identities as they are experienced on a daily basis and for focusing on the relative impact of coping strategies in response to negative identity activation. In a twenty-one-day daily diary study, black, white, and Asian first-year college students were provided with a checklist of identity options, including choices of both personal (personality and physical looks) and group (race, gender, religious, and sexual orientation) identities, and were asked to record the frequency with which various identity "categories" were activated while the subjects negotiated a broad range of situations, both positive and negative, typical of the transition to college. Across the three weeks the typical student attributed the most significant event of the day to a combination of various personal and collective identities. That is, on some days the most significant event was attributed to personality, on some days to physical appearance (especially attractiveness to a potential dating partner), and on some days to race or gender. However, members of historically devalued or excluded groups—racial and ethnic minorities and women—were more likely to attribute the most significant event of the day to the devalued identity. Thus, for members of traditionally disadvantaged groups, the daily negotiation of the transition to college was often experienced through the lens of their social group memberships, creating challenges to feelings of social inclusion and belonging with peers and professors within the university setting.

An important finding was that the outcome of negative events, whether attributed to one's race or one's personality, depended on how one coped with them. Self-silencing was linked with a lower sense of belonging and a more negative mood, whereas transforming the situation was linked with an increased sense of belonging and more positive mood. Interestingly, confronting the situation or person did not moderate the effect of the stressor. The diary approach highlights a way of examining the frequency with which personal and social identities are linked with the most important event of the day. A logical next step would be to examine the identity profile or configuration for each participant. It may be possible to discuss "stable" and "persistent" aspects of the self-concept not in terms of the frequency of employing identity categories one at a time but as a profile that links the person's proclivities across identity domains, inclusive, perhaps, of points of intersectionality, where two or more identity categories are evoked simultaneously.

Last, London et al. report frequent use of the category of "personality," or what Strauss and Cross (chapter 4) call "acting like oneself or "just being me." This finding is replicated in Strauss and Cross's daily-diary study, and negotiating individuality also emerged in the qualitative data described in chapter 6, by Celina M. Chatman and Jacquelynne Eccles. When the primary focus is on "minority" identity adjustment, the importance of individuality can get lost. This finding is a reminder that there is no inherent tension between individuality and group belonging. In fact, being free to openly explore both the "I" and "we" aspects of one's self-concept can perhaps be considered a basic requirement of an authentic multicultural environment.

In sum, the chapters in part I show that even the most accomplished students can feel vulnerable in the face of certain contextual challenges when their membership in a devalued category is activated. But they also identify generic coping resources—both global beliefs and specific tactics—than can diffuse potentially toxic and debilitating experiences. Thus, social identities matter both for how students' experiences are shaped within academic settings and how they ultimately adapt in those settings.

PART II: HOW IDENTITIES FUNCTION TO AID THE ACCOMPLISHMENT OF LIFE TASKS

In part II, the focus shifts from the challenging aspects of a societally devalued social identity to the adaptive functions of such an identity. That is, three chapters explore how aspects of social identity, specifically ethnic and racial identity, can assist in coping and in the accomplishment of life goals. Ethnic identity is depicted as an added resource for ethnic minority individuals and identity negotiation is conceived, in Strauss and Cross's words, as more than "stigma management." Indeed, ethnic identity is described as being formed and enacted in settings where experiences of marginalization, exclusion, and discrimination are normal, and includes strategies for getting along in the mainstream, for managing intragroup relations, and for protecting and expressing one's individuality.

Together, the chapters provide an evidence-based portrait of the functionality of strong group attachment and affiliation, especially in the face of negative race-related experiences. Shelton et al., in chapter 5, draw on three distinct and rich research programs to develop a convincing argument that a strong positive group identity moderates the link between negative stigma-related stressors and distress and academic disengagement. The findings replicate across different age groups (adults and adolescents), different methods (daily-diary and survey-based measures), and different ethnic groups (Chinese American and African American). In their daily-diary study of black students at a predominantly white college, Strauss and Cross detail how racial identity can function to promote resilience in challenging environments. Using both quantitative and qualitative data from a large longitudinal study of students from the seventh to the eleventh grades, Chatman and Eccles also show how youths negotiate the subjective meaning of race and ethnicity in increasingly challenging contexts and how this impacts their behavioral and psychological adjustment.

The authors compellingly portray individuals as deliberate, flexible, competent, and capable of exercising agency as they draw differentially on components of their ethnic identity in response to contextual demands. For instance, Strauss and Cross find that bonding is more common in settings in which other blacks are present, whereas buffering and code switching are more common in situations where whites are present. Chatman and Eccles similarly find that some strategies are more likely than others to emerge when participants are in the minority or exposed to group stereotypes, and that there is a co-occurrence of particular identity strategies with particular identity functions.

The authors showcase innovative methodological approaches, which allow for sophisticated, transactional, and in-depth articulations of ethnic-identity processes and the ways they develop and shift across time and contexts. Both Strauss and Cross, and Chatman and Eccles use content-analytic approaches to organize text from in-depth interviews. This enables them to identify instances in which a strategy or tactic and a function or goal (Chatman and Eccles) or a function and a situation (Strauss and Cross) were jointly present in texts. Strauss and Cross and Tiffany Yip and Andrew Fuligni (2002), described in Shelton et al., used daily-diary methods to assess within-person variability in ethnic feelings across contexts. Chatman and Eccles used cluster analysis to construct ethnic-identity profiles and show how they change over time. The idiographic approach to categorizing identity profiles that Chatman and Eccles used reveals how simultaneous variation in multiple aspects of identity are related to outcome profiles. For instance, the group that is socioculturally embedded is strong academically but doing less well psychosocially. The members of this group were highly connected with and proud of their ethnic group and viewed it as an important part of themselves. Yet they were also aware of the negative stereotypes attached to their group and of the prospect of discrimination. Chatman and Eccles suggest that expectations of being treated unfairly may undermine their commitment to behaving according to mainstream standards, a point that is echoed in chapter 10, by Susan M. Andersen, Geraldine Downey, and Tom Tyler, who posit that people voluntarily obey the rules of groups whose authority figures treat them in a respectful, unbiased and warm manner.

The chapters in part II are an excellent starting point for the difficult task of isolating the specific components of ethnic identity that moderate the stress of being a member of a racial or ethnic minority. In fact, the data from all three research programs described in Shelton et al. (chapter 5) converge in showing the benefits of viewing race as central to one's self-definition for mental health and school engagement. The work of Robert Sellers et al. (1997), described in Shelton et al. (in this volume), also showed that viewing one's group as an oppressed minority may protect black college students against mental health difficulties.

The chapters also begin to specify the mechanisms whereby ethnic identity has its salutary effects. Shelton and her colleagues suggest, for example, that individuals who view their group as an oppressed racial minority may have a wide repertoire of coping mechanisms for dealing with discrimination because discrimination is consistent with their worldview. But this viewpoint may entail a cost: genuine intergroup friendships. Further, those for whom race is central to self-definition may be better positioned to focus on the positive aspects of their racial group than those for whom race is less central. In addition to these sorts of mechanisms, strong ethnic identity may prompt ethnic-minority individuals to rely on members of their own group as a reference point for their self-appraisal. Blacks who are more strongly identified are also probably more fully embedded in a social network of other blacks who can support them in the face of discrimination.

Finally, the chapters show that identity processes and functions shift across context. Chatman and Eccles also show considerable change in identity profiles within individuals across time. The cluster analytic techniques mentioned above yielded the same six ethnic identity profiles in eighth- and eleventh-grade students. However, many students shifted from one profile to another, probably a reflection of transitions in school context over this time period. This malleability in identity profiles points to many interesting questions for future research. What aspects of school context account for identity shifts? Are some identity constellations more or less likely in schools that are diverse than those that are ethnically segregated? Does tracking within schools influence youths' identity profiles? Addressing these questions require the type of in-depth focus on context seen in the two chapters in the next section.

PART III: CONTEXTUAL DEMANDS
AND COMPETING IDENTITIES

In the chapters by Allen et al. and by Stewart and Dottolo, the emphasis shifts from unpacking the structure, content, and processes of identity to describing the contexts in which social identities are enacted. The basic premise is that contexts, whether neighborhoods or academic disciplines, high schools or universities, place demands on the kinds of identities that people enact and on how people think about themselves and their identities. Using markedly different methodologies, the two chapters document how contextual pressure to enact certain identities is socially, relationally, and emotionally more stressful for some people than others. In particular, these two chapters demonstrate that when contexts are incongruent with individuals' important social identities, those identities may be challenged or threatened.

Allen et al. describe a large longitudinal survey study of ethnically and racially diverse high-school students living or being educated in either racially and ethnically congruent or incongruent contexts. In general, the results of their study indicated that those youths whose racial or ethnic group was the minority in their school or neighborhood context reported higher levels of depression than did youths who found their identities to be more congruent with the racial and ethnic composition of their schools and neighborhoods. Moreover, among black and white youths in racially and ethnically incongruent schools and neighborhoods, racial- and ethnic-group esteem served as a protective factor in the relation between racial and ethnic congruence and psychological adjustment. That is, when they were less ethnically and racially similar to their school and neighborhood peers, black and white youth with high ethnic and racial group esteem reported fewer depressive symptoms than those with lower ethnic or racial group esteem. For Latino youths, however, higher ethnic and racial group esteem was related to greater depressive symptoms when the neighborhood or school context was more ethnically or racially congruent.

In chapter 7, Allen et al. illustrate how the demographic makeup of developmental contexts can influence racial and ethnic identity, but also how these identities can both attenuate and exacerbate the negative effects of racial and ethnic incongruence on adolescents' psychological adjustment. The data do not, however, offer information about the mediating factors in these relations. Chapter 8, by Stewart and Dottolo, complements the Allen et al. chapter in that Stewart and Dottolo examined the influence of context on strategies for coping with challenges to social identity. Their in-depth interviews with doctoral students showed that demands for divestiture of some valued aspects of the self were pervasive for those students with nontypical preexisting identities (particularly women, people of color, and sexual minorities). Specifically, in graduate programs students are socialized according to preexisting paradigms characteristic of both academia in general and their particular disciplines. Typically, these ways of thinking and being have been shaped and developed by white males, largely to the exclusion of women, people of color, and sexual minorities. The demand to conform to a scholar identity, as it were, were met by the students in the Stewart and Dottolo study with strategic resistance, including instrumental inaction, that is, apparent non-actions that help the self cope, indirect action, and collective action, but not with direct confrontation. Together, chapters 7 and 8 show how having a threatened identity or a social identity that is not supported within a given social context can create vulnerability to certain contextually created challenges. They also show how identity can help explain why people are not doing as poorly as one might expect, given the adverse circumstances.

The extent to which contexts are shaped by the distribution of power also comes across in both studies. That the white, Latino, and black youths in Allen et al.'s study were differently affected by context, and that the white youth, in particular, did not have a strongly articulated sense of racial or ethnic identity, suggests that being part of a group privileged in systems of political and economic power may have an impact on how contexts are engaged. That the graduate students of color and the white women in Stewart and Dottolo's study felt they were required to divest themselves of identities of color or femaleness suggests a system in which certain ways of knowing, doing, and believing are privileged to the point of invisibility to the actors who benefit from that privilege. Differences in power of different social identities therefore determine the possible identities one can enact to achieve success in these contexts. Whereas the power structures in these contexts do not preclude the possibility that opportunities to learn are also available, they do make it less likely that individuals alone will be able to change the contexts at work in their lives, as many of the graduate students in Stewart and Dottolo's study recognized.

PART IV: BRIDGING WORLDS: INTERPLAY BETWEEN SOCIAL IDENTITIES AND SOCIAL RELATIONSHIPS

The focus of much of identity research has been on the ways in which a strong sense of identity or attachment to a social group enhances the possibilities for relationships. The authors of the chapters in this section take on the task of theorizing and empirically testing how relationships in turn shape people's sense of themselves and their social identities, such as their ability to form attachments to social groups. Indeed, social identities can be reciprocally influenced by many forms of relationships, including those of a hierarchical or lateral nature.

Andersen, Downey, and Tyler in chapter 10 seek to understand the influence of dyadic relationships on how individuals develop group identities and become engaged in their communities. The more specific goal is to identify the circumstances under which outsiders or members of historically subordinate groups come to develop a strong, positive superordinate identification. Toward this end, the authors draw on two theories of dyadic relationships—Andersen's theory of the relational self and Downey's theory of rejection sensitivity—and explore how they can profitably be applied to augment Tyler's group-value theory of social identity. Group-value theory posits that people identify with groups when treated in a respectful, fair, and unbiased way by group representatives. Once identified with a group, people use these dimensions of relational treatment to determine how the group views them and to regulate their self-esteem. The integrated theory provides a compelling framework for understanding the complex processes that link relationships and social identities, grounded in the significance of basic needs for a sense of belonging in dyadic relationships and in identity development. Evidence for the importance of trusting, respectful, and, especially, warm dyadic relationships in the development of attachments to social groups is shown across several studies using a wide range of methodologies. Especially noteworthy is the point that when individuals meet, they react to each other in terms of each person's personal and relational characteristics as well as their respective social-category memberships.

McLaughlin-Volpe and her colleagues also show how dyadic relationships, specifically friendships with members of other ethnic and racial groups, influence the health and well-being of young people of color. They emphasize the ways in which relationships shape the possibilities for connections to groups and institutions. Drawing on data from three research programs, they find that young people of color who resist the dominant cultural norm, which is to have relationships only with people in the same ethnic or racial group, by having mixed ethnic and racial friendships are healthier, and are more likely to feel connected to primarily white universities than their peers who do not make such choices. They find that such close cross-race friendships are particularly helpful to students of color who are most doubtful about their place in primarily white universities. Much like Andersen and her colleagues, they conclude that relationships are critical to understanding social identities, but that particular types of dyadic relationships, for example, cross-ethnic and cross-racial friendships, have the potential to strengthen the attachments that young people form to institutions. The finding critically underscores the point made in other chapters, that it is essential to consider the possibilities and limits in relationships that are imposed implicitly and explicitly by the institutional contexts in which they occur.

Institutions can structure possibilities for relationship building and, if positive relationships cannot flourish, healthy development of attachments and identities may be compromised. Compelling evidence of the importance of investigating the impact of institutional climate on social relations is provided in research by Kerstin Pahl, Melissa Greene, and Niobe Way (2000) on two urban schools. In a school with a generally alienating climate where the administration implicitly discourages relationships (whether or not cross-ethnic or cross-racial), students segregated along ethnic lines and experienced difficulty connecting with schoolmates, whether within or outside of their own ethnic or racial group. They were also uncomfortable discussing race and identity. In a school where the administration has actively made decisions intended to disrupt racial-ethnic segregation and to foster supportive connections among students and teachers, students reported having close friendships that are predominantly but not exclusively with same- ethnic or same-race peers. The students also openly and freely discuss feeling attached to their own ethnic or racial group. In sum, the institutional context sets the tone for personal relationships.

Institutional contexts that are supportive of cross-ethnic and cross-racial relationships can affect social identities not just through close friendships but also through dyadic relationships with people who neither are close nor are considered "significant others." Susan Harter (1996) proposed that adolescents believe that close friends are supposed to like you, whereas classmates do not have the same responsibility—therefore, the opinions of classmates often play a more important role in the adolescents' self-assessment than do the opinions of close friends. A similar process may be evident in the development of social identity. Whether an adolescent becomes attached to a particular social group or social identity and if so, how attached may depend on the quality of his and her relationships with peers in that social group who are not expected to completely accept him or her. If the quality of these "general" friendships or relationships is trusting and respectful, Andersen and her colleagues argue, the young person may become more attached to a particular social group than he or she would if only close friends treat them this way.

WHAT DO THE AUTHORS TELL US?

First, the authors make a compelling case that social identity matters for both good and for ill. Although membership in social groups and the associated identities can predispose people to stressors such as others' stereotype-based expectations, discrimination, and other forms of social disadvantage, they can also provide resources for coping with such circumstances. Understanding how membership in and identification with social groups can have these diametrical implications for people's lives requires a view of identity as dynamic and multidimensional.

Specifically, individuals are understood to have multiple and sometimes conflicting identities rather than a single, monolithic identity. Second, the authors also make a strong case that context determines whether and how identities matter. They do so by looking at immediate micro-settings within institutions, such as the nature of the instructions given to someone taking a test, and at the racial-ethnic composition of neighborhoods and in the everyday situations in which people live out much of their lives. Third, the authors suggest that identities are continually being formed and changed in the ongoing course of everyday life and especially in the course of social interactions and relationships. We learn about our social identities from the people with whom we interact. Fourth, by focusing on intragroup identity, the authors clearly show that people can identify with the same group in many different ways and that the ways in which people differ in this respect have implications for important outcomes. Finally, while showing how particular challenged identities matter, the chapters also highlight the integrative and individualistic nature of the self. The self of each individual combines personal, relational, and group identities. We need to remember this as we focus on explicating how social or group identity matters in daily life.

WHAT WE DON'T KNOW

In the course of telling us what is known about how social identity matters, the authors also tell us what remains unknown. First, although it is clear that contexts that challenge an important identity have negative consequences for achievement and well-being, far less is known about precisely when and why a given context is experienced or perceived as more or less challenging. A more detailed understanding of social context requires that research look beyond a demographic characterization of those who populate the context and begin to identify what specific environmental cues activate perceptions of threat (for examples, see chapters 3, 4, and 9).

Second, most of the authors assume that whereas the motivation to develop social identities may be inherent, the content and form of those identities are socially constructed and reflect individuals' socialization histories in their families, communities, and societies. Thus, perhaps to a greater extent than other aspects of development, our social identities reflect our society's views of the groups to which we belong. We need to develop a greater understanding of how identity-relevant experiences shape identity-relevant meaning systems as well as more general meaning systems. We need also to investigate more thoroughly how ethnic-identity profiles and identity negotiation strategies are shaped by different socializing forces in families and other institutions. We know from prior research that parents, community members, and others play a critical role in shaping youths' ethnic identity. However, these studies have conceived of and measured ethnic identity as a stable trait rather than as a multidimensional, dynamic, and transactional phenomenon.

Third, the chapters have focused on identities associated with devalued- or underprivileged-group membership. What the authors have not done is clarify the ways in which members of the privileged majority interpret and enact membership in social groups. To some extent, the authors have indicated that majority-group members have a less elaborated sense of what their membership in social groups means for their sense of self and of the implications of that group membership in their everyday lives. The suggestion here is that members of majority groups are privileged not only in terms of the economic and social advantages afforded them but also in their not having to explicitly consider the need to negotiate their social identities in daily life. Because their identity negotiation is less overt, investigation of it may require more implicit techniques.

Fourth, although the authors acknowledge that people have multiple identities, they are examined one at a time or when in conflict. Thus, such questions as what it means to be a black woman from Brooklyn rather than a black man from Kentucky remain to be investigated. One implication of the various identities that people hold is that particular identities or identity combinations may become more or less salient at different developmental periods and in different institutional contexts. Understanding how people manage their multiple identities may require focusing on quite different questions about how identity matters than have been addressed in this volume.

IMPLICATIONS FOR POLICY

The most important policy-relevant contribution of this volume is its evidence-based message that identities matter in individuals' navigation of a diverse society. The influence of identities on how people experience stressors, coping, belongingness, and achievement of goals in particular social contexts extends far beyond simple membership in a particular social category. Thus, for policies to be effective, they must take into consideration the different ways in which people interpret and enact their membership in social groups as well as the features of contexts that can affect these interpretations and enactments.

Often, contemporary approaches to diversity treat people's membership in social groups as categorical, and membership in a given social group is viewed as sufficient explanation for differences in a variety of domains. For example, advertising companies market their products to specific social groups—say, African Americans, women, and white males—by drawing on language and symbols they assume to be representative of those groups' subcultural orientations. Likewise, multicultural student services are emerging on college campuses nationwide that base their programming on what they perceive to be the typical needs of students from particular ethnic minority groups. Alternatively, a particularly pernicious practice is the use of racial or ethnic profiling to identify threats and criminals based on the salient demographic characteristics of the "typical offender." The research described in this volume documents the damaging effects of imposed social categorization on the individual, as well as the resulting strain on intergroup relations. In sum, the work reported in this volume shows that people's subjective representations of self in the context of their group memberships matter in many more ways than their mere categorization as members of those groups.

This volume also demonstrates that while membership in certain social groups can expose people to stressors such as negative stereotypes or discrimination, what is more important in such situations is the ways people cope with these stressors. This suggests the need for institutions to pay greater attention to building and nurturing the coping skills needed to navigate a diverse society. Schools are a particularly appropriate context for providing youths with identity-related resources that can serve to buffer the potentially damaging effects of stereotypes and discrimination based on group membership. School curricula might be revised to include explicit discussions of race and ethnicity and the history of racial and ethnic groups in the United States. Such curricular inclusion may serve to equalize the experiences of majority- and minority-group members and may also serve to give majority-group members needed resources for navigating contexts and negotiating self in a rapidly changing and increasingly diverse and complex society.

Yet attention must also shift from how well the individual navigates—or copes with—the demands of new contexts and potentially competing identities to how he or she shapes the context to maximize learning and identity navigation. One way to change contexts is to increase the representation of diverse groups at all levels of institutions, and this is the goal of affirmative-action programs. These programs have successfully increased access to institutions that have historically excluded members of traditionally marginalized groups, and thus have provided previously inaccessible opportunities for socioeconomic advancement. Yet, as several of the authors point out (see chapters 3, 5, 8, 9), institutions often fall short of providing the support that members of traditionally marginalized groups need in order to succeed. For example, the benefits of gaining admission to a top law or medical school might be significantly dampened by the threat experienced as a result of continued marginalization and exclusion within that context. Moreover, individuals most vulnerable to experiencing such threat may be least likely to enter institutions where, judging by the institution's past history, they expect to experience marginalization. The chapters of McLaughlin-Volpe, Mendoza-Denton, and Shelton, and Andersen, Downey, and Tyler in particular suggest that the institutional "welcome mat" needs to lead into a relational atmosphere where individuals are treated fairly, respectfully, and warmly, irrespective of their social identities, and where opportunities for developing friendships across racial, ethnic, and other lines of category demarcation are supported.

The authors suggest the futility of basing the creation of such an atmosphere on a color-blind philosophy. This philosophy underlay the media campaigns in the 1980s and '90s that promoted the idea of the "cultural melting pot" in order to create a sense of unity and harmony among members of different social and cultural groups residing in the United States. More recently, such campaigns have been replaced with efforts to celebrate diversity without losing focus on the individual group identities as an important defining characteristic of the self. Models of society as a "mosaic" allow individuals to maintain their individual group identities while also identifying with the larger society. Research reported in this volume supports the notion that the connection with ethnic, racial, or other social identities is a central part of who we are and such connection can provide a valuable buffer against the negative outcomes associated with prejudice and discrimination. The aim of the melting-pot ideology was to promote unity. However, such efforts to deemphasize difference may not be necessary if individuals are encouraged and supported in maintaining their positive social identities and are provided with a basis for relinquishing their concerns about not being accepted, comfortable, valued, and safe. The authors show that under such circumstances, people with diverse identities can establish a positive affiliation with the larger society in ways that increase true engagement with members of different groups.

REFERENCES

Ashmore, Richard, Kay Deaux, and Tracy McLaughlin-Volpe. 2004. "An Organizing Framework for Collective Identity: Articulation and Significance of Multidimensionality." *Psychological Bulletin* 130(1): 80–114.

Bennett, Albert, Beatrice Bridglall, Ana Mari Cauce, Howard Everson, Edmund Gordan, Carol Lee, Rodolfo Mendoza-Denton, Joseph Renzulli, and Judy Stewart. 2004. "All Students Reaching the Top: Strategies for Closing Academic Achievement Gaps." Report of the National Study Group for the Affirmative Development of Academic Ability. Washington: U.S. Department of Education, North Central Regional Educational Laboratory.

Bhanpui, Hoor, and Ginger Reynolds. 2003. *Understanding and Addressing the Issue of the High School Dropout Age.* Washington: U.S. Department of Education, North Central Regional Educational Laboratory.

Bowen, William, and Derek Bok. 1998. *The Shape of the River: Long-Term Consequences of Considering Race in College and University Admissions.* Princeton: Princeton University Press.

Butchart, Ronald E. 1980. *Northern Schools, Southern Blacks, and Reconstruction: Freedmen's Education, 1862–1875.* Westport, Conn.: Greenwood Press.

College Board. 1998. *College-Bound Seniors: Ethnic and Gender Profile of SAT and Achievement Test Takers for the Nation.* New York: College Board.

Crocker, Jennifer, and Connie Wolfe. 2001. Contingencies of Self-Worth. *Psychological Review* 108(3): 593–623.

Deaux, Kay, Claude Steele, A. Gilkes, N. Bikmen, A. Ventumeac, Y. Joseph, and Yassir Payne. Forthcoming. "Becoming American: Stereotype Threat Effects in Black Immigrant Groups."

DuBois, W. E. Burghardt. 1935. *Black Reconstruction in America 1860–1880.* New York: Free Press.

Dweck, Carol. 1999. *Self-Theories: Their Role in Motivation, Personality and Development.* Philadelphia: Psychology Press/Taylor and Francis.

Eagly, Alice, and Steven Karau. 2002. Role Congruity Theory of Prejudice Toward Female Leaders. *Psychological Review* 109(3): 573–98.

Harter, Susan. 1996. "Teacher and Classmate Influences on Scholastic Motivation, Self-Esteem, and Level of Voice in Adolescents." In *Social Motivation: Understanding Children's School Adjustment,* edited by Jaana Juvonen and Kathryn Wentzel. Cambridge Studies in Social and Emotional development. New York: Cambridge University Press.

Mendoza-Denton, Rodolfo, Geraldine Downey, Valerie Purdie, Angelina Davis, and Janina Pietrzak. 2002. "Sensitivity to Status-Based Rejection: Implications for African American Students' College Experience." *Journal of Personality and Social Psychology* 83: 896–918.

Ocampo, Katheryn A., Martha Bernal, and George P. Knight. 1993. "Gender, Race, and Ethnicity: The Sequencing of Social Constancies." In *Ethnic Identity: Formation and Transmission Among Hispanics and Other Minorities,* edited by Martha E. Bernal and George P. Knight. Albany, N.Y.: State University of New York Press.

Pahl, Kerstin, Melissa Greene, and Niobe Way. 2000. "Self-Esteem Trajectories Among Urban, Low-Income, Ethnic Minority High School Students." Poster, presented at the Biennial Meeting of the Society for Research on Adolescence. Chicago (March 1, 2000).

Sellers, Robert, Stephanie Rowley, Tabbye Chavous, J. Nicole Shelton, and Mia A. Smith. 1997. "Multidimensional Inventory of Black Identity: Preliminary Investigation of Reliability and Construct Validity." *Journal of Personality and Social Psychology* 73(4): 805–15.

Steele, Claude, and Joshua Aronson. 1995. "Stereotype Threat and the Intellectual Test Performance of African Americans." *Journal of Personality and Social Psychology* 69: 797–811.

Webber, Thomas L. 1978. *Deep Life the Rivers: Education in the Slave Quarter Community,* 1831–1865. New York: Norton.

Yip, Tiffany, and Andrew Fuligni. 2002. "Daily Variation in Ethnic Identity, Ethnic Behaviors, and Psychological Well-Being Among American Adolescents of Chinese Descent." *Child Development* 73(5): 1557–72.

PART I

IDENTITY AS A SOURCE OF STRESS: CHALLENGES FROM MEMBERSHIP IN STIGMATIZED SOCIAL GROUPS

CHAPTER 2

STEREOTYPES NEGATIVELY INFLUENCE THE MEANING STUDENTS GIVE TO ACADEMIC SETTINGS

Jason S. Lawrence, Jennifer Crocker, and Carol S. Dweck

Answering questions, asking for help, taking tests, receiving feedback from teachers—these are common activities of students. But for students from social groups stereotyped as low-ability in an academic domain, such as blacks and Latinos in academics overall and females in math and science, these activities can take on ominous meaning—meaning that nonstereotyped students do not give to the same activities. It is during such activities that stereotyped students believe they could be judged by or confirm the low-ability stereotype about their group. To a female math major, for example, a math exam can be much more than a test of class content. She may also believe a poor performance will prove to her teacher and male classmates that females have low math ability and that she does not belong in the major.

People generally dislike being stereotyped, but the prospect that others think one is incompetent or unable to achieve in a domain chosen for a career seems especially pernicious. As such, these aversive thoughts can lead stereotyped students to feel an apprehension that Claude M. Steele and colleagues call stereotype threat (see Aronson, Quinn, and Spencer 1998; Steele 1997). Regardless of whether or not these students are objectively stereotyped, or whether or not they believe the stereotype's veracity, their suspicion that they could be stereotyped and the threat that follows can negatively affect their educational experiences (see Steele 1997).

In this chapter we focus on members of these stereotyped gender- and ethnic-group categories, and describe how the prospect of being stereotyped negatively impacts their education. (This makes this chapter unlike the other chapters in this book, which focus on how strongly individuals identify with their group and the positivity of identity.) We will first review the various situations that evoke stereotype threat, and propose that stereotype threat affects students' achievement goals. Then we address how the stereotype negatively impacts stereotyped students in situations pertaining to academic performance, feedback, helping, and self-worth contingency. We also discuss individual differences that affect the meaning that students give to academic situations and that increase the likelihood of stereotype threat's negative impact. Finally, we propose ways to eliminate or weaken stereotype threat among stereotyped students.

A SITUATIONAL THREAT

Stereotyped students are unlikely to perpetually think about the stereotype impugning their group's ability. Instead, the situation can profoundly impact the meaning these students give to academic settings. Stereotype-threat theory and research suggest three situations likely to induce stereotype threat (Davies et al. 2002; Steele 1997; Steele and Aronson 1995; Steele, Spencer, and Aronson 2002).

Unsurprisingly, stereotype threat is likely in academic settings where stereotyped students are exposed to stereotypes about their group. This can occur when the low-ability stereotype is alluded to (Davies et al. 2002; Pronin, Steele, and Ross 2004). In interview studies, stereotyped students report that their ability or their group's ability is sometimes openly doubted by their teachers and classmates (Chesler, Wilson, and Malani 1993; Diversity Report 1990). In one study, black and Latino students at the University of California–Berkeley reported that other students said that black and Latino students were only accepted to Berkeley because of affirmative action and not because they were able to do the work (Diversity Report 1990). But exposure to the stereotype need not be this direct or explicit to be threatening. Paul G. Davies and colleagues (2002) found that female college students who viewed a TV commercial featuring a "ditsy" young woman showed more signs of stereotype threat as compared to female students who viewed a neutral TV commercial: when given a choice, stereotype-exposed females worked on more verbal problems than math problems, and they reported less interest in math-related domains. Another possibility— although untested—is that exposure to group stereotypes unrelated to ability can evoke stereotype threat for stereotyped students. A black male student, for example, may worry about confirming the low-ability stereotype when stereotypes about black male aggression or athletic ability are salient.

Stereotype threat is also likely in academic settings where stereotyped students' group membership is salient. This assumption is based on the notion that bringing to mind (that is, activation) group categories also activates stereotypes about that category (see Fiske 1998). A teacher's class practices may activate students' group membership. In interview studies, for example, stereotyped students often report being singled out in class to give their social group's perspective (Chesler, Wilson, and Malani 1993; Diversity Report 1990). Group membership is also activated in settings where stereotyped students are in the numerical minority (McGuire, McGuire, and Winton 1979; Pollak and Niemann 1998)—which is common for stereotyped students. Females are likely to be members of a small group of females in math and science classrooms, and a black or Latino student at a predominantly white university is likely to be one of a few blacks and Latinos in the classroom. Group membership can also be activated in more subtle ways, as when individuals indicate group affiliation on a demographic form or describe their group just before working on an academic task (Steele and Aronson 1995; Shih, Pittinsky, and Ambady 1999).

Finally, stereotype threat is likely in academic settings where stereotyped students' ability is scrutinized. They may feel that their ability is under evaluation in various academic settings, but stereotype threat may be most likely when stereotyped students take IQ or standardized achievement tests. This should not come as a surprise; black and Latino individuals on average perform less well on these tests than white individuals, and (among the highest achievers) females perform on average less well on standardized math tests than males (Camara and Schmidt 1999; Cole 1997). Various social scientists have claimed that these performance gaps reflect innate ability gaps (Benbow and Stanley 1980; Eysenck 1971; Herrnstein and Murray 1994; Jensen 1969). Stereotyped students are probably aware of both facts, given the publicity of both the achievement gap and the claims of certain groups' intellectual inferiority.

Stereotype-threat research powerfully shows that changing a test's description can alter the meaning stereotyped students give to the test. When test givers assure stereotyped students that a test is not diagnostic of ability, or that the test shows no differences between stereotyped and nonstereotyped groups, stereotyped students are less likely to feel stereotype threat (Spencer, Steele, and Quinn 1999; Steele and Aronson 1995). Steele and Joshua Aronson (1995) tested this hypothesis in an experiment in which black and white participants expected to take a verbal test. Half the participants learned that the test was diagnostic of ability; the rest learned that the test assessed problem-solving styles (in other words, it was nondiagnostic). All participants subsequently viewed difficult sample problems they would ostensibly face. Then they completed word fragments as well as a questionnaire assessing their participation in stereotypically black activities such as playing basketball and listening to rap music. Indicating stereotype activation, results showed that in the diagnostic condition, black participants completed more word fragments with race- and stereotype-related words than did participants in other conditions. The black participants in the diagnostic condition also reported less engagement in stereotypically black activities than did participants in the other conditions, suggesting that they wanted to avoid being associated with race-related stereotypes in general.

It is important to note that, according to stereotype-threat theory, the above-described situations may be insufficient to evoke or sustain a heightened sense of threat for stereotyped students (Steele and Aronson 1995). Stereotype threat's likelihood increases in these situations when stereotyped students face difficult academic tasks. When stereotyped students face a difficult academic task, underperformance becomes likely, thereby raising their concerns of confirming low-ability stereotypes to outgroup others. In contrast, their concerns about confirming stereotypes are weak or nonexistent when (1) they face academic difficulty in nondiagnostic settings, where group membership or the stereotype is not salient; or (2) when they do not face difficulty on an academic task, regardless of diagnosticity, because a poor performance is unlikely.

THREAT AND ABILITY GOALS

In order to understand the meaning stereotyped students give to academic settings, it is important to know that subtle and not so subtle situational changes can either induce or reduce stereotype threat. But what happens once stereotyped students believe they are in a situation in which they can be judged according to the stereotype? We propose that one consequence is that stereotyped students are likely to adopt ability-based performance goals (ability goals for short) (see also Smith 2004). In other words, under stereotype threat their main focus becomes performing well in order to disconfirm the stereotype, or avoid a poor performance to avoid confirming the stereotype (also see Seibt and Förster 2004). Under such circumstances they would be less likely to adopt learning goals, the goals of acquiring and developing skills and knowledge (see Dweck and Elliott 1983; Dweck and Leggett 1988; Nicholls 1984; Urdan 1997). Supporting this notion, Jason S. Lawrence and Carol S. Dweck (2002) found in a survey study that the more black students believed they were expected to perform poorly in college because of their ethnicity the more they wanted to demonstrate high ability.

More specifically, when either the stereotype or group membership is salient, stereotyped students are likely to adopt ability goals. This should also be true for diagnostic academic settings. It is important to note, however, that achievement goal theory proposes that most students—regardless of whether they are stereotyped—tend to adopt ability goals in these situations (see Urdan 1997; Utman 1997). But because stereotyped students have to face the prospect of confirming the stereotype, we propose that they are more likely to adopt ability goals and to do so more extremely than nonstereotyped students.

This may at first glance seem beneficial. If stereotyped students want to demonstrate high ability or avoid demonstrations of inability then they will surely be motivated to achieve. But adopting ability goals could increase stereotyped students' risks for a number of negative school outcomes. As well documented by achievement research, on difficult academic tasks, students who adopt ability goals as opposed to learning goals tend to feel anxious, blame their ability, withdraw effort, and underperform (Grant and Dweck 2003; Utman 1997; see Urdan 1997). Students with ability goals focus on whether they are achieving their goal of proving their ability, and any sign of failure to achieve this goal disconcerts them.

It is also important to note the possibility that stereotyped students who focus more on avoiding demonstrations of low ability (that is, avoidance ability goals), are at greater risk for negative school outcomes than are those focused on demonstrations of high ability (that is, approach ability goals). As Andrew J. Elliot and colleagues (Elliot and Church 1997; Elliot and Harackiewicz 1996; Elliot and McGregor 2001) show, these are two distinct goals with distinct consequences: avoidance ability goals lead students to feel an apprehension that can impair achievement, whereas approach ability goals motivate students and can lead to high achievement. However, there is evidence that under difficulty even students with approach ability goals can have negative academic outcomes (Grant and Dweck 2003; Lawrence and Dweck 2003). Although this issue is unresolved, we assume—for now—that both approach and avoidance ability goals can be problematic for students.

UNDERPERFORMANCE—
THE STEREOTYPE-THREAT EFFECT

Several negative consequences follow once stereotyped students believe they could be judged by the low-ability stereotype. According to Steele and colleagues, one consequence is that stereotype threat can be unsettling enough to impair stereotyped students' performance, especially on difficult academic tasks (see Blascovich et al. 2001; Spencer, Steele, and Quinn 1999; Steele, 1997; Steele and Aronson 1995). To test the stereotype-threat effect, Steele and Aronson (1995) gave black and white students a difficult verbal exam under either diagnostic or nondiagnostic conditions. Results showed that black participants in the diagnostic condition performed less well than black participants in the nondiagnostic condition. White participants performed equally well across conditions.

The stereotype-threat effect has proved to be both reliable and generalizable. Many studies have replicated this underperformance with other stereotyped groups, such as women in math (Brown and Josephs 1997; Inzlicht and Ben-Zeev 2000; Spencer, Steele, and Quinn 1999), Latino students (Aronson and Salinas 2001; Gonzales, Blanton, and Williams 2002), and students from low socioeconomic backgrounds (Croizet and Claire 1998). Some studies demonstrate the stereotype-threat effect with a variety of methodologies (Inzlicht and Ben-Zeev 2000; Shih, Pittinsky, and Ambady 1999), whereas other studies show that the stereotype-threat effect can be found in domains other than academics (Kray, Thompson, and Galinsky 2001; Stone et al. 1999).

How does stereotype threat lead to underperformance? Anxiety, evaluation apprehension, low expectations, stereotype suppression, cognitive load are but a few mediators proffered by investigators (see Aronson, Quinn, and Spencer 1998; Steele, Spencer, and Aronson 2002). Although research on most of these mediators has proved inconclusive, there is growing support for cognitive load as an important mediator (Croizet et al. 2004; Schmader and Johns 2003). In a study by Toni Schmader and Michael Johns (2003), college women who were either under stereotype threat or not took a working memory test followed by a math test. Results showed that women in the threat condition had reduced working memory capacity, which in turn depressed math performance.

Although this work has greatly added to knowledge of the stereotype-threat effect, it is unclear whether the mere thought of the stereotype is cognitively taxing (see Davies et al. 2002) or whether other factors also have an influence. It is, therefore, reasonable to test the link between other potential factors such as anxiety and evaluation apprehension and cognitive load.

It is also important to continue searching for mediators that have not been emphasized or proposed. One rarely explored reason that stereotyped students' performance suffers under stereotype threat is that they try too hard and consequently use poor test-taking strategies (but see Smith 2004). This notion is based on Steele and Aronson's (1995) finding that black students in the diagnostic condition spent more time on each problem than did black students in a nondiagnostic condition and white participants in either condition (see Seibt and Förster 2004 for one reason stereotyped students may be overly careful). Consequently, the black students in the diagnostic condition ran out of time and did not complete the test, so their performance suffered.

Ability goals may also disrupt stereotyped students' performance. Recall that stereotype threat may lead stereotyped students to adopt ability goals and that ability goals have been shown to lead to underperformance (Utman 1997). Note also that diagnostic instructions used in stereotype-threat studies are the same kinds of instructions achievement-goal researchers assume lead most students to adopt ability goals (see Urdan 1997; Utman 1997). Like the stereotype-threat literature, the achievement-goal literature maintains that underperformance occurs when students work on difficult tasks in diagnostic settings (Utman 1997). Of course, if ability goals do mediate the stereotype threat effect, it still leaves unexplained how ability goals lead to underperformance (see Utman 1997). Nevertheless, testing the link between ability goals and underperformance would add to our understanding of the stereotype-threat effect (also see Smith 2004).

Mediation studies may also be more fruitful if researchers take the perspective that the stereotype-threat effect is multiplicatively determined (see Steele, Spencer, and Aronson 2002). As noted by Steele, Spencer, and Aronson (2002), it is possible that mediators for underperformance are different for different stereotyped groups. For example, females' underperformance in math may be due to cognitive load, whereas black students' underperformance may be due to evaluation apprehension. It is also possible that within different stereotyped groups, mediation occurs differently for different students. For instance, on a diagnostic math task, some female students underperform because of anxiety, whereas others underperform because of over-effort and using poor test-taking strategies. Thus it is important to identify individual differences (which we discuss later) and then test different potential mediators on the basis of these individual differences (for example, Ford et al. 2004). Researchers could, for example, examine the possibility that for students who seek to demonstrate ability, poor performance is due to overeffort and poor test-taking strategies, whereas for those who seek to avoid demonstrations of inability, poor performance is due to anxiety (but see Elliot and Harackiewicz 1996).

Another possibility is that underperformance occurs differently within students over the time of an academic task. A stereotyped student may start, for example, by trying too hard to perform well, thereby engaging in poor test-taking strategies which in turn hurt performance, and then end by experiencing anxiety as he realizes that he is running out of time and will fail to achieve the goal of disconfirming the stereotype; this anxiety impairs performance further. If it is the case that underperformance within the same student could be due to different causes at different points of the problem-solving process, then it is understandable that many mediation studies are inconclusive, given that measures of mediation are usually taken either before or after students work on academic problems (see Spencer, Steele, and Quinn 1999).

INTERPRETATION OF FEEDBACK

Most stereotype-threat research has focused on its negative impact on students' performance. But stereotype threat should also impact the meaning stereotyped students give to other educational circumstances. Because the prospect of being stereotyped is so aversive, stereotyped students are likely to be vigilant for situations in which they may be stereotyped (Crocker, Major, and Steele 1998). One situation where they believe they could be stereotyped is when they receive academic feedback—negative or positive—from teachers and peers (for example, Crocker and Major 1989).

When teachers tell students that their academic performance is poor, it should threaten most students' self-esteem and academic self-concept. Many students, in order to deflect this threat, would be motivated to attribute this negative feedback to factors other than their ability. But because negative feedback can signal to stereotyped students that they have confirmed the low-ability stereotype, they may be especially threatened and likely to explain away negative academic feedback.

Geoffrey L. Cohen, Steele, and Lee Ross (1999) examined how stereotyped students interpret negative academic feedback. In one experiment, black and white participants wrote an essay that was ostensibly evaluated by a white person. All participants received a negative evaluation for their essay under one of three conditions. In the positive-buffer condition, participants received generally positive comments prior to the negative feedback. In the high standards–expectancy condition, participants learned that the evaluator had high standards and that he believed they were capable of meeting those standards. In the control condition, no information was provided prior to the negative feedback. Results showed that the black participants judged the feedback to be more biased in the positive-buffer and the control conditions than in the high standards–expectancy condition. White participants did not differ in their judgments of bias between conditions. These results suggest not only that stereotyped students are more threatened by negative feedback than nonstereotyped students but also that they have difficulty trusting that their ability is not doubted by others and thus need some reassurance that they are free from being stereotyped (see Steele 1999).

Surprisingly, stereotyped students may also feel threatened when they receive positive academic feedback. When they perform objectively well, for instance, they may attribute praise from an outgroup evaluator to the evaluator's surprise at their good performance. According to Wulf-Uwe Meyer and colleagues, there is a risk that both stereotyped and nonstereotyped students will attribute praise to an evaluator's low expectations (Meyer 1982; Meyer 1992; Meyer et al. 1979; Meyer, Mittag, and Engler 1986; see also Barker and Graham 1987; Lord, Umezaki, and Darley 1990; Miller and Hom 1997). This is most likely when students believe the evaluator has formed an expectation on the basis of previous performances (Meyer, Mittag, and Engler 1986). But stereotyped students may attribute academic praise to low expectations even when they know that the evaluator is unaware of previous performances, because they know it is possible for an evaluator to base an expectancy on the low-ability stereotype.

Jason S. Lawrence, Jennifer Crocker, and Hart Blanton (2000) tested the idea that stereotyped students were especially likely to attribute academic praise to an evaluator's low expectations. In this study, black and white participants completed fourteen academic problems. Half the participants received written feedback indicating they solved twelve out of the fourteen problems; the rest received the same feedback plus the written comment "Great Job!!" Results showed that the black participants who received praise believed the evaluator had lower expectations of them than did the black participants who did not receive praise. Conversely, white participants who received praise believed that the evaluator had higher expectations of them than did white participants who did not receive praise.

If both negative and positive feedback is genuine, then attributing it to bias toward one's group membership may have several negative consequences. Although threatening, negative feedback can often provide students with useful information on how to improve. If stereotyped students believe this assessment is the result of bias, they are unlikely to accept that information constructively and try to improve. Moreover, both attributing negative feedback to bias and attributing praise to an evaluator's stereotypically based low expectations can hobble the relationship between stereotyped students and the evaluator. In the praise study, black participants who did not receive praise reported that they liked the evaluator more than did black participants who received praise. This finding is important because positive faculty-student interactions can reduce students' risk of dropping out of school (Tinto 1975). Another possible consequence is that once stereotyped students suspect that their ability has been questioned, they are more likely to experience stereotype threat in future interactions with the evaluator. Finally, students are unlikely to feel a sense of belonging in the classroom or in school, which is critical to academic achievement (Tinto 1975).

HELP SEEKING AND RECEIVING

The suspicion that others hold a low-ability stereotype may also affect the meaning that stereotyped students give to academic help. Achievement researchers have found that individuals generally believe that help seeking demonstrates low ability (Shapiro 1983). As a result, students—regardless of group membership—should tend to avoid seeking academic help because they do not want others to think they are incompetent. It is also telling that students with ability goals are more likely to avoid help seeking than are students with learning goals (Butler and Neuman 1995; see Newman 1991). But as with academic feedback, we propose that stereotyped students are more likely than are nonstereotyped students to avoid academic help seeking because they worry that this may confirm the stereotype to others.

Stereotyped students should also be averse to receiving academic help from an outgroup member, as such help could signify the outgroup other's stereotype-influenced low expectations. Monica E. Schneider et al. (1996) provided support for this idea. In this experiment, black and white participants worked on an academic task and either did or did not receive unsolicited help from a white peer. Results showed that black participants' self-worth decreased when they received unsolicited help, whereas white participants' self-esteem was unaffected by unsolicited help.

If stereotyped students avoid help seeking, it can have several negative consequences. According to several theorists, help seeking allows students to acquire knowledge and develop skills (Nelson–Le Gall 1981; Newman 1991). Indeed, high-achieving students are more likely to seek help than low-achieving students (Rohwer and Thomas 1989; Zimmerman and Martinez-Pons 1986). Avoiding help seeking can also prevent stereotyped students from developing a connection with their classmates and teachers (see Newman 1994). This can decrease stereotyped students' sense of belonging and increase their risk of becoming school dropouts (Tinto 1975).

SELF-WORTH CONTINGENCY

Another possible consequence of stereotype threat is that stereotyped students' sense of self-worth is strongly linked to their school outcomes, such that they have positive self-feelings following good outcomes and negative self-feelings following poor outcomes. Although some degree of contingency is likely to be common among students regardless of their group membership, we propose that this link will under some circumstances be stronger for stereotyped students because they have to contend with the low-ability stereotype and the possibility that a poor performance means that they confirmed the stereotype to outgroup others (although see Osborne 1995).

There is evidence that the link between self-worth and school outcomes is different for stereotyped students and nonstereotyped students. Recall, for example, that Schneider et al. (1996) found that black students' self-worth was negatively affected after they received unsolicited academic help from a white peer, whereas white students' self-worth was unaffected by receiving help.

There is, however, a qualification: stereotyped students may need to think the process is bias-free in order to engage their self-esteem. In other words, if they perceive an evaluator or an academic task is biased, they may attribute negative outcomes to the evaluator rather than to their ability (Cohen, Steele, and Ross 1999). Supporting this idea, Brenda Major, Steven Spencer, and Toni Schmader (1998, study 2) found that black students' self-worth was unaffected by a poor performance on an IQ test when ethnic group differences on IQ tests and notion of bias against minorities were made salient prior to taking the test. When ethnic-group differences and test bias were not made salient, however, black students' self-worth was affected by a poor performance.

It is important to determine whether or not stereotyped students engage their self-worth in academics, because such an academic contingency is thought to affect student motivation and achievement, although researchers disagree as to whether or not this effect is positive. According to stereotype threat and disidentification theory, a connection between self-worth and academic achievement is necessary for students to succeed (see Major and Schmader 1998; Osborne 1995, 1997; Steele 1997). The assumption is that because self-worth decreases after poor performances and self-worth increases after good performances, students will be motivated to avoid the former outcome and seek out the latter outcome, so they will work hard and study in order to ensure success.

Achievement theorists also believe that having an academic contingency is motivating for students, but these theorists believe that academically contingent students are at risk for lowered motivation and performance (see Burhans and Dweck 1995; Covington 1984; Deci and Ryan 1987; Dykman 1998; Molden and Dweck 2000; Ryan 1982). Richard M. Ryan (1982), for instance, argues that an academic contingency is experienced as controlling by the self. Consequently, these students tend to experience pressure and to be extrinsically motivated rather than intrinsically motivated. Martin V. Covington (1984) posits that in order to maintain self-worth, academically contingent students engage in several maladaptive strategies such as avoiding challenges, sabotaging their performance (that is, self-handicapping), and cheating. Carol S. Dweck and colleagues propose that academically contingent students are likely to adopt ability goals and respond maladaptively in the face of difficulty (see Burhans and Dweck 1995; Molden and Dweck 2000).

Another negative consequence of an academic contingency is that depression may follow a decrease in students' sense of self-worth (Crocker and Wolfe 2001; Dykman 1998). This is obvious from psychologists' conceptions of drops in self-worth. William James (1890/1950) describes self-worth drops from poor performance as "mortifying." A person with low self-esteem is inclined to agree strongly with statements such as "All and all I'm inclined to think I'm a failure" (Rosenberg 1979). Thus, a student with an academic contingency who fails a test will not just think she did poorly on the test but also that she is a general failure. If academically contingent students are prone to depression, then they also risk lowered motivation.

MODERATORS OF STEREOTYPE THREAT'S CONSEQUENCES

Not all stereotyped students are susceptible to stereotype threat's consequences. Some stereotyped students are more vulnerable because they already hold a set of beliefs about school success and failure—we call achievement meaning systems— that can negatively impact most students. Although many of these meaning systems are related to each other, Lawrence and Dweck (2002) found in a factor analysis that they are distinct. It is important to note that we only focus on individual differences in meaning systems and thus this is not exhaustive of all the individual differences that interact with stereotype threat (see Ford et al. 2004; Schmader 2002).

Academic Identification

Students who include achievement as a central part of their self-concept—termed academically identified—should be vulnerable to stereotype threat's consequences (Steele 1997). Because ability is important to their self-concepts, these students probably want to demonstrate high ability or avoid demonstrations of low ability. In other words, they are likely to have ability goals. As Joachim C. Brunstein and Peter M. Gollwitzer (1996) note, "Committed individuals set out to accumulate evidence that points to their possession of the attributes and skills associated with the particular self-definition or identity in question" (396) and such individuals feel a need to demonstrate these attributes to others (see Swann 1983). Similarly, Sheldon Stryker (1968) maintains that individuals are perpetually motivated to validate their identities (also see Foote 1951). Aronson et al. (1999, 35) posit that academically identified students "either care about having the ability or at least care about the social consequences of being seen as lacking the ability" (see also Brown and Josephs 1999).

To obtain evidence of the connection between academic identification and ability goals, Carol S. Dweck and Jason S. Lawrence conducted a survey study (Lawrence and Dweck 2002) in which college students completed an academic identification measure ("How important is having strong intellectual ability to you?"; "How important is intellectual ability to your sense of who you are?") and Heidi Grant and Dweck's (2003) approach ability goal measure ("In school I'm focused on demonstrating my intellectual ability"; "It is important for me to validate my intelligence through my schoolwork"). The results supported the above hypothesis: the higher students' academic identification, the more they endorsed ability goals (r = .44, p < .001).

Academically identified students from stereotyped groups should also be vulnerable to stereotype threat–induced underperformance because poor performances challenge this self-concept and are therefore highly disturbing and disruptive (see Marx, Brown, and Steele 1999; Steele 1997). Testing this proposition, Lawrence, Bryant T. Marks, and James S. Jackson (2000) conducted an experiment in which black students, who had earlier completed a verbal identification measure, took a verbal test. Before taking the test, some students read that the test was diagnostic; the rest read that the test was nondiagnostic. Results showed that in the diagnostic condition, the more the students identified with verbal achievement the worse they performed. In the nondiagnostic condition, the students' degree of identification was unrelated to their performance (see also Aronson et al. 1999; Stone et al. 1999).

Academically identified students are also likely to base their self-worth on achievement.[1] This idea is based on the assumption that these students' academic outcomes affect self-regard because these outcomes can confirm or disconfirm these students' central and important self-views as high achievers. In line with this notion, Lawrence and Dweck (2003) found that the more students identified with academics the more they reported basing their self-worth on achievement (r = .24, p < .05, controlling for ability goals).

Ability Goals, Motivation, and Performance

Stereotyped students who chronically adopt ability goals would likely be vulnerable to stereotype threat's consequences. By definition, ability goal–oriented students, from any group membership, should want to demonstrate their ability or avoid demonstrating inability across a variety of academic settings, especially diagnostic ones. We propose that stereotyped students with chronic ability goals may be especially vulnerable to adopting ability goals in achievement settings because they have the burden, not shared by nonstereotyped students, of having their ability potentially doubted by others.

Ability goal–oriented students from stereotyped groups should also be vulnerable to stereotype threat–induced underperformance. As we noted earlier, performance tends to be undermined when ability goal–oriented students, from any group, experience difficulty (Dweck and Leggett 1988; Grant and Dweck 2003; Utman 1997). For these students, poor performance signals a failure to demonstrate ability, and they often attribute difficulty and failure to low ability (Grant and Dweck 2003; Jagacinski and Nicholls 1987)—which may lead to a withdrawal of effort ("If I lack ability, why try?") and depression (Diener and Dweck 1978; Elliott and Dweck 1988; Grant and Dweck 2003).

Recently, Lawrence and Dweck (2003, study 1) tested the idea that under diagnostic conditions ability goal–oriented students perform less well than under nondiagnostic conditions (see Molden and Dweck 2000). In order to emphasize that ability goals can hinder performance in general, we excluded stereotyped group members as participants. In this study, white students who had previously completed a survey to measure the extent of their ability-goal orientation (Grant and Dweck 2003) took a difficult verbal test with either diagnostic or nondiagnostic instructions. Results showed that the more students endorsed ability goals, the worse they performed in the diagnostic condition ($\beta = -.38$, $p < .01$), whereas in the nondiagnostic condition the relationship between ability goals and performance was nonsignificant ($\beta = .18$, $p < .20$). These results suggest that ability goal–oriented students are especially vulnerable to diagnostic instructions. If ability goal–oriented students from a nonstereotyped group underperform in diagnostic settings then perhaps ability goal–oriented stereotyped students would be especially vulnerable to underperformance.

Ability goal–oriented students should also be prone to basing their self-worth on achievement (Molden and Dweck 2000). These students tend to attribute their performances to ability; success means they are high in ability and failure means they are low in ability. Because ability goals are so important to them, their self-worth should rise and fall with their performances. In a test of this hypothesis (Lawrence and Dweck 2002), college students completed an ability-goal measure and an academic contingency measure ("I would feel like a loser if I were to receive a poor grade in class"; "I would feel terrific about myself if I answered a question in class correctly"). The results supported the above hypotheses, showing that the higher students' academic contingency, the more they endorsed ability goals ($r = .53$, $p < .001$).

Academic Contingency

Stereotyped students who chronically base their self-worth on academic achievement—termed academically contingent—should also be vulnerable to stereotype threat's consequences. As noted in the previous section, academically contingent students are likely to adopt ability goals (see Burhans and Dweck 1995; Dykman 1998; Molden and Dweck 2000). Demonstrating high ability gives these students positive self-feelings, and avoiding demonstrations of low ability allows them to avoid negative self-feelings.

Some academically contingent students may be especially vulnerable to adopting ability goals, for their self-worth is not based on just any type of achievement. Instead, they focus on "objective indicators" of ability such as standardized achievement and IQ test performances. Jason W. Osborne (1995; 1997) views academically contingent students as those with a strong positive relationship between global self-esteem and achievement test scores. Major, Spencer, and Schmader (1998) view academically contingent students as those whose self-worth is affected by success or failure feedback on intelligence tests. Major and Schmader's (1998) academic contingency measure focuses on the importance of doing well on standardized achievement and intelligence tests (for example, "No intelligence test will ever change my opinion of how intelligent I am"; "I really don't care what tests say about my intelligence"—lower scores mean higher academic contingency). Aronson, Quinn, and Spencer (1998) equate academic contingency with basing self-worth on intelligence test performance when they say, "African Americans . . . show more evidence of disidentification than their European American counterparts in that they are less likely to base their self-esteem on performance on intelligence tests" (p. 88).

Academically contingent students should also be vulnerable to stereotype threat–induced underperformance. This proposition is based on the notion that even nonstereotyped students with an academic contingency are vulnerable to underperforming in diagnostic settings. Indeed, Lawrence and Dweck (2003, study 3) found support for this notion. In this study, white students who had earlier completed an academic contingency measure took a difficult verbal test under either diagnostic or nondiagnostic instructions. Results showed that, the higher students' academic contingency the worse their performance under diagnostic instructions ($\beta = -.42$, $p = .01$). Under nondiagnostic instructions there was no relationship between academic contingency and performance ($\beta = .24$, ns).

By definition, academically contingent students should have their self-worth attached to their achievement. Crocker, Samuel R. Sommers, and Riia K. Luhtanen (2002) conducted a study in which students applying for graduate school daily reported their feelings of self-worth and tracked when they received an acceptance or rejection notice from graduate schools. Before collecting this data, however, the students reported the degree to which they based their self-worth on achievement. Results showed that the more students reported basing their self-worth on achievement, the more their self-worth increased on days in which they were accepted into a program and the more their self-worth decreased when they were not accepted.

We propose, however, that stereotyped students experience self-worth decreases following poor performances more than nonstereotyped students. One reason is that stereotyped students may feel that underperformance confirms the stereotype to outgroup others. A second reason is that when one's group is underrepresented in a field, questions may arise about whether people with one's social identity have the ability to succeed in this field. Furthermore, negative stereotypes may lead stereotyped students to question their ability at precisely those moments when their abilities are most challenged (Spencer, Steele, and Quinn 1999; Steele 1997). For stereotyped students, unexpectedly bad grades may lead to conclusions that one is lacking in ability; for those whose self-worth is staked on their academic performance, this may lead to sharp drops in self-esteem.

In a recent study (Crocker, Sommers, and Luhtanen 2002), male and female college students who were enrolled in engineering classes reported their self-esteem as well as the grades they received on papers and exams over a three-week period. Results showed that in general both male and female students' self-worth was lower on days when grades were lower than expected. Students with a high academic contingency experienced these decreases in self-worth more than did students with a low academic contingency. But females majoring in engineering with a high academic contingency showed the biggest drops in self-worth after receiving grades that were lower than expected.

Theories of Intelligence

People who think intelligence is fixed are called entity theorists, as opposed to incremental theorists, who think that intelligence is malleable and can change with effort. Stereotyped students who are entity theorists should be vulnerable to stereotype threat's consequences. Entity theorists are likely to want to demonstrate their ability and avoid demonstrations of inability (see Dweck and Elliott 1983; Molden and Dweck 2000). Evidence of this behavioral link comes from an experiment by Janine

Bempechat, Perry London, and Dweck (1991), showing that children induced to adopt an entity theory of intelligence tended to choose an easy academic task in which success was possible but offered little chance for growth (also see Stone 1998). In contrast, children induced to adopt an incremental theory of intelligence tended to choose a difficult academic task with little chance for success, but in which learning was possible (see also Dweck, Tenney, and Dinces 1982, cited in Dweck and Leggett 1988). Other evidence comes from correlational studies revealing that the more individuals believed intelligence was fixed, the more they endorsed ability goals (Rhodewalt 1994; Stipek and Gralinski 1996).

Stereotyped students with entity theories should also be vulnerable to stereotype threat–induced underperformance. As noted by Dweck and colleagues, entity theorists are likely to respond maladaptively to difficulty and failure, hence they are prone to underperform in difficult situations (see Dweck and Elliott 1983; Rhodewalt 1994).

Stereotyped students with an entity theory of intelligence should also tend to base their self-worth on achievement outcomes (see Molden and Dweck 2000). Indeed, in a survey study, Lawrence and Dweck (2002) found that the more students believed intelligence was fixed, the more they reported basing their self-worth on academic achievement. In an experiment, Daniel C. Molden, Heidi Grant, and Dweck (2005) showed that entity theorists reported greater drops in self-worth following failure feedback on an academic task than those who believe intelligence is malleable.

Academic Contingency and Entity Theory Combined

Recent findings suggest that entity theorists do not always have an academic contingency. Stereotyped students who are both entity theorists and are academically contingent would be most likely to experience the negative consequences associated with stereotype threat. In one study, Yu Niiya, Jennifer Crocker, and Elizabeth N. Bartmess (2004) measured the extent to which students' self-worth was based on academics, manipulated entity versus incremental theories of intelligence, and then gave students success or failure feedback on a Graduate Record Exam. For students whose self-worth was based on academics and who were primed with an entity theory of intelligence, self-esteem was lower and affect was negative following failure. Priming students with incremental theories of intelligence completely eliminated the drops in self-esteem following failure for highly contingent students. Thus, the combination of contingent self-worth and entity theories of ability appears to be particularly damaging to self-esteem, and this may be even truer for stereotyped students.

Others' Theory of Intelligence

Another possible moderator of stereotype threat is students' beliefs about other people's theories of intelligence. Stereotyped students should be at risk of showing many of stereotype threat's consequences when they believe they are in an environment in which others doing the evaluating tend to think ability is fixed. First, believing that an evaluator is an entity theorist is likely to make students want to demonstrate high ability and avoid demonstrations of low ability. Recently, Lawrence and Dweck (2002) found that black college students tend to adopt ability goals when they believe college is a place where intelligence is thought to be fixed. It is significant that these students' own theory of intelligence was unrelated to their beliefs about other people's theories. Second, students who believe that an evaluator is an entity theorist will likely be less willing to seek academic help from that evaluator and feel threatened by unsolicited academic help because help can be construed as signifying low ability. Third, under-performance would be likely when students are evaluated by an entity theorist because an entity theorist is most likely to be evaluating ability. Finally, self-worth may drop if stereotyped students think they have confirmed the low-ability stereo-type to an entity theorist, someone likely to generalize such a performance to other stereotyped students.

PREVENTING STEREOTYPE THREAT AND ITS NEGATIVE CONSEQUENCES

Stereotype-threat and achievement-goal theorists both recommend ways to reduce stereotyped students' experiences of stereotype threat and its negative impact. Stereotype-threat theorists, guided by the notion that stereotype threat is situationally determined, recommend remedies that focus on school structure. According to Steele (1997), stereotype threat is reduced in school environments that convey optimism for stereotyped students' ability to meet academic challenges; provide stereotyped students with challenging work, not remedial work; persuade stereotyped students to adopt an incremental theory of intelligence over an entity theory of intelligence.

Researchers are beginning to explore these environmental characteristics' effectiveness in reducing stereotype threat. Cohen, Steele, and Ross (1999), as noted earlier, found that black students who received a message of high standards as well as optimism about their ability to meet those standards were less likely to attribute negative academic feedback to bias than black students who only received a message of high standards. In Aronson, Fried, and Good (2002), black and white students were persuaded to endorse an incremental theory of intelligence. Results showed that although the incremental theory manipulation did not reduce black students' beliefs that low-ability stereotypes are applied to them, they were less likely to experience negative consequences associated with stereotype threat. Specifically, over the course of the study, black students who had been encouraged to endorse an incremental theory of intelligence showed increases in both school enjoyment and grades.

Although not directly addressing stereotype threat, achievement-goal theorists' recommendations for generally improving student motivation and achievement may also reduce stereotyped students' experiences of stereotype threat. Like stereotype-threat theorists, achievement-goal theorists focus on school structure. Indeed, achievement-goal theorists' recommendations appear to provide a general framework and a detailed set of procedures for accomplishing stereotype-threat theorists' recommendations.

The two approaches differ slightly on one point: instead of communicating to stereotyped students that they are thought to be high in ability, achievement-goal theorists recommend that ability not be focused on at all. The aim is to create an environment in which students adopt learning goals over ability goals (see Ames 1992). Environments that evoke learning goals focus on the process of learning the material's content, the development of new skills, and the effort needed to accomplish these goals. In contrast, environments that evoke ability goals focus on social comparison, demonstrations of ability, and quantifiable outcomes such as test grades.

Both ability-goal and learning-goal environments can be created within the classroom through one of three routes (see Ames 1992; Ames and Archer 1988). First, the type of task assigned can influence students' goals. Students adopt learning goals when tasks are diverse, challenging, and meaningful to students. Second, the evaluations used can influence students' goals. Evaluations that lead to students' adopting learning goals are ones that downplay social comparison and focus more on process than on outcomes. Also, evaluations that focus on effort rather than ability are likely to induce students to adopt learning goals. Claudia M. Mueller and Dweck (1998), for example, showed that young children who were praised for intelligence tended to adopt ability goals, whereas young children who were praised for effort tended to adopt learning goals. Finally, classrooms in which students are given autonomy and choices are likely to lead students to adopt learning goals over ability goals.

The school at large can also influence the goals students adopt (see Maehr 1991). Even if a classroom has a learning-goal structure, students within the class may adopt ability goals if the school at large emphasizes grades and competition (see Anderman and Maehr 1994).

The likelihood that stereotyped students experience stereotype threat should be reduced in learning-goal environments. In an environment that does not focus on ability, stereotyped students need not worry about being judged in terms of low-ability stereotypes. Learning-goal environments should also reduce the degree to which students endorse an entity theory of intelligence, have an academic contingency, and believe others in the school endorse an entity theory of intelligence. In such environments stereotyped students are less likely to experience the negative school-related consequences associated with stereotype threat.

CONCLUSION

This chapter's theme is that the meaning students bring to academic situations has implications for academic outcomes (see also Ames 1992; Crocker 1999; Dweck 1999; Maehr 1991; Molden and Dweck 2000; Steele 1997). Members of groups stereotyped as low-ability may view the same objective situations differently than students who are not part of groups alleged to be low in ability. In addition, students' achievement meaning systems affect how they perceive and therefore react in academic situations. For example, students with an academic contingency believe their academic performances reflect their self-worth, and students who believe intelligence is fixed tend to believe their performances reflect on their ability. These meaning systems have the potential to lead students, especially stereotyped students, to engage in maladaptive strategies. However, we believe that changes in school structure can lead students to adopt more adaptive learning strategies, thereby increasing their motivation and chances for academic success as well as enjoyment of their studies.

NOTE

1. Some researchers use academic identification and basing self-worth on achievement interchangeably (see Osborne 1995).

REFERENCES

Ames, Carol. 1992. "Classrooms: Goals, Structures, and Student Motivation." *Journal of Educational Psychology* 84(3): 261–71.

Ames, Carol, and Jennifer Archer. 1988. "Achievement Goals in the Classroom: Students' Learning Strategies and Motivation Processes." *Journal of Educational Psychology* 80(3): 260–67.

Anderman, Eric M., and Martin L. Maehr. 1994. "Motivation and Schooling in the Middle Grades." *Review of Educational Research* 64(2): 287–309.

Aronson, Joshua, Carrie B. Fried, and Catherine Good. 2002. "Reducing the Effects of Stereotype Threat on African American College Students by Shaping Theories of Intelligence." *Journal of Experimental Social Psychology* 38(2): 113–25.

Aronson, Joshua, Michael J. Lustina, Catherine Good, Kelli Keough, Joseph L. Brown, and Claude M. Steele. 1999. "When White Men Can't Do Math: Necessary and Sufficient Factors in Stereotype Threat." *Journal of Experimental Social Psychology* 35(1): 29–46.

Aronson, Joshua, Diane M. Quinn, and Steven Spencer. 1998. "Stereotype Threat and the Academic Underperformance of Minorities and Women." In *Prejudice: The Target's Perspective*, edited by Janet Swim and Charles Stangor. San Diego: Academic Press.

Aronson, Joshua, and Moises F. Salinas. 2001. "Stereotype Threat, Attributional Ambiguity, and Latino Underperformance." Unpublished manuscript.

Barker, George, and Sandra Graham. 1987. "Developmental Study of Praise and Blame as Attributional Cues." *Journal of Educational Psychology* 79(1): 62–66.

Bempechat, Janine, Perry London, and Carol S. Dweck. 1991. "Children's Conceptions of Ability in Major Domains: An Interview and Experimental Study." *Child Study Journal* 21(1): 11–36.

Benbow, Camilla P., and Julian C. Stanley. 1980. "Sex Differences in Mathematical Ability: Fact or Artifact?" *Science* 210(December 12): 1262–64.

Blascovich, Jim, Steven J. Spencer, Diane M. Quinn, and Claude M. Steele. 2001. "African Americans and High Blood Pressure: The Role of Stereotype Threat." *Psychological Science* 12(3): 225–29.

Brown, Ryan P., and Robert A. Josephs. 1999. "A Burden of Proof: Stereotype Relevance and Gender Differences in Math Performance." *Journal of Personality and Social Psychology* 76(2): 246–57.

Brunstein, Joachim C., and Peter M. Gollwitzer. 1996. "Effects of Failure on Subsequent Performance: The Importance of Self-Defining Goals." *Journal of Personality and Social Psychology* 70(2): 395–407.

Burhans, Karen K., and Carol S. Dweck. 1995. "Helplessness in Early Childhood: The Role of Contingent Worth." *Child Development* 66(6): 1719–38.

Butler, Ruth, and Orna Neuman. 1995. "Effects of Task and Ego Achievement Goals on Help-Seeking Behaviors and Attitudes." *Journal of Educational Psychology* 87(2): 261–71.

Camara, W. J., and A. E. Schmidt. 1999. "Group Differences in Standardized Testing and Social Stratification." College Board Report no. 95–5. New York: College Entrance Examination Board.

Chesler, Mark, Mark Wilson, and Ann Malani. 1993. "Perceptions of Faculty Behavior by Students of Color." *Michigan Journal of Political Science* 16: 54–79.

Cohen, Geoffrey L., Claude M. Steele, and Lee Ross. 1999. "The Mentor's Dilemma: Providing Feedback Across the Racial Divide." *Personality and Social Psychology Bulletin* 25(10): 1302–18.

Cole, N. S. 1997. "The ETS Gender Study: How Females and Males Perform in Educational Settings." Princeton, N.J.: Educational Testing Service.

Covington, Martin V. 1984. "The Self-Worth Theory of Achievement: Findings and Implications." *Elementary School Journal* 85(1): 5–20.

Crocker, Jennifer. 1999. "Social Stigma and Self-Esteem: Situational Construction of Self-Worth." *Journal of Experimental Social Psychology* 35(1): 89–107.

Crocker, Jennifer, and Brenda Major. 1989. "Social Stigma and Self-Esteem: The Self-Protective Properties of Stigma." *Psychological Review* 96(4): 608–30.

Crocker, Jennifer, Brenda Major, and Claude M. Steele. 1998. "Social Stigma." In *Handbook of Social Psychology,* edited by Daniel Gilbert, Susan T. Fiske, and G. Lindzey. Boston: McGraw-Hill.

Crocker, Jennifer, Samuel R. Sommers, and Riia K. Luhtanen. 2002. "Hopes Dashed and Dreams Fulfilled: Contingencies of Self-Esteem and Admissions to Graduate School." *Personality and Social Psychology Bulletin* 28(9): 1275–86.

Crocker, Jennifer, and Connie T. Wolfe. 2001. "Contingencies of Self-Worth." *Psychological Review* 108(3): 593–623.

Croizet, Jean-Claude, and Theresa Claire. 1998. "Extending the Concept of Stereotype Threat to Social Class: The Intellectual Underperformance of Students from Low Socioeconomic Backgrounds." *Personality and Social Psychology Bulletin* 24(6): 588–94.

Croizet, Jean-Claude, Gerard Deprés, Marie-Eve Gauzins, Pascal Huguet, Jacques-Philippe Leyens, and A. Meot. 2004. "Stereotype Threat Undermines Intellectual Performance by Triggering a Disruptive Mental Load." *Personality and Social Psychology Bulletin* 30(6): 721–31.

Davies, Paul G., Steven J. Spencer, Diane M. Quinn, and Rebecca Gerhardstein. 2002. "Consuming Images: How Television Commercials That Elicit Stereotype Threat Can Restrain Women Academically and Professionally." *Personality and Social Psychology Bulletin* 28(12): 1615–28.

Deci, Edward L., and Richard M. Ryan. 1987. "The Support of Autonomy and the Control of Behavior." *Journal of Personality and Social Psychology* 53(6): 1027–37.

Diener, Carol I., and Carol S. Dweck. 1978. "An Analysis of Learned Helplessness: Continuous Changes in Performance, Strategy, and Achievement Cognitions Following Failure." *Journal of Personality and Social Psychology* 36(5): 451–62.

Diversity Report. 1990. "Final Report: Institute for the Study of Social Change." University of California, Berkeley.

Dweck, Carol S. 1999. *Self-Theories: Their Role in Motivation, Personality, and Development.* Philadelphia: Taylor and Francis/Psychology Press.

Dweck, Carol S., and Elaine S. Elliott. 1983. "Achievement Motivation." In *Socialization, Personality, and Social Development,* edited by E. M. Hetherington. New York: Wiley.

Dweck, Carol S., and Ellen L. Leggett. 1988. "A Social-Cognitive Approach to Motivation and Personality." *Psychological Review* 95(2): 256–73.

Dweck, Carol S., Y. Tenney, and N. Dinces. 1982. "Implicit Theories of Intelligence as Determinants of Achievement Goal Choice." Unpublished data.

Dykman, Benjamin M. 1998. "Integrating Cognitive and Motivational Factors in Depression: Initial Tests of a Goal-Orientation Approach." *Journal of Personality and Social Psychology* 74(1): 139–58.

Elliot, Andrew J., and Marcy A. Church. 1997. "A Hierarchical Model of Approach and Avoidance Achievement Motivation." *Journal of Personality and Social Psychology* 72(1): 218–32.

Elliot, Andrew J., and Judith M. Harackiewicz. 1996. "Approach and Avoidance Achievement Goals and Intrinsic Motivation: A Mediational Analysis." *Journal of Personality and Social Psychology* 70(3): 461–75.

Elliot, Andrew J., and Holly A. McGregor. 2001. "A 2 × 2 Achievement Goal Framework." *Journal of Personality and Social Psychology* 80(3): 501–19.

Elliott, Elaine S., and Carol S. Dweck. 1988. "Goals: An Approach to Motivation and Achievement." *Journal of Personality and Social Psychology* 54(1): 5–12.

Eysenck, Hans J. 1971. *The IQ Argument: Race, Intelligence, and Education.* New York: Library Press.

Fiske, Susan. 1998. "Stereotyping, Prejudice, and Discrimination." In *The Handbook of Social Psychology,* edited by Daniel T. Gilbert, Susan T. Fiske, and G. Lindzey. Volume 2. 4th edition. New York: McGraw-Hill.

Foote, Nelson. 1951. "Identification as the Basis for a Theory of Motivation." *American Sociological Review* 16(1): 14–21.

Ford, Thomas E., Mark A. Ferguson, Jenna L. Brooks, and Kate M. Hagadone. 2004. "Coping Sense of Humor Reduces Effects of Stereotype Threat on Women's Math Performance." *Personality and Social Psychology Bulletin* 30(5): 643–53.

Gonzales, Patricia M., Hart Blanton, and Kevin J. Williams. 2002. "The Effects of Stereotype Threat and Double Minority Status on the Test Performance of Latino Women." *Personality and Social Psychology Bulletin* 28(5): 659–70.

Grant, Heidi, and Carol S. Dweck. 2003. "Clarifying Achievement Goals and Their Impact." *Journal of Personality and Social Psychology* 85(3): 541–53.

Herrnstein, Richard, and Charles Murray. 1994. *The Bell Curve: Intelligence and Class Structure in American Society.* New York: Free Press.

Inzlicht, Michael, and Talia Ben-Zeev. 2000. "A Threatening Intellectual Environment: Why Females Are Susceptible to Experiencing Problem-Solving Deficits in the Presence of Males." *Psychological Science* 11(5): 365–71.

Jagacinski, Carolyn M., and John G. Nicholls. 1987. "Competence and Affect in Task Involvement and Ego Involvement." *Journal of Educational Psychology* 79(2): 107–14.

James, William. 1890/1950. *The Principles of Psychology.* New York: Dover.

Jensen. Arthur J. 1969. "How Much Can We Boost IQ and Scholastic Achievement?" *Harvard Educational Review* 39(1): 1–123.

Kray, Laura J., Leigh Thompson, and Adam Galinsky. 2001. "Battle of the Sexes: Gender Stereotype Confirmation and Reactance in Negotiations." *Journal of Personality in Social Psychology* 80(6): 942–58.

Lawrence, Jason S., Jennifer Crocker, and Hart Blanton. 2000. "Does Academic Praise Communicate Stereotypic Expectancies to Black Students?" Unpublished manuscript.

Lawrence, Jason S., and Carol S. Dweck. 2002. "The Link Between Academic Identification, Contingencies of Self-Worth, and Ability Goals." Unpublished data. University of Massachusetts, Lowell.

———. 2003. "Validation and Performance: Students with Ability Goals or Base Self-Worth on Achievement Underperform on Evaluative Tests." Unpublished manuscript.

Lawrence, Jason S., Bryant T. Marks, and James S. Jackson. 2000. "The Role of Verbal Identification in Black Students' Test Performance: Are Low Identified Students Resilient to Stereotype Threat?" Unpublished manuscript.

Lord, Charles G., and D. S. Sanz. 1985. "Memory Deficits and Memory Surfeits: Differential Cognitive Consequences of Tokenism for Tokens and Observers." *Journal of Personality and Social Psychology* 49: 918–26.

Lord, Charles G., Kentaro Umezaki, and John M. Darley. 1990. "Developmental Differences in Decoding the Meanings of the Appraisal Actions of Teachers." *Child Development* 61(1): 191–200.

Maehr, Martin L. 1991. "The Psychological Environment of the School: A Focus for School Leadership." In *Advances in Educational Administration*, edited by P. Thurston and P. Zodhiates. Greenwich, Conn.: JAI Press.

Major, Brenda, and Toni Schmader. 1998. "Coping with Stigma Through Psychological Disengagement." In *Prejudice: The Target's Perspective*, edited by Janet Swim and Charles Stangor. San Diego: Academic Press.

Major, Brenda, Steven Spencer, and Toni Schmader. 1998. "Coping with Negative Stereotypes About Intellectual Performance: The Role of Psychological Disengagement." *Personality and Social Psychology Bulletin* 24(1): 34–50.

Marx, David M., Joseph L. Brown, and Claude M. Steele. 1999. "Allport's Legacy and the Situational Press of Stereotypes." *Journal of Social Issues* 55(3): 491–502.

McGuire, William J., Claire V. McGuire, and Ward Winton. 1979. "Effects of Household Sex Composition on the Salience of One's Gender in the Spontaneous Self-Concept." *Journal of Experimental Social Psychology* 15(1): 77–90.

Meyer, Wulf-Uwe. 1982. "Indirect Communication About Perceived Ability Estimates." *Journal of Educational Psychology* 74(6): 888–97.

———. 1992. "Paradoxical Effects of Praise and Criticism on Perceived Ability." *European Review of Social Psychology* 3: 259–83.

Meyer, Wulf-Uwe., M. Bachmann, U. Biermann, M. Hempelmann, F.-O. Ploger, and H. Spiller. 1979. "The Informational Value of Evaluative Behavior: Influences of Praise and Blame on Perceptions of Ability." *Journal of Educational Psychology* 71: 259–68.

Meyer, Wulf-Uwe., Waldemar Mittag, and Udo Engler. 1986. "Some Effects of Praise and Blame on Perceived Ability and Affect." *Social Cognition* 4(3): 293–308.

Miller, Arden T., and Harry L. Hom Jr. 1997. "Conceptions of Ability and the Interpretation of Praise, Blame, and Material Rewards." *Journal of Experimental Education* 65(2): 163–77.

Molden, Daniel C., and Carol S. Dweck. 2000. "Meaning and Motivation." In *Intrinsic Motivation*, edited by Carol Sansone and Judith Harackiewicz. New York: Academic Press.

Molden, Daniel C., Heidi Grant, and Carol S. Dweck. 2005. "Theories of Intelligence and Self-Worth Responses to Failure Feedback." Unpublished data.

Mueller, Claudia M., and Carol S. Dweck. 1998. "Praise for Intelligence Can Undermine Children's Motivation and Performance." *Journal of Personality and Social Psychology* 75(1): 33–52.

Nelson–Le Gall, Sharon. 1981. "Help–Seeking: An Understudied Problem-Solving Skill in Children." *Developmental Review* 1(3): 224–46.

Newman, Richard S. 1991. "Goals and Self-Regulated Learning: What Motivates Children to Seek Academic Help." In *Advances in Motivation and Achievement,* edited by Martin L. Maehr and Paul R. Pintrich. Greenwich, Conn.: JAI Press.

———. 1994. "Adaptive Help-Seeking: A Strategy of Self-Regulated Learning." In *Self-Regulation of Learning and Performance: Issues and Educational Application,* edited by Dale H. Schunk and Barry J. Zimmerman. Hillsdale, N.J.: Erlbaum.

Nicholls, John G. 1984. "Achievement Motivation: Conceptions of Ability, Subjective Experience, Task Choice, and Performance." *Psychological Review* 91(3): 328–46.

Niiya, Yu, Jennifer Crocker, and Elizabeth N. Bartmess. 2004. "From Vulnerability to Resilience: Learning Orientations Buffer Contingent Self-Esteem from Failure." *Psychological Science* 15(12): 801–5.

Osborne, Jason W. 1995. "Academics, Self-Esteem, and Race: A Look at the Underlying Assumptions of the Disidentification Hypothesis." *Personality and Social Psychology Bulletin* 21(5): 449–55.

———. 1997. "Race and Academic Disidentification." *Journal of Educational Psychology* 89(4): 728–35.

Pollak, Kathryn I., and Yolanda F. Niemann. 1998. "Black and White Tokens in Academia: A Difference of Chronic Versus Acute Distinctiveness." *Journal of Applied Social Psychology* 28(11): 954–72.

Pronin, Emily, Claude M. Steele, and Lee Ross. 2004. "Identity Bifurcation in Response to Stereotype Threat: Women and Mathematics." *Journal of Experimental Social Psychology* 40(2): 152–68.

Rhodewalt, Frederick. 1994. "Conceptions of Ability, Achievement Goals, and Individual Differences in Self-Handicapping Behavior: On the Application of Implicit Theories." *Journal of Personality* 62(1): 67–85.

Rohwer, William D., and John W. Thomas. 1989. "The Role of Autonomous Problem-Solving Activities in Learning to Program." *Journal of Educational Psychology* 81: 584–93.

Rosenberg, Morris. 1979. *Conceiving of the Self.* New York: Basic Books.

Ryan, Richard M. 1982. "Control and Information in the Intrapersonal Sphere: An Extension of Cognitive Evaluation." *Journal of Personality and Social Psychology* 43: 450–61.

Schmader, Toni. 2002. "Gender Identification Moderates Stereotype Threat Effects on Women's Math Performance." *Journal of Experimental Social Psychology* 38(2): 194–201.

Schmader, Toni, and Michael Johns. 2003. "Converging Evidence That Stereotype Threat Reduces Working Memory Capacity." *Journal of Personality and Social Psychology* 85(3): 440–52.

Schneider, Monica E., Brenda Major, Riia Luhtanen, and Jennifer Crocker. 1996. "Social Stigma and the Potential Costs of Assumptive Help." *Personality and Social Psychology Bulletin* 22(2): 201–9.

Seibt, Beate, and Jens Förster. 2004. "Stereotype Threat and Performance: How Self-Stereotypes Influence Processing by Inducing Regulatory Foci." *Journal of Personality and Social Psychology* 87(1): 38–56.

Shapiro, E. G. 1983. "Embarrassment and Help Seeking." *New Directions in Helping,* edited by Arie Nadler and Jeffrey D. Fisher. New York: Academic Press.

Shih, Margaret, Todd L. Pittinsky, and Nalini Ambady. 1999. "Stereotype Susceptibility: Identity Salience and Shifts in Quantitative Performance." *Psychological Science* 10(1): 80–83.

Smith, Jessi L. 2004. "Understanding the Process of Stereotype Threat: A Review of Mediational Variables and New Performance Goal Direction." *Educational Psychology Review* 16(3): 177–206.

Spencer, Steven J., Claude M. Steele, and Diane M. Quinn. 1999. "Stereotype Threat and Women's Math Performance." *Journal of Experimental Social Psychology* 35(1): 4–28.

Steele, Claude M. 1997. "A Threat in the Air: How Stereotypes Shape the Intellectual Identities and Performance of Women and African Americans." *American Psychologist* 52: 613–29.

———. 1999. "Thin Ice: Stereotype Threat and Black College Students." *The Atlantic Monthly* 248(August): 44–54.

Steele, Claude M., and Joshua Aronson. 1995. "Stereotype Threat and the Intellectual Test Performance of African-Americans." *Journal of Personality and Social Psychology* 69(5): 797–811.

Steele, Claude M., Steven J. Spencer, and Joshua Aronson. 2002. "Contending with Group Image: The Psychology of Stereotype and Social Identity Threat." In *Advances in Experimental Social Psychology,* edited by Mark P. Zanna. San Diego: Academic Press.

Stipek, Deborah, and J. Heidi Gralinski. 1996. "Children's Beliefs About Intelligence and School Performance." *Journal of Educational Psychology* 88(3): 397–407.

Stone, Jeff. 1998. "Theories of Intelligence and the Meaning of Achievement Goals." Ph.D. dissertation, New York University.

Stone, Jeff, Christian I. Lynch, Mike Sjomeling, and John M. Darley. 1999. "Stereotype Threat Effects on Black and White Athletic Performance." *Journal of Personality and Social Psychology* 77(6): 1213–27.

Stryker, Sheldon. 1968. "Identity Salience and Role Performance: The Relevance of Symbolic Interaction Theory for Family Research." *Journal of Marriage and the Family* 30(4): 558–64.

Swann, William B., Jr. 1983. "Self-Verification: Bringing Social Reality into Harmony with the Self." In *Psychological Perspectives on the Self,* edited by Jerry Suls and Anthony G. Greenwald. Volume 2. Hillsdale, N.J.: Erlbaum.

Tinto, V. 1975. "Dropout from Higher Education: A Theoretical Synthesis of Recent Research." *Review of Educational Research* 45: 89–125.

Urdan, Timothy. 1997. Achievement Goal Theory: Past Results, Future Directions. In *Advances in Motivation and Achievement,* edited by Martin L. Maehr and Paul R. Pintrich. Greenwich, Conn.: JAI Press.

Utman, Christopher H. 1997. "Performance Effects of Motivational States: A Meta-Analysis." *Personality and Social Psychology Review* 1(2): 170–82.

Zimmerman, Barry J., and Manuel Martinez-Pons. 1986. "Development of a Structured Interview for Assessing Student Use of Self-Regulated Learning Strategies." *American Educational Research Journal* 23: 614–328.

CHAPTER 3

A FRAMEWORK FOR STUDYING
SOCIAL IDENTITY AND COPING WITH
DAILY STRESS DURING THE
TRANSITION TO COLLEGE

Bonita London, Geraldine Downey, Niall Bolger,
and Elizabeth Velilla

Over the past several decades, psychological theory and research have substantially improved our understanding of how stressful life experiences can undermine health, well-being, and the accomplishment of valued goals (Anderson, McNeilly, and Myers 1993; Clark et al. 1999; Lazarus and Folkman 1984). Whereas initially this research focused on reactions to major but infrequent life events, more recently it has focused on the mundane and chronic stress that emerges in daily life (Bolger and Eckenrode 1991; Bolger and Zuckerman 1995; Swim, Cohen, and Hyers 1998). One source of chronic stress that research has begun to examine is membership in a traditionally stigmatized or devalued social group (Clark et al. 1999; Cross, Smith, and Payne 2001; Cross and Strauss 1998; Major et al. 2003; Major and O'Brien 2005; Miller and Kaiser 2001; Miller and Major 2000). By focusing on stress processes in daily life researchers can investigate the microprocesses linking membership in historically devalued social categories with greater risk for stress-related physical and mental illnesses and relative underachievement (Clark et al. 1999; Steele and Aronson 1995). This work is a critical means of answering the important question of why, given the minimization of structural barriers to equality, members of traditionally stigmatized groups continue to experience relatively poorer health, lower achievement outcomes, and greater psychological alienation than members of non-stigmatized groups.

In this chapter we describe a framework for studying how membership in a devalued group is experienced in daily life during an important life transition. We draw on the stress and coping literature to help understand the processes linking membership in such a group to negative psychological outcomes during the transition. We also draw on the social- and personal-identities literature to link the experiences of stigmatized individuals with the ways they identify with the social groups they belong to and with their conceptualization of themselves as individuals. Although negative experiences have typically been the focus of the research on stigmatized group members, we will also consider the positive experiences associated with group membership.

Having outlined a framework for studying stress, coping, and identity activation in daily life, we will use that framework to examine how one's membership in historically devalued groups (for example, ethnic-racial, gender, sexual-orientation, or religious minority groups) influence daily life during the transition to college by presenting and reviewing data from a daily-diary study of undergraduate students entering college. These students provided daily reports of the activation of their social and personal identities in positive and negative contexts, as well as the strategies they used to cope with each situation. Using the data, we assessed the effects of each coping strategy on the well-being and adjustment of students and explored how these effects varied according to students' social and personal identities.

PERSONAL AND SOCIAL
IDENTITY ACTIVATION

The term "identity" has been used to signify the core features of the self that individuals carry with them throughout their daily experiences and that provide a lens for viewing the world. They reflect how individuals view themselves as well as how they think others view them (Erikson 1968, 1980). An individual may have multiple identities, some based on membership in a social group such as those defined by race or gender, and some based on unique personal characteristics such as personality or physical appearance (Brewer 1991; Chatman and Eccles, chapter 5, this volume; Ellemers, Spears, and Doosje 2002; Luhtanen and Crocker 1992). Although these identities are often stable characteristics of the individual, contextual cues determine which of an individual's identities is active or salient at any particular point in time (Deaux and Major 1987; Steele and Aronson 1995). For example, in contexts where an Asian American woman may be the only female, gender may become her most salient identity, whereas for the same individual, being in an environment where she is the only Asian American among females, ethnicity may become the most salient identity. Further, the specific identity that is activated within a context may influence whether individuals appraise a situation as stressful, and if so, how they cope with it. For example, a feature of one's personal identity, such as the tendency to view the self as likely to be rejected by potential romantic partners, may be activated in situations where acceptance or rejection by an intimate partner or new friend is a possibility. This expectation of rejection would also influence how the individual copes in the situation, for example, using ingratiation to ensure acceptance or self-silencing to avoid rejection (Downey and Feldman 1996). Alternatively, a stigmatized identity such as race or gender may be activated within the same individual in the context of an academic stressor, as when being evaluated by a university professor. This activation may lead to expectations of discrimination on the basis of the stigmatized identity and to the subsequent deployment of coping strategies, such as academic disengagement or a motivated challenge response to prove the professor wrong (London, Downey, and Dweck 2005; Mendoza-Denton et al. 2002).

The relatively separate literatures of personality (emphasizing unique individual characteristics) and social stigma (emphasizing group-based identities) have focused on how identity affects the appraisals and experiences of individuals. However, there is the need for a more comprehensive view of the self that incorporates both personal and social identities simultaneously and that clarifies their role in appraisals and coping (Andersen, Downey, and Tyler, chapter 10, this volume).

Indeed, in the literature, much research has focused on how stigmatizing characteristics, especially visible stigmas such as ethnicity and gender, may increase exposure to stress by subjecting the stigmatized to the scrutiny and potentially discriminatory behavior of prejudiced others (Miller and Major 2000). Researchers are now beginning to examine under what circumstances and for whom membership in a stigmatized group is stressful. For example, Claude Steele and colleagues provide empirical evidence of the contextual cues that may activate a threatened social identity in such a way as to undermine academic performance and heighten physiological stress responses (Blascovich et al. 2001; Steele and Aronson 1995; see Lawrence, Crocker, and Dweck, chapter 2, this volume, for a review). Margaret Shih et al. (2002) have extended this work to show that when different identities within the same person are made salient (even within the same context), individuals can differ in their performance and engagement. Capitalizing on the fact that Asians are positively stereotyped in math whereas women are negatively stereotyped in math, Shih et al. (2002) examined the performance of Asian women on a math task. When participants' Asian identity was activated, they performed better than when their female identity was activated. Thus, the same stressor can yield different outcomes in the same person depending on which of their identities is activated.

The laboratory-based research of Steele, Shih, and others illustrates the complex role of social-identity activation by demonstrating variability in the impact of the same objective situation on members of stigmatized groups. However, findings from field research on members of such groups importantly caution against focusing only on social identity when investigating how individuals negotiate important challenges (Strauss and Cross, chapter 4, this volume). Thus, while in this chapter we focus on the experiences of members of traditional stigmatized groups through the activation of their stigmatized social identities, we are also careful to explore their attributions to personal characteristics outside of their stigmatized social identities.

APPLYING THE STRESS AND COPING FRAMEWORK TO STUDYING THE IDENTITY PROCESS DURING THE TRANSITION TO COLLEGE

An individual's entry into a new context is a ripe opportunity for studying the relations among identity activation, stress, coping, and adaptation. During important transitions, people often draw on their preexisting frameworks (that is, identities, beliefs, and experiences) to understand their new roles and environment (Lazarus and

Folkman 1984; see Ruble and Seidman 1996). Many students experience the transition to college as an acute stressor that is marked by frequent, but often minor negative events, low levels of social support, and declines in physical and mental well-being (Gall, Evans, and Bellerose 2000). Researchers emphasize that a new college environment may challenge the meaning and value of an identity because it involves a move away from family and support networks to a new and unfamiliar environment that is initially less comfortable and supportive (Deaux and Major 1987).

Although entering college is a significant stressor for all students, a central finding of the stress and coping literature is that the same objective stressor may not be experienced uniformly (see Lazarus and Folkman 1984). To account for individual variability in the perception and impact of objectively similar stressors (such as entering college or the death of a loved one), Richard Lazarus and Susan Folkman (1984) outlined a model of the psychological process mediating the occurrence of a stressful event and one's appraisal of and reaction to it. The model highlighted the importance of how the individual evaluates an experience on two levels. Primary appraisal involves assessing whether a situation presents a challenge, threat, or potential for loss. This appraisal yields an evaluation of the perceived stressfulness of the situation. Secondary appraisal, or coping, involves evaluating the potential actions that might be used to manage the experience, as well as the potential success of each strategy employed. This model provides a framework for considering not only the context in which stress occurs, such as the transition to college in this research, but also factors that may mediate exposure to stress and negative outcomes, for example, drawing on personal or social identities to make sense of and deal with the stressor. Therefore, what the individual brings to the transition to college, in the way of identity-relevant schemas, should play a significant role in the transition experience.

Researchers studying life transitions indicate that "variables such as race, economic comfort levels, and gender influence whether a transition is represented as involving demands, alterations in relationships, and so on" (Ruble and Seidman 1996, 838). Thus, social and personal identities may play a major role in how individuals experience and cope with the transition to college. For example, Lisa Aspinwall and Shelley Taylor (1992) report that women experience decreased physical health and increased negative mood during the initial period of their first year in college. Thus, this transition presents an important challenge for psychological adjustment, particularly for members of stigmatized groups.

For members of traditionally stigmatized ethnic or racial groups, the transition to a new environment, particularly in a university that is predominantly white, may be especially stressful. Awareness of being members of a visible minority may leave them feeling vulnerable to additional negative stressors such as prejudice and discrimination beyond the transition itself (Bowen and Bok 1998; Deaux and Major 1987). For example, as ethnic minority students make the transition from a heterogeneous high school environment to a predominantly white university, race is likely to be a more salient identity used to understand the negative experiences they encounter. This may be evidenced by ethnic-minority students' reporting more negative experiences with new classmates or roommates, discomfort with their white professors, or their experiencing exclusion from events or new relationships because of their race (Mendoza-Denton et al. 2002). However, identification with the stigmatized identity may also hold opportunities for positive experiences. For example, in the study described in this paper, many black students report feeling heightened positive affect and a sense of belonging to the university following positive race-related activities such as attending cultural pride parades within the community or attending meetings of black student organizations (Mendoza-Denton et al. 2002). Further, the desire to gain acceptance within the novel environment may dictate the kinds of coping strategies used. Thus, the following questions are particularly relevant to this line of research: What personal and social identities become activated during the transition to college? And what happens when each of these distinct identities is activated? Drawing on the literature on stigmatized social identities and psychological well-being, we focus on traditionally stigmatized identities as one subgroup of social identities, in addition to the activation of personal identities for students during this transition.

COPING

The stress and coping literature posits that the impact of a stressor depends not only on its appraised severity but also on how the individual copes with it. The stress literature initially focused on dispositional coping strategies, proposing that individuals tend to choose and use a particular strategy when faced with a stressor and that certain coping choices produce better outcomes than others. Research on rumination versus distraction (Nolen-Hoeksema 1987) and problem-focused versus emotion-focused coping (Carver, Scheier, and Weintraub 1989) exemplify this approach. For example, Susan Nolen-Hoeksema (1987) found that ruminating about one's difficulties, in contrast to distracting oneself, generally increased depression. In the same vein, the benefits and detriments of adopting problem-focused versus emotion-focused coping strategies have been extensively examined (Carver, Scheier, and Weintraub 1989), where problem-focused coping is associated with optimism, sense of control, and hardiness, while emotion-focused coping is positively associated with anxiety and negatively associated with feelings of situational control, hardiness, and self-esteem (Carver, Scheier, and Weintraub 1989).

Considerably less attention has been paid to contextual influences on coping, despite Lazarus and Folkman's original emphasis on the importance of both person and context. The stigma literature is beginning to redress the imbalance by examining how members of stigmatized groups respond to threats to their stigmatized identity within particular contexts. For example, Brenda Major and Toni Schmader (1998) found that African American students cope with the threat of negative evaluation through devaluation of and disengagement from the domain in which they are stigmatized (see also Major et al. 1998). For African American students, the activation of their ethnicity in an evaluative situation which holds historically negative achievement expectations may prompt a coping strategy that has negative effects on achievement, but positive and protective effects on self-worth. These observations highlight the importance of addressing the following question: When an identity is activated, what particular coping strategies are employed to combat the threat, and to what end are these strategies used across different situations? The effectiveness of the strategy used also depends on the goal of the individual, for example self-protection versus advancement. Both the choice of strategy and the effectiveness of the strategy chosen are important, yet they are relatively neglected features of responses to identity threat (Bolger and Zuckerman 1995).

Though the coping literature identifies a wide range of coping strategies in response to stress, in this chapter we focus on three potential strategies for dealing with threats to one's identity: (a) confrontation (b) self-silencing, and (c) transformation and diffusion. We chose to focus on these distinctive strategies on the basis of pilot testing as well as on a measure of behavioral responses to perceived racism developed by Maya D. McNeilly et al. (1996). Factor analysis of the daily diary data confirmed their distinctiveness. Confrontation, operationalized as actively speaking out or confronting the source or circumstance of the threat, may be used in situations where the individual believes him- or herself to have been treated unfairly and where the presumed objective is educating or influencing a perceived perpetrator of the injustice. Self-silencing, operationalized as keeping the circumstances of the event to yourself, or accepting the situation, involves not expressing or acting on the perceived injustice or hurt. Here the likely objective is to maintain the relationship or to avoid further conflict or hurt. Finally, transformation and diffusion involves actively reframing or changing the subject of an interaction or using humor in a situation. This strategy may allow individuals to effectively deflate a threat.

Each of these strategies has potential costs and benefits. Speaking out may facilitate feelings of power and control over an interaction, giving the target a sense of vindication and accomplishment in righting a perceived wrong. However, it may also lead to alienation from others if the reaction is perceived as overly aggressive, or is not met with understanding or support from the perpetrator. Self-silencing may promote harmonious interactions, but at the cost of an undermined sense of well-being and control and increased rumination about the event. Finally, transforming the situation may allow for a diffusion of the potentially heightened negativity in an interaction and give the individual a sense of control; however, it may leave the individual susceptible to further threats from the same source if the threat was not directly addressed.

OVERVIEW

The literature that we have reviewed suggests that an adequate framework for understanding the experience of a stigmatized individual, particularly when making a transition to a new environment, involves:

1. Identifying exposure to stressors

2. Consideration of whether the stressor activates a particular identity or set of identities

3. Identifying the coping strategies employed to deal with the stressors

4. Understanding how various psychological outcomes are affected by these strategies

Within this model, the activation of a particular identity from among the individual's many personal and social identities will reflect both the individual and the context and potentially influence the strategies used to cope with the threat and the outcome of the stressor.

USING A DAILY-DIARY METHODOLOGY TO CAPTURE IDENTITY ACTIVATION AND COPING

The design and analysis of our daily-diary study of social identity in the transition to college closely mirrors Niall Bolger and Adam Zuckerman's (1995) study of personality in the stress process. This approach realizes Lazarus and Folkman's (1984; Lazarus 1993) call for a microanalytic, process approach to stress and coping, and provides an important methodological attempt at patterning signatures of activation and coping within individuals (Lazarus 2000). It integrates both a nomothetic approach that allows comparisons across individuals (such as across males and females, and members of different racial groups) and an ideographic approach that examines relations among variables within an individual (such as activation of different identities or use of different coping strategies within the same individual; Allport 1937; Bolger, Davis, and Rafaeli 2003). The approach allows researchers to examine perceived exposure to different types of identity-relevant events in relation to social-category membership, the impact of exposure to such events on outcomes relevant to the accomplishment of an important life task, and the moderating effect of coping choices. Further, the methodology of reporting the occurrence of events on a daily basis limits the biases that retrospection may produce.

In the data that we review here, thirty-seven Caucasian, sixty-seven African American, and seventeen Asian students were recruited prior to the first day of classes to participate in a twenty-one-day daily-diary study. A little over half of the participants were female. They completed background measures and were then given a package containing seven-day structured daily-diary questionnaires to be completed nightly for the first twenty-one days of their first college academic year. The daily-diary questionnaires were two-page semistructured questions designed to assess the activation of various identities in relation to positive and negative events in daily life, and the coping strategies used to negotiate such events. In addition, the diary questionnaire assessed participants' attitudes, current mood, and sense of belonging at the university each day.

The data were analyzed to answer two questions. The first question concerned the association between perceived exposure to positive and negative identity-related events and social-category membership, that is, do members of stigmatized groups experience the college transition through the lens of their social identity? This phenomenon was examined using generalized estimating equation methods, or GEE (Diggle, Liang, and Zeger 1994). This approach takes account of the fact that there are multiple observations per person in estimating the effect of between-person characteristics such as gender and race on the occurrence of identity-related events.

The second question concerned the impact of positive and negative identity-related events on well-being and sense of belonging at the institution. In the case of negative events, we also assessed the extent to which the impact of an event was moderated by the use of each of the three coping strategies described. Analyses of the links between identity-related events, coping, sense of well-being, acceptance, and belonging at the institution were conducted using a multilevel or hierarchical linear model, or HLM (Bolger, Davis and Rafaeli 2003; Bryk and Raudenbush 1992; Kenny, Kashy, and Bolger 1998). A detailed account of the specific analytic strategy is given in Bolger and Zuckerman (1995). Since the frequency of events related to each type of identity for the typical individual was low, the data looking at the impact of events were pooled across persons. Thus, in the analyses reported below the effects of identity-related events are treated as common across individuals, but each individual was allowed to have his or her unique level of a particular outcome given a random intercept.

Personal- and Social-Identity Activation During the Transition to College

Individuals have a great many potential identities on which to draw from to explain events they encounter. We limit our focus to six identities determined through extensive pilot testing to be relatively common and salient in an undergraduate population: race, gender, religion, sexual orientation, personality, and physical looks. These categories span both social identities (race, gender, religion, and sexual orientation) and personal identities (personality and physical appearance) and include concealable (religion and sexual orientation) and visible (race, gender, and physical appearance) identities. Each day, students wrote about a salient positive or negative experience they had that day and then indicated which of the six possible identities were activated in that experience (see the appendix for identity-activation examples). They could attribute the event to single or multiple identities (Brewer 1991).

The range of positive and negative identity-related events during the first three weeks of college spanned interactions on campus with new roommates, classmates, and professors, as well as events in the surrounding community such as parades, community activities, and parties. For example, positive race-related events reported by students were attending meetings of the black students' organization and going to the Caribbean Day parade in the community. Such interactions appear to reflect important daily enactments of identity around "bonding" with members of one's ethnic group, as described by Linda Strauss and William E. Cross (chapter 4, this volume). Negative race-related events included reporting feeling alienated as a result of being excluded from conversations or activities because of race (see the appendix for other examples of identity-related events reported).

Overall, during this transition, 64 percent of the events described were positive and 36 percent were negative. Participants reported important events relevant to one or more of the six identities on 19 percent of days. Neither the total number of identity-related events nor the number of positive or negative events reported differed by ethnicity or by gender. The only exception to this general pattern was that white males reported approximately equal numbers of positive and negative events while others reported more positive than negative events. This suggests that, contrary to much of the literature reviewed earlier, within this sample of students the transition to college was generally associated with positive identity-related events, including for those students from traditionally stigmatized groups. However, it may be the case that experiencing negative identity-related events on just a minority of days is sufficiently stressful to significantly undermine well-being. Very few events were attributed to either sexual orientation or religion. This may either reflect the fact that these identities are concealable or that the sample included few members of sexual minorities or of religions that are actively stigmatized.

When a negative experience was reported during the transition, African American and Asian students attributed such experiences to their race or ethnic identity to a greater extent than did Caucasian students. For example, an African American student reported, "I had a hard time making new friends today because I think that people are intimidated by the fact that I am a black person from New York." African American and Asian students did not differ in the frequency of activation of race-ethnicity for negative experiences (although the specific experiences that activated this identity may have been very different for each group). Thus, for these two groups of students, being a member of a traditionally stigmatized group was related to the negative activation of their ethnicities to a greater extent than for Caucasian students. Similarly, women were more likely to report negative gender-related events than were men. When Caucasian students experienced negative events, they reported marginally greater activation of their gender identity—for example, "I felt intimidated in class because of my gender"—than did Asian students in negative contexts, and significantly greater activation of their religious identity than did African American students. Finally, there were no differences by race or gender in the frequency of activation of the personal identities (personality and physical appearance).

These findings provide evidence of the activation patterns of personal and social identities for African American, Asian, and Caucasian students during the transition to college. When negative events occur, students are more likely to attribute them to devalued social identities, such as being a woman or a member of a racial or ethnic minority, than to their personal identities (personality and physical appearance). Thus, in these three weeks, negative experiences tend to center around social identities rather than more personal characteristics of the individual, for members of traditionally stigmatized groups.

For positive events, there was a trend for race to be mentioned more frequently by Asian Americans than by African Americans. Race was also activated significantly more often by both Asian Americans and African Americans than for Caucasians under positive circumstances. For example, an African American student reported, "I joined the Minority Recruitment Council" as a positive event, while another student reported, "I attended a party hosted by two black fraternities. It felt very good to be having a good time with so many people who looked like me." One Asian student reported, "I went to a Chinese students club meeting and met a lot of people. I also learned a few things." Thus, these two groups also experienced greater positive race-ethnicity identity activation than Caucasian students, suggesting that they may use their identities to understand both positive and negative experiences to a greater extent than white students do. Finally, women used gender significantly more than men to understand positive as well as negative events, again suggesting that a stigmatized identity may be more centrally meaningful in the life of the individual, and thus it may be used more frequently as a frame for understanding both positive and negative experiences.

Psychological Well-Being and Sense of Belonging During the Transition to College

The diary assessed a variety of emotions potentially experienced by students in reaction to events they reported. Our study focused on feelings of well-being and feelings of rejection. A well-being index was based on the following eleven emotions: feeling supported, cared for, accepted, appreciated, loved, happy, confident, pleased, successful, satisfied, and content. A rejection index was created from three emotions: feeling rejected, alienated, and unwelcome.

Because a key task during the transition to college is to develop a sense of comfort and belonging within the institution, we explored the level of connection students felt toward the university in general and toward their classmates, roommates, and professors each day. The items for belonging at the university instructed the participants to indicate the degree to which they felt thrilled to be at the university, felt that they fit in, and felt welcome at the university.

Experiencing positive or negative gender events did not impact well-being outcomes for men or women. However, this was not the case for race-related events. On days when students recorded a negative race-related event (for example, "I was in [the bookstore] and the security seemed to be following me"; "I felt a little out of place when I was talking to a group of people because I was the only black person"), students felt a marginally lower sense of belonging at the university, that is, they felt less connected, comfortable, and welcome. The effect of a negative race-based event on feelings of either rejection or happiness were significant only for men, who felt a reduced sense of belonging, greater feelings of rejection, and more unhappiness following such events.

Clearly, experiencing negativity because of one's race could undermine well-being and sense of belonging; and the opposite is true for positive race-relevant experiences. When students reported a positive race-related event (for example, going to the black student union, or having a conversation with suite mates) they experienced a significant increase in sense of belonging at the university. The effects of positive race-related events did not differ by sex. This finding lends support for the view that identity-affirming events can lead to a greater sense of connection and comfort within one's environment. Tracy McLaughlin-Volpe, Rodolfo Mendoza-Denton, and J. Nicole Shelton (chapter 9, this volume) discuss the benefits of positive intergroup friendships for developing a sense of belonging and well-being in their chapter.

Together these results suggest a continuing vulnerability to experiencing alienation on the part of members of ethnic and racial groups that remain minorities in institutions that have historically devalued their group. For women, having numerical equality within the context may dampen the negative effects of gender-related negativity on sense of belonging. Although this seems to be the case here, ongoing research shows that women who anxiously expect rejection because of their gender have greater feelings of alienation and discomfort within the university setting than those low in gender-based rejection anxiety (London et al. 2005).

In terms of personal identities, there was a consistent significant effect of experiencing negative personality-related events on the well-being of students during the transition. Positive and negative events attributed to personality included being complimented on one's personality and having others show personal interest in the student or communicate trust in and comfort with the student, as opposed to being excluded from events with friends and suite mates. When a negative event was attributed to their personality, students felt a reduced sense of belonging and felt more rejected and less happy. Positive personality-related events showed a trend toward a beneficial impact, but the effects were neither as strong nor as consistent as the effects of negative events attributed to one's personality. Events related to one's physical looks did not significantly impact the outcomes examined. Thus, both social and personal identity attributions have a strong impact on how connected students feel to their surroundings.

Coping with Identity Activation: Implications for Well-Being and Sense of Belonging

Next, we assessed the implications of the three strategies described previously for coping with a negative event captured in the diary. Silencing was indexed by two items, "accepting it" or "keeping it to myself." Confrontation was indexed by six items, including "speaking out" and "trying to prove them wrong." Transformation and diffusion of the stressor was indexed by two items: "using humor" and "changing the subject." There were no significant race or gender differences in the frequency of use of each type of coping strategy; however, as to be expected, to the extent that individuals used self-silencing responses they were less likely to use confrontation strategies. Neither of these types of strategies was significantly associated with the use of transformation and diffusion.

The moderating effects of coping strategy were most pronounced for race- and personality-related events. Following a negative race-related event, students felt a significantly greater sense of belonging to the university when they used transformation as a coping strategy, but felt a significantly reduced sense of belonging when they used self-silencing. The effect of confrontation was nonsignificant. The same pattern emerged for feelings of rejection and for total happiness, although in the case of total happiness the positive effect of transformation was not significant.

In the case of a negative event based on personality, individuals felt greater feelings of rejection and reduced sense of happiness irrespective of the type of coping used. However, the type of strategy used moderated the effect of such an event on sense of belonging. Both confrontation and self-silencing were associated with a reduced sense of belonging, whereas transformation reduced the negative impact of a personality-related event.

How often did students actually use these coping strategies when either a race- or personality-based negative event occurred? Confrontation was used in 13 percent of the events; self-silencing was used in 24 percent of the events, and transformation was used in 11 percent of the events. These usage patterns were comparable across types of event. Thus, the most effective coping strategy, transformation—because it reduced the negative impact of the events—was used less frequently than silencing, which was consistently the most used and least effective mode of coping.

CONCLUSION

This chapter began with the question, How do people's identities shape their daily experience as they negotiate important life tasks such as the transition to college? To answer this question we sought to forge a link between the stress and coping litera-ture and the literature on stigma and identity. The study that we have described illus-trates the utility of a framework that considers the relative exposure of individuals to stressful situations, the ways people appraise situations in relation to their multiple social and personal identities, and the ways they cope in situations they deem threat-ening to their identity.

Perceived Exposure to Identity-Relevant Events

Although the number of positive and negative events reported by students during the transition to college were the same irrespective of race and gender, members of historically devalued groups, women and minorities, were more likely than those who were not, men and Caucasians, to attribute significant daily events to gender and race. Thus, it would appear that social-category membership is consciously used as an interpretative framework to the extent that the category is devalued. It is note-worthy that African American and Asian American students experienced both more positive and more negative events that they viewed as race-related during the tran-sition to college than did Caucasian students. In addition, across the sample the level of belonging to the university was relatively high. Thus, the transition period may provide many opportunities for positive race experiences for members of historically devalued groups (see Strauss and Cross, chapter 4, this volume).

Significant daily events were ascribed as frequently to personal identity (physical appearance and personality) as to social identity. This was true within gender and racial groups. This finding echoes Strauss and Cross's (chapter 4, this volume) find-ing that among African American students, "individualism," which is a focus on the self as an individual rather than within a social framework, was most often reported as the behavioral enactment used to negotiate situations. Thus, our findings support Strauss and Cross's declaration that social-identity research should not lose sight of the centrality of individuality in the efforts of members of devalued groups to make sense of their world.

Not surprisingly, gender differences emerged in the appraisal of identity-related events. To the extent that men used a social identity to explain an event, they used race. Women were equally likely to use race and gender. These findings highlight the importance of considering how people draw on the multiple identities at their dis-posal to view and understand their experiences.

It is important to note that study participants identified positive or negative events related to the six identities targeted in the study on fewer days than they reported no such events. This suggests either that significant daily events are typi-cally not appraised in terms of identity or that we omitted other important identi-ties that students use. Many significant events may have been viewed as having occurred by chance or because of contextual factors, and it is possible, too, that nor-matively important identities may have been omitted (for example, social-class membership). Also omitted were uncommon but highly salient identities, such as being physically disabled. Future work may better approach investigating identities in daily life by having individuals describe their central identities prior to the diary component of the study and to investigate daily experience relevant to these identities in the diary study.

The diary approach does not permit us to distinguish how social-category membership shapes objective exposure to certain experiences from how it impacts the subjective interpretation of the same objective event. Availability of objective observations of the type of daily events described by study participants would probably not resolve this problem. Although we know of no study with adults, observational studies of the daily interpersonal experiences of children at school have been undertaken. In a study of children's exposure to rejection in daily life, Stephen Asher, Amanda Rose, and Sonda Gabriel (2001) found that many of the rejection incidents they observed were ambiguous to the observer with respect to underlying intent. Thus, the children necessarily drew on an interpretative framework to understand their experiences as do the students in this study. In the initial stages of college, a context that frowns on overt expressions of race- or gender-relevant negativity, individuals may be particularly reliant on preexisting interpretive frameworks to understand their new world.

Finally, people differ considerably in the extent to which they invoke social and personal identities to explain their daily experience. This suggests the importance of looking for sources of individual differences in identity activation. For example, sensitivity to status-based rejection would appear to be one important source of within-status group variability in perceived exposure to identity-linked events. We have found this to be the case for race in the present data set. To the extent that African Americans are high in sensitivity to race-based rejection, they report experiencing more race-based negative (but not positive) events during the diary period (Mendoza-Denton et al. 2002). In work currently under way in our laboratory, Bonita London et al. (2005) have shown that to the extent that women are sensitive to gender-based rejection they also report experiencing more gender-based discrimination.

Consequences of Identity-Relevant Events

With the daily-diary approach it was possible to compare students' sense of belonging at college and their general sense of well-being and feelings of rejection on days when they experienced an identity-related event compared to days when they did not. Of the social identity–related events, only race-related experiences had a consistent impact on the outcomes examined. This identity may be the most salient as members of traditionally stigmatized groups, in this case African Americans and Asian Americans, enter an environment in which they are in the minority. Further, the impact of events ascribed to personal identity, specifically personality, was actually stronger than that of events ascribed to social identity. When an event is interpreted as personal, its benefits or costs cannot be attributed to arbitrary membership in a social group. Judging a negative event as being based on one's membership in a stigmatized group may protect the individual from the sense of self-devaluation that personal rejection elicits (Crocker and Major 1989). On the other hand, attributing positive events to group membership rather than to the self may deprive the individual of the sense of efficacy that should emanate from being able to link positive outcomes with personal efforts.

The three outcomes we examined were chosen because they were predictive of long-term outcomes. However, it will be important for future research to investigate a broader array of outcomes, including behavioral variables, such as time spent studying, academic or other types of help seeking, and physical health symptoms.

Moderating Role of Coping

Prior research on social identity has paid little attention to how people cope with the negative identity-relevant events in daily life (for an exception, see Strauss and Cross, chapter 4, this volume). Research using the daily-diary methodology to study stress and coping has established that how people cope with daily stressors influences their well-being (Bolger and Zuckerman 1995; Tennen et al. 2000). In the present study we examined three coping strategies that appeared especially pertinent to dealing with unpleasant social situations, especially situations involving interpersonal rejection and discrimination: confrontation, self-silencing, and transformation. The use of confrontation as a coping strategy did not improve things when the event was race-related and it harmed things when the event was deemed to be due to one's personality. Although confrontation may be necessary and useful in certain situations in order for an individual to communicate his or her beliefs, concerns, and emotions, it did not appear to facilitate a smooth transition to college. Self-silencing, inhibiting one's reactions, may protect against an escalation of the negative interaction, however, it does so at a cost. When individuals self-silenced, they experienced a diminished sense of belonging, perhaps because this reaction fostered rumination. Finding that self-silencing had a cost on well-being is in line with prior evidence that silencing the self can lead to depression and anxiety and is often negatively related to adjustment during the college transition (Haemmerlie et al. 2001).

The more beneficial third strategy, transformation, was not used as often as confrontation and self-silencing by students during the transition. Actions that transform a negative situation, via the use of humor or changing the subject, may allow individuals to benefit from the event, perhaps because such actions may promote a sense of being in control of the situation (see Stewart and Dottolo, chapter 8, this volume, for an in-depth view of coping with graduate school). Transformation may have a downside, however, as it can also result in individuals' not actively dealing with the threat, and may foster negative outcomes for self- and group-esteem, which we have not measured here.

Thus, our review of this research suggests that coping matters and that the impact of negative identity-related events, such as a race-related event, are best understood in light of how the situation was coped with. Nonetheless, the study leaves a number of questions unanswered. For example, it does not indicate why one coping strategy is chosen over another. Possibly, events that elicit a transformative reaction are less negative than those that elicit less beneficial coping strategies, however our examination of brief qualitative descriptions of the events did not support this view. It is also possible that the individuals' general sense of belonging at the university or their overall well-being influences the coping resources available to the individual when facing any particular event. Thus, those who feel marginalized, unwelcome, or depressed may be unable to muster the energy or effort needed to engage in the type of strategic, flexible, and discriminative coping that allows them to regulate and thus transform the social situation. Instead, when feeling distressed or unwelcome, people may be more likely to engage in more impulse-driven fight-or-flight reactions that emerge in confrontation or self-silencing. It is also important to acknowledge that the measure of coping that we used was limited. A stronger test of the moderating impact of coping on identity-relevant stressors awaits the development of better measures of how individuals cope with such stressors (see Strauss and Cross, chapter 4, this volume).

The study permits us to make general claims about the efficacy of each type of coping, but the measures do not capture the fact that in some situations, a particular coping strategy—remaining silent or confrontation—may be the most appropriate. This leaves us with the dilemma of how to distinguish effective from ineffective coping without peeking at the outcome of interest. We would argue that a critical distinction is whether the coping strategy used is consciously chosen (reflective) as being in line with one's long-term goals or impulsive and geared toward immediate goals or reactions. Our current research showing that self-regulatory competency protects high-rejection-sensitive people from the personal and interpersonal difficulties characteristic of that disposition supports this distinction (Ayduk et al. 2000; Ayduk, Mischel, and Downey 2002).

Caveats

Two important caveats need to be considered when evaluating the study described in this review. First, because we examined same-day associations between the occurrence of an event and outcomes of interest, it was not possible to determine unambiguously the direction of causality in the associations that we documented. One way around this would be to examine whether the occurrence of an event today predicted change from today to tomorrow in outcomes of interest. Analyses revealed no significant cross-day effects. This was true whether we used today's event to predict cross-day change in belonging, happiness, and rejection or today's sense of belonging, happiness, and rejection to predict the occurrence of an event tomorrow.

Second, the fact that identity-related events occurred relatively rarely placed important limits on the types of analyses that we could undertake. Ideally we would have liked to treat each type of event and each type of coping (where relevant) as random effects in the multilevel analyses that we undertook. However, events of interest (and consequent coping strategies) did not occur with sufficient frequency for this to be possible. The limited number of events in combination with the limited sample size also meant that the statistical power to test whether identity-related processes differed by identity group was low and thus the absence of significant effects should be treated cautiously.

These caveats notwithstanding, we demonstrate the value of drawing on theory and methods from the stress and coping literature to further our understanding of how individuals draw on their multiple identities, both social and personal, during the negotiation of an important life task, making the transition to college.

APPENDIX: EXAMPLES OF IDENTITY ACTIVATION

Race or Ethnicity Activation

NEGATIVE

- I had a hard time making new friends today because I think that people are intimidated by the fact that I am a black person from New York.
- I felt uncomfortable with some people from my floor because they were having a conversation, which I was excluded from because of my race.

POSITIVE

- Had a meeting with the black student organization, made me feel welcome and the people involved were very receptive.
- I attended a party hosted by two black fraternities [or sororities]. It felt very good to be having a good time with so many people who looked like me.

Gender Activation

NEGATIVE

- I felt intimidated in class because of my gender.
- I was teased about "being a girl" (weak and so forth) by a floormate.

POSITIVE

- I think a lady in the office of admission extended a job application deadline because I was a black female.
- I received a rose because I was female.

Personality Activation

NEGATIVE

- I'm starting to suspect that my French teacher is scared to call on or talk to me. Today, the only reason he called on me is because, for a length of time, I was the only one raising my hand.
- Some friends at home sent me a rather offensive e-mail for some strange reason, which bothered me.

POSITIVE

- Somebody complimented me on my personality.
- My suite mates seemed interested in me.

Physical-Appearance Activation

NEGATIVE

- I felt uncomfortable in physical education because of my weight.

- Was followed by a young man trying to get my phone number.

POSITIVE

- I wore a summer dress and people told me I should be a model. They told me I had the face and body for it.

- Because of my looks, I was invited to a party.

REFERENCES

Allport, Gordon Willard. 1937. *Personality: A Psychological Interpretation*. Oxford, England: Holt.

Anderson Norman, Maya McNeilly, and Hector Myers. 1993. "A Biopsychosocial Model of Race Differences in Vascular Reactivity." In *Cardiovascular Reactivity to Psychological Stress and Disease*, edited by James J. Blascovich and Edward S. Katkin. Washington, D.C.: American Psychological Association.

Asher, Steven, Amanda Rose, and Sonda Gabriel. 2001. "Peer Rejection in Everyday Life." In *Interpersonal Rejection*, edited by Mark Leary. London: Oxford University Press.

Aspinwall, Lisa, and Shelley Taylor. 1992. "Modeling Cognitive Adaptation: A Longitudinal Investigation of the Impact of Individual Differences and Coping on College Adjustment and Performance." *Journal of Personality and Social Psychology* 63(6): 989–1003.

Ayduk, Ozlem, Rodolfo Mendoza-Denton, Walter Mischel, Geraldine Downey, Philip Peake, and Monica Rodriguez. 2000. "Regulating the Interpersonal Self: Strategic Self-Regulation for Coping with Rejection Sensitivity." *Journal of Personality and Social Psychology* 79(5): 776–92.

Ayduk, Ozlem, Walter Mischel, and Geraldine Downey. 2002. "Attentional Mechanisms Linking Rejection to Hostile Reactivity: The Role of 'Hot' Versus 'Cool' Focus." *Psychological Science* 13: 443–48.

Blascovich, James, Steven Spencer, Diane Quinn, and Claude Steele. 2001. "African Americans and High Blood Pressure: The Role of Stereotype Threat." *Psychological Science* 12(3): 225–29.

Bolger, Niall, Angelina Davis, and Eshkol Rafaeli. 2003. "Diary Methods: Capturing Life As It Is Lived." *Annual Review of Psychology* 54: 579–616.

Bolger, Niall, and John Eckenrode. 1991. "Social Relationships, Personality, and Anxiety During a Major Stressful Event." *Journal of Personality and Social Psychology* 61: 440–49.

Bolger, Niall, and Adam Zuckerman. 1995. "A Framework for Studying Personality in the Stress Process." *Journal of Personality and Social Psychology* 69: 890–902.

Bowen, William, and Derek Bok. 1998. *The Shape of the River: Long Term Consequences of Considering Race in College and University Admissions*. Princeton: Princeton University Press.

Brewer, Marilynn. 1991. "The Social Self: On Being the Same and Different at the Same Time." *Personality and Social Psychology Bulletin* 17(5): 475–82.

Bryk, Anthony, and Stephen Raudenbush. 1992. *Hierarchical Linear Models: Applications and Data Analysis Methods*. Newbury Park, Calif.: Sage.

Carver, Charles, Michael Scheier, and Jagdish Weintraub. 1989. "Assessing Coping Strategies: A Theoretically Based Approach." *Journal of Personality and Social Psychology* 56: 267–83.

Clark, Rodney, Norman Anderson, Vernessa Clark, and David Williams. 1999. "Racism as a Stressor for African Americans: A Biopsychosocial Model." *American Psychologist* 54: 805–16.

Crocker, Jennifer, and Brenda Major. 1989. "Social Stigma and Self-Esteem: The Self-Protective Properties of Stigma." *Psychological Review* 96: 608–30.

Cross, William, Lakersha Smith, and Yassir Payne. 2001. "Black Identity: A Repertoire of Daily Enactments." In *Counseling Across Cultures,* edited by Paul Pederson, Juris G. Draguns, Walter Lonner, and Joseph Trimball. Thousand Oaks, Calif.: Sage.

Cross, William, and Linda Strauss. 1998. "The Everyday Functions of African American Identity." In *Prejudice: The Target's Perspective,* edited by Janet Swim and Charles Stangor. San Diego: Academic Press.

Deaux, Kay, and Brenda Major. 1987. "Putting Gender into Context: An Interactive Model of Gender-Related Behavior." *Psychological Review* 94(3): 369–89.

Diggle, Peter, Kung-Yee Liang, and Scott Zeger. 1994. *Analysis of Longitudinal Data.* Oxford: Oxford University Press.

Downey, Geraldine, and Scott Feldman. 1996. "Implications of Rejection Sensitivity for Intimate Relationships." *Journal of Personality and Social Psychology* 70: 1327–43.

Ellemers, Naomi, Russell Spears, and Bertjan Doosje. 2002. "Self and Identity." *Annual Review of Psychology* 53(1): 161–86.

Erikson, Erik. 1968. *Identity: Youth and Crisis.* Oxford, England: Norton.

———. 1980. *Identity and the Life Cycle.* New York: Norton.

Gall, Terry Lynn, David Evans, and Satya Bellerose. 2000. "Transition to First-Year University: Patterns of Change in Adjustment Across Life Domains and Time." *Journal of Social and Clinical Psychology* 19(4): 544–67.

Haemmerlie, Frances, Robert Montgomery, A. Williams, and K. A. Winborn. 2001. "Silencing the Self in College Settings and Adjustment." *Psychological Reports* 88: 587–94.

Kenny, David, Deborah Kashy, and Niall Bolger. 1998. "Data Analysis in Social Psychology." In *The Handbook of Social Psychology,* edited by Daniel Gilbert and Susan Fiske. Volume 1. 4th edition. Boston: McGraw-Hill.

Lazarus, Richard. 1993. "Coping Theory and Research: Past, Present, and Future." *Psychosomatic Medicine* 55: 234–47.

———. 2000. "Toward Better Research on Stress and Coping." *American Psychologist* 55(6): 665–73.

Lazarus, Richard, and Susan Folkman. 1984. *Stress Appraisal and Coping.* New York: Springer.

London, Bonita, Geraldine Downey, and Carol Dweck. 2005. "Appraisal and Coping with Race-Based Threat." Unpublished paper. New York: Columbia University.

London, Bonita, Geraldine Downey, Aneeta Rattan, and Diana Tyson. 2005. "Sensitivity to Gender Based Rejection: Theory, Validation, and Implications for Psychosocial Well-Being." Unpublished paper. New York: Columbia University.

Luhtanen, Riia, and Jennifer Crocker. 1992. "A Collective Self-Esteem Scale: Self-Evaluation of One's Social Identity." *Personality and Social Psychology Bulletin* 18(3): 302–18.

Major, Brenda, Shannon McCoy, Cheryl Kaiser, and Wendy Quintan. 2003. "Prejudice and Self-Esteem: A Transactional Model." In *European Review of Social Psychology,* edited by Wolfgang Stroebe and Miles Hewstone. Hove, England: Psychology Press.

Major, Brenda, and Laurie O'Brien. 2005. "The Social Psychology of Stigma." *Annual Review of Psychology* 56: 393–421.

Major, Brenda, and Toni Schmader. 1998. "Coping with Stigma Through Psychological Disengagement." In *Prejudice: The Target's Perspective*, edited by Janet Swim and Charles Stangor. San Diego: Academic Press.

Major, Brenda, Steven Spencer, Toni Schmader, Connie Wolfe, and Jennifer Crocker. 1998. "Coping with Negative Stereotypes About Intellectual Performance: The Role of Psychological Disengagement." *Personality and Social Psychology Bulletin* 24: 34–50.

McNeilly, Maya D., Norman Anderson, Elwood L. Robinson, Cecil H. McManus, Cheryl Armstead, Rodney Clark, Carl F. Pieper, C. Simons, and Terry D. Saulter. 1996. "Convergent, Discriminant, and Concurrent Validity of the Perceived Racism Scale: A Multidimensional Assessment of the Experience of Racism Among African-Americans." In *Handbook of Tests and Measurements for Black Populations*, edited by Reginald Jones. Hampton, Va.: Cobb & Henry.

Mendoza-Denton, Rodolfo, Geraldine Downey, Valerie Purdie, Angelina Davis, and Janina Pietrzak. 2002. "Sensitivity to Status-Based Rejection: Implications for African American Students' College Experience." *Journal of Personality and Social Psychology* 83: 896–918.

Miller, Carol, and Cheryl Kaiser. 2001. "A Theoretical Perspective on Coping with Stigma." *Journal of Social Issues* 51: 73–92.

Miller, Carol, and Brenda Major. 2000. "Coping with Stigma and Prejudice." In *The Social Psychology of Stigma*, edited by Todd Heatherton, Robert Kleck, Michelle Hebl, and Jay Hull. New York: Guilford Press.

Nolen-Hoeksema, Susan. 1987. "Sex Differences in Unipolar Depression." *Psychological Bulletin* 109: 259–82.

Ruble, Diane, and Edward Seidman. 1996. "Social Transitions: Windows into Social Psychological Processes. In *Social Psychology: Handbook of Basic Principles*, edited by Edward Tory Higgins and Arie Kruglanski. New York: Guilford Press.

Shih, Margaret, Nalini Ambady, Jennifer Richeson, Kentaro Fujita, and Heather Gray. 2002. "Stereotype Susceptibility: Identity Salience and Shifts in Quantitative Performance." *Psychological Science* 10: 80–83.

Steele, Claude, and Joshua Aronson. 1995. "Stereotype Threat and the Intellectual Performance of African Americans." *Journal of Personality and Social Psychology* 69: 797–811.

Swim, Janet, Laurie Cohen, and Lauri Hyers. 1998. "Experiencing Everyday Prejudice and Discrimination." In *Prejudice: The Target's Perspective*, edited by Janet K. Swim and Charles Stangor. San Diego: Academic Press.

Tennen, Howard, Glenn Affleck, Stephen Armeli, and Margaret Carney. 2000. "A Daily Process Approach to Coping: Linking Theory, Research, and Practice." *American Psychologist* 55: 626–36.

PART II

HOW IDENTITIES FUNCTION TO AID
THE ACCOMPLISHMENT OF LIFE TASKS

CHAPTER 4

TRANSACTING BLACK IDENTITY:
A TWO-WEEK DAILY-DIARY STUDY

Linda C. Strauss and William E. Cross Jr.

The study described in this chapter is premised on a theory of black identity that links racial socialization, identity orientation, and everyday identity transactions. A small group of mostly black women participated in a two-week daily-diary study to investigate whether they engaged none, some, or all of the identity enactments suggested by both the developmental literature on racial socialization and a particular theory of black identity (nigrescence theory). Scores from a premeasure were used to assign participants to one of three identity categories to explore whether positionality predicts frequency of transaction engagement. Following a review of the developmental literature on racial socialization, we summarize nigrescence theory and outline the study.

Racial Socialization from Infancy Through Adulthood

In her exploration of black families (Tatum 1987) and identity development in black children and youth (Tatum 1997), Beverly D. Tatum reports that black parents differ in the importance they accord race and black culture in the socialization of their children, with some assigning little significance, others taking a moderate stance, and still others injecting race messages into a broad range of socialization activities. Focusing on black parents who accord moderate to high race salience in their socialization practices, Howard C. Stevenson and his students at the University of Pennsylvania found that racial socialization is driven by two concerns: protective socialization and proactive socialization (Stevenson, Reed, and Bodison 1996; Stevenson et al. 1997; Stevenson et al. 2002). Protective socialization involves practices, messages, and enactments that heighten awareness to societal oppression, whereas proactive socialization includes conversations, activities, and messages promoting an appreciation of black culture at the affective (pride), intellectual (historical awareness), and behavioral (attendance and participation in black cultural events) levels. Black parents use the two concerns to fashion in their children a self-concept capable of carrying out, sustaining, and refining three types of identity transactions: protection against racism; pride, connectivity with black people, and immersion in black culture; and success within mainstream (white) culture (Stevenson and Davis, forthcoming).

The themes of protection, within-group connectivity and pride, and mainstream success dovetail with the tripartite model of minority identity (Oyserman and Harrison 1998), and the triple-quandary theory of black identity (Boykin and Toms 1985). Both theories suggest that by early adolescence, and continuing across the life span, black youth evidence a multifaceted identity structure that makes possible the negotiation of three worlds or types of situations and exchanges: racist situations (the world of oppression and discrimination); African American cultural experiences and exchanges (the world of African American culture); and mainstream experiences, situations, and institutions (the world of white-controlled America). Multicultural educational theorists such as James A. Banks and Cherry A. Banks (1995), along with observers working in the field of social justice education (Adams, Bell, and Griffin 1997), would likely expand the concept of "mainstream" to include a broad range of immigrant and other groups that are part of a broadly multicultural society—Koreans, Japanese, and Chinese and those from the African diaspora such as West Indians, Africans, and Panamanians. By widening the concept of mainstream, we are better able to understand the complexity of demands being made on today's black youth when they transact mainstream circumstances.

Finally, Margaret B. Spencer's (1995) theorizing and research demonstrate the interconnectivity between a black youth's racial sense of self and the search for individuality. Her work tends to stress the socialization of racial-cultural issues (protection, proactive, mainstream) as well as socialization pathways black parents employ to bring out and shape the unique personality and talents of each child. Stevenson, whose earlier research, discussed above, has found his way to a similar position and in a recent work (Stevenson and Davis, forthcoming), affirms that the overall objective of black parents is to help each black child achieve self-actualization. Complementing Spencer's emphasis on individuality and Stevenson's concern for self-actualization is the recent finding that young black adults, who fit into various racial-cultural categories (Afro-centric, multicultural, and assimilated), show considerable personality variability within and across such categories (Vandiver et al. 2002). In effect, racial socialization does not appear to result in the suppression of black individuality at the level of general personality and self-esteem (Cross and Fhagen-Smith 2001).

In summary, protection against racism, pride and heritage about black people and the black experience, and the need for success within mainstream America are the three race- and culture-related objectives commonplace to the racial socialization practices of black parents. These foci are designed to promote transactional competence in racist situations (transactions with oppression), in all-black situations (transactions with African Americana), and mainstream circumstances (transactions with the larger and increasingly multicultural American society). Interwoven throughout racial socialization is the more comprehensive shading of the person's emerging individuality, such that the self-concepts of many black people juxtapose signs of both collectivist thinking and individualism (Carter and Helms 1987).

Nigrescence Theory (NT)

The current work is premised on nigrescence theory, a term that requires a brief historical note. During the colonial period of the mid-twentieth century, Léopold Senghor, a poet and eventual statesman (he became president of Senegal) born in French West Africa (later Senegal), joined with the Francophone writers Aimé Césaire and Léon Damas to start a social, political, and literary movement that affirmed the validity of an African aesthetic and charged Africans with beginning a personal journey toward "nigrescence." This journey's purpose was to expunge negative attitudes about being black and African and replace them with positive and proactive attitudes (Jack 1996; Senghor 1988). In the early 1970s the French term "nigrescence" effectively captured the African American search for identity, and today "nigrescence theory" is synonymous with theory and research on African American identity development.

Nigrescence theory (NT) highlights the range of black identity attitudes found in everyday black life; the labels "pre-encounter," "immersion-emersion," and "internalization" mark the degree to which an attitude reflects (1) the level of racial salience, the extent to which "race and black culture" are accorded either positive or negative importance; (2) the degree of racial zeal or militancy; and (3) the level of identity achievement (presupposing that one is not born with an "attitude" and thus must acquire or "achieve" it). In the current study, one focus will be on identity beliefs that accord limited importance to race and black culture, and this assimilated perspective is labeled "pre-encounter." Attitudes that connote anger, rage, militancy, racial zeal, and hatred toward whites are labeled "immersion-emersion." Finally, attitudes according considerable importance to race and black culture and reflecting a sense of resolution, habituation, and identity achievement are referred to as "internalization."

NT shows how differences in socialization experiences—across infancy, childhood, preadolescence, and adolescence—result in some young black adults entering early adulthood with pre-encounter attitudes, others with immersion-emersion attitudes, and still others with internalization attitudes (Cross and Fhagen-Smith 2001). However, going a step further, NT links these "meta" racial-cultural meaning-making systems or "ideologies" to a propensity to engage one, a few, or all of what, for the time being, we will call transactional propensities. These transactional propensities are the "products" of years of racial-cultural socialization that pressure the black person to become "good at" transacting the world of racism, the world of the mainstream, and the world of the black experience. In effect, NT suggests that racial-cultural themes, inculcated in black youth over the course of their socialization, emerge in late adolescence and early adulthood as a set of transactional competencies that make possible the negotiation of a range of race- and culture-sensitive contexts, challenges, and opportunities.[1]

Everyday Identity Transactions, or Enactments

Where the identity and attitudinal dimensions of NT reveal connections to the writings of Erik Erikson (1950) (identity-development theory), Urie Bronfenbrenner (2005) (theory on the ecology of human development), and Henry Tajfel (1974) (social-identity theory), racial-cultural socialization themes and transactional competencies in everyday black life are grounded in the works of Erving Goffman (identity "performance") (1959) and, more specifically, Lev Vygotsky (identity "enactments" or "activities"). Vygotsky (1978) in his activity theory argued that a parent, teacher, or mentor assists the learner (child, adolescent, or doctoral student) through practice, imitation, replication, and "doing." Culture is conceived as an intrinsic component of the core learning activities, which means the learner is not simply absorbing period-specific acts. Rather, she or he is taking part in the passing forward and transformation of history and culture. The transformative component reflects the fact that the learner's reality is not a mirror image of the mentor's, and the learner modifies or transforms the enactments to better meet the demands of contemporary contexts. Each activity has psychological properties (context, cognitions, affect). Activity theory emphasizes the nexus, or point of interconnectivity, where all the elements come together and produce lived experiences, all filtered through the individual.

NT conceives of black identity "as the passing down from one generation to the next of the learned experiences and identity activities that facilitate black adjustment and humanity under conditions often framed by race, racism, and the proactive dimensions of black culture" (Cross, Smith, and Payne 2002, 94). Through the concept of identity enactment, or transaction, NT becomes dynamic by linking the psychological characteristics of the person (cognition, affect, behavior choices) to the properties of the situation (number and racial characteristics of people present; nature of the setting such as workplace, school, neighborhood, government institution, or restaurant; level of threat and emotional valence). Contexts infused with stigma stimuli are said to trigger one type of response, while situations that are race- and culture-sensitive but devoid of stigma implications elicit other modes of expression. Consequently, the person's identity does not change from situation to situation; instead, the integrated black identity involves a repertoire of enactments, transactions, or modes of expression, including stigma management (buffering); mainstream management (code switching); intimacy with selected whites (bridging); positive connectivity with black people and immersion in the black experience (bonding); and experiences with the personal self (individualism).

The first transaction category, buffering, includes identity transactions designed to provide relief from the full brunt of a hostile, aggressive, threatening, racist person or situation. We define buffering as engaging in strategies to protect oneself from an actual occurrence of prejudice or to respond to the possibility of encountering prejudice. An example of buffering would be a black student who feels he has been singled out by the campus police in the aftermath of a campus incident that actually involved many people. The student might withdraw from all interactions with campus police or more extreme, develop an anti–campus police attitude. The buffering mechanism results from the protective theme of black socialization, as discussed by Jennifer Crocker and Brenda Major (1989) in their study on stigma as a protective mechanism against racism. Code switching reflects bicultural competence and allows the black person to smoothly, effectively, and competitively operate within mainstream institutions, and to fluidly shift back and forth between black cultural and mainstream circumstances. This function is often employed for the individual to successfully achieve a desired outcome in a mainstream situation. Another extreme example would be a change from traditional affirmative to a more western outfit for a job interview. This might be evidenced by a change in a black student's speech pattern while he or she is interacting with a white faculty member. This mechanism is central to Daphna Oyserman and Kathy Harrison's (1998) prescription for minority success in the mainstream and A. Wade Boykin and Forrest D. Toms's (1985) discussion on the need for blacks to negotiate relations and experiences within the white world. In some instances, code switching can be enacted in situations of threat (buffering), but more typically code switching is less reactive and more intentional and strategic. Code switching is used in the context of long-term needs such as educational advancement, promotions, credentialing, and employment, whereas buffering is used in the context of a fairly immediate need for safety and literal protection from either psychological or physical harm. (As will be discussed, code switching was added at the suggestion of a black focus group that helped pretest the list of transactions used in this study; more recently, William Cross, Lakesha Smith, and Yasser Payne [2002] have modified the theory to incorporate code switching as a key transaction.) Bridging is the identity activity that makes possible a black person's intimate and deeply felt friendship with a person from another group, including whites. We define bridging as feeling comfortable with racial identity, able to interact in a reciprocal manner with other people having different racial identities and being open about the differences. A black student's inviting her white roommate to a holiday celebration with her family is an example of bridging. Bridging is not driven by colorblind dynamics, because racial-cultural differences are part and partial of the dyad's sense of intimacy and connection; each person is explicitly respectful, curious, and intrigued by the other's "difference" (intimacy achieved through the explicit recognition and exploration of difference, rather than its avoidance, denial, or repression).

The first three transaction modalities are designed to carry out protective as well as mainstream transactions with the "other." However, blackness is about more than stigma management. The fourth transaction, bonding, or attachment, defines the primary psychological transaction blacks employ to sustain, enrich, and protect their sense of connection to black people, the black community, and the larger black experience. We define bonding as feeling a sense of comfort and security that comes from being around members of the same race and a desire to support one another and share in the joy of a shared culture. It can provide a personal sense of cultural meaning, be part of a person's explanatory system or world-view, and be a source of motivation and creativity to write poems, novels, and plays about black life. It can be a source of one's aesthetics, which can draw one to a hip-hop concert or an exhibition of paintings by a new or traditional black artist, or the internal trigger that prompts a person to turn on the radio and tune in a local jazz station. Because much of bonding is intrinsic, measuring it poses a challenge; it is rather easy to set up a social experiment on stigma wherein one manipulates an external trigger that elicits a buffering response, but the impulse toward bonding is often inside the person's head. Without any type of apparent external stimulus, a black writer wakes up in the morning and begins to play with his internal thoughts and eventually composes a poem about black love; how can that be repeated in a social experiment? This probably explains why blackness in the sense of bonding as an intrinsic motivating phenomenon is not as readily studied as blackness in the sense of an expression of buffering or code switching. However, unlocking this puzzle will provide insights into the origins of jazz, the creativity of Zora Neale Hurston, the vision of Romare Bearden, or the drive behind David Levering Lewis's amazing dedication to researching the life and times of W. E. B. DuBois, a project that took ten years and has resulted in a two-volume biography that has drawn national and international praise and garnered for its author a Pulitzer Prize.

Buffering, code switching, bridging, and bonding explain the "enaction" of "race and black culture" on an everyday basis, that is, the "doing of race and culture" day in and day out. But not every situation a black person encounters in life is necessarily race- and black culture–related. NT accounts for "acting as an individual" or expressing and enacting one's sense of individuality by the enactment category of individualism. The individualism category is meant to capture those exchanges, interactions, and experiences in which the person feels as though she or he is "just being myself" or just being "me." Adding the category of individualism is important in another sense. Recall from our earlier discussion that the pre-encounter identity defines a frame of reference in which the person's sense of individuality takes priority over collectivist thinking; black people with an identity dominated by pre-encounter attitudes are likely to enact their identity through individualism and make less use of the other categories.

POSITIONALITY AND TRANSACTION PROFILES   NT depicts buffering, code switching, bridging, and bonding as race and culture enactments carried out by blacks holding ideological positions that accord varying degrees of salience to race and black culture. Individualism, by contrast, is likely to be favored by blacks who embrace an identity that is framed by something other than race. NT suggests that a person's positionality (ideological stance) can be defined or understood as a particular configuration of the transaction categories. That is, if each category were to be operationalized by a subscale, and each person's set of scores were examined as a configuration, then it would be possible to isolate "positionality × transaction profiles." For example, a pre-encounter (assimilationist) profile will accentuate individualism and make infrequent use of the race-sensitive transactions. Militant blacks (immersion-emersion) will be dismissive of bridging (having no desire to be close to whites and possibly even hating them), will show muted individualism scores (they will use the individualism category but less than will pre-encounter blacks), and record high scores on buffering, code switching, and bonding. Those who have been socialized into the identity attitude of internalization (a form of advanced identity development) can be expected to have muted individualism scores (a reflection of their more collectivist orientation), along with high scores across all the race-sensitive mechanism, including bridging or closeness to some white friends, as this type of identity reflects a sense of identity resolution and achievement across a range of issues. Table 4.1 depicts the "positionality × enactments" relationships.

In summary, NT shows black identity varying according to the ideology or identity type into which the person has been socialized. One's ideology, or positionality, is not simply a label, because each typology is linked to the frequency with which a person engages or makes use of a constellation of identity enactments. These enactment proclivities help a person "function," "negotiate," "transact," or "enact" identity within and across three worlds: the world of the mainstream, the world of

Table 4.1   Positionality and Enactments Configurations

| Positionality | Identity Transactions | | | | | |
	Buffering	Code Switching	Bridging	Bonding	Individualism	Other
Pre-encounter	–	–	–	–	+	+
Immersion-emersion	+	+	–	+	–	+
Internalization	+	+	+	+	+	+

Source: Authors' compilation.
Note: A minus sign indicates a tendency not to use or engage a transaction modality; a plus sign means this transaction modality is frequently engaged.

oppression, and the world of black folk and community. Traversing these three worlds does not trigger three different identities; rather, different transactional modalities provide the infrastructure for an integrated identity. Focusing on any one transactional category can lead to the distorted perception of a fragmented identity structure. Finally, the configuration of enactment categories is another way of giving definition to positionality or ideology. Consequently, knowing a person's positionality should make it possible to predict the frequency of transactional activity over a long period of time (week, two weeks, a month, or many months).

DAILY-DIARY STUDY

As a way of demonstrating how black people use the different modalities and the fact that transactional configurations are predicted by positionality, we shall now describe the results of a two-week daily-diary study, involving thirty-five African Americans. The diary format involves the subjects recording daily a single incident or interaction and then answering a series of questions that essentially lead the participant to deconstruct or interrogate the experience, using various close-ended scales and checklists. The selection of variables and traits to probe was based on a review of the social-identity literature; consequently, the variables explored dovetail with those found in the social experimental studies of racial-cultural coping (Crocker and Major 1989; Shelton and Sellers 2000; Swim and Stangor 1998) and the functions of identity (Deaux et al. 1999). There were scales and checklists for the following:

- Type of identity transaction used in the situation (buffering, code switching, bridging, bonding, acting as an individual)
- Number and characteristics of the people present (Saenz 1994)
- Characteristics of the situation such as racial salience (Shelton and Sellers 2000)
- Affective dimensions of the situations (Feldman 1995)
- Self-perceived stress level (Feldman-Barrett and Swim 1998)

Predictions and Hypotheses of the Study

To simplify the presentation of the hypotheses, we present three broad categories consistent with the major components measured in our study. More specific hypotheses are included in the results section under each component.

TRANSACTIONS AND THE CONTEXTUAL CHARACTERISTICS OF THE SITUATION   Our first predictions pertain to the activation of transactions in situations where racial salience is triggered by the composition of the group of other individuals in the situation. Consistent with self-categorization theory (reviewed in this volume by Bonita London et al., chapter 3, and Allen et al., chapter 7), we predict transactions associated with race and culture such as buffering, code switching, bridging, and bonding will be more probable than the transaction not centering on race and culture (acting as an individual). Specifically, when race salience is activated by the person being in the numerical minority, transactions reflective of protection and mainstream identity themes will be prevalent (Abrams, Thomas, and Hogg 1990). Conversely we do not expect bonding to occur. This prediction is also consistent with the work of LaRue Allen et al. (chapter 7, this volume). Contrarily, with more African Americans present—referred to by Boykin and Toms (1985) as operating within the world of blackness—the individual may rejoice in sharing the same race and cultural experiences (Sue, Mak, and Sue 1998) or race may not be perceptually salient. In these situations, we predict bonding or acting as an individual.

As an aside, it should be noted that in a recent theoretical work it has been argued that beyond bonding and acting as an individual, some within-group or black-on-black transactions may involve buffering, code switching, or bridging (Cross, Smith, and Payne 2002). Cross, Smith, and Payne (2002) arrived at this supposition after most of the data analysis for the current study had already been completed. Consequently, post hoc analyses are presented to determine whether there is any evidence of blacks transacting buffering, code switching, and bridging among themselves, in contexts where the only person present in the situation is another black person.

TRANSACTIONS AND AFFECTIVE DIMENSIONS   As discussed in this chapter, NT is dynamic in linking the psychological characteristics of the person with the properties of the situation. This hypotheses section includes the second key element of our predictions, the emotional components of the situation. We hypothesize relationships between the transactions and the following emotive components of the situation: specific emotions, emotional valences, emotions toward European Americans, level of stress in the situation, level of threat in the situation, and perception of free choice to be in the situation.

In general, situations associated with the more "negative" emotive components are predicted to evoke buffering. This hypothesis is consistent with the work of Crocker and Major (1989) and Nicole Shelton et al. (chapter 5, this volume), where the self-protective function of buffering is utilized by the individual.

Code switching should be the primary mechanism for transactions with the mainstream (Oyserman and Harrison 1998; Boykin and Toms 1985), and should be associated with more moderately focused emotive components. Because the study takes place on a predominately white college campus, most of the black participants can be expected to have considerable practice and experience with both buffering and code switching. It is important to note that the "content" of these two transactions may overlap. For example, one may use Standard English (code switching) in many campus-based transactions with whites and nonblacks (professors, teaching assistants, residence advisers, administrators), but one may also resort to Standard English (buffering) during an interaction with a white policeman late at night at a location miles from the campus. However, because the campus-based interactions are generally less likely to be associated with negative emotions and negative stress, stress and negative emotions should predict buffering, while neutral and positive emotions should predict code switching.

Bridging should occur in situations with low levels of threat—situations where the individual feels confident to reach out to members of different groups. These may include situations where the individual feels participation is a free choice. Positive emotions and an overall emotional valence should also be associated with bridging, especially in the context of social interactions with European Americans. Bonding should have similar emotional predictions to bridging (that is, less threat, low stress, positive emotional valence, and positive emotions). However, we predict bonding will link positive emotions with activities carried out with other African Americans and not with European Americans.

TRANSACTIONS AND GROUP IDENTITY   In our final set of hypotheses, we predict an association between the transactions and both race centrality (Sellers et al. 1997) and identity positionality. Race centrality will predict the general use of three race and culture transactions—buffering, code switching, and bonding—but not bridging. Race centrality scales tend to be negatively related to bicultural and multicultural orientations (Vandiver et al. 2002; Chavous 2000); consequently, we predict that race centrality will be negatively related to bridging, as this transaction represents the operationalization of bicultural and multicultural attitudes.

The predicted configurations of transactions and identity positions are noted in Table 4.1. We predict that transactional configurations will differ by positionality, as blacks positioned in one of three identity categories will evidence differential usage of the transactions. In other words, the "lived experience of blackness" will differ in accordance to one's ideology. Persons positioned at pre-encounter will tend to underutilize the race-sensitive transactions (buffering, code switching, bridging, and bonding), and rely more heavily on individualism. Immersion-emersion, or black militants, who tend to be very race-vigilant and hostile toward whites, will turn to code switching and buffering for transactions with whites, and will avoid bridging. Also, their emphasis on collectivism should result in fewer individualism transactions (Oyserman and Harrison 1998). The internalization category, which depicts advanced and habituated blackness (achieved identity) as well as bicultural and multicultural proclivities, should make use of all the race-sensitive mechanisms, including bridging. The differential use of bridging should in large measure define the difference between militants (infrequent bridging) and internalizers (frequent bridging). Since internalization is a form of advanced and mature identity development (Cross 1991; Helms 1990; Phinney 1989), this identity category should make less frequent use of individualism.

Method

In the present study a group of African American students recorded over a two-week period the number of times they transacted buffering, bonding, bridging, code switching, and acting as an individual. They did this in three ways. Using a daily-diary form, participants described one event per day that occurred during a randomly assigned time period. They also indicated at the end of the day and at the end of the study (a postmeasure) the extent to which they perceived that they had engaged in each of the four transactions and acted as an individual. The current study is limited to an analysis of the daily-diary and end-of-day reports.

PARTICIPANTS   Participants for the study were 35 African American students, 29 female and 6 male, who attended a predominately white mid-Atlantic university. There were 15 entries for each participant, for each of the 15 days, yielding 525 cases in the study. The participants ranged from sophomores to seniors, and were 18 to 21 years old. A roster of sophomore, junior, and senior African American students was generated from the university database. First-year students were not included in the study because of their involvement in another research project. Participants were contacted by phone by the first author to partake in the study. Participants were selected from the list in a random fashion. Interested participants were asked to attend an orientation meeting. All participants were paid ten dollars for participating in the study.

PREMEASURE MATERIALS AND ASSESSMENT OF RACIAL-CULTURAL IDENTITY   An initial premeasure packet included demographic information (age, gender, racial group), racial-background composition information, and ratings of participants' current emotional state. The racial background questions asked the participants to indicate the racial compositions of their high schools, hometowns, and college. Following the demographic page, the participants' current emotional state was measured by a list of twenty emotions. These twenty emotions are elaborated on in the description of the daily diary.

As a premeasure, participants also completed a sixty-eight item questionnaire based on a modification of the RIAS (RIAS: Parham and Helms, 1981), a scale used to measure dimensions of nigrescence theory. Responses to the items on this questionnaire ranged from one ("strongly disagree") to seven ("strongly agree"). The identity instrument helped position individuals into one of three racial-cultural identity categories (pre-encounter, immersion-emersion, and internalization), and responses were coded such that higher numbers indicated greater likelihood of being in a particular identity category. Pre-encounter statements describe African Americans for whom race is not a central focus of their identity ("We are Americans first, and then we are black"). Immersion-emersion describes those for whom racial militancy and racial vigilance are central ("It is absolutely necessary that I present myself to other African Americans in an Afro-centric manner"). The final category, internalization, is characterized by a stable, habituated identity in which race is salient, but not all-encompassing ("Because I feel comfortable with my black identity, I seek interactions with people who represent other racial and ethnic groups"). In addition to these identity categories, a racial-centrality score was recorded for each participant ("In general, being African American is an important part of my self image"). The reliabilities for the four subscales were pre-encounter: [.64], immersion-emersion: [.91], internalization-commitment: [.78], and racial centrality: [.67].

DAILY-DIARY FORMS   Each daily-diary form had four sections.

1. Situation and transaction identification. Section 1 was a "Situation and Transaction Identification" field at the top of each diary, containing a participant code, date, and assigned time to complete the diary, and instructions to the participant to identify and describe an important event experienced during the time assigned for that day, and explain why the event was important. Participants could use the back of the diary form to write long descriptions, and they often did. The participant was then instructed to indicate the extent to which the four transaction categories plus acting as an individual were used during the event (they could also check "none of the above"). Each transaction and acting as an individual could be rated from zero (not at all) to six (extreme). This allowed the participant to indicate more than one response for the same situation. Participants could also record that they engaged a mechanism other than the four enactments and acting as individual, by checking the category: none of the above. Participants were instructed to refer to the important event they recorded on the form, when completing the diary form for that day.

2. Individuals in the situation. The second main section was called "People Present" and asked for responses in three areas. The first item had three parts, to record the number of black people present, the number of European Americans present, and the number of "persons of other ethnicity" present. The second item was about classifying people present in terms of friend or roommate; girl or boyfriend; relative or family member; classmate or acquaintance; college staff, faculty, or teaching assistant; business person or resident of city; stranger; other. The third item was about how close the participant felt to the people present, using a scale of 0 (not at all close) to 5 (very close).

3. Situational characteristics. The third section used four questions to explore the situational characteristics of the event. The first item was about race salience ("I felt that this situation was race neutral; ambiguous; or race related"), to be assessed by means of a Likert scale of 0 to 6. The scale values and labels were juxtaposed such that the respondents could see that low scores (0 or 1) meant race-neutral; values of 2, 3, and 4 corresponded to ambiguous, and 5 or 6 meant strongly race-related.

   The second item asked the respondent to check one of the following three categories as a measure of degree of self-control and self-initiation of the referent situation: "something you initiated"; "something that you were required to do"; "something that just happened."

   The third item in the situational section assessed how important the situation was to the participant. Scale values of 0 to 6 were juxtaposed with key labels such that checking a low score meant "not very important," midrange values meant "somewhat important," and high scores meant "very important." The last item in this section asked the participant to assess the stress level related to the situation, and the values 0 to 6 were juxtaposed with labels such that marking low values meant "not very stressful," medium-range values meant "somewhat stressful," and high values meant "very stressful."

4. Emotions. The final section of the diary was designed to generate data on the emotions the participant felt in the situation, and was introduced with the question "To what extent do the following emotions describe how you felt in this situation?" followed by a list of twenty emotions (sleepy, sluggish, aroused, sad, calm, nervous, quiet, still, peppy, relaxed, happy, satisfied, enthusiastic, afraid, surprised, disappointed, peaceful, proud, threatened, and encumbered). The participant used the values 0 to 6 to rate the degree of felt emotion for each of the twenty items, with low scores indicating "not at all," medium scores indicating "moderate feelings," and high values indicating "extreme feelings." After reverse-scoring the negative items, a total emotional score was developed by adding the scores for the twenty items and dividing by twenty, giving a total emotion score that was an average of all the scores, somewhere between 0 and 6.

In addition to a total emotion score, a valence subscale score was constructed in accordance to the system developed by Lisa A. Feldman (1995). The emotions representing positive valence were "happy" and "satisfied." The negative emotions were "sad" and "disappointed."

The next item in the emotion sections assessed the participant's feelings toward European Americans and led off with the question "Whether [European Americans were] present in the situation or not, to what extent did you feel the following emotions toward European Americans during this event?" Using the scoring system just described, a participant accorded a score of 0 to 6 for each of these emotions: positive, neutral, ambivalent, hating, negative, curious, jealous. The participant had the option of checking: "Did not consider European Americans."

The last item assessed the participant's feelings toward black people as a group, and the lead-off statement was "My feelings about my racial group in this situation were . . ." Using the 0-to-6 scoring system already described, the participant assigned a value to the following descriptors: "neutral," "confused," "self-doubting," "slightly aware," "very aware," and "sensitive," "did not consider my racial group in this situation." This was the last item on the daily diary form.

END-OF-THE-DAY SUMMARY The participants were asked to fill out an end-of-the-day summary at the conclusion of each day they participated in the study. Participants were asked to complete a table indicating their experiences with the transactions during the day. In the first column of the table, participants indicated the number of times each transaction occurred during the day. The participant recorded the importance of each transaction in the second column of the table. The participant rated each transaction on a scale of 0 ("not important") to 6 ("important"). In the third column the participant indicated the valence of emotions experienced in concert with each of the transactions. The rating choices were "very negative," represented by three minus signs ($---$) to "very positive," represented by three plus signs ($+++$). Next the participant rated the stressfulness of the day 0 ("not stressful") to 6 ("very stressful").

The last question was an emotional checklist with the lead-off question "To what extent do the following emotions describe how you felt today?" The list of emotions that followed was the same as those on the daily-diary form.

Procedure

Interested participants attended an evening orientation meeting. At this meeting, the initial packets were distributed. Each packet contained definitions of the four transactions of racial identity and the concept of acting as an individual, the premeasure items, fifteen daily-diary forms, and a postmeasure questionnaire. The participants were given the following definitions of the transactions:

1. Buffering: Engaging in strategies to protect oneself from an actual occurrence of prejudice or to respond to the possibility of encountering prejudice

2. Bonding: Feeling a sense of comfort and security that comes from being around members of the same race and a desire to support one another and share in the joy of a shared culture

3. Bridging: Feeling comfortable with racial identity, able to interact in a reciprocal manner with other people having different racial identities and being open about the differences

4. Code switching: Feeling obligated to interact according to norms characteristic of another racial group, and at the same time playing down ways one would normally act with others of the same racial group

5. Acting as an individual: Acting as an individual and seeing others as individuals, without regard to the color of their skin

The participant was also able to check "none of the above" and use all aspects of the diary response system to amplify what he or she meant by "none of the above."

These definitions were verified with the help of two focus groups. First, the second author held a discussion as part of a course on racial-identity development. Consensus was reached about buffering, bonding, and bridging. However, members of the class felt that a transaction category was missing and proposed the code switching concept. The four transactions, along with the concept of acting as an individual, were presented to a second focus group. Some minor adjustments to the definitions were made, but in general participants felt that the four transactions captured their everyday thoughts, feelings, and behaviors in different situations. The second group was presented with a series of vignettes to verify that the participants understood the transactions as the researchers had intended. The results indicated that the definitions were adequate to convey the necessary ideas. After completing the initial measures, the participants in the study discussed the definitions and completed the first daily-diary measure.

The participant was asked to complete the fifteen forms during specific times of the day. One-third of the forms were to be completed during morning hours (wake-up until noon), one-third during the afternoon (noon until dinnertime), and one-third during the evening. Each participant received five surveys at each time of day. These times were randomly distributed for each participant.

Each participant left the orientation with fifteen daily-diary forms and the postmeasure. Participants were asked to complete one daily-diary form on every day of the study. The participant was asked to pick an important event and provide a written description of the event on the daily-diary form, explaining why that situation was important. Participants were asked to return their diary forms on a daily basis. Any participant not turning in forms for two days was contacted by phone and asked whether he or she was still participating in the study. Twelve participants dropped out of the study after attending the initial orientation session.

When the participant completed the last daily-diary form and the postmeasures, he or she was thanked for participating in the study. Any participant requesting further information met with the first author to discuss the study.

Results and Analysis

The study explored the personal and situational characteristics that might predict the everyday transactions of racial-cultural identity. Each transaction had a possible value from 0 to 6. The results were re-coded so that the highest valued transaction for each situation was the focus of analysis. If a participant responded that two (or more) transactions were equally appropriate for a situation, then both (or more) transactions were recorded for that situation. The statistical technique was OLS (ordinary least squares) regression analysis, entered in blocks delineated by the characteristics of the situation and the emotions of the participant in the situation. Separate analyses are presented using hierarchical linear modeling (HLM) to explore the relationship between positionality and the transactions. The majority of analyses are OLS regressions entered in blocks appropriate to the variables under consideration. Because the daily diary (DD) utilized repeated-measures design and included a premeasure of global characteristics, HLM was utilized for data from these sources in several instances. Specifically, when comparing racial-cultural identity obtained in the premeasure with the measures obtained through the fifteen repeated daily-diary observations, HLM fit the data structure most appropriately. These HLM analyses are specifically identified in the next section. The data were stored on and analyzed using SPSS version 10.0 for PC and HLM version 5.02.

Many of the situations the participants wrote about involved multiple or simultaneous transactions and the participants were able to capture this situational complexity by recording all the transactions they perceived themselves to have transacted during a single event. The following case, number 2227, is an example:

> A girl [good friend] I went to [high] school with last year has a sister [here at the college] and she [the sister] is a member of a sorority upstairs from me. We happened to be in the elevator at the same time and she offered me a ride to class. I accepted. The ride was weird because those white sorority girls give me the dirtiest looks, when I go to their floor to do laundry, but [in the car] they were polite because I knew one of their friends. When my friend introduced me . . . they couldn't look at

me. I was really uncomfortable. And as we were driving, I was hoping that no one would see me in the car with these white girls. That's really bad. I feel ashamed now. But they probably did not think twice about it.

To describe her transactions in this situation, the participant checked both "buffering" and "bridging," with buffering getting the highest rating, 6, and bridging getting 2. The remainder of the diary inputs were keyed to the interactions with the white sorority sisters (buffering), and not the exchange with her friend (bridging). Thus, the situation was viewed as race-related (race salience), something that just happened, something that was very important, and something that was very stressful. At the emotional level, the participant's feelings toward whites reflected mild ambivalence, high negativity, and a touch of curiosity. The important thing to note is that even though multiple transactions were recorded, the totality of the diary input was keyed to the participant's main concern (in this case, buffering).

In case number 1648, four transactions were recorded as relevant to the situation. Again, the high and dominant rating became the frame for the diary input: "Chemical engineering 304—today we had to get in groups of three for a project due at the end of the semester. Of course, no one picked me and so I had to go to the teacher to let him know I did not have a group."

In his ratings, this black male participant saw himself, at different points in the story, code switching (probably with the teacher), bridging (he knew several classmates), and bonding (one person was a friend), but buffering, which he accorded a rating of 6, drove his diary input.

Altogether, 318 usable cases were analyzed, and many reflected the simultaneous use of multiple transactions. In 137 cases, however, only one person was present, and in such cases typically only one transaction was underscored. As stated, for all analyses, transactions were re-coded so that the highest valued transaction for each situation was included for the analysis. If a participant responded that two or more transactions were equally appropriate to a situation, both transactions were recorded for that situation. An examination of the daily-diary data revealed a skewed distribution in that some transactions were engaged far more frequently than others. To meet the assumptions of normality for the statistical analyses, a log transformation was utilized.

The descriptive frequencies for each of the transactions and acting as an individual were examined. Two separate measurements were used: the number of transactions used in each situation on the diary report and the reported frequency count on the end of the day summary. The frequencies are reported in table 4.2.

Table 4.2 shows that the transactions were applied with similar frequency across both the daily-diary (DD) and the end-of-day (EOD) summary. Rank-ordering the transactions indicates that for both DD and EOD, the participants were most likely to report acting as an individual. As reported in the DD data, the next most frequent mechanism was bonding, and buffering was the least frequently engaged mechanism. Table 4.2 also shows the average importance ratings assigned to each transaction for the EOD form. The pattern for importance mirrors the frequency data, with the exception that bonding is rated the most important transaction and acting as an individual is second. Thus, in this study, which gave expression to a range of black identity transactions, the modalities listed as most frequently transacted and rated as

Table 4.2   Function Frequency and Importance Rankings

| | Daily Diary | | End of Day | | | |
	Mean Intercept	Rank	Mean Proportion	Rank	Mean Importance	Rank
Buffering	1.28	3	.067	4	1.20	5
Bonding	2.62	2	.315	2	3.50	1
Bridging	1.09	5	.174	3	2.52	3
Code switching	1.27	4	.064	5	1.22	4
Acting as an individual	3.45	1	.354	1	3.44	2

Source: Authors' compilation.

most important turn out to be the ones that have been the least studied in the social psychological literature, where the emphasis has been on stigma management (buffering).

To check on the generalizability of the time sample, participants indicated the normality of the fifteen days at the end of the study. Most participants rated the fifteen days as normal (scale of 0 to 6, with, 0 being not normal and 6 being normal). The mean was 4.6, and 80 percent of the responses were 4 or higher. No participant rated the fifteen-day period as not normal (0 rating).

The degree of transaction overlap (DD reports) was assessed by correlation analysis and the results are shown in table 4.3. Buffering significantly negatively correlated with both bonding and acting as an individual ($p < .01$), suggesting that it is not to be confused with positive attachment activities involving other blacks, nor with situations in which one is just being oneself. Bonding correlated positively with code

Table 4.3   Correlations of Functions Used in the Daily Diaries

	Buffering	Bonding	Bridging	Code Switching	Acting as an Individual
Buffering					
Bonding	−.142				
Bridging					
Code switching		.528	−.233		
Individual	−.104	−.213	.105	−.632	
No functions		−.278	−.151	−.205	−.338
Functions	.18	.707	.384	.522	−.361

Source: Authors' compilation.
Note: All significant at $p < .01$.

switching, which can be traced to the numerous code-switching transactions carried out with other blacks. There were 100 instances where the only person present was another black person, and bonding characterized the majority of black-on-black transactions (fifty-eight instances), aside from acting as an individual. However, thirty-three of the remaining transactions involved code switching with other blacks present. Continuing with the correlation results, we note that bonding negatively correlated with buffering and acting as an individual (for both, $p < .01$), underscoring the group-enhancement dynamics of this mechanism, rather than identity protection and individualism. Bridging significantly negatively correlated with buffering and positively correlated with acting as an individual ($p < .01$), indicating that far from being an identity-protection mechanism, this transaction depicts closeness to whites that can meld into a very individualistic or humanistic sense of connection. Acting as an individual or individualism correlated with all the other mechanisms; however, the most consequential involved highly negative relationships with bonding (−.213) and code switching (−.632). The negative relationship between individualism and bonding is the opposite of one of our predictions. Apparently, when bonding was engaged and a strong sense of cultural connection to other blacks was experienced, a sense of one's individuality was not an accompanying theme, as had been predicted. The negative correlation between individualism and code switching suggests that when people were transacting the mainstream, a keen sense of moving back and forth between one culture code to another precluded any sense of acting as an individual.

PREDICTORS OF GENERAL TRANSACTION USE   As previously noted, there were 318 cases where the individual indicated the situation was race-sensitive. The OLS regression analysis yielded five significant predictors for general use of the transactions. Reporting a situation as race-related (that is, race salient) was a positive predictor of general transaction use ($\beta = .127$, $p = .02$), whereas situations perceived as stressful were negatively related to general transaction use ($\beta = -.146$, $p = .02$). Positively valenced emotions ($\beta = .187$, $p = .01$) and a sense of group pride ($\beta = .095$, $p = .07$) predicted general transaction use in a positive direction. Overall, the majority of incidents recorded in the daily diaries were nonstressful, somewhat group-focused, and framed by positive emotions. This suggests that general transaction use is not inherently defensive, reactive, or negatively triggered. One mild tendency toward negativity was evident in that ambivalent feelings toward whites predicted general transaction use ($\beta = .094$, $p = .04$).

PREDICTORS OF EACH SPECIFIC TRANSACTION AND ACTING AS INDIVIDUAL

Including all cases in the data set, each transaction was analyzed to examine the relationship between the transaction, characteristics of the situation, and emotions reported in the situation. The results also covered acting as an individual as well as both the "other" and the "none of the above" categories. The results of this analysis are contained in table 4.4. Unless otherwise stated, the results reflect the DD data, and EOD results will only be mentioned where necessary.

Table 4.4   Results of OLS and HLM Analyses for Black-Identity Daily-Diary Study

Variables	Buffering	Code Switching	Bridging	Bonding	Individualism
Pre-encounter [assimilation][a]					B = −.235, p = .072
Immersion-emersion [militant][a]	B = .255, p = .001	B = .296, p = .002			
Internalization [bicult-multcult][a]					
Race centrality[a]	B = .021, p = .020	B = .014, p = .040	B = −.039, p = .493	B = .010, p = .015	
People present: whites					
People present: blacks				B = .002, p = .042	
Situation: race-related	B = .014, p = .010	B = .027, p = .039			
Situation: self-initiated				B = .030, p = .064	
Situation: important					B = .108, p = .077
Situation: stressful		B = −.032, p = .023		B = −.034, p = .022	
Emotions: positive					
Emotions: negative					
Valence: positive		B = .138, p = .043		B = .044, p = .009	
Valence: negative					
Feelings toward whites: positive	B = .037, p = .000		B = .022, p = .030		
Feelings toward whites: negative					B = .119, p = .032
Feelings toward whites: neutral					B = −.107, p = .025
Feelings toward whites: ambivalent					B = −.128, p = .033
Feelings toward whites: hateful			B = .032, p = .025		
Feelings toward whites: curious					
Feelings toward whites: did not consider					
Affect toward my group: positive					
Affect toward my group: neutral					
Affect toward my group: confused					
Affect toward my group: proud					
Level of awareness: slightly aware					
Level of awareness: very aware					
Level of awareness: not on my mind					

Source: Authors' compilation.

[a]Scales created from the modified RAIS.

BUFFERING   Our specific hypotheses about the use of buffering included:

- Being in the minority
- Race-related situations
- Perceived threat
- Negatively valenced emotions
- Negative affect toward European Americans

Our results indicate that identification of the situation as race-related ($\beta = .014$) and stressful ($\beta = .036$) significantly predicted buffering. This mechanism was linked to holding negative feelings toward European Americans ($\beta = .037$). These findings are consistent with shielding or identity-protection transactions. Participants checked sad, nervous, surprised, and especially "threatened" to describe the emotions they felt while transacting buffering; the results for the emotional checklist are shown in table 4.5. In addition, negative correlations suggested that in the midst of such circumstances they felt the opposite of calm, relaxed, happy, or peaceful.

CODE SWITCHING   To summarize our hypotheses about code switching, we perceived the following situational characteristics as predictive:

- Being in the minority
- Race-related situations
- Neutral to moderately positive emotions
- Overall positive valence of emotions
- A nonstressful situation

Two characteristics of the situation predicted code switching. As with buffering, the more a participant perceived the situation as race-related, the more code switching was reported ($\beta = .027$, $p = .039$). However, unlike buffering, which was related to stress, the less stressful the race-related situation, the more code switching occurred ($\beta = -.032$, $p = .023$). Affectively, a positive valence ($\beta = .138$, $p = .043$) framed those persons who were the target of code-switching transactions. On the emotional checklist, peppy, happy, enthusiastic, and the opposite of quiet were associated with code-switching transactions.

BRIDGING   The main predictors of bridging that we hypothesized were:

- Race-related situations
- Being in the minority

Table 4.5 Function and Adjective Checklist Correlations for Daily-Diary and End-of-Day Results

	Daily-Diary Correlations				End-of-Day Correlations			
	Buffering	Bridging	Bonding	Code Switching	Buffering	Bridging	Bonding	Code Switching
Sleepy								
Sluggish								
Aroused			.104[a]		.116[a]			
Sad	.164[b]		-.111[a]		.183[b]			
Calm	-.123[a]							
Nervous	.133[a]				.113[a]			
Quiet			-.134[a]	-.214[b]				
Still			.176[b]			-.149[a]	-.112[a]	
Peppy			.192[b]	.113[a]		.251[b]	.241[b]	
Relaxed	-.154[b]					.113[a]		
Happy	-.216[b]		.327[b]	.156[b]		.172[b]	.088[a]	
Satisfied								
Enthusiastic			.240[b]	.182[b]		.242[b]	.200[b]	
Afraid					.178[b]			.089[a]
Surprised	.090[a]							.138[a]
Disappointed					.156[b]			
Peaceful	-.174[b]		.200[b]					
Proud			.163[b]					
Threatened	.380[b]		-.097[a]					
Encumbered								

Source: Authors' compilation.

[a] <.05
[b] <.01

- Low-threat situations

- Situations where participation is a free choice

- Positive emotions

- Positive emotional valence

- Positive emotions toward European Americans

There were two significant emotional predictors of bridging: Positive affect toward European Americans (β = .022) and expressing curiosity about European Americans (β = .032). Interestingly, none of the emotions from the emotional checklist was significant for the daily-diary data, but on the EOD data, bridging was linked to peppy, relaxed, happy, and satisfied, and the opposite of still.

BONDING   We hypothesized the following predictors for bonding transactions:

- Race-related situation

- Being in the majority

- Low-threat situations

- Situations where participation is a free choice

- Positive emotions

- Positive emotional valence

Situations evoking the bonding transaction had four significant predictors: many African Americans present (β = .002, p = .042), low levels of stress (β = −.034, p = .022), and positively valenced emotions (β = .044, p = .009), and participant initiation of the situation (β = .030, p = .063). On the emotional checklist, aroused, peppy, relaxed, happy, enthusiastic, peaceful, and proud played a role in transacting bonding, as well as the opposite of these emotions: sad, quiet, and threatened.

ACTING AS AN INDIVIDUAL   Although acting as an individual was not a race-related transaction, we had several hypotheses concerning this transaction:

- Situation that is not race-related

- Not in a minority

- Situation is important to the individual

- Ambiguous feelings toward European Americans

None of the situational variables was associated with this transaction (race salience, people present, whether situation was self-initiated), but three emotional factors, all related to the perceptions of whites, were significant. Holding neutral feelings toward European Americans was significantly and positively related to the use of the mechanism of acting as an individual (β = .119, p = .032). Conversely, there were significant negative relationships between ambivalent (β = −.107, p = .025) and hateful feelings toward European Americans and acting as an individual (β = −.128, p = .033), meaning that when a participant felt negatively or ambivalently toward the white person or white people in the situation, acting as an individual was not likely to be transacted. On the checklist, the specific emotions calm, quiet, satisfied, and peaceful, and the opposite of threatened and encumbered were associated with acting as an individual.

"NO-TRANSACTION-USE" OR "OTHER-TRANSACTIONS" CATEGORIES   For the "no-transaction-use" or "other-transactions" category we did not have any a priori hypotheses. However, the analysis of when the participants checked "no transaction use" produced significant findings. The category was used in situations perceived as race-related (β = .032, p = .045), low in stress (β = −.035, p = .022), and characterized by a positive valence (β = .046, p = .012). These results suggest that this category was applied in a systematic fashion, as the participants seemed to be thinking of positive race- and culture-sensitive activities that did not fit any of the predefined categories. On the other hand, table 4.5 shows the list of emotions found to be correlated with the "other" category and the list is not very coherent, suggesting that in other instances participants used this category to classify miscellaneous transactions. The "no transaction" category was also used in situations where participants felt ambivalence about European Americans (β = .033, p = .006). Recalling an earlier finding, this means that feelings of ambivalence toward European Americans played a role in triggering either the code-switching or no-transaction categories. These results point to the need to isolate other transaction categories not identified by this research project.

Race Centrality, Positionality, Gender, and Specific Transaction Use

Given the two-level nature of the measurements (premeasure and daily diary, or DD), the following analyses were conducted using HLM.

RACE CENTRALITY AND THE TRANSACTION   We predicted racial centrality would positively predict buffering, code switching, and bonding. Consistent with our predictions, higher levels of race centrality predicted buffering (β = .025, p = .021), code switching (β = .014, p = .043), and bonding (β = .011, p = .016), and these transactions are associated with protective, mainstream, and cultural transactions, respectively. Although not statistically significant, the trend of the relationship between race centrality and bridging was, as predicted, negative (β = −.039, p = .493). Such a negative trend is consistent with the interpretation that global measures of race centrality are insensitive to bicultural or multicultural tendencies (Vandiver et al. 2002), and, of course, the object of bridging is the transaction of biculturally and multiculturally social interactions (Cross, Smith, and Payne 2002).

POSITIONALITY AND TRANSACTION USE   It was hypothesized that the pre-encounter, immersion-emersion, and internalization identity frames, or positionalities, would be associated with three different transactional usage profiles. Significant results were recorded for only one identity frame. As predicted, immersion-emersion, or black militancy, predicted buffering (β = .255, p = .001), code switching (β = .296, p = .002), and acting as an individual (β = –.235, p = .072), suggestive of racial vigilance, arms-length relationships with whites, and a proclivity to be less individualistic and more group-focused in everyday activities. Militants tended to avoid bridging with whites and showed a surprising tendency not to bond with other blacks, though this was a statistically insignificant trend.

After the fact, we realized that it was probably too ambitious to assume that our small sample could pinpoint the relationship between positionality and every single transaction, as opposed to positionality and general transaction use. In hindsight, we realized that it might have been better to begin with a prediction that pre-encounter would tend not to use the transactions, whereas militants and internalizers would show heavy usage. Looking at both correlation data and HLM analysis, pre-encounter was associated with the tendency to make less frequent use of the identity transactions, whereas both immersion-emersion and internalization showed more frequent usage. However, the overall pattern was merely suggestive and accounted for very little variance.

GENDER   We did not hypothesize any gender differences, but there was one significant relationship between females and males. Using HLM, buffering was positively associated with gender: males made more frequent use than females of buffering to frame their experiences. Gender did not significantly predict any of the other measures.

DISCUSSION

This fifteen-day daily-diary study explored the range of gestalt-like psychological transactions black people use to transact racial-cultural identity across a broad range of everyday situations. Factors such as racial-cultural mind-set, perception of the situation, perception of the demand characteristics of the situation, and the emotions experienced in response to the situation were used as predictors of transaction usage. The transaction definitions employed by the participants to categorize their transactions were theory-driven and pretested in focus groups made up of African Americans whose characteristics were similar to those of the actual study participants.

The participants selected the concept "buffering" to define the way they transacted race-sensitive situations that were threatening, emotionally negative, and typically dominated by white people or a single white person perceived by the respondent to be acting in a hostile or threatening way.

The transaction "code switching" was also engaged in race-sensitive situations, where the participant felt little threat and in fact felt neutral to positive feelings about the people present.

As predicted, the concept "bridging" framed transactions, carried out mostly with whites, in which friendship, curiosity, and positive emotions were in play. Bridging was significantly correlated with "acting as an individual," suggesting an ebb and flow between seeing one's white friend as "white" and experiencing him or her simply as a human being. Although it was not the focus of a specific hypothesis, the level of bridging recorded was much higher than the researchers expected. The campus on which the study was conducted had its share of racial tensions; nevertheless, bridging proved to be common.

"Bonding" was the concept participants used to transact positive interactions with other blacks. Such situations were bathed in positive emotions and low levels of threat and typically the participant initiated the exchanges.

The most frequently reported transaction was defined as "acting as an individual," a rather dramatic indication that the average participant experienced the "nonracial" aspects of her or his self-concept and sense of individuality. When whites were involved, the emotions felt were either very positive or at least neutral. Conversely, when the feelings felt toward whites were ambivalent or hateful, acting as an individual was not used by the participants to define the nature of the transaction.

Lastly, the participants were free to check "none of the above" as a way of expressing that neither the four transactions nor acting as an individual clearly defined the nature of the transaction. There was always the possibility that participants might use this category to "dump" miscellaneous transactions, and the hodgepodge of emotions (emotion checklist) associated with the "other" category bore out this prediction. However, other trends in the data showed the participants using the "other" category to frame experiences that were race-salient, nonstressful, and enveloped by a positive emotional valence, pointing to the likely possibility that there are other race-sensitive transactions that the current study did not isolate. For example, J. Taylor (2003) as well as Robert J. Jagers et al. (1997) have addressed a religious or spirituality transaction that functions as both a coping mechanism and a motivating force in one's everyday interactions, and they characterize this identity transaction as race- and culture-related (race-salient), a source of both psychological protection and personal inspiration (nonstressful), and energized by positive affect (positive emotional valence).

Participant scores on a pre-measure provided mixed to modest support for the notion that identity predicts which transactions a participant will favor or downplay. Racial centrality provided the strongest support for this line of thinking, in that, as predicted, participants who scored high on centrality, which is an indication that race and black culture are important anchors in a person's meaning-making system, were more likely to report transacting buffering, code switching, and bonding. Also, as predicted, racial centrality was not statistically related to the use of bridging, but indicated, as predicted, that individuals for whom race is less sensitive bridged more. A second measure used to sort participants into three racial-identity categories—assimilated, militant, and internalized or habituated blackness—proved less successful. Neither the assimilated nor internalized identity categories produced distinctive frequency-of-transaction-use profiles. However, as hypothesized, the militant identity category showed statistically significant signs of racial vigilance (buffering) and arms-length interactions with whites (code switching). Militants also downplayed bridging (intimacy) with whites, and militancy being a form of strong group identity, not surprisingly, their tendency was to make fewer acting-as-an-individual transactions. Finally, in terms of gender identity, only one significant result was recorded but it was important and ominous. Black males, who currently are the object of hysterical levels of stigmatization by the larger society, were more likely than black females to report buffering transactions.

Going into the study, we conceptualized most exchanges between blacks as forms of bonding. However, as predicted in a new theoretical work by Cross, Smith, and Payne (2002), a post hoc analysis revealed that in addition to bonding, blacks also use buffering, code switching, and bridging to transact their black-to-black interactions.

Finally, the overall pattern of our results suggests that the use of any one type of transaction is not to be mistaken for transacting a separate identity. We have already noted that race centrality was associated with three mechanisms: buffering, code switching, and bonding. Furthermore, examination of the actual cases showed it was common for a participant to report simultaneously transacting two or three transactions within the same situation, depending on the number and type of people present and the nature of the participant's relationship with each person present. In such instances, our data do not suggest identity fragmentation; rather, "one" identity seems to be "expressed" or "lived" through a repertoire of identity transactions.

THEORETICAL IMPLICATIONS

Results from the developmental literature that focus on racial-cultural socialization show that black parents prepare their children to transact "race" and "black culture" in three ways (Stevenson 1995; Stevenson et al. 2002):

1. Identity and self-concept protection, or shielding

2. Connectivity to the mainstream

3. A sense of attachment to black people and the black experience

Such parental objectives overlap and complement the theoretical orientations of both Oyserman and Harrison (1998, for the tripartite model of minority identity and adjustment) and Boykin and Toms (1985, for the triple-quandary theory of black identity), who suggest that on a daily basis black youth find themselves moving in and out of experiences with oppression, mainstream culture, and black culture. A logical question to ask is whether such socialization has long-term consequences? Aside from the need and value of longitudinal studies, the current work took it as reasonable to assume that embedded in the ways black adults enact black identity in everyday life are transactional modes that very closely match what might be considered the multiple consequences of racial-cultural socialization. When our subjects perceived situations as race-salient and hostile, they described themselves as engaging the psychological shield called buffering, and it was buffering that helped them "transact" racism. Thus, their "stigma identity" did not provide them with protection; rather, encounters with stigma triggered a broad range of reaction strategies designed to shield them from the full thrust of the stigma assault. Our findings only touch the surface of buffering; for example, we did not explore situations of buffering breakdown, such as stereotype threat (Steele and Aronson 1995). In stereotype-threat circumstances, the black person may be caught totally off-guard and performance may suffer, reflecting a breakdown in buffering (breakdown in self-protection).

Examining the situations eliciting code switching, we see high race-salience. This indicates that in these situations the participants did not "switch off" their black identity (though they may have appeared to do so) and resort to individualism, nor did they define these situations as race-neutral, which might have led them to favor acting-as-an-individual transactions. At the "surface level," however, the person acted in a way that might make others in the situation feel that race and black culture were the last things being negotiated.

Bridging represents the achievement of intimacy, trust, and profound closeness to whites (or "others"), yet the theme of becoming close to whites is not dominant in the socialization practices of blacks as a group (Stevenson 1995; Stevenson et al. 2002). We have defined code switching as a bicultural competence to achieve desired outcomes in mainstream situations. However, we decided to include bridging as an object of study so that our results might extend to blacks who go beyond the more manipulative aspects of code switching to open themselves to close relationships across the racial-cultural divide and actually practice biculturalism. Despite the fact that a central source of tension in American society, the "black-white thing," has yet to be resolved, the ability to transact multicultural situations is increasingly becoming a demand characteristic of modern life for all Americans, including African American youths.

The exchanges that blacks have with each other are often assumed to emanate from a single cultural competency, but Boykin and Toms (1985) stress that learning to live and be functional within the black community is not accomplished without considerable socialization, experience, and personal effort to learn black culture. When this sense of group connection is achieved, it results in cultural attachment and bonding, which, as it happened, was one of the most frequently transacted experiences in the entire study. While we correctly predicted the importance of bonding, we were not prepared for the findings that underscore Boykin and Toms's call for more in-depth analysis of the multiple ways blacks transact blackness within the black community. We were surprised by evidence suggesting that blacks may buffer, code-switch, and even bridge with each other, results that are in accord with the recent extension of the identity enactments schema to black-on-black exchanges (Cross, Smith, and Payne 2002). That blacks might buffer or code-switch with each other is somewhat readily understood; the black community has a long history of within-group tensions based on regional, social class, and differences of skin color and physical appearance, and such fractures can cause one black person to feel the need to invoke buffering with a fellow black person who is acting in a racially hostile manner. Furthermore, many blacks are now part of the mainstream. A black person may record a code-switching episode involving a person of authority, power, or influence at the center of the mainstream context who is another black person. Exchanges between blacks who are not friends but merely acquaintances may also trigger the use of code switching.

Less obvious but nevertheless present is the need for bridging in black-on-black interactions. For example, if a friendship between Tuere, an African college student from Senegal, and Nikka, a black American college student from New York City, is ever to be achieved, their cultural differences will have to be negotiated, or "bridged," despite the fact that they share African physical characteristics. The same can be said of dyads involving a black person from the United States and a black person from

Haiti, Jamaica, Panama, or Brazil. Bridging among blacks involves the same sort of cultural-difference-intimacy negotiations more typically associated with black-white friendships.

Within the psychological makeup of an average adult may be found not one but a cluster of social identities (Stryker and Statham 1985; Markus and Wurf 1987; Deaux and Perkins 2000), and the sum total of these multiple identities accounts in large measure for a key superordinate component of a person's overall self-concept: the group identity or reference-group sector of the self. Jay W. Jackson and Eliot R. Smith (1999) make reference to a person's total identity matrix wherein each "cell" of the matrix defines the boundaries and dynamics of a separate social identity. The current work seeks to further extend the identity matrix concept by suggesting that buffering, code switching, bridging, bonding, and "acting as an individual" are probably intrinsic to the social dynamics of every social-identity cell. Thus, the identity matrix for an adult male who is black, gay, and physically very short will contain a separate "cell" for each social marker, and within each cell will be found the repertoire of identity enactments. The current work provides a glimpse of the inner workings of each cell of the matrix.

NOTE

1. Research on identity development conducted by other scholars pertains to other besides black groups, but the research and results presented here are limited to black individuals.

REFERENCES

Abrams, Dominic, Joanne Thomas, and Michael A. Hogg. 1990. "Numerical Distinctiveness, Social Identity, and Gender Salience." *British Journal of Social Psychology* 29(1): 87–92.

Adams, Maureen, LeeAnn A. Bell, and Pat Griffin. 1997. *Teaching for Diversity and Social Justice: A Source Book.* New York: Routledge.

Banks, James A., and Cherry A. Banks. 1995. *Handbook of Research on Multicultural Education.* New York: Macmillan.

Boykin, A. Wade, and Forrest D. Toms. 1985. "Black Child Socialization: A Conceptual Framework." In *Black Children,* edited by Harriette P. McAdoo and John L. McAdoo. Newbury, Calif.: Sage.

Bronfenbrenner, Urie. 2005. *Making Human Beings Human: Biological Perspectives on Human Development.* Thousand Oaks, Calif.: Sage.

Carter, Robert T., and Janet E. Helms. 1987. "The Relationship of Black Value-Orientation to Racial Attitudes." *Measurement and Evaluation in Counseling and Development* 19(4): 185–95.

Chavous, Tabbye M. 2000. "The Relationship Among Racial Identity, Perceived Ethnic Fit, and Organizational Involvement for African American Students at a Predominantly White University." *Journal of Black Psychology* 26(1): 79–100.

Crocker, Jennifer, and Brenda Major. 1989. "Social Stigma and Self-Esteem: The Self-Protective Properties of Stigma." *Psychological Review* 96: 608–30.

Cross, William E., Jr. 1991. *Shades of Black.* Philadelphia: Temple University Press.

Cross, William. E., Jr., and Peony Fhagen-Smith. 2001. "Patterns of African American Identity Development: A Life Span Perspective." In *New Perspectives on Racial Identity Development,* edited by Charmaine L. Wijeysinghe and Bailey W. Jackson, III. New York: New York University Press.

Cross, William E., Jr., Lakesha Smith, and Yasser Payne. 2002. "Black Identity: A Repertoire of Daily Enactments." In *Counseling Across Cultures,* edited by Paul B. Pedersen, Juris G. Draguns, Walter J. Lonner, and Joseph E. Trimble. 5th edition. Thousand Oaks, Calif.: Sage.

Deaux, Kay, and T. S. Perkins. 2000. "The Kaleidoscope Self." In *Individual Self, Relational Self, and Collective Self: Partners, Opponents or Strangers,* edited by Constantine Sedikides and Marilynn B. Brewer. Philadelphia: Psychology Press.

Deaux, Kay, Anne Reid, Kim Mizrahi, and Dave Cotting. 1999. "Connecting the Person to the Social: The Functions of Social Identification." In *The Psychology of the Social Self,* edited by Tom R. Tyler, Roderick Kramer, and Oliver Jons. Hillsdale, N.J.: Erlbaum.

Erikson, Erik. 1950. *Childhood and Society.* New York: Norton.

Feldman, Lisa A. 1995. "Valence Focus and Arousal Focus: Individual Differences in the Structure of Affective Experience." *Journal of Personality and Social Psychology* 69(1): 153–66.

Feldman-Barrett, Lisa, and Janet K. Swim. 1998. "Appraisals of Prejudice and Discrimination." In *Prejudice: The Target's Perspective,* edited by Janet K. Swim and Charles Stangor. New York: Academic Press.

Goffman, Erving. 1959. *The Presentation of Self in Everyday Life.* Garden City, N.Y.: Doubleday Anchor.

Helms, Janet E. 1990. "Black and White Racial Identity Development: Theory, Research, and Practice." Westport, Conn.: Greenwood Press.

Jack, Belinda E. 1996. *Negritude and Literary Criticism: The History and Theory of "Negro-African" Literature in French.* Westport, Conn.: Greenwood Press.

Jackson, Jay W., and Eliot R. Smith. 1999. "Conceptualizing Social Identity: A New Framework and Evidence for the Impact of Different Dimensions." *Personality and Social Psychology Bulletin* 25(1): 120–35.

Jagers, Robert J., Paula Smith, Lynne O. Mock, and Ebony Dill. 1997. "An Afrocultural Social Ethos: Component Orientation and Some Social Implications." *Journal of Black Psychology* 23(4): 328–43.

Markus, Hazel, and Elissa Wurf. 1987. "The Dynamic Self-Concept: Social Psychological Perspective." *Annual Review of Psychology* 38: 299–337.

Oyserman, Daphna, and Kathy Harrison. 1998. "Implications of Cultural Context: African American Identity and Possible Selves." In *Prejudice: The Target's Perspective,* edited by Janet K. Swim and Charles Stangor. New York: Academic Press.

Parham, Thomas A., and Janet E. Helms. 1981. "Influence of a Black Student's Racial Identity Attitudes on Preference for Counselor's Race." *Journal of Counseling Psychology* 28: 250–57.

Phinney, Jean. 1989. "The Stages of Ethnic Identity Development in Minority Group Children." *Journal of Early Adolescence* 9(1–2): 34–49.

Saenz, Delia S. 1994. "Token Status and Problem-Solving Deficits: Detrimental Effects of Distinctiveness and Performance Monitoring." *Social Cognition* 12(1): 61–74.

Sellers, Robert M., Stephanie A. Rowley, Tabbye M. Chavous, J. Nicole Shelton, and Mia A. Smith. 1997. "Multidimensional Inventory of Black Identity: Preliminary Investigation of Reliability and Construct Validity." *Journal of Personality and Social Psychology* 73(4): 805–15.

Senghor, Léonard S. 1988. *Ce que je crois: Negritude, francite et civilization de l'universel.* Paris: B. Grasset.

Shelton, J. Nicole, and Robert M. Sellers. 2000. "Situational Stability and Variability in African American Racial Identity." *Journal of Black Psychology* 26(1): 27–50.

Spencer, Margaret B. 1995. "Old and New Theorizing About African American Youth: A Phenomenological Variant of Ecological Systems Theory." In *African American Youth,* edited by Ronald Taylor. Westport, Conn.: Praeger.

Steele, Claude M., and Joshua Aronson. 1995. "Stereotype Threat and the Intellectual Test Performance of African Americans." *Journal of Personality and Social Psychology* 69(5): 797–812.

Stevenson, Howard C. 1995. "The Relationship of Racial Socialization and Racial Identity in African American Adolescents." *Journal of Black Psychology* 21(1): 49–70.

Stevenson, Howard C., Rick Cameron, Teri Herrero-Taylor, and Gwendolyn Y. Davis. 2002. "Development of the Teenage Experience of Racial Socialization Scale: Correlates of Race-Related Socialization from the Perspective of Black Youth." *Journal of Black Psychology* 28(2): 84–106.

Stevenson, Howard C., and Gwendolyn Y. Davis. Forthcoming. "Applied Cultural Socialization and the Catch 33: The Meta-Art of Balancing Intolerance, Survival, and Self-Actualization." In *Black Psychology,* edited by Reginald Jones. 4th edition.

Stevenson, Howard C., Jocelyn Reed, and Preston Bodison. 1996. "Kinship, Social Support, and Adolescent Perceptions of Racial Socialization: Extending Self to Family." *Journal of Black Psychology* 22: 498–508.

Stevenson, Howard C., Jocelyn Reed, Preston Bodison, and Angela Bishop. 1997. "Racism Stress Management: Racial Socialization Beliefs and Experience of Depression and Anger for African American Adolescents." *Youth and Society* 29(2): 197–222.

Stryker, Sheldon, and Anne Statham. 1985. "Symbolic Interaction and Role Theory." In *The Handbook of Social Psychology,* edited by G. Lindzey and E. Aronson. 3rd edition. New York: Random House.

Sue, David, Winnie S. Mak, and Derald W. Sue. 1998. "Ethnic Identity." In *Handbook of Asian American Psychology,* edited by Lee Lee and Nolan W. S. Zane. Thousand Oaks, Calif.: Sage.

Swim, Janet. K., and Charles Stangor, eds. 1998. *Prejudice: The Target's Perspective.* New York: Academic Press.

Tajfel, Henry. 1974. "Social Identity and Intergroup Behavior." *Social Science Information* 13: 65–93.

Tatum, Beverly D. 1987. *Assimilation Blues: Black Families in a White Community.* Northampton, Mass.: Hazel-Maxwell Publishing.

———. 1997. *Why Are All the Black Kids Sitting Together in the Cafeteria, and Other Conversations About Race.* New York: Basic Books.

Taylor, J. 2003. "How Values for Life Promote Spiritual and Cultural Well-Being." Presentation at the National Black Child Development Institute. Pittsburgh (June 12, 2003).

Vandiver, Beverly J., William E. Cross Jr., Frank C. Worrell, and Peony E. Fhagen-Smith. 2002. "Validating the Cross Racial Identity Scale." *Journal of Counseling Psychology* 49(1): 71–85.

Vygotsky, Lev S. 1978. *Mind in Society: The Development of Higher Psychological Processes.* Cambridge, Mass.: Harvard University Press.

CHAPTER 5

ETHNIC IDENTITY AS A BUFFER OF PSYCHOLOGICAL ADJUSTMENT TO STRESS

J. Nicole Shelton, Tiffany Yip, Jacquelynne S. Eccles,
Celina M. Chatman, Andrew J. Fuligni, and Carol Wong

Being an ethnic minority in the United States can be stressful. Having to contend with negative stereotypes and beliefs about one's group can be emotionally and psychologically draining for ethnic minorities. In fact, researchers once suggested that ethnic minorities internalized the dominant culture's stereotypes and beliefs about their groups, which led to negative self-concepts (see Cross 1991 for a review). Moreover, having to deal with unfair treatment and resource inequities can lead to poor physical and psychological health for ethnic minorities (Allison 1998).

The aim of this chapter is to demonstrate that ethnic identity has the potential to protect ethnic minorities from the negative consequences of ethnic prejudice and discrimination and general daily stressors. We argue that although ethnicity (ethnic group membership) may put ethnic minorities at risk for experiencing discrimination, which in turn is associated with negative psychological consequences, ethnic *identity* buffers individuals from these consequences (see figure 5.1 for a conceptual model).

The first part of the chapter provides an overview of research that focuses on ethnicity as a risk factor for psychological well-being. The next section reviews research that demonstrates that ethnic identity can buffer ethnic minorities from the risks associated with being an ethnic minority. Throughout this latter section, we draw on empirical findings from three different programs of research to illustrate incidents when and mechanisms whereby ethnic identity serves as a protective function in individuals' lives. These data sets allow us to make comparisons between African Americans and Chinese Americans. In addition, the data sets allow us to examine the protective function of ethnic identity in young adolescents thirteen to eighteen years old and older, college-age young adults eighteen to twenty-two years old. Taken together, the data sets provide us with converging evidence that various dimensions of ethnic identity protect ethnic minorities from the psychological consequences related to discrimina-

Figure 5.1 Conceptual Model of Racial Identity and Experiences with
Discrimination

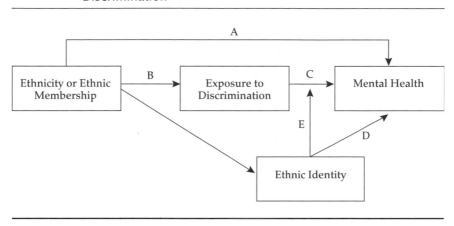

Source: Authors' compilation.

tion and negative events more generally. We close the chapter with directions for future
research and recommendations for policy intervention.

ETHNICITY AS A RISK FACTOR FOR POOR PSYCHOLOGICAL ADJUSTMENT

Much of the early research on ethnic minorities, particularly African Americans, was
geared toward demonstrating that being an ethnic minority was related to negative
psychological outcomes (see, for example, Kardiner and Ovesey 1951). This research
suggested that being an ethnic minority is related to poor psychological outcomes
through two routes. First, researchers assumed that there was a direct relation
between ethnic minority group membership and mental health (see Cross 1991 for a
review). Second, researchers argued that being an ethnic minority places individuals
at risk for higher levels of stress, including those associated with ethnic discrimination, which in turn could lead to poor psychological outcomes. We discuss these two
views in more detail in the next section.

Ethnicity and Mental Health

Is ethnic-group membership directly related to negative psychological adjustment
(see path A in figure 5.1)? If so, then there should be consistent group differences
between whites and ethnic minorities in measures of psychological well-being. If not,
then research should indicate that ethnic minorities are not psychologically worse off
than whites. Most of the early theoretical work on ethnic minorities suggests the former, but most of the past and recent empirical research suggests the latter.

A substantial portion of the research on group differences in mental health has
focused on differences in self-esteem. In general, empirical evidence in this literature
indicates that African Americans have higher personal self-esteem than whites (see

Crocker and Major 1989; Porter and Washington 1979; and Twenge and Crocker 2002 for reviews). In fact, a recent meta-analysis of research published between 1960 and 1998 on racial differences in self-esteem revealed that African American children, adolescents, and young adults have higher self-esteem than their white counterparts (Gray-Little and Hafdahl 2001; see also Twenge and Crocker 2002 for a meta-analytic review). Interestingly, Bernadette Gray-Little and Adam R. Hafdahl (2001) note that because it is practically unacceptable or hard to imagine that African Americans have higher self-esteem than whites, various arguments, such as response style artifact, a group-by-item interaction favoring African American respondents, and defensive responding have been postulated as explanations as to why this finding must be incorrect. In essence, there seems to be an implicit bias toward examining ethnic minorities within a risk-factor framework.

The evidence comparing self-esteem of whites and other ethnic minority groups such as Asian Americans, Hispanics, and Native Americans is not as favorable as that comparing whites and African Americans. Some Latin American groups, for example, Mexican Americans, tend to have self-esteem equivalent to white Americans, whereas others, for example, Puerto Ricans, tend to have lower self-esteem. In a meta-analytical review, Jean M. Twenge and Jennifer Crocker (2002) found that Hispanics and Native Americans tend to have lower self-esteem than whites. Furthermore, of all of the ethnic groups represented in these studies, Asian Americans tend to have the lowest levels of self-esteem compared to whites. As Jennifer Crocker and her colleagues (Crocker and Lawrence 1999; Crocker and Wolfe 2001) note, however, these findings do not necessarily indicate that all ethnic minorities are at risk for low self-esteem. In fact, making the comparison between whites and ethnic minorities in terms of mental health outcomes may be too simplistic an approach to assess the extent to which ethnic minority status is a risk factor for poor psychological functioning. There may be differences within groups that are important to consider in this process.

Ethnicity and Exposure to Discrimination

Does belonging to an ethnic minority group increase the risk of being exposed to discrimination (see path B in figure 5.1)? The answer to this question seems to be a resounding yes. Ethnic minorities, compared to whites, are disproportionately exposed to stimuli that may be sources of stress (Clark et al. 1999). Objective and subjective reports on incidents of ethnic discrimination corroborate this point. Objective findings show that ethnic minorities are discriminated against in higher education (Farrell and Jones 1988), the housing market (Bobo 1983; Massey and Denton 1992; Yinger 1988), as well as hiring and employment (Tomaskovic-Devey 1993). Additionally, subjective, self-report findings indicate that ethnic minorities are more likely than whites to believe they are targets of intergroup discrimination and prejudice. For example, Nancy Krieger (1990) found that approximately 60 percent of the noncollege adult African American respondents in her sample reported one or more instances of negative race-based treatment in their lives, whereas approximately 84 percent of the white respondents reported *never* experiencing negative race-based treatment. Additional research suggests that 60 percent or more of ethnic minority adults report that they typically encounter ethnic discrimination in their lives (D'Augelli and Hershberger 1993; Kessler, Mickelson, and Williams 1999; Landrine and Klonoff 1996; Sanders-Thompson 1996; Williams et al. 1997).

The statistics are just as disturbing for ethnic minority groups other than African Americans. For instance, approximately 20 percent of Latino job seekers are discriminated against because of their ethnicity (Bendick et al. 1991). Similarly, 30 percent of Asian Americans indicate they have experienced discrimination in employment situations, 15 percent indicate that they have experienced discrimination in seeking housing, and 39 percent indicate that they have experienced discrimination in other situations (Kuo 1995). More specifically, approximately 20 percent of Chinese Americans indicate that they have received some form of unfair treatment because of their ethnicity in their lifetime (Goto, Gee, and Takeuchi 2002). Taken together, these findings provide objective and subjective support that large numbers of ethnic minorities are frequently exposed to discrimination-related stress.

Additional research shows that exposure to racial discrimination is directly linked to a variety of negative physical health outcomes among ethnic minorities (see path C in figure 5.1; Allison 1998; Clark et al. 1999; Landrine and Klonoff 1996). Perceived prejudice and discrimination contribute to the disproportionately high rates of hypertension among African Americans (Clark et al. 1999; Guyll, Matthews, and Bromberger 2001; Krieger 1990; Krieger and Sidney 1996; McNeilly et al. 1995). Evidence also shows that for African Americans, experiencing high levels of discrimination is adversely related to cardiovascular health, compared to experiencing moderate or low levels of discrimination.

Researchers have pinpointed various psychological consequences of experiencing discrimination (see path C in figure 5.1). For example, experiencing racial discrimination is associated with a higher incidence of psychiatric symptoms—depression, anxiety, obsession-compulsion, and somatization—among African Americans (Landrine and Klonoff 1996; Sanders-Thompson 1996). Moreover, the more African Americans and Hispanics experience discrimination the more they feel anger, lower levels of life satisfaction, and lower levels of happiness (Jackson et al. 1996; Salgado de Snyder 1987). Maya McNeilly et al. (1995) found that racist provocation produced resentment, anxiety, and cynicism among African Americans. Finally, experiences with racial discrimination over time have a cumulative negative impact on African Americans' subjective well-being. Taken together, the findings from these studies indicate that experiencing racial discrimination can have serious mental health consequences.

In summary, empirical evidence is mixed regarding the extent to which ethnicity is associated with poor psychological adjustment. Despite earlier theoretical arguments, there is little empirical research to support the direct link between ethnic-group membership and poor mental health. In fact, at least with respect to self-esteem, the data indicate that some ethnic minority groups fare psychologically similarly to or better than whites. There is research, however, indicating that ethnic minorities are at a higher risk than whites for experiencing and perceiving discrimination, which leads to poor psychological outcomes.

ETHNIC IDENTITY AS A PROTECTIVE FACTOR

Thus far, the discussion has focused primarily on ethnicity as a social-category label. That is, the previously discussed research examines ethnic minority status in terms of whether or not a person belongs to a certain social category. Being an ethnic minority is more complex than such thinking. Consistent with the idea that being an ethnic minority is complex, as research on and about ethnic minorities has started to flourish, researchers have given more thought to what it means to be an ethnic minority. Scholars are developing sophisticated and intricate models and measures specifically about ethnic minority identity that examine ethnicity as more than a social category (for examples, see Cross, Parham, and Helms 1998; Phinney 1990, 1992; Sellers et al. 1998).

Despite differences in definitions and labels to describe the components of ethnic identity that have arisen from these ethnic-identity models, there seems to be consensus from this research that ethnic minority groups are not homogeneous.[1] (See Chatman, Eccles, and Malanchuk, chapter 6, this volume, as well as Allen et al., chapter 7, this volume, for additional discourse on definitions of ethnic identity.) There is a great deal of variability in the value ethnic minorities place on their ethnicity and how important their ethnicity is to their overall self-concept. For some ethnic minorities, ethnic-group membership is not an important reflection of who they are whereas for others it is the most significant component of their identity (Cross 1991; Luhtanen and Crocker 1992; Sellers et al. 1997). Similarly, some ethnic minorities have positive regard for other members of their ethnic group whereas others have negative regard (Luhtanen and Crocker 1992; Sellers et al. 1997). Moreover, as Robert M. Sellers and his colleagues note, there is variability in the beliefs and attitudes ethnic minorities have about what it means to be a member of their ethnic group. Interestingly, the grounded-theory approach used by Celina M. Chatman, Jacquelynne Eccles, and Oksana Malanchuk (chapter 6, this volume) to assess the meaning of ethnic identity for adolescents revealed similar components (racial ideology and racial pride), suggesting that these concepts are indeed how individuals think about their ethnic identity.

Research that has advanced from the ethnic-identity models has demonstrated that the variability in ethnic identity is associated, both directly and indirectly, with positive mental health outcomes. First, researchers have demonstrated a direct relationship between ethnic identity and mental health. Second, researchers have demonstrated that ethnic identity buffers the previously discussed relationship between exposure to discrimination and mental health. We discuss examples from our programs of research that illustrate these two points in more detail in the following sections.

Ethnic Identity and Mental Health

Is there a direct relationship between ethnic identity and mental health? If so, is it positive or negative (see path D in figure 5.1)? Empirical evidence indicates that the more ethnicity is an important component of ethnic minorities' social identity, the higher their levels of psychological well-being (Lorenzo-Hernandez and Ouellette 1998; Martinez and Dukes 1997; Phinney 1996; Smith 1991; Yip and Fuligni 2002a). Research shows that for African Americans in particular, the esteem associated with ethnic-group membership is positively related to personal self-esteem, but only among those individuals for whom ethnicity is an important part of the self-concept (Rowley et al. 1998). A similar relationship was found among Chinese adolescents who participated in a daily-diary study (Yip and Fuligni 2002a, 2002b) and Chinese college students who participated in an experience-sampling study (Yip 2004) on ethnic-identity salience and psychological well-being. In these studies, ethnic-identity salience was considered to be the dynamic dimension of ethnic identity that fluctuates in response to contextual cues. Tiffany Yip and Andrew J. Fuligni (2002a, 2002b) found that Chinese adolescents (mean age = sixteen years) with a strong attachment to their ethnic group showed the highest association between daily levels of ethnic salience and psychological well-being such that increased ethnic salience was paired with more positive feelings. In contrast, adolescents with a weaker attachment to their ethnic group reported no daily association between ethnic salience and psychological well-being. Similarly, at the level of the situation, Yip (2004) found that ethnic-identity salience was positively associated with psychological well-being among older Chinese students, but primarily among those individuals with high regard for their ethnic group. Specifically, Yip (2004) found that older Chinese students with high regard for their ethnic group reported positive associations between situation levels of ethnic-identity salience and psychological well-being, while students with moderate levels of regard for their group reported much weaker positive associations, and students with low regard for their group reported negative associations between ethnic-identity salience and psychological well-being.

Taken together, these findings show that people of color who choose to make ethnicity an important aspect of their social identity or have positive views about their group seem to exhibit better psychological adjustment. Interestingly, it does not seem to be the case that those who do not have a strong sense of ethnic identity are more poorly adjusted, rather it appears that their well-being is not tied to their feelings about their ethnic group. Therefore, we propose that ethnic identity may in fact protect and promote esteem and positive mental health for ethnic minorities who integrate ethnicity in the construction of their identity.

Ethnic Identity as a Buffer Against Racial Discrimination

Does ethnic identity buffer ethnic minorities from the adverse effects of discrimination and prejudice (see path E in figure 5.1)? We, along with other scholars (Bowler, Rauch, and Schwarzer 1986; Chatman, Eccles, and Malanchuk, chapter 6, this volume; Crocker and Major 1989), posit that it does. Specifically, a certain type of ethnic identity seems to provide individual members of ethnic minority groups with a repertoire of strategies that allow them to negotiate difficult situations such as being faced with negative stereotypes, discrimination, and unfair treatment. Perhaps in the presence of discrimination, individuals who are connected to their group can feel good about themselves by focusing on the positive aspects of their group. We discuss the results of two programs of research, one dealing with young adults and the other with adolescents, to illustrate the buffering effects of ethnic identity in the lives of ethnic minorities.

BUFFERING EFFECTS FOR YOUNG ADULTS   Using the Multidimensional Model of Racial Identity (MMRI) as a theoretical framework, Sellers and his colleagues (Sellers and Shelton 2003; Neblett, Shelton, and Sellers 2004) found support for the buffering thesis with a sample of African American young adults. Sellers and colleagues define racial identity as the significance and qualitative meaning that individuals attribute to being black in their conceptualization of self (Sellers et al. 1997; Sellers et al. 1998).

They refer to the significance component of racial identity as "racial centrality," and refer to the qualitative meaning of racial identity as "racial ideology" and "racial regard." More specifically, "racial centrality" refers to how important race is to an individual's overall self-concept. As noted previously, for some African Americans, race is not an important part of who they are, but for others it is the most defining component of their identity. Sellers and his colleagues suggest, however, that two people can be equally identified with their racial group but have very distinct beliefs about what it means to be a member of that group—in other words, have different racial ideologies—as well as have very different affective judgments about their group. According to this research there are at least four ideologies that capture African Americans' views on what it means to be an African American:

1. A nationalist ideology, which stresses the uniqueness of being of African descent

2. An oppressed-minority ideology, which stresses the similarities between African Americans and other oppressed groups

3. An assimilationist ideology, which stresses the similarities between African Americans and American mainstream society

4. A humanist ideology, which stresses the commonalities of all humans

(See Sellers et al. 1998 for a richer description of each ideology.) In addition to these ideologies, Sellers and his colleagues suggest that some African Americans may have positive private regard for African Americans whereas others may have negative private regard; similarly, some African Americans believe that other people have positive regard for African Americans whereas some African Americans believe that other people have negative regard (public regard).

In accordance with a buffering framework, these three dimensions of racial identity (centrality, regard, and ideology) should moderate the relationship between experiencing racial discrimination and mental health outcomes. As noted previously, individuals who are strongly identified with their racial group may be able to focus on the positive aspects of their racial group in the face of discrimination. As a result, they may be buffered from the effects of discrimination. Similarly, Sellers and his colleagues suggest that racial discrimination may be consistent with some individuals' racial ideological worldview and that individuals for whom this is the case may be buffered from the ill effects of discrimination. For example, African Americans with a racial ideology that stressed their uniqueness (nationalist ideology) or one whereby they see themselves as members of an oppressed minority group may expect others to treat them negatively because of their racial group membership. Because it is consistent with their perspective on life, these individuals may have developed strong coping strategies to deal with discrimination. As a result, when they experience discrimination in their lives it may not be as psychologically taxing for them as it is for African Americans with other racial ideologies. Finally, African Americans who believe that other groups make negative affective judgments about African Americans may be less affected by discrimination because it is not foreign to the way they view the world. Similar to individuals who endorse a nationalist or an oppressed-minority ideology, these individuals may have developed coping strategies to deal with discrimination. In the next section, we discuss recent research that supports these predictions.

RACIAL CENTRALITY AS A BUFFER AGAINST RACIAL DISCRIMINATION   Using data from the Racial Identity Longitudinal Survey (RILS), Enrique Neblett, J. Nicole Shelton, and Robert M. Sellers (2004) examined racial centrality as a moderator of experiencing racial discrimination and psychological distress. At the time of their data analyses, the participants in the RILS were 108 self-identified African American freshman college students from two predominately white universities located in the Midwest and Southeast and one historically black college located in the Southeast. All students who participated in the RILS completed a racial-identity measure, a racial-discrimination daily hassles questionnaire, and several psychological well-being measures. Students also completed the Multidimensional Inventory of Black Identity (MIBI), which is a fifty-six-item measure that assesses an individual's racial centrality, racial ideology, and racial regard (Sellers et al. 1997). In addition, students completed the Daily Life Experience questionnaire, a self-report measure whereby students indicate the frequency of experiencing eighteen types of micro-aggressions due to race in the past year (Harrell 1994) and how much the events bothered them. The micro-aggressions include being observed or being followed while in public places; and being ignored or overlooked, or not being given service. Finally, students completed the Center for Epidemiological Studies Depression Scale (CES-D), the Perceived Stress Scale (PSS), and the Spielberger Trait Anxiety Inventory (STAI). Students completed all of these measures during their first semester of college and again at the end of their second semester of college.

The analyses from this portion of the RILS revealed that there was a direct relationship between experiences with daily racial hassles and anxiety, stress, and depression. Specifically, the more racial discrimination students reported experiencing at the first time point, the more anxiety, stress, and depression they reported experiencing at the second time point. Racial centrality, however, moderated these relationships. The sample was divided into low, medium, and high groups based on how important race was to individuals' overall self-concept. The results suggest a buffering effect of centrality on the relationship between experiencing daily racial hassles and mental health outcomes. Among students for whom race was not important or moderately important to their overall self-concept, experiencing daily racial hassles was related to more anxiety, stress, and depression. By contrast, among students for whom race was a very important aspect of their overall self-concept, experiencing daily racial hassles was unrelated to anxiety, stress, and depression. In other words, highly identified African Americans were buffered from the adverse impact of daily racial hassles on mental health.

RACIAL IDEOLOGY AND RACIAL REGARD AS BUFFERS AGAINST RACIAL DISCRIMINATION
The findings from the RILS suggest that not all African Americans suffer from the adverse mental health consequences of racial discrimination. Racial centrality seems to buffer some individuals from these negative outcomes. Expanding upon that finding, Sellers and Shelton (2003) demonstrated that other dimensions of racial identity besides racial centrality—racial ideology and racial regard—also protect individuals from the negative consequences of racial discrimination.

Similar to Neblett, Shelton, and Sellers (2004), Sellers and Shelton's (2003) research also utilized African American students from the RILS. However, several differences regarding the sample and the methodology must be noted. First, by the time Sellers and Shelton's work was conducted, the RILS comprised a larger sample size than the one used by Neblett, Shelton, and Sellers (2004); Sellers and Shelton's research involves 267 African American students, instead of 108. Second, in addition to examining the global mental health consequences of experiencing racial discrimination, Sellers and Shelton investigated the event-specific consequences. Specifically, students indicated how bothered they were by daily racial hassles as an index of the event-specific consequences. In addition, Sellers and Shelton created an overall psychological distress variable that was a composite of the three mental health scales—anxiety, stress, and depression scales—as opposed to examining each scale separately as conducted by Neblett, Shelton, and Sellers (2004). Students completed the racial identity, daily racial hassles, and psychological well-being measures at two time points, at the beginning and at the end of their freshmen year in college.

Sellers and Shelton (2003) found that experiencing racial discrimination more frequently at the first time point resulted in more negative psychological outcomes at both the event-specific and global levels of psychological distress at the second time point. Participants' own appraisal of the discriminatory situation (for example, their answers to the question "How much did it bother you?") as well as their overall psychological well-being indicated that experiencing racial discrimination was devastating for individuals' mental health. However, as Sellers and Shelton predicted, individuals' attitudes regarding the meaning of race influenced the extent to which they were psychologically influenced by racial discrimination. Specifically, individuals who endorsed a nationalist ideology, which stresses the uniqueness of being black, were buffered from the adverse impact of racial discrimination at event-specific and global distress levels. That is, the more individuals believed that African Americans should join together and provide emotional, financial, and spiritual support to one another, the less they were negatively impacted by racial discrimination. Likewise, individuals who believed that other groups perceived African Americans negatively were buffered from the negative impact of racial discrimination. That is, the more individuals recognized that whites hold negative views of African Americans generally, the less they were negatively impacted by racial discrimination.

Taken together, the findings by Sellers and his colleagues (Neblett, Shelton, and Sellers 2004; Sellers and Shelton 2003) provide empirical support to the accumulating theoretical work that suggests that ethnic identity protects minorities from the deleterious impact of racism. Their data show that for African Americans who see race as a central component of their self-concept, and for those African Americans who endorse a nationalist ideology, as well as for those African Americans who think others view their group negatively or encountered negative racial events, they were not as psychologically taxed as other African Americans.

BUFFERING EFFECTS FOR ADOLESCENTS   Sellers and his colleagues' research focused exclusively on African American college-age youth. Recent research by Eccles and her colleagues (Wong, Eccles, and Sameroff 2003) explored the protective functions of aspects of ethnic identity among African American adolescents in their school experiences. Their findings are based on longitudinal analyses of data from the Maryland Adolescent Development in Contexts Study (MADICS).

The participants in this study were living in a county in Maryland that has undergone tremendous demographic and political changes since 1960 (Cook et al. 1999). For example, prior to 1960, 85 percent of the residents in this county were white and political control was held by whites; by 1995, 51 percent of the households were African American and 43 percent were white, and whites and African Americans had equal political control. In addition, because of the fairly comparable social-class profile of the white and African American households in this county, it was possible to study the development of African American adolescents from poor and from middle- and upper-class families.

The first wave of MADICS data was collected from 1,480 families when the adolescents were in seventh grade (1991). The second wave was collected from 1,067 families the summer following the adolescents' completion of eighth grade (1993). Only the 336 African American males and 293 African American females who participated in both waves of data collection in both of the larger studies are included in the present study. The median-income range for the African American adolescents' families in 1991 was $45,000 to $49,999 and for the white adolescents' families, $50,000 to $54,999. The primary caregivers' average levels of education were the same in the two ethnic groups: 54 percent had received a high school degree and 40 percent had obtained a college degree.

The adolescents attended public junior high schools in which the racial composition of the student body ranged from 99 percent African Americans and less than 1 percent white to 33 percent African Americans and 60 percent white students. The racial composition of the school faculties ranged from 25 percent African American and 70 percent white teachers to 52 percent African American and 47 percent white teachers.

In the following sections we first show that there is a negative relationship between discrimination and mental health and also between discrimination and developmental outcomes. Secondly, consistent with our argument, we show that ethnic identity buffers adolescents from these negative outcomes.

PERCEIVED DISCRIMINATION AND ADOLESCENT DEVELOPMENT   Consistent with Sellers and colleagues' research with college-age students, the findings from Carol A. Wong, Eccles, and Arnold Sameroff's (2003) research indicates that during early adolescence, experiences of ethnic discrimination at the first time point influence mental health and developmental outcomes at the second time point. Specifically, the findings reveal the negative effects of perceived racial discrimination from peers and teachers (as a single scale) on adolescents' academic motivation and achievement (declines in school grades, self-concept of academic ability, perceived importance of and perceived utility of school success), and mental health (declines in psychological resilience and self-esteem and increases in depression and anger). In addition, perceived discrimination was associated with increases in the probability of engaging in problem behaviors and having a high proportion of friends who also engage in problem behaviors. These relationships were obtained after controlling for each of the outcome variables and family socioeconomic status at the first time point.

These results indicate that experiences of racial discrimination in junior high school are environmental risks that potentially can threaten African American adolescents' academic and socio-emotional well-being. This is noteworthy because at this age adolescents are at an increased risk for declining motivation, poorer self-perceptions, greater susceptibility to conforming to peers' negative influence, and proneness to problem behaviors (Berndt 1979; Eccles and Midgley 1989; Eccles et al. 1993). Experiencing ethnic stressors such as experiences of discrimination in addition to the non-ethnic-related stressors commonly faced by early adolescents can further increase the probability of negative psychological outcomes (Simmons et al. 1987). Furthermore, prior research indicates that risks during early adolescence have long-term implications. For example, Eccles and her colleagues found that adolescents who report decreases in self-esteem as they make the transition to junior high school continue to have lowered self-esteem throughout their high school years, along with increased depression, anxiety, and alcohol consumption (Eccles et al. 1997).

THE PROTECTIVE ROLE OF ETHNIC IDENTITY AMONG ADOLESCENTS   Although the above findings reveal a negative relationship between exposure to discrimination and psychological and developmental outcomes, we argue that ethnic identity may serve as a protective factor for adolescents, in a similar vein to what Sellers and his colleagues have found with college-age students. Wong, Eccles, and Sameroff (2003) focused specifically on connection to one's ethnic group as the principal component of ethnic identity. Adolescents' feeling of connection to their ethnic group was measured with four questions developed by the staff of the MADIC study: whether respondents felt close to friends because of similar race or ethnicity; whether they believed that people of their race or ethnicity had a rich heritage; whether they felt they had rich traditions because of their race or ethnicity; and whether they felt supported by people of their own race or ethnicity.

Wong, Eccles, and Sameroff (2003) demonstrated that connection to one's ethnic group had both main and interactive effects on psychological adjustment for these African American adolescents. First, connection to one's ethnic group predicted increases in one's psychological resilience and school grades and a higher proportion of friends who were positive about school. In each case, the size of the beta for the connection indicator was approximately equal to the size of the negative beta for perceived discrimination. These results suggest that a strong positive connection to one's ethnic group is a promotive asset that can compensate for the negative impact of perceived discrimination on these aspects of adolescent development.

Second, the interaction term between connection to one's ethnic group and perceived discrimination provides an estimate of the buffering or moderating effect of connection to one's ethnic group on the negative impact of perceived discrimination on adolescent development. This interaction term was significant for four adolescent outcomes: self-concept of academic ability, school grades, involvement in problem behaviors, and the proportion of one's friends that value school. In each case, perceived discrimination had no impact on change in these aspects of adolescent development if the adolescent had a strong connection to their ethnic group. Thus, these African American youths' connection to their ethnic group acted as a protective factor by both compensating for and buffering against the impact of perceived discrimination.

Like the work by Sellers and colleagues, described above, results from the MADICS indicate that although perceptions and experiences of ethnic discrimination can negatively influence well-being among African Americans, certain aspects of ethnic identity can act as a buffer against those effects. Taken together, the Sellers and colleagues and Eccles and Wong studies suggest that the protective function of ethnic identity against the negative effects of discrimination is relatively robust, applying to both adolescents and adults in varying contexts (school, college, workplace), across time, and with regard to many different outcomes (for example, psychological adjustment, academic motivation).

Ethnic Identity as a Buffer Against General Stress

It is clear from the two programs of research described thus far that ethnic identity can protect individuals from discrimination-related stress. But is it possible that ethnic identity can also protect individuals from the deleterious consequences associated with threatening events more generally? That is, is it possible that members of ethnic minorities, because of their marginalized status in society, may be more exposed to general stressors in addition to stressors related to exposure to race-related discrimination? Recent research by Yip and Fuligni (2002a, 2002b) suggests that ethnic identity does indeed buffer against the potentially damaging effects of daily stressors. Approximately 100 Chinese adolescents (mean age = sixteen years) completed the ethnic-identity achievement subscale of the Multigroup Ethnic Identity Measure (Phinney 1992). Individuals who scored high on the identity achievement subscale showed evidence of having explored and come to terms with what it means to be an ethnic minority. Hence, these individuals have a clear understanding of the role of ethnicity in their lives as well as a secure sense of themselves as members of ethnic minority groups. Individuals reporting a low ethnic-identity achievement score may be grappling with the role and meaning of ethnicity in their lives. In addition to reporting on their ethnic identity, participants also completed a measure of daily stressors (Bolger and Zuckerman 1995) and anxiety (Profile of Mood States, Lorr and McNair 1971) at the end of the day for one week. Respondents indicated the occurrence of general stressors for that day. More specifically, participants checked whether they "had a lot of work at home," "had a lot of work at job or school," "had a lot of demands made by your family," and "had a lot of demands made by other relatives or friends" (M = 0.80, SD = .72). Anxiety was assessed using five items (for example, "on edge," "uneasy," "nervous"), to which participants responded using a five-point Likert-type scale (M = 2.03, SD = .68).

In general, on days when participants reported more stressors, they also reported feeling more anxious, but this association was buffered by individual differences in ethnic-identity achievement. For youths who had a clear sense of their ethnic identity, daily stressors were not associated with anxiety, and this pattern of results remained even after controlling for individual differences in personal (Rosenberg 1986) and collective self-esteem (Luhtanen and Crocker 1992). Therefore, it seems that the buffering effect was due to the specific dynamics of ethnic-identity achievement, and not general feelings of esteem. Ethnic identity was also found to buffer the effect of stressors on anxiety after adjusting for feelings of family closeness. High levels of ethnic identity seemed to account for decreased anxiety in the face of daily stressors, independent of youths' level of intimacy with their parents. For youths reporting moderate and low scores on ethnic-identity achievement, stressors maintained a positive association with anxiety.

From these data, it seems that having a strong sense of ethnic identity may help to protect Chinese adolescents and perhaps more generally other ethnic minority youth against the mental health consequences of exposure to everyday stressors. Not having a strong sense of ethnic-identity achievement seemed to predict increased anxiety in reaction to stress on a daily basis, as these youths were not able to draw upon their ethnic identity as a stress-buffering resource. It is not clear what the consequences of this increased anxiety may be over time.

SUMMARY OF PROTECTIVE FUNCTION OF ETHNIC IDENTITY

Taken together, the findings from three programs of research (Sellers and his colleagues, and Eccles and her colleagues, Yip and Fuligni) show that ethnic identity can serve a positive and protective role in the lives of ethnic minorities. In the past, most of the research on ethnic minorities has attended to only the deficits, weaknesses, and risks associated with being an ethnic minority. By contrast, the evidence in the work presented in this chapter illuminates the protective factors associated with ethnic identity. This work shows how ethnic identity plays an important role in ethnic minorities' psychological development, particularly under threatening circumstances.

It is important to stress that we are not arguing that experiencing ethnic discrimination does not have negative consequences for ethnic minorities who feel connected to their identity group or who endorse certain ideological views about race. The consequences of discrimination may take on other forms for these individuals. Perhaps these individuals' racial attitudes or perceptions of intergroup dynamics are influenced. Or perhaps these individuals are affected in an unconscious manner. Moreover, in our work, we have focused primarily on *intra*personal consequences of discrimination (mental health and goals) and how identity may play a role. Future research needs to address the extent to which there are *inter*personal consequences in which ethnic identity may not be a protective factor. Finally, we are not arguing that a certain type of ethnic identity (being strongly identified with one's group) always serves as a protective function for ethnic minorities. In some contexts a certain type of ethnic identity may be detrimental to individuals' physical and mental health. Our research shows, however, that in the context of stressful events, particularly those related to prejudice and discrimination, being highly identified with and feeling positive regard for one's ethnic group is associated with positive well-being.

DIRECTIONS FOR FUTURE RESEARCH

The goal of this chapter was to illustrate that ethnic identity protects ethnic minorities against the deleterious consequences associated with the stressors of being an eth-

nic minority in the United States. Although being an ethnic minority can be a risk factor for negative physical and psychological outcomes, we argued that there is great
variability in ethnic minorities' experiences and beliefs regarding their ethnicity. Our
research shows that ethnic minorities who value their ethnicity seem to be protected
from the adverse consequences of such stressors. Unfortunately, not much is known
about the specific processes and mechanisms by which ethnic identity serves as a
buffering factor for ethnic identity in the face of stress. Research presented in other
chapters in this book, especially chapter 4, by Linda Strauss and William Cross, and
chapter 3, by Bonita London, Geraldine Downey, Niall Bolger, and Elizabeth Velilla,
may shed light on this issue.

The Strauss and Cross suggest that African Americans cope with positive and negative
events associated with their black identity through the use of identity transactions.
They provide evidence that social situations identified as race-related and stressful
trigger African Americans to use a buffering transaction, a strategy designed to protect
oneself from a hostile situation. In addition, Strauss and Cross demonstrated that the
more important their racial identity is to African Americans' self-concept, the more
likely they are to rely on the buffering transaction, regardless of the type of situation.
Given these findings, it is feasible that ethnic minorities for whom their ethnic identity
is an important component of their self-concept rely on buffering when they experience discrimination, which protects them from the negative psychological implications
of discrimination. In addition, individuals who feel connected to their ethnic group
may be better able to draw on (think about) positive experiences with other in-group
members when they are faced with discrimination than are those who are not connected, which helps reduce the negative effects of discrimination on mental health.
This process may be closely linked to what Strauss and Cross refer to as bonding.
Future research is needed to explore the possibility that identity transactions explain
why ethnic identity buffers the ill effects of discrimination on mental health.

London, Downey, Bolger, and Velilla (this volume) also investigated stress and coping issues among university students who are members of devalued social-identity
groups. Specifically, they examined the relationship between encounters with stressors related to one's devalued social identity and feelings of belonging to the university, and how individuals' coping strategies impact that relationship. They found that
coping with a negative race-related event by transforming the situation into one that
is less focused on negativity (perhaps through the use of humor or changing the subject) allows individuals to feel a greater sense of belonging to the university. It is feasible that ethnic minorities who are highly identified with their ethnic group engage
in such transformation coping strategies when they encounter discrimination, which
buffers them from the negative consequences of the event. Future research is needed
to explore the role of transformation as a means of explaining the buffering effect of
ethnic identity on experiences with discrimination and mental health.

In this chapter, we opted to focus on how ethnic identity can serve as a protective
factor in experiences with *inter*group treatment. Recent work has begun to show the
importance of studying *intra*group relations among ethnic minorities. For example,
Chatman, Eccles, and Malanchuk (chapter 6, this volume) as well as Strauss and
Cross (chapter 4, this volume) suggest that ethnic identity may influence self-
presentation strategies ethnic minorities use in intragroup contexts. These strategies
in intragroup contexts may have important implications for ethnic minorities' psy-

chological well-being. In addition, recent research suggests that intragroup discrimination and rejection can negatively impact ethnic minorities' psychological well-being. Tom Postmes and Nyla Branscombe (2002), for example, found that the more African American college students (study 1) and noncollege adults (study 2) felt rejected by other African Americans, the lower their collective self-esteem, personal self-esteem, and life satisfaction. In similar work on intragroup relations, Signithia Fordham (see Fordham and Ogbu 1986; Fordham 1988) argue that behaviors that distance African American youth from other African Americans result in feelings of cultural alienation, and these feelings of cultural alienation are related to depression and anxiety. Likewise, Richard J. Contrada et al. (2001) found that the more ethnic minorities felt pressured by their in-group to conform to certain behaviors, the more depressive symptoms and negative physical symptoms they experienced.

Taken together, these findings suggest that negative intragroup treatment may be just as important as intergroup treatment for ethnic minorities' well-being. Does being highly identified with one's ethnic group protect individuals' from the negative consequences noted above? Or does being highly identified exacerbate the problem? Given the adverse consequences associated with negative intragroup treatment, future research needs to address the extent to which the protective function of ethnic identity discussed in this chapter extends to stress associated with intragroup experiences.

IMPLICATIONS FOR POLICY AND INTERVENTIONS

In the census year 2000, much discussion surrounded the treatment of race and ethnicity in the United States national census. In 2004, the Illinois Democratic candidate for the U.S. Senate, Barack Obama, who was born to a Kenyan father and white American mother and who identifies himself as an African American, re-sparked the debate over who should be considered an African American in America. In a *New York Times* article entitled "'African American' Becomes a Term for Debate" (August 29, 2004), the Illinois Republican candidate for the U.S. Senate, Alan Keyes, asked whether it was correct for Obama to claim an African American identity. Although the policy ramifications of the labels used in the census and the resulting labels used for ethnic minorities such as Barack Obama are extremely important, the findings presented in this chapter suggest that when it comes to understanding the everyday lived experiences of ethnic minorities it is also important to take into consideration the *meaning* ethnic minorities associate with their identity. We are in no way suggesting that the Census Bureau should assess individuals' ethnic identity as we have done in our research (that is, with multiple-item scales that assess ethnic-identity centrality and ideology). But policymakers should keep in mind that the meaning an individual attaches to his or her ethnic-identity label may be just as important as if not more important than the label itself. The findings from the programs of research presented in this chapter suggest that the meaning associated with individuals' ethnic identity has serious implications for the way they experience daily and race-related stressors in a particular context.

Along with the debate about ethnic-identity labels has occurred a long-standing debate about how to improve intergroup relations in the United States. Some researchers suggest that the best strategy to foster intergroup harmony is to de-emphasize group differences and to highlight commonalities across groups. Other researchers, however, oppose de-emphasizing group differences and instead suggest that it is important to emphasize and celebrate group differences. In truth, the best strategy is probably a combination of the de-emphasizing and emphasizing differences. This chapter's findings support allowing ethnic minorities to vary in the meaning they associate with their ethnic identity. If ethnic minorities in the United States were forced to de-emphasize their ethnic identity or redefine their ethnic identity solely in terms of another identity, such as a national identity, they may not benefit from the protection that feeling connected to one's ethnic group and having a certain racial ideology seem to afford them when they encounter stress, especially prejudice-related stress.

Given that it may be difficult to eradicate negative perceptions and treatment of ethnic minorities, policies and practices targeting race- and ethnicity-related stressors and their effects on individuals' lives may be best informed by surveying the ethnic minorities who experience these stressors. If nothing more, we hope we have convinced interested parties that the same intervention and prevention strategies will not work for all ethnic minorities. If exposure to negative treatment (general stressors as well as discrimination) has differential impact on different members of ethnic minority groups, then the same intervention and prevention strategies will not work for all individuals. It is of critical importance to undertake research that takes this variation within ethnic groups into account, in order to identify the specific strategies that will be maximally effective for different types of people.

That said, we caution readers about interventions aimed at encouraging ethnic minorities to identify with and feel connected to their ethnic group (perhaps this process may even be detrimental). In general, our findings show that ethnic minorities who feel attached to their ethnic group are protected from the deleterious consequences of discrimination on their psychological well-being. Our findings, however, do not suggest that ethnic minorities who do not feel attached to their ethnic group incur more psychological harm when they encounter discrimination. In fact, in most of the studies we presented in this chapter, there was no relationship between encountering discrimination and psychological well-being for ethnic minorities who do not feel attached to their group. Thus, the theme that emerges from our research is that it is vital for intervention researchers to develop ways for ethnic minorities who already feel attached to their group to continue to embrace and nurture their ethnic identity.

FINAL THOUGHTS

In closing, we turn to what is perhaps the definitive pivotal finding that sparked research on ethnic identity. Approximately fifty years ago, Kenneth and Mamie Clark's classic "doll studies" changed the course of American history when their results were incorporated into the United States Supreme Court decision in Brown v. Board of Education, which mandated desegregation of American institutions. The core finding of the "doll studies" was that black children, when given a choice between white and brown dolls, showed a preference for the white dolls when asked which ones they preferred and liked the most (Clark and Clark 1947). These studies provided the scientific evidence that segregation was detrimental to the self-esteem and psyches of black Americans. During the past fifty years there have been numerous debates over how to interpret the Clarks' finding. The interpretation used in the Court's decision was crucial for promoting social change at the time. Nevertheless, over the years the zeitgeist has changed, and researchers have focused more on the adaptive functions of being an ethnic minority in the United States. We hope our work, which was very much inspired by some of the original questions that challenged Kenneth and Mamie Clark, enriches scholars' understanding of the complexity of ethnicity and ethnic identity in the lives of ethnic minorities in the United States.

NOTE

1. Because of these differences we do not provide a general definition of ethnic identity. Instead we provide definitions and detailed information about the component or dimension of ethnic identity we are referring to when we discuss empirical findings from our three different programs of research.

REFERENCES

Allison, Kevin W. 1998. "Stress and Oppressed Social Category Membership." In *Prejudice: The Target's Perspective,* edited by Janet K. Swim and Charles Stangor. New York: Academic Press.

Bendick, Marc, Jr., Charles W. Jackson, Victor A. Reinoso, and Laura E. Hodges. 1991. "Discrimination Against Latino Job Applicants: A Controlled Experiment." *Human Resource Management* 30(4): 469–84.

Berndt, Thomas J. 1979. "Developmental Changes in Conformity to Peers and Parents." *Developmental Psychology* 15(6): 608–16.

Bobo, Lawrence. 1983. "Whites' Opposition to Busing: Symbolic Racism or Realistic Group Conflict?" *Journal of Personality and Social Psychology* 45(6): 1196–1210.

Bolger, Niall, and Adam Zuckerman. 1995. "A Framework for Studying Personality in the Stress Process." *Journal of Personality and Social Psychology* 69(5): 890–902.

Bowler, Rosemarie, Stephen Rauch, and Ralf Schwarzer. 1986. "Self-Esteem and Interracial Attitudes in black High School Students: A Comparison of Five Ethnic Groups." *Urban Education* 21:3–19.

Clark, Kenneth B., and Mamie P. Clark. 1947. "Racial Identification and Preferences in Negro Children." In *Readings in Social Psychology,* edited by T. M. Newcombe and E. L. Hartley. New York: Holt.

Clark, Rodney, Norman B. Anderson, Vernessa B. Clark, and David R. Williams. 1999. "Racism as a Stressor for African Americans: A Biopsychosocial Model." *American Psychologist* 54(10): 805–16.

Contrada, Richard J., Richard D. Ashmore, Melvin L. Gary, Elliot Coups, Jill D. Egeth, Andrea Sewell, Kevin Ewell, Tanya M. Goyal, and Valerie Chasse. 2001. "Measures of Ethnicity-Related Stress: Psychometric Properties, Ethnic Group Differences, and Associations with Well-Being." *Journal of Applied Social Psychology* 31(9): 1775–1820.

Cook, Thomas D., Farah-Naaz Habib, Meredith Phillips, Richard A. Settersten, Shobha C. Shagle, and Serdar M. Degirmencioglu. 1999. "Comer's School Development Program in Prince George's County, Maryland: A Theory-Based Evaluation." *American Educational Research Journal* 36(3): 543–97.

Crocker, Jennifer, and Jason S. Lawrence. 1999. "Social Stigma and Self-Esteem: The Role of Contingencies of Worth." In *Cultural Divides: Understanding and Overcoming Group Conflict,* edited by Deborah Prentice and Dale Miller. New York: Russell Sage Foundation.

Crocker, Jennifer, and Brenda Major. 1989. "Social Stigma and Self-Esteem: The Self-Protective Properties of Stigma." *Psychological Review* 96(4): 608–30.

Crocker, Jennifer, and Connie T. Wolfe. 2001. "Contingencies of Self-Worth." *Psychological Review* 108(3): 593–623.

Cross, William E. 1991. *Shades of black: Diversity in African-American Identity.* Philadelphia: Temple University Press.

Cross, William E., Thomas A. Parham, and Janet E. Helms. 1998. "Nigrescence Revisited: Theory and Research." In *African American Identity Development: Theory, Research, and Intervention,* edited by R. L. Jones. Hampton, Va.: Cobb & Henry.

D'Augelli, Anthony R., and Scott L. Hershberger. 1993. "African American Undergraduates on a Predominately White Campus: Academic Factors, Social Networks, and Campus Climate." *Journal of Negro Education* 62(1): 67–81.

Eccles, Jacquelynne S., Sarah Lord, Robert Roeser, Bonnie Barber, and Jose Hernandez-Jozefowicz. 1997. "The Association of School Transitions in Early Adolescence with Developmental Trajectories Through High School." In *Health Risks and Developmental Transitions During Adolescence,* edited by John Schulenberg and Jennifer Maggs. New York: Cambridge University Press.

Eccles, Jacquelynne S., and C. Midgley. 1989. "Stage/Environment Fit: Developmentally Appropriate Classrooms for Early Adolescents." In *Research on Motivation in Education: Goals and Cognitions,* edited by R. E. Ames and C. Ames. Volume 3. New York: Academic Press.

Eccles, Jacquelynne S., Allan Wigfield, Rena D. Harold, and Phyllis Blumenfeld. 1993. "Age and Gender Differences in Children's Self- and Task Perceptions During Elementary School." *Child Development* 64(3): 830–47.

Farrell, Walter, and Cloyzelle Jones. 1988. "Recent Racial Incidents in Higher Education: A Preliminary Perspective." *Urban Review* 20(3): 211–26.

Fordham, Signithia. 1988. "Racelessness as a Factor in Black Students' School Success: Pragmatic Strategy of Pyrrhic Victory?" *Harvard Educational Review* 58(1): 54–84.

Fordham, Signithia, and John Ogbu. 1986. "Black Students' School Success: Coping with the Burden of 'Acting White.'" *The Urban Review* 18(3): 176–206.

Goto, Sharon G., Gilbert C. Gee, and David T. Takeuchi. 2002. "Strangers Still? The Experience of Discrimination Among Chinese Americans." *Journal of Community Psychology* 30(2): 211–24.

Gray-Little, Bernadette, and Adam R. Hafdahl. 2001. "Factors Influencing Racial Comparisons of Self-Esteem: A Questionnaire Review." *Psychological Bulletin* 126(1): 26–54.

Guyll, Max, Karen A. Matthews, and Joyce T. Bromberger. 2001. "Discrimination and Unfair Treatment: Relationship to Cardiovascular Reactivity Among African American and European American Women." *Health Psychology* 20(5): 315–25.

Harrell, Shelly P. 1994. "The Racism and Life Experience Scales." Unpublished manuscript. Cambridge, Mass.: Harvard University.

Jackson, James S., Tony N. Brown, David R. Williams, M. Torres, Robert Sellers, and Kendrick Brown. 1996. "Racism and the Physical and Mental Health Status of African Americans: A Thirteen-Year National Panel Study." *Ethnicity and Disease* 6(1–2): 132–47.

Kardiner, Abram, and Lionel Ovesey. 1951. *The Mark of Oppression.* New York: Norton.

Kessler, Ronald C., Kristin D. Mickelson, and David R. Williams. 1999. "The Prevalence, Distribution, and Mental Health Correlates of Perceived Discrimination in the United States." *Journal of Health and Social Behavior* 40(3): 208–30.

Krieger, Nancy. 1990. "Racial and Gender Discrimination: Risk Factors for High Blood Pressure?" *Social Science Medicine* 30(12): 1273–81.

Krieger, Nancy, and Stephen Sidney. 1996. "Racial Discrimination and Blood Pressure: The CARDIA Study of Young Black and White Adults." *American Journal of Public Health* 86(10): 1370–78.

Kuo, Wen H. 1995. "Coping with Racial Discrimination: The Case of Asian Americans." *Ethnic and Racial Studies* 18(1): 109–27.

Landrine, Hope, and Elizabeth A. Klonoff. 1996. "The Schedule of Racist Events: A Measure of Racial Discrimination and a Study of Its Negative Physical and Mental Health Consequences." *The Journal of Black Psychology* 22(2): 144–68.

Lorenzo-Hernandez, Jose, and Suzanne C. Ouellette. 1998. "Ethnic Identity, Self-Esteem, and Values in Dominicans, Puerto Ricans, and African Americans." *Journal of Applied Social Psychology* 2(21): 2007–24.

Lorr, Maurice, and Douglas M. McNair. 1971. *The Profile of Mood States Manual*. San Francisco: Educational and Industrial Testing Service.

Luhtanen, Riia, and Jennifer Crocker. 1992. "A Collective Self-Esteem Scale: Self-Evaluation of One's Social Identity." *Personality and Social Psychology Bulletin* 18(3): 302–18.

Martinez, Ruben O., and Richard L. Dukes. 1997. "The Effects of Ethnic Identity, Ethnicity, and Gender on Adolescent Well-Being." *Journal of Youth and Adolescence* 26(5): 503–16.

Massey, Douglas S., and Nancy A. Denton. 1992. "Racial Identity and the Spatial Assimilation of Mexicans in the United States." *Social Science Research* 21(3): 235–60.

McNeilly, Maya D., Elwood Robinson, Norman B. Anderson, Carl Pieper, Akbar Shah, Paul S. Toth, Pamela Martin, Dreama Jackson, Terrence Saulter, Cynthia White, Magaratha Kuchibatl, Shirley M. Collado, and William Gerin. 1995. "Effects of Racist Provocation and Social Support on Cardiovascular Reactivity in African American Women." *International Journal of Behavioral Medicine* 2(4): 321–38.

Neblett, Enrique, J. Nicole Shelton, and Robert M. Sellers. 2004. "The Role of Racial Identity in Managing Daily Racial Hassles." In *Race and Identity: The Legacy of Kenneth Clark*, edited by G. Philogene. Washington, D.C.: American Psychological Association Press.

Phinney, Jean S. 1990. "Ethnic Identity in Adolescence and Adulthood: A Review and Integration." Psychological Bulletin 108(3): 499–514.

———. 1992. "The Multigroup Ethnic Identity Measure: A New Scale for Use with Diverse Groups." *Journal of Adolescent Research* 7(2): 156–76.

———. 1996. "When We Talk About American Ethnic Groups, What Do We Mean?" *American Psychologist* 51(9): 918–27.

Porter, Judith R., and Robert E. Washington. 1979. "Black Identity and Self-Esteem: A Review of Studies of Black Self Concept, 1968–1978." *Annual Review of Sociology* 19:139–61.

Postmes, Tom, and Nyla R. Branscombe. 2002. "Influence of Long-Term Racial Environmental Composition on Subjective Well-Being in African Americans." *Journal of Personality and Social Psychology* 83(2): 735–51.

Rosenberg, Morris. 1986. *Conceiving the Self*. Melbourne, Fla.: Krieger.

Rowley, Stephanie J., Robert M. Sellers, Tabbye M. Chavous, and Mia Smith. 1998. "The Relationship Between Racial Identity and Self-Esteem in African American College and High School Students." *Journal of Personality and Social Psychology* 74(3): 715–24.

Salgado de Snyder, V. Nelly. 1987. "Factors Associated with Acculturative Stress and Depressive Symptomatology Among Married Mexican Immigrant Women." *Psychology of Women Quarterly* 11(4): 475–88.

Sanders-Thompson, Vetta. 1996. "Perceived Experiences of Racism as Stressful Life Events." *Community Mental Health Journal* 32(3): 223–33.

Sellers, Robert M., Laura Morgan, and Tony Brown. 2000. "A Multidimensional Approach to Racial Identity: Implications for African American Children." In *Forging Links: African American Children Clinical Developmental Perspectives,* edited by A. Neal-Barnett, J. Contreras, and K. Kerns. Westport, Conn.: Praeger.

Sellers, Robert M., Stephanie J. Rowley, Tabbye M. Chavous, J. Nicole Shelton, and Mia Smith. 1997. "Multidimensional Inventory of Black Identity: Preliminary Investigation of Reliability and Construct Validity." *Journal of Personality and Social Psychology* 73(4): 805–15.

Sellers, Robert M., and J. Nicole Shelton. 2003. "The Role of Racial Identity in Perceived Racial Discrimination." *Journal of Personality and Social Psychology* 84(5): 1079–92.

Sellers, Robert M., Mia Smith, J. Nicole Shelton, Stephanie J. Rowley, and Tabbye M. Chavous. 1998. "Multidimensional Model of Racial Identity: A Reconceptualization of African American Racial Identity." *Personality and Social Psychology Review* 2(1): 18–39.

Simmons, Roberta G., Richard Burgeson, Steven Carlton-Ford, Dale A. Blyth. 1987. "The Impact of Cumulative Change in Early Adolescence." *Child Development* 58(5): 1220–34.

Smith, Elsie J. 1991. "Ethnic Identity Development: Toward the Development of a Theory Within the Context of Majority/Minority Status." *Journal of Counseling and Development* 70(1): 181–87.

Tomaskovic-Devey, Donald. 1993. "The Gender and Race Composition of Jobs and the Male/Female, White/Black Pay Gaps." *Social Forces* 72(1): 45–76.

Twenge, Jean M., and Jennifer Crocker. 2002. "Race and Self-Esteem: Meta-Analyses Comparing whites, blacks, Hispanics, Asians, and American Indians and Comment on Gray-Little and Hafdahl (2000)." *Psychological Bulletin* 128(3): 371–408.

Williams, David R., Y. Yu, D. S. Jackson, and Norman B. Anderson. 1997. "Racial Differences in Physical and Mental Health: Socioeconomic Status, Stress, and Discrimination." Unpublished manuscript. Ann Arbor: University of Michigan.

Wong, Carol A., Jacquelynne S. Eccles, and Arnold Sameroff. 2003. The Influence of Ethnic Discrimination and Ethnic Identification on African American Adolescents' School and Socio-Emotional Adjustment." *Journal of Personality* 71(6): 1197–32.

Yinger, John. 1988. "Examining Racial Discrimination with Fair Housing Audits." In *Lessons from Selected Program and Policy Areas,* edited by David S. Cordray and Howard S. Blood. San Francisco: Jossey-Bass.

Yip, Tiffany. 2004. "Sources of Situational Variation in Ethnic Identity and Psychological Well-Being: A Palm Pilot Study of Chinese American Students." Manuscript submitted for publication.

Yip, Tiffany, and Andrew J. Fuligni. 2002a. "Daily Variation in Ethnic Identity, Ethnic Behaviors, and Psychological Well-Being Among American Adolescents of Chinese Descent." *Child Development* 73(5): 1557–72.

———. 2002b. "Ethnic Identity as a Stress Buffer: A Daily Diary Study of Chinese American Youths." Paper presented at the Society for Research in Child Development Biennial Conference. Minneapolis (April 20, 2001).

CHAPTER 6

IDENTITY NEGOTIATION IN EVERYDAY SETTINGS

Celina M. Chatman, Jacquelynne S. Eccles,
and Oksana Malanchuk

Throughout their lives, individuals are continually faced with new experiences and situations that, somehow, must be integrated with existing aspects of the self (see James 1890/1910; Erikson 1968). Some of these experiences involve major life events such as entering new contexts where people may espouse attitudes, beliefs, and values that are different from one's own. Other experiences involve single encounters with new people or new information that may create conflicts with one's existing set of beliefs and values. In either case, these events and experiences can challenge individuals to reevaluate aspects of the self and subsequently engage in various negotiation strategies in order to maintain a sense of continuity in the self while adapting to changing circumstances (see James 1890/1910; Erikson 1968). The focus of this chapter is to show that such processes can be particularly adaptive for members of racial and ethnic minority groups in the United States. Our aim is to show that members of racial and ethnic minority groups are afforded additional identity-relevant resources from which to draw upon as they negotiate new contexts, situations, and information, thereby facilitating their positive overall adjustment.

We begin by defining our key terms for this chapter, following with an overview of identity formation as an adaptive process, as this sets up the framework for our discussion of the adaptive function of ethnic identity in particular. We follow with an overview of the role that contextual factors play in this process, and finally we go into an extended discussion on the special case of ethnic identity as a resource in individuals' negotiations of the self across contexts. Throughout this chapter, we will draw on empirical findings from a study of African American adolescents living in the mid-Atlantic coastal region of the United States. These findings are based on both survey data and in-depth interviews among these youths, and some are longitudinal. Finally, we close with directions for future research and recommendations for policy and practice regarding healthy adolescent development, with an emphasis on healthy transitions.

IDENTITY AS AN ADAPTIVE PROCESS

In both the lay and scholarly discourses, identity has been treated—albeit often implicitly—as essential, as some "thing" that resides within persons. As researchers, our central objective has been to understand what that "thing" is and how it is formed. In this chapter, we distinguish between the what and the how of identity: content and process. Identity processes refer to sequences of psychological events (both conscious and unconscious) that unfold over time and that serve to maintain a system of self-coherence and a sense of self-sameness, whereas identity content refers to the specific elements (also both conscious and unconscious) that constitute that coherence and sameness. We believe it is critical to maintain both conceptual and operational distinctions between these two phenomena because each provides unique information about individuals' psychological functioning and behavior. We focus mainly on identity as a process of negotiations between self and context, with identity content serving as the resources upon which individuals draw in this process. Given this emphasis, more precise definitions of our key concepts will be useful.

IDENTITY   Despite the popularity of identity as a construct both within and outside psychology, the term often evades definition. There does, however, seem to be a point of convergence among those who study identity that it inherently involves issues around the self in context (Grotevant 1992; for reviews on definition and use of the term "identity," see Brubaker and Cooper 2000; Gleason 1983). Here we adopt a definition in the Eriksonian (Erikson 1968) tradition, which views identity as an ongoing dynamic process whereby individuals establish, evaluate, reevaluate, and reestablish who they are and are not relative to others in their environments (for examples, see Erikson 1968, 1980; Kleiber 1999; Harter 1990; Waterman 1993). Such a process is inherently dependent on the contexts in which individuals find themselves. Thus, as individuals encounter new physical and social contexts, they are challenged with the task of maintaining a balance between self-continuity and re-definition. To the extent that individuals are able to reconcile conflicts between the self and these changing contexts, they maintain a sense of positive well-being (Erikson 1968; Grotevant 1987).

The dynamic nature of identity formation means that the specific mechanisms by which this process occurs are many and complex. We return to a more detailed discussion of these mechanisms later, but for now offer this simple explanation: identity as a process is best thought of as individuals' formulations of answers to the question "Who am I?" Identity content would be the substance of those answers. Contained therein are the resources upon which individuals rely when faced with such questions. These resources might include individuals' likes and dislikes, attitudes, beliefs, values, ideologies and worldviews, skills and competencies, as well as their social roles and descriptive attributes such as race, ethnicity, gender, social class, and religion. Whatever the case, individuals' unique configurations on these sets of attributes are said to constitute the content of their personal identities.

SOCIAL IDENTITY   Traditionally, psychologists have distinguished between personal and social identity. Personal identity has been treated as an individuated representation of the self (see Brewer 1991; Luhtanen and Crocker 1992; Thoits and Virshup 1997; Turner et al. 1987), reflecting the set of personality characteristics, behaviors, and other attributes that individuals believe distinguishes them from others. This is consistent with our description of identity content. Social identity, on the other hand, has been treated as a collective representation of the self (Brewer 1991; Luhtanen and Crocker 1992; Tajfel and Turner 1986; Turner et al. 1987), deriving from individuals' memberships in social groups and participation in social roles (Burke and Tully 1977; McCall and Simmons 1966; Stryker and Serpe 1994). Simply put, personal identities distinguish individuals as unique persons, whereas social identities connect them with others on the basis of shared attributes.

Many researchers have begun to ask whether social identities are in fact so distinct from the set of attributes with which individuals define themselves. For example, some have argued that social roles and group memberships are themselves attributes that are included in the personal identity "set" that distinguishes each individual from others (Thoits and Virshup 1997). This position is consistent with our description of identity content, but implies that social roles and group memberships are reduced to descriptors. That is, roles such as mother, psychologist, and husband as well as characteristics such as race, ethnicity, and gender simply mark individuals as belonging in a particular role or social category but do not necessarily take on any deeper meaning for individuals' sense of self.

But for many people, social group memberships go beyond personal description. Membership in social groups can be imbued with personal meanings that help to define a person as a unique individual, thereby functioning as an aspect of personal identity. Thus, although individuals may or may not consider the self as interchangeable with the collective whole of the social group, they may personally identify with the beliefs, values, and ideals they perceive to characterize that group. Moreover, individuals can be selective in this process, rejecting some aspects of the group's position and accepting others. Similarly, individuals may also create their own meanings around their membership in social groups, without regard to the existing meanings to which they have been exposed (Fordham 1988; Waters 1990, 1996). We are particularly concerned here with the societally shared meaning systems around race and ethnicity, and the ways in which individuals negotiate and incorporate such meanings in their own identities.

RACIAL OR ETHNIC IDENTITY   Race has been described by some researchers as a "master" category because it is perceptually salient and believed by some people to be immutable (McGuire et al. 1978; Stryker and Serpe 1994). Moreover, members of ethnic minority groups are more likely to develop ethnic identities than are white Americans (see Crocker et al. 1994; Phinney 1992), on the basis of their distinctiveness in their environments (McGuire et al. 1978). Thus, race and ethnicity may predispose some individuals to develop racial and ethnic identities, special cases of social identity wherein the racial or ethnic group is the specific referent.[1]

Ethnic identity has been described broadly as "one's sense of belonging to an ethnic group and the part of one's thinking, perceptions, feelings, and behavior that is due to ethnic group membership" (Rotheram and Phinney 1987, 13). Racial identity is similarly defined, in Robert Sellers et al.'s (1998) Multidimensional Model of Racial Identity (MMRI), as "the significance and qualitative meaning that individuals attribute to their membership within the Black racial group within their self-concepts" (23). Inherent in both definitions is the view that racial and ethnic identities are multidimensional. We adopt this multidimensional orientation for both social identity in general and racial and ethnic identity in particular. More specifically, we define racial and ethnic identity as a process whereby individuals link their racial and ethnic group memberships to their thoughts, feelings, and experiences regarding the self. This process is informed by and responsive to existing racial and ethnic meanings in the contexts, both broad and proximal, in which individuals find themselves in their daily lives.

ADAPTIVE FUNCTIONS OF IDENTITY-FORMATION PROCESSES

Having defined our central concepts—identity, social identity, and racial and ethnic identity—we shift now to describe the adaptive functions of identity in the contexts of everyday activities. To be clear, although we describe these functions as they relate to identity in general, social and racial or ethnic identities in particular are inherently implicated. Social and racial or ethnic identities are aspects of identity that derive from people's memberships in and identification with social groups or categories and that cannot easily be separated or distinguished from identity as we have defined it here. In other words, because we describe identity as a dynamic process of negotiating self and context, it is difficult to isolate any single "component" as a separate entity. Therefore, we first describe the general processes whereby identities are formed and negotiated, and follow with a more detailed discussion of the specific cases of social and racial or ethnic identities.

Identity Formation and Negotiation

Individuals are presumed to be motivated in part by a subconscious need to maintain a sense of self-sameness (Erikson 1968; Epstein 1990; James 1890/1910; Swann 1987), one manifestation of which is the effort made to maintain congruency between behavior and identity (Eccles 1987; Steele 1988; Swann 1987). Moreover, individuals are presumed to possess multiple identities (Brewer 1991; Burke and Tully 1977; Deaux 1993; Frable 1997), all of which vary in their degree of importance or centrality to an individual's overall self-concept (Markus and Wurf 1987; Stryker and Serpe 1994; Turnbull, Miller, and McFarland 1990). To the extent that one identity is more important to an individual than others, the content of that identity is likely to drive the individual's behavior, as well as his or her selection of contexts in which to engage (Eccles et al. 1983; Eccles 1987). All of these processes are ongoing across specific contexts and across the life course and function to provide people with a sense of self-coherence across time and space.

But where does the initial content of individuals' identities come from? How do people come to perceive the self in a particular way? In the developmental literature the answers are varied. Although many have argued, as does Erik Erikson, that identity is formed during adolescence, others have argued that the process begins much earlier and goes on over the whole life span. Whichever the case, there is sufficient agreement that initial identity content is based on feedback from parents and caregivers (Bronfenbrenner 1979, 1992; Eccles 1993; Erikson 1968), as well as from other people who are intimately involved in children's daily lives. As children grow older and experience new people, new contexts, new information—about both themselves and the rest of the world—the picture of self becomes simultaneously more distinct and more blurred.

According to Erikson, adolescents are faced with resolving the dilemma posed by the accumulation of multiple sources of self-defining knowledge. As they approach adulthood—the period when they are expected to be self-sufficient, independent, and productive members of society—adolescents are burdened with the task of choosing their course. Who am I? Where do I fit in? What am I supposed to do? Traditionally this process of finding one's place has been viewed as one filled with angst, especially when a person fails to resolve it. But it can also be seen as adaptive. As adolescents forge ahead in their lives, they can try out many of the messages they have received and learn what works for them and what does not (Eccles and Barber 1999; Erikson 1968). These messages can be seen as the resources upon which youths may rely as they try to identify where they do and do not belong, how they are different from the rest of the world, and what they have in common with others around them.

A Sense of Belonging in Social Groups

In trying to forge an identity that is unique yet not so different from others that one would be viewed as deviant, individuals seek a sense of belonging to identifiable social groups in their environments (Baumeister and Leary 1995; Brewer 1991; Eccles and Barber 1999; Eccles et al. 2003; Erikson 1968; Youniss and Yates 1997). These group memberships can be either ascribed (imposed by others, for example, at birth) or chosen (such as joining an organization or associating with a clique, an organization, or a team). In either case, individuals vary both in the extent to which they feel a sense of belonging to and identification with the group and in the specific aspects of that group membership with which they choose to identify. But it is this process of negotiation—deciding for oneself how much and in what ways one "fits" with a given group—that provides individuals with a sense of achievement in the domain of self-knowledge (Eccles et al. 2003; Phinney 1990; Youniss and Yates 1997). A certain degree of confidence in one's knowledge about oneself is in turn related to many positive outcomes (Pelham 1991).

Resources Specific to Racial- and Ethnic-Group Membership

Members of racial and ethnic minority groups are faced with the additional developmental task of considering race and ethnicity in their identity formation (Cross 1991; Erikson 1968; Phinney 1990; Phinney and Rotheram 1987). They are faced with the challenge of reconciling other aspects of the self with their difference from and similarities to others around them (even when those others are not physically present in their life space). On the one hand, perceived differences from others can lead to feelings of marginalization, which makes it difficult to fulfill one's need for belonging. On the other hand, being part of an ethnic group provides individuals with an abundance of cultural and social resources that can be used to help individuals successfully negotiate the self in different contexts and situations, thereby facilitating positive outcomes and buffering the negative consequences of discrimination and marginalization in those contexts.

For example, several different dimensions of ethnic identity are positively related to individuals' psychological adjustment, and both academic engagement and achievement (Arroyo and Zigler 1995; Oyserman, Gant, and Ager 1995; Taylor et al. 1994; Wong, Eccles and Sameroff 2003): the extent to which individuals have explored and achieved a solid and positive sense of ethnic identity is positively related to academic performance (their grade-point averages) among African American public high school students. Similarly, African American students who report that race is an important part of their self-concept and that they are worthy members of their racial group have more positive attitudes toward academic achievement and higher self-efficacy beliefs. Finally, the negative effects of discrimination on African American early adolescents' mental health, academic motivation, and school grades is buffered by strong positive feelings of a culturally connected ethnic identity. In each of these studies, racial- and ethnic-group identity buffered against the impact of negative race-related experiences.

IDENTITY NEGOTIATION IN YOUTHS' EVERYDAY LIVES

For the remainder of this chapter, we present findings from our analyses of data gathered from adolescents living in southeastern Maryland in 1991. We have followed these youths through their junior and senior high school years and on into early adulthood. We conducted analyses of both quantitative and qualitative data related to racial- and ethnic-identity formation and the relation of these processes and identities to multiple outcomes. Here we describe findings supporting our notions of identity as an adaptive process. These data illustrate how African American and white youths negotiate racial and ethnic identity across various situations and across time.

The Participants and Their Setting

The participants in the Maryland Adolescent Development in Context Study, or MADICS (Jacquelynne S. Eccles and Arnold J. Sameroff, principal investigators), were living in a county in Maryland that has undergone tremendous demographic and political changes since 1960 (Cook et al. 1999). For example, prior to 1960, 85 percent of the residents in this county were white and political control was held by whites; by 1995, 51 percent of the households were African American and 43 percent were European American, and these two groups had equal political control. In addition, because of the fairly comparable social-class profile of the white and African American communities in this county—with both communities composed of low-, middle-, and upper-class households—it was possible to study the development of African American adolescents from lower-, middle-, and upper-class families.

The data we describe here are based on both synchronous and longitudinal analyses. The first wave of data was collected in 1991, when the youths were in seventh grade. Subsequent waves of data collection occurred at the end of seventh grade (wave 2), the summer following eighth grade (wave 3), the summer following eleventh grade (wave 4), one year after high school graduation (wave 5), and then three years after high school graduation (wave 6). The analyses we describe in this chapter are based almost exclusively on the data in waves 3 and 4, collected right after the eighth and eleventh grades. Both qualitative and quantitative information was collected. The survey questionnaires were administered in the youths' homes. The quantitative analyses reported in this chapter are based on a sample size of 599 African American youths. The in-depth qualitative interviews were also conducted at the youths' homes (unless the youth preferred it be conducted elsewhere) at a different time than the questionnaires. The qualitative analyses reported in this chapter are based on 23 African Americans and 8 European Americans.

Different but related threads of research have been undertaken based on the larger study described earlier. Although each of these studies asks a different set of research questions, all ultimately address the overarching issue of the ways in which youth negotiate race, ethnicity, and identity in a variety of everyday settings and situations. Together, these smaller studies illustrate, first, the different forms of meaning adolescents attach to racial and ethnic identity and, second, the ways in which they negotiate these meanings across contexts and specific situations. These observations serve as empirical support for the processes elaborated earlier in this chapter.

The Construction of Meaning in Identity— Race and Ethnicity as Resources

In order to understand how racial and ethnic identities are negotiated, we first need to understand the meanings that individuals attach to being African or European American. That is, what specific forms of racial and ethnic identity content do they bring into different situations? Given the complexity of this question, we conducted in-depth interviews with a subset (N = 35) of the MADICS sample, beginning in the summer following their eleventh-grade year. We conducted follow-up interviews with these youths when they were one year out of high school. We then analyzed these data both independently and in conjunction with our quantitative data to examine the subjective meanings these youths attach to their racial and ethnic identities.

CONTENT-ANALYTIC APPROACHES   Previous research (Sellers et al. 1997) has demonstrated the importance of several distinct ideological orientations regarding race in predicting various outcomes among African American young adults. Similarly, research across the social sciences has indicated that people attach specific interpersonal and behavioral characteristics to their racial- and ethnic-group memberships (Ethier and Deaux 1990, 1994; Fordham and Ogbu 1986; Keefe 1992; Landrine and Klonoff 1994; Matute-Bianchi 1986; Waters 1990, 1996). These studies have demonstrated that such subjective meanings have important direct implications for behavioral outcomes such as school engagement and performance, intergroup interactions, physical health, and participation in cultural activities. Thus, the subjective meanings of race and ethnicity can be seen as resources for youths' development.

Because the subjective meaning of racial and ethnic identity has only recently emerged as a popular area of investigation, there is no consensus as to what meaning actually entails. Some researchers have described meaning in terms of individuals' ideological orientations toward race-related issues (Sellers et al. 1997, 1998); others, in terms of individuals' affective orientations toward their group membership (Luhtanen and Crocker 1992; Sellers et al. 1997, 1998); and still others, in terms of specific cultural attributes and behaviors, including stereotypes (Ethier and Deaux 1990, 1994; Fordham and Ogbu 1986; Keefe 1992; Landrine and Klonoff 1994; Matute-Bianchi 1986; Waters 1990, 1996). Accordingly, we used a partially grounded approach in our analysis of in-depth interviews with African American adolescents to explore the specific meanings individuals attach to their racial and ethnic identities. First, we conducted semistructured one-on-one interviews at our participants' homes during the summer following their eleventh-grade year in high school. These interviews were conducted by trained interviewers of same race and gender as the interviewee. We have now used a variety of qualitative techniques to analyze the transcripts of these interviews.

In one approach we used an iterative process of independent and group analyses with the goal of developing a coding scheme for interview text regarding the meaning of one's ethnicity. This process revealed four emergent themes in the data:

1. Stereotypes and other challenges related to racial or ethnic stigma

2. Racial and ethnic pride and affirmation

3. Cultural differentiations between African Americans and other ethnic and racial groups

4. Race and ethnicity as an individualistic orientation

We applied codes to sections of the interview texts on the basis of their "fit" to these categories and explored alternative interpretations among our team of researchers especially in the case of ambiguous data.

Consistent with previous research on the subjective meanings of race and ethnicity, ideology (particularly as it pertains to stereotypes and other race and ethnicity-based challenges), racial and ethnic pride, and culture emerged as particularly prevalent subjective themes. Specifically, respondents consistently conveyed concerns about being judged by others on the basis of stereotypes about and prejudice against blacks and about having to deal with these experiences in their everyday lives. Also, almost all of the youth reported being proud of their racial or ethnic group membership, but an important finding was that individuals differed in the source of their racial or ethnic pride. For some it was a sense of pride in the accomplishments of their African and African American ancestors, particularly in "rising above" slavery and other forms of oppression. For others it was a sense of pride in their skin color simply as an attribute of the self, just as one might be proud of one's height or hair color. Finally, many described the meaning of being black in terms of the behaviors, speech styles, and musical and stylistic preferences associated with African American culture. Some of the youths believed that these cultural indicators constituted the boundaries between them and other racial and ethnic groups. Some saw these boundaries as cultural bridges; others saw them as facilitating racial and ethnic separateness.

We were also struck by the number of our participants who included a strong sense of individualism as part of the subjective meanings they attached to their racial and ethnic group membership. The role of individualism in racial and ethnic identity formation has also been noted quite recently by Linda Strauss and William E. Cross (chapter 4, this volume) in their work on identity enactments and by Sellers and his colleagues in their discussion of a humanist ideology (Sellers et al. 1998). Individualism manifested itself in our youths' interviews through their use of a range of strategies for reconciling the individuated self with racial- and ethnic-group membership. Their comments ranged from recognizing race only as a personal attribute (akin to having brown eyes) to "de-racializing" personal attributes in an attempt to maintain connection to the group (for example, attributing speech and clothing styles to racial group "culture"). Motivations for adopting an individualist orientation included the need to distance oneself from negative stereotypes, redefine stereotypes to maintain group connection, or acknowledge that one's race is fundamentally linked to one's view of self. Adopting an individualistic orientation did not preclude respondents being aware of stereotypes, having pride in their ethnicity, or acknowledging cultural differences.

Discursive Approaches

We have also conducted extensive analyses of these data using a discursive approach, which focuses on the language forms individuals adopted in expressing their self-representations during the interviews. In the social-constructionist epistemology on which discursive analysis is based, it is assumed that individuals are exposed to multiple messages about the meaning of their race or ethnicity, and that over the life course much of the work in constructing a sense of self requires that individuals negotiate these messages and reconcile any inherent contradictions. Discursive analysis focuses on the ideological dilemmas presented in discourse (in this case, the youths' interviews) and the ways in which people position themselves with respect to these dilemmas.

Our team's discursive analyses have focused on both our European American and African American youths' construction of racial- and ethnic-identity meaning systems (O'Neill and Chatman 2003). This analysis corroborated and extended findings from the content-analytic approach described earlier. That is, both groups of youths discussed stereotypes and other race- and ethnicity-based challenges and biases, racial and ethnic pride, cultural differences between their own and other groups, and individualism as an aspect of racial and ethnic identity. The discursive approach increased the depth and complexity of our understanding of these phenomena. Although the youth were able to give accounts of events and issues related to their racial and ethnic group membership, they struggled to define what it means to be black or white. Most did attempt to do so, drawing on the discourses available to them to make sense of race in the context of the interview setting. Moreover, many of the youths expressed some apparent tension between representing themselves as individuals and as part of the collective.

These tensions are apparent in the following excerpt from an interview with a high school student we will call Antoinette. Antoinette is a very articulate, introspective African American female who had given a lot of thought to her racial- and ethnic-group membership and what it meant for the self. Yet, when asked what it means to be black, she struggled to provide a definition:

That's a little bit of a weird question. I mean because before I'm even black, I am me. But sometimes I . . . I mean, I'm not, I know I'm black, but it's not something that I constantly harp on like go out and say "oh, I'm black," because people are going to see that when they see me.

For Antoinette, being black was a part of her self that both she and others around her took for granted. There was no definition for it—it just "was." She explicitly denied any influence of her race on who she was as a person, saying: "So, it . . . it . . . it really . . . it really hasn't changed me that much." Nevertheless she continually alluded to racial differences, her identification with those differences, and the constraints race often put on her self-expression. "I'm proud to be black every day, because when I think about it— I mean, no offense or nothing—but I wouldn't want to be white." The interviewer responded with agreement: "Uh-hmmm." Then Antoinette stated: "I'm happy to be black every day of my life."

In sum, both our content and discursive analyses of interviews with African American youths indicated that they attach different subjective meanings to race and ethnicity. These meanings seemed to fall into four different realms:

1. Ideology around issues of social inequality

2. Racial and ethnic pride

3. Cultural characteristics

4. Individualism

In addition, several tensions were evident in the ways these youth talked about race and ethnicity in their lives. For example, many if not all found it difficult to articulate subjective meanings of race and ethnicity, alluding in their discourses to an inability to separate race and ethnicity from self. Some of the youths in the study took offense at their perception of the interviewer's imposing racial and ethnic identities on them. Similarly, many expressed tensions between being perceived and identifying as an individual versus as a member of a collective.

Negotiating Across Contexts

How do youths rely on these meanings as resources for negotiating identity across contexts? Kay Deaux and K. A. Ethier (1998) proposed that identity-negotiation strategies often occur in response to perceived identity threats. Such threats are often encountered by members of racial and ethnic minority groups, and include such instances as being a member of a minority group or being exposed to negative stereotypes about one's group. We have argued that racial and ethnic meanings can serve as resources to members of racial and ethnic minority groups as they negotiate identity across contexts. In this section we describe findings illustrating some of the mechanisms by which meanings may operate as resources in identity-negotiation processes. We draw on ideas from Linda Strauss and William E. Cross's identity functions framework (see Cross and Strauss 1998; Strauss and Cross, chapter 4, this volume).

Deaux and Ethier (1998) proposed that identity-negotiation strategies in response to threat can take two basic forms: those that enhance identity and those that negate identity. Identity-enhancement strategies identified by the authors include attaching increased importance to a particular identity (reaffirmation), employing new outlets and supports for the identity (remooring), increasing one's contact with members of the identity group (intensified group contact), and changing the social system to facilitate one's expression of the identity (social change). Identity-negation strategies include abandonment of an identity, the belief that one can escape categorization (elimination), rejection of a label imposed externally (denial), and de-emphasizing the importance of an identity without relinquishing it entirely (decreasing importance).

Cross and Strauss (1998) described several identity functions that are served by black identity in particular. Whereas identity strategies focus on the means by which individuals negotiate self and context (goal-directed behaviors), identity functions focus on the self-relevant goals they are trying to achieve through these means (identity end-states). The functions described by Cross and Strauss (1998) include buffering, bonding, code switching, bridging, and individualism. Buffering occurs when identification with the identity group protects the self-concept from negative effects of stigmatization. Bonding occurs when identification with the group promotes and sustains a sense of connection. Bridging refers to the connections with members of out-groups that are forged directly as a result of racial and ethnic differences. And finally, individualism refers to a sense of being different from other members of one's racial or ethnic group as a result of personal attributes not attached to ethnic-group membership, and facilitates a unique view of the self.

In our preliminary analyses of the interview data, we used the identity strategies and functions described earlier as categories for coding the text. These preliminary analyses yielded additional emergent strategies that we used in the subsequent and final coding scheme. These strategies included individualism, redefinition, humanist orientation, discounting, and code switching. Individualism as a strategy is distinguished from individualism as a function because it refers to an agentic, personal resistance to stereotypes based on emphasizing one's own unique attributes ("I'm not like that"). In this sense, individualism is a strategy for negotiating identity across contexts, not an everyday function. Redefinition refers to an active and conscious resistance to stereotypes by emphasizing the group's attributes ("We're not like that"). A humanistic orientation refers to individuals' emphasizing the similarities among all humans without regard to race (Sellers et al. 1998). Discounting refers to the devaluing of the source from which stigma is expressed (Crocker and Major 1989). And finally, code switching refers to the conscious turning on and off of those attributes and behaviors associated with group membership in response to situational demands (Cross and Strauss 1998). Although Cross and Strauss conceptualize code switching as a function of identity, we view it more as a strategy because it is a means by which individuals are trying to achieve identity fit in a given context. In this sense, however, code switching as a strategy is very similar to Cross and Strauss's concept of identity enactments (see chapter 4, this volume).

To better understand the circumstances under which African American youths employed the identity-negotiation strategies and to what end, we coded the interview text for instances in which both strategies and functions were apparent. We also noted

Table 6.1   Identity-Negotiation Strategies as a Function of Context

Strategy Employed	Contextual Characteristics				
	In-Group in Majority	In-Group in Minority	Interracial Contact	Domain-Specific Stereotypes	General Experiences
Elimination					
Denial					
Decreased importance					
Reaffirmation	XXX	XX		X	XXXX
Remooring					
Intensified group contact		XX	XX		XXX
Social change					
Code switching		XXXX		XXX	
Individualism	XXX	XXX	X	XX	XXXXXXX
Redefinition		XXXXX	X	XXX	XXXXXXX
Humanist worldview		XXX		X	XXXXXX
Discounting		XX	X	X	X

Source: Authors' compilation.
Note: Number of X's indicates respondents' mentions of a strategy.

(using information from preliminary analyses) whether the contexts in which the strategies and functions occurred were characterized by the respondents' in-group being the minority or majority, were instances of interracial contact or in-group stereotypic cues, or were general everyday experiences unrelated to race or ethnicity.

Our results provided only partial support for the strategies identified by Deaux and Ethier (1998). On the one hand, no instances of identity-negation strategies were reported by our participants, even in contexts described by Ethier and Deaux (1994) as potential threats to identity (for example, in-group as minority; see table 6.1). On the contrary, our respondents overwhelmingly expressed pride in their race or color as a personal attribute, regardless of the particular contextual circumstances. On the other hand, identity-enhancement strategies were frequently employed across a variety of situations. Few strategies were employed when respondents were in contexts where their group was in the majority. If ethnicity is less salient in such situations, then there should be less need for identity negotiation. In contrast, several strategies were adopted in situations in which ethnicity was salient.

Although Deaux and Ethier (1998) described identity-negotiation strategies as responses to situationally specific instances of threat, respondents revealed the ubiquity of ethnic stigma in their everyday lives, regardless of ethnic salience in the immediate context. For example, our participants most frequently reported using various strategies to deal with their awareness of negative media images of African Americans.

Table 6.2   Identity-Negotiation Strategies and Functions

Strategy Employed	Function			
	Buffering	Bonding	Bridging	Individualism
Elimination				
Denial				
Decreased importance				
Reaffirmation	XX	XXXXXXX		X
Remooring				
Intensified group contact	X	XXXX	X	X
Social change				
Code switching	XX		XXXX	X
Individualism	XXXXXX		XX	XXXXXXXX
Redefinition	XXXXXXXXX			
Humanist worldview	XXXX		XX	XXXXXX
Discounting	XXXXX			

Source: Authors' compilation.
Note: Number of X's indicates respondents' mentions of a strategy.

Respondents were often proactive in their use of strategies such as intensified group contact to select themselves into certain contexts. For example, they might choose to attend a predominantly black college rather than simply react in the face of immediate threat.

Not all functions corresponded with specific strategies (see table 6.2). The redefinition and discounting strategies functioned only as buffers to counteract the negative effects of stigmatization. Respondents were acutely aware of the stereotypes associated with their ethnic group and these strategies likely protected them from the potentially damaging effects of harmful messages. The individualism and humanist-worldview strategies served several functions for identity, but they did not bond group members together. This is to be expected, as respondents employing individualism as a strategy determine which characteristics make them unique by comparing themselves to other group members.

Identity Negotiation and Adaptation

In the preceding sections we have described the subjective content of youths' racial and ethnic identities and some of the strategies they employ as they negotiate their identities across various contexts and situations. Another of our objectives was to illustrate instances in which these identity-negotiation strategies, relying on subjective meanings as identity resources, are adaptive for developing youths. Although our findings related to the racial-identity functions described by Cross and Strauss (1998) lend themselves to such an argument, they are limited to the domain of identity management. In this section, we describe findings illustrating adaptive functions of identity negotiation in other domains, such as academic motivation and achievement and psychological adjustment.

In this research we took a pattern-oriented approach to operationalizing ethnic and racial identity. In the descriptions of racial and ethnic identity meanings and the ways these meanings are used to negotiate identity across contexts, three consistent themes resonate. First, many of the youths have not elaborated a sense of self as a member of their racial or ethnic group, and treat race and ethnicity simply as a personal attribute (skin color or ancestral lineage) in a set of many that distinguishes them as individuals from other individuals. Thus, when asked whether race and ethnicity are important to their sense of self and whether they are proud of their race and ethnicity, such individuals respond affirmatively, but their responses are not indicative of any ties to the racial or ethnic group. Here we used cluster analyses to identify a typology of racial- and ethnic-identity profiles among a sample of early adolescents (eighth grade, average age thirteen years), ranging from the type we have just described to more elaborated forms based on connections to the racial and ethnic group culture or an awareness of the racial and ethnic group's social disadvantage in society (for a full description of this work, see Chatman, Malanchuk, and Eccles 2003).

Our cluster analyses supported a typology of six different ethnic-identity profiles (see figure 6.1):

1. Low identification

2. Personal pride

3. Nominal identification

4. Socially embedded identification

5. Culturally embedded identification

6. Socioculturally embedded identification

The personal-pride group was the second largest of the six profiles (N = 136)—and the only one we failed to predict. Youths falling in this cluster reported that they were proud of being African American and acknowledged mean levels of cultural and social significance to their racial-group membership but did not see their race as being an important aspect of their sense of self. In retrospect, we realized that this pattern is consistent with developmental theory on racial- and ethnic-identity development (Phinney 1992; Quintana and Segura-Herrera 2003). Given their relative youth, the young adolescents in this study likely have just begun to consider the meaning of their racial- and ethnic-group membership to their sense of self, beyond personal identification markers such as skin color, ancestral lineage, and self-categorization. The other five profiles are consistent with previous conceptualizations of ethnic and racial identity based on factors such as cultural affirmation and pride, sense of belonging, and racial ideology (placing the racial group in the broader context of its relation to other groups and society) (Cross 1978, 1991; Oyserman, Gant, and Ager 1995; Phinney 1990, 1992; Sellers et al. 1998; Strauss and Cross, chapter 4, this volume).

Analyses of variance testing for whether the six ethnic-identity profiles differed in terms of psychological adjustment, problem behaviors, and academic achievement three years later, just after the respondents' eleventh-grade year in high school,

Figure 6.1   Ethnic-Identity Profiles Among African American
              Eighth-Grade Youths

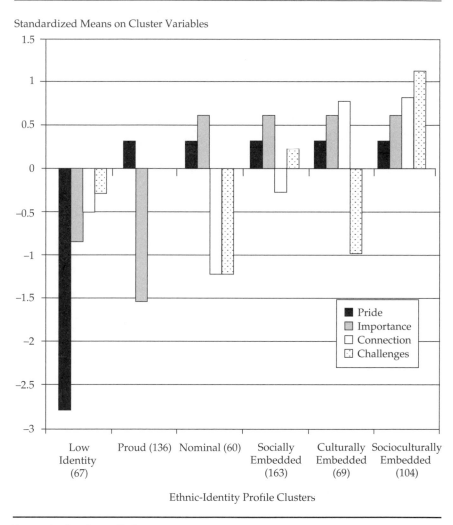

Standardized Means on Cluster Variables

Ethnic-Identity Profile Clusters

Source: Authors' compilation.

indicated complex relations between racial and ethnic identity and individual development (Chatman, Malanchuk, and Eccles 2001) (see table 6.3). For example, although those youth whose ethnic identities were socioculturally embedded had higher GPAs, on average, than all the other groups, they also reported lower psychological adjustment and higher involvement in problem behaviors than the other groups. These findings, however, are best interpreted in context. For example, the average levels of psychological adjustment are quite high, so being lower than the other groups represents a relative difference among very high functioning adolescents. Similarly, the average rates of problem behaviors are quite low—so being

Table 6.3   Mean Scores on Achievement, Psychological Adjustment, and
Problem Behaviors for Ethnic-Identity Profiles

	Low Identity	Nominal	Proud Identity	Socially Embedded	Culturally Embedded	Fully Embedded
Grade-point average	−.16[a]	−.07	−.12[a]	−.14[a]	.16[b]	.36[b]
Psychological adjustment	−.13[a]	−.12[a]	.21[b]	−.07[a]	.40[b]	−.04[a]
Problem behaviors	−.03	0	−.24[a]	.15[b]	−.21[a]	.09[b]

Source: Authors' compilation.
Note: Standardized scores are reported for all measures; figures with different superscripts across each row denote statistically significant differences.

higher than other groups represents a relative difference among a population of adolescents with very low rates of problem behaviors.

We interpret these findings in terms of the impact that anticipated future racial discrimination might have on adolescents' development. In other analyses with this data set, we found that expecting future racial discrimination predicts increases in academic motivation and achievement (Wong, Eccles, and Sameroff 2003). Apparently, these youths respond to anticipated future racial discrimination in an agentic manner, increasing their academic striving in order to best equip themselves to personally combat the impact of racial discrimination on their own lives. Thus, it is not surprising that the socioculturally embedded group had a very high grade-point average.

But it is also likely that anticipated future racial discrimination might affect other aspects of adolescents' behavior and psychological states. For example, anticipated future discrimination might increase anger and lead to such problem behaviors as fighting and using alcohol in order to cope with these future external challenges. Developmentalists such as Diana D. Baumrind (1987), Michelle Fine (1991) and Niobe Way (1998) talk about healthy "acting out" and risk taking. The youths who exhibit what might be considered the most mature and integrated ethnic identities (those in the socioculturally embedded group) may also be "acting out" in ways that reflect a relatively healthy adolescent reaction to perceived oppression. On the one hand, they are maintaining high academic engagement; on the other, they are reacting emotionally and behaviorally to being a member of an oppressed minority. As expected, the youths who did not report relatively high levels of concern about future racial discrimination also did not report these emotional and behavioral reactions. The long-term consequences of these patterns of identity beliefs and behavioral and emotional reactions remain to be seen and should depend on a variety of other psychological and social characteristics of the individual adolescents, as well as on the subsequent development of their racial identity and their coping strategies.

We next looked at developmental changes in identity profiles and found considerable individual variation over time. That is, although we were able to identify the same six profiles in the data at wave 4, many of the youths' specific profiles had changed, suggesting that between waves 3 and 4 these adolescents are using different forms of ethnic-identity negotiation strategies. Because the significant developmental transition from middle school to high school occurs between these two points, the youths are likely responding to changes in context as well as their own increasing maturity. In high school, these youths were more systematically exposed to their ethnic group's history and cultural heritage through specific courses and extracurricular activities. In addition, the salience of the task of both personal and social identity formation normally accelerates during this age period. Thus the pressure to "become black," as described by Cross's (1978, 1991) nigrescence theory, is likely to have increased for these youth as they tried to find their place. As proposed both by Deaux and Ethier (1998) and by Cross and Strauss (1998), these changes will have led some of the youths to a shift toward a more complex socially and culturally embedded ethnic identity and other youths to shift toward detachment from their ethnic identity. We plan to investigate the factors that explain these different developmental trajectories.

CONCLUDING THOUGHTS ON IDENTITY NEGOTIATION

In this chapter we have argued that individuals' subjective meanings about race and ethnicity can serve as resources for negotiating identity across contexts and across developmental time. We have presented data from a sample of African American youths demonstrating some of the ways in which such negotiation may occur. These data illustrated youths' use of a variety of strategies to make sense of race and ethnicity and its relevance for the self. In some instances, identity-negotiation strategies were shown to be facilitative of positive psychological and behavioral adjustment.

The findings we have presented corroborate previous research on racial and ethnic identity and integrate much of that work within a framework describing the content of such identities as resources for identity negotiation. Our use of multiple and mixed methodological approaches allowed us to highlight and better understand some of the processes by which such negotiation may occur. As youths develop over the course of childhood and adolescence, they are exposed to a host of new sources of information that they are pressed to integrate into existing knowledge structures. As they try to better understand who they are and where they fit in their proximal and distal worlds, they must evaluate both the new and preexisting knowledge they have acquired and position themselves as they best see fit. To the extent that they can do so, they are able to maintain a positive and coherent sense of self and identity.

Our approach highlights the dynamic nature of identity. Individuals are constantly faced with new information, new situations, and new contexts, both as they make major life transitions (such as from school to family, college, and work life) and as they progress in their day-to-day activities. This new information may bear on their sense of who they are and are not relative to others around them and on the way they have seen themselves in the past. Thus, individuals are constantly negotiating identity as they mature and traverse the course of daily life. This is in contrast to the base of theoretical work presenting identity as existing knowledge structures that can be located within the person and that interact with features of various contexts. Our approach departs from such a perspective in that identity is viewed as a process that must be tracked across time and contexts, and contexts are viewed as having features that are negotiated and often are integrated with existing knowledge about the self. In other words, we emphasize what individuals *do* with identity content in different contexts and situations rather than focusing only on the specific content of identity and its interactions with contextual features.

Future research on identity might examine the processes we have outlined here among adult populations. Although identity development has traditionally been presented as a major task of adolescence and early adulthood (Erikson 1968), several researchers now suggest that identities change throughout the life span, particularly in response to changes in the context of individual lives (Cross 1991; Eccles and Bryan 1994). Although research in social psychology emphasizes contextual cues that may make particular identities more or less salient, leading individuals to "activate" those identities in a given context, this approach still presents identity as a fixed structure located within individuals' psychic makeup. Such approaches do not take into account identity negotiations whereby identity content may be reevaluated and sometimes altered. Approaches that do take such content negotiation into consideration can be informative as to the ways in which identities may be adaptive resources in individuals' lives.

Implications for Policy and Practice

The research presented in this chapter has several implications for policy and practice in an increasingly multicultural society. First, youths vary both in the degree to which they identify with racial and ethnic groups and in the subjective meanings they attach to their membership in those groups. Although it is common practice in contemporary society to assume that individuals sharing racial- and ethnic-group membership necessarily also share racial and ethnic identity, the research presented in this chapter and throughout this volume indicates that this practice is faulty and can have adverse consequences. For example, one of the most prevalent themes in the data we have presented here, and in other chapters in this volume (particularly chapter 3, by Downey, London, Bolger, and Velilla, and chapter 4, by Strauss and Cross), is that adolescents and young adults experience great tensions in expressing individualism in the context of group membership. Although they do not wish to disassociate from the racial and ethnic group, they are also resistant to being labeled and stereotyped on the basis of their group membership.

Second, as adolescents mature and enter new contexts in which they are increasingly exposed to societal messages around racial inequalities, their response may be to become angry and to "act out." Our research converges with previous findings suggesting that providing youths with a sense of cultural connection and heritage can buffer these feelings and behaviors to some extent. Clearly, however, developing youths are in need of additional resources to help them cope with conflicting messages about race, ethnicity, and self. Beverly Tatum (1997) suggests that the best way to do this, for both minority and majority individuals as well as society as a whole, is to put racial and ethnic issues on the table. Open discussions about race and ethnicity can facilitate progress on social inequality through providing a broader range of discourses on which youths may draw in negotiating personal meaning and self (O'Neill and Chatman 2003).

Finally, as has been argued elegantly and comprehensively by many contemporary scholars studying race and ethnicity in developmental context (for example, Boykin and Toms 1985; Cross 1991; Garcia Coll et al. 1996; Quintana and Segura-Herrera 2003; Spencer and Markstrom-Adams 1990; Tatum 1997), children take many varied paths in integrating relevant experiences. It should never be assumed, for example, that all youths will respond to discrimination with anger, frustration, or a sense of helplessness. It is, however, important that children who do experience such race- and ethnicity-based disadvantage (including discourses regarding their group's status) be helped to succeed by being given supports in the way of affirming their group's culture and its significance to their own sense of self as a member of the group.

APPENDIX

I. Racial Configuration Measures

- Importance: "How important is it for you to know about your racial background?"

- Pride: "How proud are you of your racial background?"

- Connection to ethnic heritage (alpha = .72):
  "I have a close community of friends because of my race or ethnicity."
  "People of my race/ethnicity have a culturally rich heritage."
  "I have meaningful traditions because of my race or ethnicity."
  "People of my race or ethnicity are very supportive of each other."

- Expectation of race-based challenges (r = .83):
  "Because of your race, no matter how hard you work, you will always have to work harder than others to prove yourself."
  "Because of your race, it is important that you do better than other kids at school in order to get ahead."

II. Ethnic and Racial Attitudes and Behaviors

- Same-ethnicity peer preferences (alpha = .78)
  "In general, you prefer to hang out with kids of your own race."

- Family involvement in own-ethnicity activities (alpha = .67)
  For example, "How often do you celebrate any special days connected to your racial background?"

- Salience of discrimination in the family (alpha = .71)
  For example, "How often do you talk in the family about discrimination you may face because of your race?"

- Perceived Racial Discrimination at School (alpha = .89)
  For example, "How often do you feel that kids do not want to hang out with you because of your race?"

- Psychological salience of race and ethnicity: Frequency count of multiple open-ended survey questions unrelated to race for instances of spontaneously mentioned race or ethnicity.

III. Outcomes

- Achievement (alpha = .86): standardized composite grade in English/Science/Math/Health and Maryland Functional Test Math Score

- Psychological adjustment (alpha = .80): Standardized Composite Score for:
  Resiliency
  Self-esteem
  Satisfaction with self and relationships
  Preference for improvement-based coping strategies
  Depression (R = reverse scored)
  Anger (R)
  General confusion (R)
  Problem paying attention (R)
  Social self-consciousness (R)

- Problem behaviors: Examples from summed score of problem behaviors ever participated in (out of twenty-four)
  Skipping class without a valid excuse
  Lying to your parents
  Cheating on tests or exams
  Damaging public or private property just for fun
  Hitting someone because you didn't like what they said or did
  Being involved in a gang fight
  Being suspended from school
  Bringing alcohol or drugs to school
  Being a member of a gang
  Stealing or trying to steal a motor vehicle
  Using crack in last six months
  Being involved with the police

The research described in this chapter was supported by grants from the National Institute for Child Health and Human Development (NICHD) and the William T. Grant Foundation.

We thank the following for their work on this data set: Todd Bartko, Elaine Belansky, Diane Early, Kari Fraser, Leslie Gutman, Yael Harlap, Katie Jodl, Ariel Kalil, Linda Kuhn, Alice Michael, Melanie Overby, Steve Peck, Rob Roeser, Sherri Steele, Erika Taylor, Cynthia Winston, and Carol Wong. Special thanks Suzie O'Neill, Melanie Overby, Cynthia Winston, Janice Templeton, and Nasha Vida for their conceptual and analytical contributions to the empirical work presented in the second part of this chapter.

NOTE

1. "Race" and "ethnicity" often have been used erroneously as interchangeable concepts. For a detailed analysis on how each has been defined, see Michael Omi and Howard Winant (1994). Although we acknowledge the differences between race and ethnicity, in this chapter we use both terms, sometimes together and sometimes separately. For many reasons, including methodology, it is difficult to disentangle the psychology of one from the other.

REFERENCES

Arroyo, C. G., and E. Zigler. 1995. "Racial Identity, Academic Achievement, and the Psychological Well-Being of Economically Disadvantaged Adolescents." *Journal of Personality and Social Psychology* 69(5): 903–14.

Baumeister, R. F., and M. R. Leary. 1995. "The Need to Belong: Desire for Interpersonal Attachments as a Fundamental Human Motivation." *Psychological Bulletin* 117(3): 497–529.

Baumrind, D. 1987. "A Developmental Perspective on Adolescent Risk Taking in Contemporary America." *New Directions for Child Development* 37: 93–125.

Boykin, A. W., and F. D. Toms. 1985. "Black Child Socialization: A Conceptual Framework. In *Black Children*, edited by H. P. McAdoo, and J. L. McAdoo. Newbury, Calif.: Sage.

Brewer, M. B. 1991. "The Social Self: On Being the Same and Different at the Same Time." *Personality and Social Psychology Bulletin* 17(5): 475–82.

Bronfenbrenner, Urie. 1979. *The Ecology of Human Development: Experiments by Nature and Design.* Cambridge, Mass.: Harvard University Press.

———. 1992. "Ecological Systems Theory." In *Six Theories of Child Development: Revised Formulations and Current Issues*, edited by R. Vasta. London: Jessica Kingsley.

Brubaker, R., and F. Cooper. 2000. "Beyond 'identity.' " *Theory and Society* 29:1–47.

Burke, P. J., and J. Tully. 1977. "The Measurement of Role/Identity." *Social Forces* 55(4): 881–97.

Chatman, Celina M., O. Malanchuk, and Jacquelynne S. Eccles. 2001. "Ethnic Identity Configurations Among African-American Adolescents." Paper presented at the biennial meeting of the Society for Research on Child Development. Albuquerque (April 20–23).

———. 2003. "Racial Formation Among African-American Early Adolescents: Profiles of Ethnic and Racial Identity." Unpublished manuscript. University of Michigan.

Cook, Thomas D., F. Habib, M. Phillips, R. A. Settersten, S. C. Shagle, and S. M. Degirmencioglu. 1999. "Comer's School Development Program in Prince George's County: A theory-based evaluation." *American Educational Research Journal* 36(3): 543–97.

Crocker, Jennifer S., and Brenda Major. 1989. "Social Stigma and Self-Esteem: The Self-Protective Properties of Stigma." *Psychological Review* 96(4): 608–30.

Crocker, Jennifer, R. Luhtanen, B. Blaine, and S. Broadnax. 1994. Collective Self-Esteem and Psychological Well-Being Among White, Black, and Asian College Students." *Personality and Social Psychology Bulletin* 20(5): 503–13.

Cross, William E. 1978. "The Thomas and Cross Models of Psychological Nigrescence: A Review." *Journal of Black Psychology* 5(1): 13–31.

———. 1991. *Shades of Black: Diversity in African-American Identity.* Philadelphia: Temple University Press.

Cross, William E., and Linda Strauss. 1998. "The Everyday Functions of African American Identity." In *Prejudice: The Target's Perspective,* edited by Janet K. Swim and Charles Stangor. San Diego: Academic Press.

Deaux, Kay. 1993. "Reconstructing Social Identity." *Personality and Social Psychology Bulletin* 19(1): 4–12.

Deaux, Kay, and K. A. Ethier. 1998. "Negotiating Social Identity." In *Prejudice: The Target's Perspective*, edited by Janet K. Swim and Charles Stangor. San Diego: Academic Press.

Eccles, Jacquelynne S. 1987. "Gender Roles and Women's Achievement-Related Decisions." *Psychology of Women Quarterly* 11(2): 135–71.

———. 1993. "School and Family Effects on the Ontogeny of Children's Interests, Self-Perceptions, and Activity Choice." In *Developmental Perspectives on Motivation*, edited by Janis E. Jacobs. Nebraska Symposium on Motivation, volume 40. University of Nebraska Press.

Eccles (Parsons), Jacquelynne S., et al. 1983. "Expectancies, Values and Academic Behaviors." In *Achievement and Achievement Motivation*, edited by J. Spence. San Francisco: W. H. Freeman.

Eccles, Jacquelynne S., and B. L. Barber. 1999. "Student Council, Volunteering, Basketball, or Marching Band: What Kind of Extracurricular Involvement Matters?" *Journal of Adolescent Research* 14:10–43.

Eccles Jacquelynne S., B. L. Barber, M. Stone, and J. Hunt. 2003. "Extracurricular Activities and Adolescent Development." *Journal of Social Issues* 59(4): 865–89.

Eccles, Jacquelynne S., and J. Bryan. 1994. "Adolescence and Gender-Role Transcendence." In *Gender-Roles Across the Life Span: A Multidisciplinary Perspective*, edited by M. Stevenson. Muncie, Ind.: Ball State University Press.

Epstein, S. 1990. "Cognitive-Experiential Self-Theory." In *Handbook of Personality: Theory and Research*, edited by L. A. Pervin. New York: Guilford Press.

Erikson, Erik H. 1968. *Identity: Youth and Crisis.* London: Faber & Faber.

———. 1980. *Identity and the Life Cycle.* New York: Norton.

Ethier, K. A., and Kay Deaux. 1990. "Hispanics in Ivy: Assessing Identity and Perceived Threat." *Sex Roles: Special Issue: Gender and Ethnicity: Perspectives on Dual Status* 22(7–8): 427–40.

———. 1994. "Negotiating Social Identity When Contexts Change: Maintaining Identification and Responding to Threat." *Journal of Personality and Social Psychology* 67(2): 243–51.

Fine, M. 1991. *Framing Dropouts: Notes on the Politics of an Urban Public High School.* Albany: State University of New York Press.

Fordham, Signithia. 1988. "Racelessness as a Factor in Black Students' School Success: Pragmatic Strategy or Pyrrhic Victory?" *Harvard Educational Review* 58(1): 54–84.

Fordham, Signithia, and John Ogbu. 1986. "Black Students' School Success: Coping with the Burden of 'Acting White.' " *The Urban Review* 18(3): 176–206.

Frable, D. 1997. "Gender, Racial, Ethnic, Sexual, and Class Identities." *Annual Review of Psychology* 48:139–62.

Garcia Coll, C. T., G. Lamberty, G. Jenkins, H. P. McAdoo, K. Crnic, B. H. Wasik, and H. V. Garcia. 1996. "An Integrative Model for the Study of Developmental Competencies in Minority Children." *Child Development* 67(5): 1891–1914.

Gleason, P. 1983. "Identifying Identity: A Semantic History." *Journal of American History* 69: 910–31.

Grotevant, H. D. 1987. "Toward a Process Model of Identity Formation." *Journal of Adolescent Research* 2(3): 203–22.

———. 1992. "Assigned and Chosen Identity Components: A Process Perspective on Their Integration." In *Advances in Adolescent Development: Adolescent Identity Formation*, edited by G. R. Adams and T. P. Gullotta. Volume 4. Thousand Oaks, Calif.: Sage.

Harter, S. 1990. "Self and Identity Development." In *At the Threshold: The Developing Adolescent*, edited by S. S. Feldman and G. R. Elliott. Cambridge, Mass.: Harvard University Press.

James, William. 1890/1910. *The Principles of Psychology.* New York: Holt.

Keefe, S. E. 1992. "Ethnic Identity: The Domain of Perceptions of and Attachment to Ethnic Groups and Cultures." *Human Organization* 51(1): 35–43.

Kleiber, D. A. 1999. *Leisure Experiences and Human Development: A Dialectical Interpretation.* New York: Basic Books.

Landrine, H., and E. A. Klonoff. 1994. The African American Acculturation Scale: Development, Reliability, and Validity. *Journal of Black Psychology* 20(2): 104–27.

Luhtanen, Riia, and Jennifer Crocker. 1992. "A Collective Self-Esteem Scale: Self-Evaluation of One's Social Identity." *Personality and Social Psychology Bulletin* 18(3): 302–18.

Markus, H., and E. Wurf. 1987. "The Dynamic Self-Concept: A Social Psychological Perspective." *Annual Review of Psychology* 38: 299–337.

Matute-Bianchi, M. 1986. "Ethnic Identities and Pattern of School Success and Failure Among Mexican-Descent and Japanese-American Students in a California High School: An Ethnographic Analysis." *American Journal of Education* 95: 233–55.

McCall, G. J., and J. L. Simmons. 1966. *Identities and Interactions.* New York: Free Press.

McGuire, W. J., C. V. McGuire, P. Child, and T. Fujioka. 1978. "Salience of Ethnicity in the Spontaneous Self-Concept as a Function of One's Ethnic Distinctiveness in the Social Environment." *Journal of Personality and Social Psychology* 36(5): 512–20.

Omi, Michael, and Howard Winant. 1994. *Racial Formation in the United States.* 2nd ed. New York: Routledge.

O'Neill, Suzie A., and Celina M. Chatman. 2003. "The Social Construction of Race, Ethnicity and Identity Among White and African-American Adolescents." Paper presented at the Biennial meeting of the Society for Research on Child Development. Tampa (April 24–27).

Oyserman, D., L. Gant, and J. Ager. 1995. "A Socially Contextualized Model of African American Identity: Possible Selves and School Persistence." *Journal of Personality and Social Psychology* 69(6): 1216–32.

Pelham, B. W. 1991. "On Confidence and Consequence: The Certainty and Importance of Self-Knowledge." *Journal of Personality and Social Psychology* 60(4): 518–30.

Phinney, Jean S. 1990. "Ethnic Identity in Adolescence and Adulthood: A Review and Integration." Psychological Bulletin 108(3): 499–514.

———. 1992. "The Multigroup Ethnic Identity Measure: A New Scale for Use with Diverse Groups." *Journal of Adolescent Research* 7(2): 156–76.

Phinney, Jean S., and Rotheram, M. J., eds. 1987. *Children's Ethnic Socialization: Pluralism and Development.* Beverly Hills: Sage.

Quintana, S. M., and T. A. Segura-Herrera. 2003. "Developmental Transformations of Self and Identity in the Context of Oppression." *Self and Identity* 2: 269–85.

Rotheram, M. J., and Jean S. Phinney. 1987. "Ethnic Behavior Patterns as an Aspect of Identity." In *Children's Ethnic Socialization: Pluralism and Development,* edited by Jean S. Phinney and M. J. Rotherham. Beverly Hills: Sage.

Sellers, Robert M., S. A. J. Rowley, T. M. Chavous, J. N. Shelton, and M. A. Smith. 1997. "Multidimensional Inventory of Black Identity: A Preliminary Investigation of Reliability and Construct Validity." *Journal of Personality and Social Psychology* 73(4): 805–15.

Sellers, Robert M., M. A. Smith, J. N. Shelton, S. A. J. Rowley, and T. M. Chavous. 1998. "Multidimensional Model of Racial Identity: A Reconceptualization of African American Racial Identity." *Personality and Social Psychology Review* 2(1): 18–39.

Spencer, M. B., and C. Markstrom-Adams, 1990. "Identity Processes Among Racial and Ethnic Minority Children in America." *Child Development* 61(2): 290–310.

Steele, C. M. 1988. "The Psychology of Self-Affirmation: Sustaining the Integrity of the Self." In *Advances in Experimental Social Psychology*. Volume 21, *Social Psychological Studies of the Self: Perspectives and Programs*, edited by Leonard Berkowitz. San Diego: Academic Press.

Stryker, S., and R. T. Serpe 1994. "Identity Salience and Psychological Centrality: Equivalent, Overlapping, or Complementary Concepts?" *Social Psychology Quarterly* 57(1): 16–35.

Swann, W. B. 1987. "Identity Negotiation: Where Two Roads Meet." *Journal of Personality and Social Psychology* (special issue: *Integrating Personality and Social Psychology*) 53(6): 1038–51.

Tajfel, H., and J. C. Turner. 1986. "The Social Identity Theory of Intergroup Behavior." In *Psychology of Intergroup Relations*, edited by S. Worchel and W. Austin. Chicago: Nelson-Hall.

Tatum, Beverly D. 1997. *Why Are All the Black Kids Sitting Together in the Cafeteria, and Other Conversations About Race*. New York: Basic Books.

Taylor, R. D., R. Casten, S. M. Flickinger, D. Roberts, and C. D. Fulmore. 1994. "Explaining the School Performance of African-American Adolescents." *Journal of Research on Adolescence* 4(1): 21–44.

Thoits, P., and L. Virshup. 1997. "Me's and We's: Forms and Functions of Social Identities." In *Self and Identity: Fundamental Issues*, edited by R. D. Ashmore and L. Jussim. New York: Oxford University Press.

Turnbull, W., D. T. Miller, and C. McFarland. 1990. "Population-Distinctiveness, Identity, and Bonding." In *Self-Inference Processes*, edited by James M. Olson. The Ontario Symposium, volume 6. Hillsdale, N.J.: Erlbaum.

Turner, J. C., M. A. Hogg, P. J. Oakes, S. D. Reicher, and M. S. Wetherell. 1987. *Rediscovering the Social Group: A Self-Categorization Theory*. Cambridge, Mass.: Basil Blackwell.

Waterman, A. S. 1993. "Finding Something to do or Someone to Be: A Eudaimonist Perspective on Identity Formation." In *Discussions on Ego Identity*, edited by J. Kroger. Hillsdale, N.J.: Erlbaum.

Waters, M. C. 1990. *Ethnic Options: Choosing Identities in America*. Berkeley: University of California Press.

———. 1996. "The Intersection of Gender, Race, and Ethnicity in Identity Development of Caribbean American Teens." In *Urban girls: Resisting Stereotypes, Creating Identities*, edited by B. Leadbetter and N. Way. New York: New York University Press.

Way, N. 1998. *Everyday Courage: The Lives and Stories of Urban Teenagers*. New York: New York University Press.

Wong, Carol A., Jacquelynne S. Eccles, and Arnold Sameroff. 2003. "Ethnic Discrimination and Ethnic Identification: The Influence on African-Americans' and Whites' School and Socio-emotional Adjustment." *Journal of Personality* 71(6): 1197–1232.

Youniss, J., and M. Yates. 1997. *Community Service and Social Responsibility in Youth*. Chicago: University of Chicago Press.

PART III

CONTEXTUAL DEMANDS
AND COMPETING IDENTITIES

CHAPTER 7

ADOLESCENT RACIAL AND ETHNIC IDENTITY IN CONTEXT

LaRue Allen, Yael Bat-Chava, J. Lawrence Aber,
and Edward Seidman

Seventy-eight percent of the United States population now lives in urban centers that are increasingly characterized as densely populated, multiracial, and multiethnic (United Nations Children's Fund 2002). Racial and ethnic identities become increasingly salient aspects of the social identity when we are thrown into close contact with those from other groups in school, at work, or in community settings (Ashmore, Deaux and McLaughlin-Volpe 2004; Kim-ju and Liem 2003; McGuire et al. 1978). A person's race, his or her ethnicity, the feelings triggered by and associated with those aspects of social identity, and the race and ethnicity of those who surround him or her are critically important to the functioning and well-being of that individual. This is especially true in adolescence, when the key task is the achievement of a positive identity (Erikson 1968). Achieving a clear sense of racial or ethnic identity, especially for adolescents from ethnic and racial minority groups, is a critical part of that search for personal and social identity (Helms 1989; Phinney 1996; Vandiver et al. 2001).

In this chapter we focus on the relationship between selected aspects of identity and a particular aspect of the absence of psychological well-being, depressive symptoms, in a sample of inner-city adolescents. Given our broad interests in the relationships between contexts of development and developmental outcomes (see Aber, Jones, and Cohen 2000; Allen et al., in preparation; and Brooks-Gunn, Duncan and Aber 1997), we offer here a look at how the relationship between identities and depressive symptoms vary as a function of characteristics of youths' neighborhood and schools. But before we describe our studies, we will discuss some key definitional issues that surround the conceptualization, function, and measurement of racial and ethnic identity.

WHAT IS ETHNIC IDENTITY? IS IT THE SAME AS RACIAL IDENTITY?

No single definition exists in the literature for the constructs of racial or ethnic identity. Margaret Beale Spencer and Carol Markstrom-Adams (1990) and Jean S. Phinney (1990) each have noted the considerable confusion in the use of the terms that describe these dimensions of social identity. The term "race" was historically used in research involving black and African American children (Asher and Allen 1969; Clark and Clark 1939; Semaj 1980) or in comparisons of black and white children that were common in the developmental literature in the 1970s and 1980s. More recently the term "ethnicity" has been used in research on a variety of groups, including Latinos, blacks, Asians, and whites (Aboud 1987; Rice, Ruiz and Padilla 1974, Smith and Brookins 1997; Waters 1990).

We believe that it is important to highlight the differences between the two terms, and note that they differ in ways that have significance for developmental researchers—that is, in their impact on the development of social identity (Ashmore, Deaux, McLaughlin-Volpe 2004). Race is the superordinate, or more numerically inclusive, category, which denotes in its literal sense a phenotypic expression of shared physical characteristics that though it has greater social than biological meaning, has powerful meaning nonetheless. Alternatively, ethnicity implies a set of characteristics, which could include cultural values, language, race, traditions, and behaviors, shared by a geographically contiguous group of people that are transmitted through socialization as well as heredity (Ocampo, Bernal, and Knight 1993). In our efforts to study the impact of various personal and ecological factors on development, we must be very clear on the factor whose impact we are examining.

There is no evidence that race and ethnicity are equally significant in the development of all groups or that the relationship between the two is constant. Indeed, a frequent finding in studies of diverse groups is that in the United States, whites score on average lower on scales that assess the strength of one's attachment to an ethnic group than do all other groups studied (for example, Martinez and Dukes 1997; Yancey, Aneshensel and Driscoll 2001). For whites, ethnic identity is described as a social process that may be related to how long a family has been in the United States, how old an individual is, or who is speaking for the individual. Being Italian American or Greek American is often the consequence of a deliberate choice to include oneself in a given cultural group (Waters 1990), a choice not usually available to those whose ethnicity is more visible.

Across groups, being a member of a low-status racial group is thought to be a risk factor for development. Thus, being black is most often an undeniable part of one's identity in ways that being white is not. Further complicating the picture is the fact that race does not have the same meaning for U.S. whites and blacks that it does for Asians, Latinos, and even immigrant blacks. Caribbean blacks from nations such as Jamaica move from a setting in which "race" is not a salient dimension of their social identity (Akbar, Chambers, and Thompson 2001) to the United States, where skin color is a prominent factor in how people perceive one another. Thus, within the United States black racial group, there are ethnic groups defined most often by national origin. There may also be African American subgroups defined, perhaps, by geographic roots. "Southern blacks" or "inner-city blacks" might prove to be examples of groups that have common food, music, clothing, and behavioral customs that unite them, even when they are geographically dispersed. Within these groups, there might also be important subgroups formed on the basis of social class. But the evidence that the entire group formerly known as black Americans constitutes a homogeneous ethnic group is weak.

Among Latinos, national origin is the most significant determinant of ethnic-group membership, with "race" varying widely in meaning. In the 2000 census, 47 percent of the Latino population identified themselves as neither white nor black but "other."

Although a number of interpretations have been offered for such findings, it is the case that race classification, immutable in the United States culture, is a classification that can change in many parts of Latin America, both over time and from country to country. Further, in Latin America race is a continuum correlated with social class, in contrast to the sharp division between racial groups that has historically obtained in the United States.

So across racial and ethnic categories, the opportunities and burdens of membership vary. Both of these memberships may be important in an adolescent's ability to confront obstacles on his or her developmental path. We might hypothesize, in fact, that race is a risk factor, at least for some lower-status groups, whereas ethnicity is protective for those who proactively include themselves in the group and seek to derive the benefits of belonging (Ashmore, Deaux, and McLaughlin-Volpe 2004).

In this chapter we use the hybrid term "racial-ethnic identity." Although we recognize that this is a rather awkward term, we advocate its use in studies such as ours, when one but not the other of these terms may have been most salient for the adolescent respondents in different groups. To do otherwise is to oversimplify and perhaps even obscure our phenomena of interest.

RACIAL AND ETHNIC IDENTITY AS A DEVELOPMENTAL CONSTRUCT

One way of conceptualizing racial and ethnic identity has been through developmental models (Arce 1981; Chatman, Eccles, and Malanchuk, chapter 6, this volume; Cross 1971; Parham 1989; Phinney 1989; Thomas 1970; Vandiver et al. 2002). In this approach, the achievement of such an identity follows a series of development stages. In the revision of William E. Cross's 1971 theory of nigrescence (for example, Vandiver et al. 2002), he and his coauthors distinguish personal identity from group identity or reference-group orientation and posit that black identity is primarily a reference-group or social-identity variable. Thus, race can vary in salience for an individual just as it can vary from negative to positive in its meaning for him or her.

The revised theory describes four stages of black racial identities, each described by the overarching theme of the stage. The first stage, pre-encounter, is characterized by the absence of any significant concern for or consideration of one's racial-group membership. During the second stage, encounter, also described as pivotal in Latino racial-ethnic identity development, the individual has a transformative experience that causes a reexamination of the meaning of racial or ethnic identity. In the next stage, immersion-emersion, the individual might immerse him- or herself in intense black involvement with over-romanticization of the black experience. Or she or he might emerge as antiwhite and reject everything related to whites and their culture.

Internalization, the fourth and final stage of the revised model, is marked by high positive race salience.

Although Cross does not deal with adolescent development directly, the theory might be applied to adolescence, assuming that researchers can determine whether the progression through stages is contingent upon cognitive or perhaps social competence levels that might or might not be available to adolescents.

Phinney (1989; Phinney and Kohatsu 1997) describes a three-stage ethnic-identity development process similar in its outlines to James E. Marcia's (1966) four-stage model of the development of identity based on Erik Erikson's theory of identity development. Phinney postulates that the process begins with individuals showing no exploration of ethnicity, reflected in either a lack of interest (ethnic-identity diffusion) or a premature adoption of an ethnic identity based on the opinions of others (ethnic-identity foreclosure). This first stage, unexamined ethnic identity, parallels two of Marcia's stages—diffusion and foreclosure. Phinney's second stage, ethnic identity search, parallels Marcia's moratorium stage, in which the individual actively seeks to understand the meaning of ethnicity for him- or herself. In the final stage, achieved ethnic identity, the person has reached a clear, confident sense of his or her own ethnicity.

Robert Sellers and his colleagues (Sellers et al. 1998), in their Multidimensional Model of Racial Identity (MMRI), integrate the two predominant approaches to racial identity—the universal approach of researchers such as Phinney (1989) and theories such as Cross's (1971) that emphasize the role of unique African American experience in identity formation—in a four-dimensional model that seeks to better explain how identity is reflected in the behavior of African Americans. Distinctive here is the fact that this model is designed not to describe the development of identity but to describe the significance and nature of racial identity at a particular point in the individual's life. Of the four dimensions, "racial salience" and "racial centrality" tell us what significance individuals attach to race when defining themselves. "Racial regard" and "racial ideology," on the other hand, tell us the meaning of this attachment.

For those who study adolescents, a developmental approach is important for tracing the emergence of group identities across this developmental period. Work such as that of Sellers, done primarily with those beyond adolescence, focuses on the attachment to and meaning of blackness and therefore is an important complement to a developmental focus on how identity emerges. The next stage for those of us who study adolescent development is to work toward an integration of these two perspectives, to achieve a deeper understanding of where an adolescent is at the moment, and what the depth of his or her attachment and feeling is at that particular stage. Such a deepening would contribute greatly to our understanding of whether categories, "stages" or "levels" of racial-ethnic identity function as risk or protective factors, a discussion to which we turn next.

RACIAL AND ETHNIC IDENTITY AS REFLECTIONS OF COPING SKILLS

The earliest work on racial identity assumed that feeling good about being a member of one's racial group would predict positive mental health, and racial-self hatred would predict the reverse (for example, Cross 1971). The empirical evidence, particularly among adolescents, does not provide overwhelming support (perhaps because racial-ethnic identity was so broadly conceptualized and measured). Nonetheless there are enough positive findings, including those from a recent meta-analytic review (Bat-Chava, Pahl, and Steen, under review) to encourage the continued effort to understand how and under what circumstances racial-ethnic identity functions as a coping resource for youth under duress.

Phinney (1989) found that adolescents at the earliest, unexamined, stage of development had significantly more negative self-concept scores than those in more advanced stages (Phinney 1989). This finding was true across African American, Asian American, and Latino subgroups. Two additional studies of diverse youth (Martinez and Dukes 1997; Phinney, Cantu, and Kurtz 1997) produced similar findings: higher stages of ethnic identity were related to higher levels of protective factors such as self-esteem, purpose in life, and self-confidence.

With regard to mental health outcome measures, higher levels of racial-ethnic identity have been associated with lower levels of depression (Crocker et al. 1994). Further, connection to one's ethnic group (for example, respondent felt close to friends because of similar race or ethnicity) has been shown to protect youth from the impact of racial discrimination, increase protective factors such as psychological resilience, and reduce the risk of outcomes such as involvement in problem behaviors (Shelton et al., chapter 5, this volume). In two related studies of problem behaviors among African American adolescents, racial identity was related to greater ability to cope with stressors such as lack of friends and difficult environmental conditions (McCreary, Slavin, and Berry 1996; Miller and MacIntosh 1999). In a final example, Cuban American adolescents who rejected their roots and became highly Americanized showed poorer psychological adjustment than their peers who retained a bicultural ethnic identity (Szapocznik, Kurtines, and Fernandez 1980).

Though it seems clear that the protective role of positive features of racial-ethnic identity deserves further exploration, at the same time it must be understood that not all youths who are at the initial stage of identity development suffer poor psychological health (Cross 1991). We would argue, rather, that for an adolescent beyond a certain developmental level, being at this identity stage would represent a risk factor that could lead to poor psychological outcome should she or he encounter insurmountable stress. It is also clear across studies that the strength of relationships between risk and outcome varies considerably across adolescent subgroups. For example, in the Phinney et al. (1997) examination of ethnic identity as a predictor of self-esteem, there were two significant predictors for African Americans, ethnic identity and grade-point average, which accounted for only 8.5 percent of the variance in their regression analyses. For Latinos, four predictors were significant (ethnic identity, other-group attitudes, gender, and grade-point average) and accounted for 16 percent of the variance. For white students, ethnic identity and identity as an American, along with gender, accounted for 48 percent of the variance. These results provide further evidence that the meaning of the construct varies across subgroups and that we need to be clear what dimensions of racial-ethnic identity we are measuring.

RACIAL AND ETHNIC IDENTITY AS MULTIDIMENSIONAL CONSTRUCTS

Empirical investigations have contributed to our understanding of the dimensions that make up the racial-ethnic–identity construct. In one, for example, Steve Hinkle,

Laurie A. Taylor, and D. Lee Fox-Cardamone (1989) delineated three dimensions: affective, cognitive, and individual–group interdependence. In another study conducted in Canada, six factors made up attitudes toward ethnicity: attitudes toward religion, endogamy, language, ethnic organizations, parochial education, and friends (Driedger 1975). Different patterns of identification on the six factors emerged for different ethnic groups. The construction of Phinney's Multigroup Ethnic Identity Measure (Phinney 1992), based on both social identity (Tajfel and Turner 1986) and developmental (Erikson 1968) thinking, was based on three theoretically derived components (affirmation and belonging, ethnic-identity achievement, and ethnic behaviors). However, research with over five thousand middle school students resulted in a two-factor structure, one labeled "affirmation, belonging and commitment," and a second labeled "exploration and ethnic behaviors" (Roberts et al. 1999; Yancey, Aneshensel and Driscoll 2001).

The need to examine the multidimensional nature of racial and ethnic identity is stressed in theoretical literature as well. In a review of racial-identity measures, A. Kathleen Burlew and Lori R. Smith (1991) point out that different measures assess different components of identity and that the choice of an identity measure reflects the particular dimension of racial identity that taps the researcher's interest. In addition, they note that relationships with other variables (for example, self-esteem, academic achievement) may vary depending on the dimension of identity measured.

The developmental and multidimensional conceptual approaches to racial and ethnic identity are, of course, not mutually exclusive. Indeed, our own findings presented here represent strong support for a multidimensional conceptualization and some suggestions that, at least for some dimensions, there are developmental processes involved in how the dimension is expressed in a given individual.

OUR OWN WORK ON RACIAL AND ETHNIC IDENTITY

In the remainder of this chapter, we will present the results from three sets of data analyses of responses given by youths in the Adolescent Pathways Project (APP). The APP is a longitudinal study of youths who attend schools that have high concentrations of poor children in Baltimore, Washington, D.C., and New York City. (See Seidman 1991 for further details about design, sample, and procedures.) When we began the study, we focused on recruiting students from schools that had high proportions of students eligible for reduced-fee or free lunch. We were able to find black and Latino students in schools where 80 percent or more of the students were so identified. In recruiting white students, we found them in schools where no more than 60 percent of the students were eligible, as would be expected from general patterns of racial and economic segregation in the United States (Massey and Denton 1993; Duncan 1994).

Our sample consisted of 1,130 adolescents at the second wave of data collection when the racial-ethnic identity measure had been administered to all youths. At this time participants were either at the end of their first year of junior high school (the young cohort, N = 752) or at the end of their first year of senior high school (the older cohort, N = 378). The inclusion in our sample of youths in two age groups allowed us to explore the developmental question. Participants ranged in age from ten to eighteen;

60 percent were female; 27 percent were black (Caribbean American and African American), 24 percent were white (primarily Greek and Italian American), and 38 percent were Latino (primarily Dominican, Puerto Rican, and Central or South American).

Our measure of racial-ethnic identity was developed to allow us to assess the degree to which racial-ethnic identity is a multidimensional or developmental construct. The measure included two parts. First, using an open-ended format, adolescents were asked to self-describe their race or ethnicity. Adolescents were primed to use responses that were based on race, ethnicity, cultural background, country of origin, and religion. The respondents used as many or as few descriptive words as they wished. Consistent with their instructions, 80 percent of the adolescents categorized themselves primarily on the basis of their country of origin (for example, Dominican Republic), religion (for example, Catholic), race (for example, white), or color (for example, tan). However, about 20 percent of respondents did not provide an ethnic or racial label, but instead used a label or labels inconsistent with the instructions (for example, "cute" and "athlete"). It should be noted that in a subsequent analysis, we discovered that whether adolescents use a racial-ethnic label(s) to respond to this request for self-description was significantly and positively correlated with self-esteem (Bat-Chava, Pahl, and Steen, under review).

For the second part of this measure we adapted an unpublished measure using twenty items to assess different features of ethnic identity (Phinney, personal communication, December 31, 1987). We selected and adapted nine items that seemed to be important for our study of pathways to adaptive and maladaptive outcomes in a racially and ethnically diverse sample of urban youths. The selection and adaptation of items was geared to age appropriateness and elimination of overlapping content. We also reworded the items to allow youths to choose to respond from either their racial- or their ethnic-identity frame of reference. Our aim was to uncover specific dimensions of racial and ethnic identity relevant to the study of pathways to academic and psychosocial outcomes. Examples of items are: "I talk with my friends about our racial/ethnic group and how it affects our lives"; "I'm confused about my racial/ethnic group and what it means to me"; and "I feel good about being in my racial/ethnic group" (see table 7.1). Adolescents were asked to respond to the nine statements on a 4-point scale, from "Not at all true" to "Very true."

In our analyses, we first explored the degree to which our measure of racial-ethnic identity is multidimensional in structure. We were interested in the structure of the measure, both within and across racial-ethnic, gender, and age subgroups. In addition, we addressed an important and too often overlooked issue in the study of development—the relationship between social contexts, racial-ethnic identity, and key developmental outcomes.

COMPONENTS OF AND TYPES OF RACIAL-ETHNIC IDENTITY IN URBAN YOUTHS

We began with an exploration of the structure of a set of items measuring behaviors characterizing racial and ethnic identity. We searched for both the components that would best describe reliable variation in racial-ethnic identity, and the way the

Table 7.1 Component Loadings, Means, Standard Deviations, and Alphas for
Racial- and Ethnic-Identity Items and Subscales

	Prominence	Group-Esteem	Ambivalent Ethnic Attitudes
Racial- and ethnic-identity items			
1. I have talked with my parents about race and ethnicity.	.82		
2. I have talked with friends about race and ethnicity.	.75		
3. I have thought about whether group membership will affect my future goals.	.71		
4. I have been taught about my background.	.63		
5. I am comfortable with my own group.		.79	
6. I feel good about my race or ethnicity.		.76	
7. I will raise my children to be aware of their race and ethnicity.		.75	
8. I would prefer to belong to another group.			.86
9. I am confused about my group.			.85
Percentage variance	35.30	19.50	10.20
Mean	2.59	3.41	1.66
Standard Deviation	.87	.72	.87
∝	.76	.71	.51[a]

Source: Authors' compilation.
[a]This statistic is a bivariate correlation coefficient.

composition of the components might differ across a sample of poor urban youths. We used factor-analytic techniques to describe this component structure (Bat-Chava et al. 1995). The nine racial-ethnic identity items were subjected to a principal-components analysis with Varimax rotation for the entire sample. A three-component solution, accounting for 65 percent of the variance, was derived (see table 7.1). The first component, that we labeled "Exploration" (also referred to in the literature as "search"), comprised four items that measure the degree to which an adolescent thought about and talked with others about his or her race and ethnicity. "Group-esteem," also referred to in the literature as "pride," comprised three items that measure how good and comfortable the adolescent felt about his or her racial or ethnic group. Finally, "conflicted ethnic attitudes" comprised two items that measure the degree to which an adolescent preferred to belong to another racial or ethnic group or was confused about his or her group. The same analysis was performed separately within each race or ethnicity, gender, and cohort subgroup. Interestingly, in each case the resulting component structure was virtually identical. Consequently, three scales were created on the basis of this structure by applying unit weights to the items and averaging them. "Exploration" was highly correlated with group-esteem ($r = .46$, $p < .001$), and, to a lesser extent with conflicted ethnic attitudes ($r = .24$, $p < .001$); the group-esteem and conflicted attitudes correlation was low but significant as well ($r = -.06$, $p < .05$).

Although the dimensional structure was consistent across all subgroup analyses, the profile of mean-level responses across subgroups did vary in meaningful ways. Older adolescents had higher group-esteem and less ambivalent attitudes than younger ones, and blacks and Latinos reported higher ambivalent attitudes than whites. In addition, older white adolescents manifested the least ambivalence: less than older black and Latino adolescents, and less than younger white adolescents.

IDENTITY IN CONTEXT

Having explored the issues involved in the conceptualization and structure of racial-ethnic identity, we are now ready to turn to the study of racial-ethnic identity in context. The primary question is whether, and for whom, dimensions of racial-ethnic identity such as having a positive feeling about one's group vary in settings that differ in racial and ethnic composition. Previous research shows that racial congruence (that is, consonance, or similarity) between individuals and residents in one's neighborhood (Tweed et al. 1990) or students in one's school (Rosenberg 1979) has positive effects on psychological well-being for black respondents. There is also evidence that positively identifying with one's racial or ethnic group is directly associated with well-being (for example, Bat-Chava, Pahl, and Steen, under review); (Shelton et al., chapter 5, this volume). Current theorizing along with empirical findings that racial-ethnic identity accounts for significant but small amounts of variance for some groups suggests that rather than considering how group identity directly affects psychological well-being, we should examine how group identity in combination with other constructs is related to various outcomes of interest (Banaji and Prentice 1994; Kinket and Verkuyten 1997; Phinney and Kohatsu 1997). We speculate that in conditions under which one is in the minority, racial-ethnic identity becomes more salient and therefore more relevant to positive outcomes.

We describe two sets of analyses (Allen et al., in preparation) in which we look at how racial or ethnic identity and the racial and ethnic composition of settings in which youths find themselves are related to psychological well-being. We examine the effects of the interaction of social context (neighborhood and school racial composition) and racial-ethnic identity on depressive symptoms. Depressive symptoms among adolescents are of acute interest, given that the prevalence of depression increases dramatically during adolescence (Fleming and Offord 1990). Population studies report that at any given point, 10 to 15 percent of the child and adolescent population have symptoms of depression (Smucker et al. 1986). Given the relationship between mood disorders such as depression and suicidal behavior, these numbers are cause for alarm and provide strong motivation to examine the role of context and racial-ethnic identity in clarifying how these symptoms vary across adolescent subgroups.

The Neighborhood Context

Work by Urie Bronfenbrenner (1979), Christopher Jencks and Susan Mayer (1990), William Julius Wilson (1987), and others has spurred interest in the effects of communities and neighborhoods and family processes on child and adolescent development (for example, Brooks-Gunn, Duncan and Aber 1997). The first wave of recent research has examined the direct effects of such neighborhood factors on child, youth, and adult outcomes, net of family effects (Crane 1991). The second wave of research has increasingly examined indirect effects of neighborhood factors on developmental outcomes via family processes—for example, home provision of resources—(Duncan, Brooks-Gunn and Klebanov 1994); and also the moderating influence of neighborhood contexts on the relationship between other risk factors—for example, harsh parenting, poor social problem-solving skills—and youth outcomes (Aber and Jones 1995; Steinberg and Cauffman 1995). The current, third, wave brings advanced statistical techniques to bear on the problem of separating the effects of multiple contexts, such as family and neighborhood influences, through multilevel analyses of designs in which time can be nested within individual youths, who can be nested within their various contexts (Gershoff and Aber 2005) and brings an occasional powerful experiment that circumvents the potential problem of families selecting themselves into certain neighborhoods through randomly assigning families to more advantaged neighborhoods (for example, Leventhal and Brooks-Gunn 2000). Because of this chapter's theoretical interest in racial and ethnic identity, we chose to examine racial-ethnic composition as our neighborhood effect. We looked at how neighborhood composition was related to depressive symptoms directly as well as in combination with various components of racial-ethnic identity.

For these analyses we included Adolescent Pathways Project youths from New York City and Washington, D.C., whose addresses could be geo-coded into census tracts. Of these adolescents, 217 were black, 361 were Latino, and 236 were white; they ranged in age from nine to seventeen, and 60 percent were female.

We used the measure of racial-ethnic identity described earlier. Our outcome measure, depressive symptoms, was measured using fourteen items adapted from the Youth Self Report (Achenbach and Edelbrock 1987; M = 1.42, SD = .35, alpha = .81). For each item the response choices were "not true," "true," or "very often or often true." This measure includes items describing feeling lonely, worthless, sad, and suicidal. The measure of neighborhood ethnic-racial congruence was derived from census data. It consisted of the percentage of residents in the adolescent's neighborhood, defined by census tract, who shared his or her race-ethnicity. This variable was distributed very differently within the three ethnic-racial groups in our sample. White adolescents lived in the most homogeneous, or congruent, neighborhoods. About 90 percent of them lived in neighborhoods where 80 to 100 percent of residents were from their racial group. The Latino and black youths lived in more racially and ethnically heterogeneous neighborhoods.

We conducted three hierarchical regression analyses, one for each racial-ethnic group, in order to examine the interaction of the three components of racial-ethnic identity with the neighborhood racial-ethnic congruence score and the relationship of these interactions to depressive symptoms. Because depressive symptoms were expected to vary with age and gender in adolescence (Allen and Mitchell 1998), we included gender and age as control variables in the first step. In the second and third

Figure 7.1   Neighborhood Racial-Ethnic Congruence Moderates the
Relationship Between Depressive Symptoms and
Group-Esteem for Black Adolescents

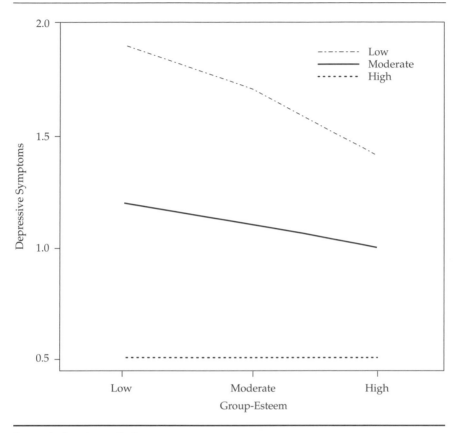

Source: Authors' compilation.

steps, neighborhood ethnic-racial congruence and the three racial-ethnic identity components were entered, respectively. Our primary focuses, the interaction of neighborhood racial-ethnic congruence with components of racial-ethnic identity, were entered in the fourth and final step.

For black adolescents, neighborhood ethnic congruence predicted depressive symptoms, such that higher ethnic congruence was related to lower levels of symptoms. In addition, the interactive effect of neighborhood racial congruence by group-esteem had a significant effect on depressive symptoms. In neighborhoods where youths were most racially congruent, group-esteem was not differentially associated with depressive symptoms. Conversely, in neighborhoods in which the youth's group membership was not congruent with the residential racial-ethnic makeup, group-esteem was directly associated with depressive symptoms, such that youths with low group-esteem manifested the highest levels of depressive symptoms (see figure 7.1).

Figure 7.2 Neighborhood Racial-Ethnic Congruence Moderates the Relationship Between Depressive Symptoms and Group-Esteem for Latino Adolescents

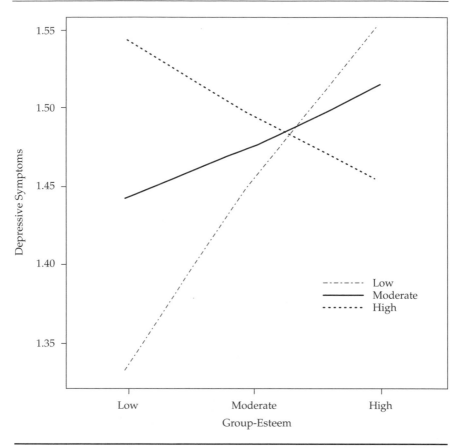

Source: Authors' compilation.

Within the Latino group, girls reported more depressive symptoms than boys. More ambivalent ethnic attitudes were associated with higher levels of depressive symptoms for the Latino group as a whole. In addition, the interactive effect of neighborhood racial-ethnic congruence by group-esteem had a significant relationship to depressive symptoms. The highest levels of symptoms were predicted by a combination of high levels of group-esteem and living in neighborhoods with low levels of racial-ethnic congruence (see figure 7.2). This finding is in contrast to the findings with black adolescents in their neighborhood, where the highest levels of depressive symptoms were among youth with *low* group-esteem who lived in neighborhoods with low levels of racial-ethnic congruence. Perhaps having high group-esteem but living in a neighborhood where one is in the minority, and especially, as a Latino, is a less visible minority than members of ethnic groups with a black racial background, creates an internal conflict between group pride and ability to express group pride. Thus, the youths may feel group pride, but when the group membership is not recognized and validated by enough of the surrounding community, the youths become depressed, wishing for people with whom to share that group pride.

To explore this conflict hypothesis we examined the interactive effect of neighborhood racial-ethnic congruence and racial-ethnic identity separately for Latino adolescents who spoke only English and those who spoke primarily Spanish. If our conflict hypothesis is correct, we should find this conflict present for teens who have been socialized in a more Latin culture—who still primarily speak Spanish—but not for those who speak only English. Our speculation was that the English speakers have more ways to connect to their surrounding community than monolingual Spanish speakers.

We used a questionnaire about the use of English and of one's native language in five different situations: reading and speaking; speaking before the start of formal education; speaking at home; thinking; and speaking with friends. Items were scored on a 5-point Likert scale, averaged, then dichotomized using a median split (median = 3.4). The above hierarchical regression analysis was conducted again separately for Latinos who spoke primarily or exclusively English and those who spoke primarily Spanish across the five situations. As hypothesized, the interaction effect predicting depressive symptoms was significant for the Latino adolescents who spoke primarily Spanish but not for those who spoke only English (see figures 7.3 and 7.4). For those who spoke primarily English, it is remarkable that all levels of group-esteem show the same positive relationship between neighborhood composition and depressive symptoms, such that higher congruence was related to higher levels of depressive symptoms. Finding themselves in neighborhoods with high proportions of Latino residents, they may show symptoms of depression as a result of not feeling "Latino enough."

White adolescent girls reported more depressive symptoms than white adolescent boys, and higher racial-ethnic exploration was associated with lower levels of symptoms. Racial-ethnic congruence, though, was not related to symptoms of depression as either a main effect or in interaction with racial-ethnic identity, perhaps owing to the low variability in the whites' neighborhood racial-congruity scores.

The School Context

Because whites live primarily in homogeneous neighborhoods whereas blacks and Latinos in our sample came from neighborhoods that were much more socially heterogeneous, we explored other contexts, where the values of our congruence variables might differ for our three groups. We settled on the school setting, where at least half of our students of color found themselves in the majority. Conversely, our white students, dominant in their neighborhoods, were not so clearly dominant in their schools and indeed were sometimes members of the smallest group present.

Data about the racial makeup of the schools were available only for youths from New York City. Participants for whom these data were available were 151 black, 313 Latino, and 205 white adolescents ranging in age from nine to seventeen; 60 percent were female. School racial-ethnic congruence was derived from New York City Board of Education records. The variable was the percentage of students in the adolescent's

Figure 7.3 Neighborhood Racial-Ethnic Congruence Moderates the
Relationship Between Depressive Symptoms and
Group-Esteem in Latinos Who Speak Spanish

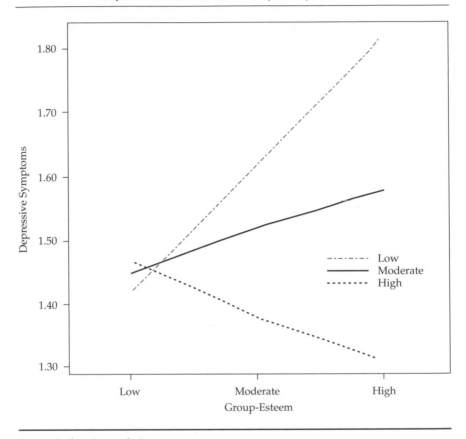

Source: Authors' compilation.

school who shared his or her race or ethnicity. Because of the Adolescent Pathways
Project's sampling frame, most black and Latino adolescents attended schools where
the majority of students shared their race-ethnicity. Most white adolescents, however,
attended schools where they were in the minority.

Examination of the racial-ethnic composition of New York City public schools,
which our adolescents attended, showed that about half of the black and Latino students attended schools in which 90 to 100 percent of the other students belonged to
the same group. Most white adolescents in our sample (about 60 percent), on the
other hand, attended schools where students from other groups constituted about 50
to 60 percent of the student body. That is, in no case did white adolescents attend
schools with an overwhelming majority of white students. This presents a picture
quite different from the neighborhood data. Whereas almost all white adolescents lived
in neighborhoods that were overwhelmingly white, almost none of them attended
schools where they made up more than half the student body. And where black and

Figure 7.4   Neighborhood Racial-Ethnic Congruence Moderates the
Relationship Between Depressive Symptoms and
Group-Esteem in Latinos Who Do Not Speak Spanish

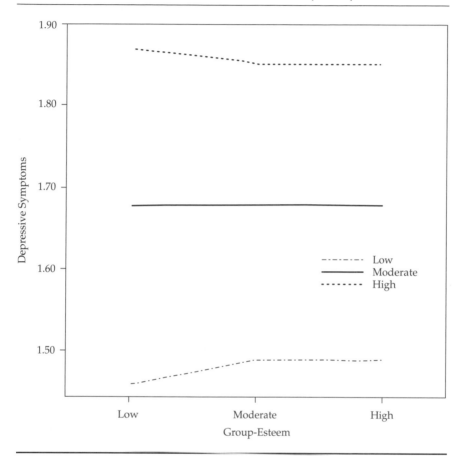

Source: Authors' compilation.

Latino adolescents lived in more heterogeneous neighborhoods, at least half of them attended schools where theirs was the majority group.

Thus, the relationship of racial-ethnic identity to symptoms of depression was assessed again in the context of one's ethnic-racial congruence with the composition of one's school peers. Most studies that have examined such relationships have included either black samples, or both black and white students. Earlier studies of the effect of school racial-ethnic composition on psychological well-being found that African Americans who attend segregated schools have higher self-esteem than those who attend integrated schools (see, for example, Busk, Ford, and Schulman 1973), and participate more in extracurricular activities (Trent and McPartland 1982). This finding is exhibited consistently from elementary school (Hunt and Hunt 1977) through junior high school (Busk, Ford, and Schulman 1973), high school (Rosenberg and Simmons

1972), and college (Gurin and Epps 1975). In our sample, we have the opportunity to update these findings (from the 1970s to the 1990s) and extend the examination to other groups.

Hierarchical regression analyses, parallel to those conducted for neighborhood context, were again conducted separately within each racial-ethnic group. For black adolescents there was one significant effect that is consistent with prior literature. Higher school racial congruence was associated with lower levels of depressive symptoms. Among Latinos, adolescent girls reported higher levels of depressive symptoms, and adolescents with higher levels of conflicted attitudes had higher levels of symptoms as well.

For white adolescents, exploration was negatively related to symptoms of depression in that more exploration was associated with fewer symptoms. In addition, the interactive effect of school racial congruence and group-esteem was associated with depressive symptoms, such that in the high levels of school racial congruence, group-esteem did not affect depression. In the low levels of school congruence, on the other hand, low levels of group-esteem were associated with higher levels of depressive symptoms (see figure 7.5).

SUMMARY

It is noteworthy that the only main effect for the racial-ethnic composition of settings occurred for black youths, in both the neighborhood and school contexts. Black adolescents who resided in neighborhoods or attended schools with which they were less congruent, that is, in more heterogeneous settings, reported higher rates of symptoms of depression. This is consistent with Dan L. Tweed et al.'s (1990) findings regarding the effect of neighborhood congruence on depression among black adults in Baltimore. School effects are also consistent with the previously reviewed literature, showing better adjustment for black students attending black schools (for example, Beers 1973; Rosenberg 1979) than for those attending more heterogeneous educational settings, effects that are attributed to the impact of racial tension on students' adjustment.

Interactions of social context by racial-ethnic identity only occurred for one dimension of ethnic identity: group-esteem. This effect occurred for blacks and Latinos in neighborhoods, and for white adolescents in the context of schools. The interaction effects for blacks and Latinos in the neighborhood, however, were in the opposite direction from each other.

Except for the level of depressive symptoms (white levels higher than black), this interaction in school among whites replicates that found for black adolescents in neighborhoods. Group-esteem did not affect depressive symptoms for white adolescents in schools with high levels of racial congruence. For youths in schools with low levels of congruence, however, low group-esteem was associated with higher levels of depressive symptoms. Looked at another way, for white adolescents who attend racially congruent schools, group-esteem is not related to depressive symptoms. But in schools where students have little racial-ethnic similarity to most of the other students, group-esteem is directly associated with depressive symptoms, such that youth with low group-esteem manifest the highest levels of symptoms. Low group-esteem

Figure 7.5   School Racial-Ethnic Congruence Moderates the Relationship
Between Depressive Symptoms and Group-Esteem for
European American Adolescents

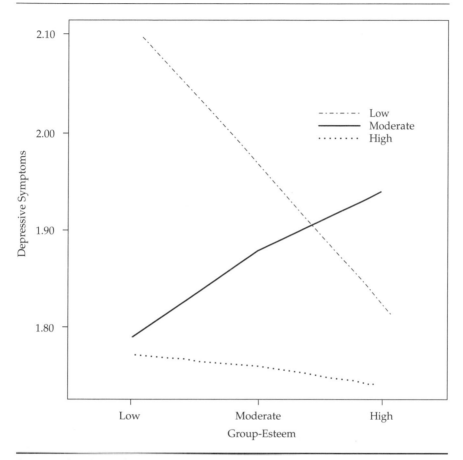

Source: Authors' compilation.

in noncongruent schools places these white inner-city adolescents at greater risk for depressive symptoms.

In another study we examined racial-ethnic identity among students making the transition from junior to senior high school (French et al. 2000). Within each racial-ethnic group, we examined the impact of changes in both peer and staff racial-ethnic congruence on students' group-esteem and exploration. For predicting group-esteem, racial-ethnic congruence with staff was significant for black and European American subsamples. However, the relationships were in opposing directions. For black students, as racial-ethnic congruence with staff decreased, their group-esteem increased (in other words, the fewer black staff members there were, the higher their group-esteem). For these students, the reduction in racial-ethnic congruence may have served as a consciousness-raising event, or "encounter," and they coped with this change by reportedly feeling better about their group. There was an opposite effect for whites:

their group-esteem rose as racial-ethnic staff congruence remained constant across the transition. The only significant relationship for racial-ethnic exploration was that as European Americans' racial-ethnic congruence with peers decreased and they found themselves a smaller proportion of the school population, exploration increased.

Whites in the United States do not often experience what it is like to be in the minority. Large urban public school systems provide one of the few places where that occurs. Here we find that when a youth is part of a minority—a black adolescent in the neighborhood, a white adolescent in school—low group-esteem puts him or her at greater risk for symptoms of depression. These results highlight the importance of minority and majority statuses within context. Group-esteem had no effect on adolescents' depressive symptoms when they are the majority ethnicity in a given context. But it did have a strong effect when adolescents were in the minority. Thus, even though white adolescents belong to the majority group in the larger society, in their schools they make up the minority of students, a fact that makes their race or ethnicity more salient to them, and makes the congruence with their fellow students important in determining psychological well-being. Whites who experienced a decrease in peer congruence across the transition from junior to senior high school also increased their exploration of the meaning of their racial-ethnic identities, another clear indication of heightened salience. Black students who experienced a decrease in staff congruence during the transition saw an increase in group-esteem. Possibly the "shock" of the change in social composition of school staff represented a confrontation that led to a focus on and increase in salience of the elements of group-esteem on the part of these students.

CONCLUSION

In this chapter we have endeavored to make a case for a multidimensional and contextual approach to the understanding of racial and ethnic identity. We demonstrated that our nine-item measure consists of three interpretable components that were found consistently across the three racial-ethnic groups in our sample of youth. In addition, we showed that ethnic-racial identity interacts with context (ethnic-racial composition of school or neighborhood) to affect depressive symptoms. Nonetheless, several questions remain unanswered about the combined roles of ethnic-racial identity and context on the lives of youths. In the remainder of this chapter, we list several questions and propose ways to study them.

Despite our relatively large sample, we were still limited in the degree to which we could explore differences among racial-ethnic and gender subgroups of youths. For example, we were not able to examine separately the effect of identity and context on subgroups within the Latino youths, such as Puerto Ricans and Dominican Americans, groups that have different histories and relationships with U.S. mainstream society. Nor were we able to examine how racial-ethnic identity functions for black and Latino males and females. Future studies could intensively sample male and female adolescents from one race or ethnic group with specific attention to subgroups, and examine the interactive effect of ethnic or racial identity, gender, and context on these various subgroups.

We would also like to see attention paid explicitly to the differential impact of racial identities, separate from that of ethnic identities. Perhaps whites, as members of the dominant group, do not consider their racial identity to be salient or important. If given the opportunity to address both race and ethnicity, we may find, as did Mary Waters (1990), that for this group, ethnic identity is more salient than racial identity. Meanwhile, blacks are being increasingly "ethnicized," as distinctions between African Americans, Caribbean Americans, and African immigrants are made more and more frequently (Epstein, Williams, Botvin 2002; Ross Leadbeater and Way 1996). If asked about both race and ethnicity, what would members of various black groups report at various developmental stages? How this pattern of relative salience might unfold developmentally could provide important answers to our questions about risk and protective factors. We would speculate that race and much of its "baggage" will constitute a risk factor and ethnic identification a source of protection. Research with college students showed that some dimensions of racial identity (for example, racial centrality) change with the context while other dimensions (for example, racial ideology) are stable across contexts (Shelton and Sellers 2000). When extended to younger adolescents, such research may shed light on how and when aspects of racial-ethnic identity function as determinants or moderators of psychological and social adjustment. Distinguishing between racial and ethnic identities for white and black respondents will necessitate a somewhat different methodology than that used in the current study. Rather than letting research participants choose identities spontaneously, participants would be directed to think specifically about their race or ethnicity and to respond to the identity questionnaire twice, once while considering their race and once while considering their ethnicity. Alternatively, the differential effect of race or ethnicity could be studied in an experimental paradigm where the salience of either race or ethnicity is manipulated, and the effect of the salient identity on answers to a racial-ethnic identity questionnaire is assessed. These questions can also be pursued ethnographically, in detailed questioning of selected youths.

Other questions require the careful selection of diverse samples of youths that vary in developmental level in order to, for example, investigate the emergence and development of race and ethnic ideas regarding the self. Katheryn A. Ocampo, Martha E. Bernal and George P. Knight (1993) report that children's ideas of racial constancy develop before their ideas of ethnic constancy. To date, however, no study has addressed these constancy and relative salience questions longitudinally.

Finally, additional indicators of well-being need to be considered. In the current study we used depressive symptoms as the outcome of interest. Other variables that have been studied as outcomes or correlates of ethnic identity are academic achievement (Chapell and Overton 2002; Steele and Aronson 1995), peer relationships (Hamm 2000), and substance abuse (Scheier et al. 1997). But *none* of these studies considered the combined effect of ethnic-racial identity and context on these variables. Assessing the combined effect of ethnic-racial identity and context on these important psychological and social indicators of adjustment would add to our understanding of these phenomena, and could lead to new ideas about more effective interventions.

The demographic predictions for our country and increasing interracial and interethnic contact around the globe lead us to conclude that questions about the role of ethnicity and race in the development of social identity of children, adolescents, and adults will only become more pressing over the next several decades. As the contexts of individual development become more varied and more diverse, those of us interested in the process of development and in the promotion of coping and well-being need to understand what the protective mechanisms are for healthy adjustment as we are increasingly confronted with others' views of ourselves.

This research was supported in part by grants from the National Institute of Mental Health (MIH43084) and the Carnegie Corporation (B4850), awarded to Edward Seidman, J. Lawrence Aber, LaRue Allen, and Christina Mitchell.

REFERENCES

Aber, J. Lawrence, and Stephanie M. Jones. 1995. "Neighborhood Influences on Adolescent Antisocial Behavior and Psychological Symptoms." Paper presented at the biennial meeting of the Society for Research in Child Development. Indianapolis (March 30–April 2).

Aber, J. Lawrence, Stephanie Jones, Jennifer Cohen. 2000. "The Impact of Poverty on the Mental Health and Development of Very Young Children." In *Handbook of Infant Mental Health,* edited by Charles H. Zeanah Jr. 2nd edition. New York: Guilford Press.

Aboud, Frances E. 1987. "The Development of Ethnic Self-Identification and Attitudes." In *Children's Ethnic Socialization,* edited by Jean S. Phinney and Mary J. Rotheram. Newbury Park, Calif.: Sage.

Achenbach, Thomas M., and Craig Edelbrock. 1987. "Manual for the Youth Self-Report and Profile." Burlington: University of Vermont, Department of Psychiatry.

Akbar, Maysa, John W. Chambers Jr., and Vetta L. Saunders Thompson. 2001. "Racial Identity, Africentric Values, and Self-Esteem in Jamaican Children." *Journal of Black Psychology* 27(3): 341–58.

Allen, LaRue, Jennifer Astuto, Stephanie M. Jones, J. Lawrence Aber, Edward Seidman, and Yael Bat-Chava. In preparation. "Racial-Ethnic Identity in Neighborhood and School Context: Longitudinal Effects of Depression Among African American, Latino, and European American Urban Adolescents."

Allen, LaRue, and Christina Mitchell. 1998. "Racial and Ethnic Differences in Patterns of Problematic and Adaptive Development: An Epidemiological Review." In *Studying Minority Adolescents: Conceptual, Methodological, and Theoretical Issues,* edited by Vonnie C. McLoyd and Laurence Steinberg. Mahwah, N.J.: Erlbaum.

Arce, Carlos. 1981. "A Reconsideration of Chicano Culture and Identity." *Daedalus* 110: 177–92.

Asher, Steven R., and Vernon L. Allen. 1969. "Racial Preference and Social Comparison Processes." *Journal of Special Issues* 25(1): 157–66.

Ashmore, Richard D., Kay Deaux, and Tracy McLaughlin-Volpe. 2004. "An Organizing Framework for Collective Identity: Articulation and Significance of Multidimensionality." *Psychological Bulletin* 130(1): 80–114.

Banaji, Mahzarin R., and Deborah A. Prentice. 1994. "The Self in Social Contexts." *Annual Review of Psychology* 45: 297–332.

Bat-Chava, Yael, LaRue Allen, Edward Seidman, J. Lawrence Aber, and Ana Maria Ventura. 1995. "Ethnic Identity Among Black, Latino, and European American Urban Adolescents: Nomothetic and Idiographic Approaches." Unpublished manuscript. New York University.

Bat-Chava, Yael, K. Pahl, and E. M. Steen. Under review. "Ethnic Identity and Self-Esteem: A Meta-Analytic Review."

Beers, Joan S. 1973. "Self-Esteem and School Interest of Black Fifth-Grade Pupils as a Function of Demographic Categorization." Paper presented at a meeting of the Eastern Psychological Association. Washington, D.C. (May).

Bronfenbrenner, Urie. 1979. *The Ecology of Human Development: Experiments by Nature and Design.* Cambridge, Mass.: Harvard University Press.

Brooks-Gunn, Jeanne, Greg Duncan, and J. Lawrence Aber, eds. 1997. *Neighborhood Poverty: Context and Consequences for Children.* Volumes 1 and 2. New York: Russell Sage Foundation.

Burlew, A. Kathleen, and Lori R. Smith. 1991. "Measures of Racial Identity: An Overview and a Proposed Framework." *Journal of Black Psychology* 17(2): 53–71.

Busk, Patricia L., Robin C. Ford, and Jerome L. Schulman. 1973. "Effects of Schools' Racial Composition on the Self-Concept of Black and White Students." *Journal of Educational Research* 67(2): 57–63.

Chapell, Mark S., and Willis F. Overton. 2002. "Development of Logical Reasoning and the School Performance of African American Adolescents in Relation to Socioeconomic Status, Ethnic Identity, and Self-Esteem." *Journal of Black Psychology* 28(4): 295–317.

Clark, Kenneth B., and Mamie P. Clark. 1939. "The Development of Consciousness of the Self and the Emergence of Racial Identification in Negro Preschool Children." *Journal of Social Psychology* 10: 591–99.

Crane, Jonathan. 1991. "The Epidemic Theory of Ghettos and Neighborhood Effects on Dropping Out and Teenage Childbearing." *American Journal of Sociology* 96(5): 32–41.

Crocker, Jennifer, Riia Luhtanen, Bruce Blaine, and Stephanie Broadnax. 1994. "Collective Self-Esteem and Psychological Well-Being Among White, Black, and Asian College Students." *Personality and Social Psychology Bulletin* 20(5): 503–13.

Cross, William E. 1991. *Shades of Black: Diversity in African-American Identity.* Philadelphia: Temple University Press.

———. 1971. "Toward a Psychology of Black Liberation: The Negro-to-Black Conversion Experience." *Black World* 20(9): 13–27.

Driedger, Leo. 1975. "In Search of Cultural Identity Factors." *Canadian Review of Sociology and Anthropology* 12:150–62.

Duncan, Greg. 1994. "Families and Neighbors as Sources of Disadvantage in the Schooling Decisions of Black and White Adolescents." *American Journal of Education* 103(4): 20–53.

Duncan, Greg, Jeanne Brooks-Gunn, and Pamela Klebanov. 1994. "Economic Deprivation and Early Childhood Development." *Child Development* 65(2): 296–318.

Epstein, Jennifer, Christopher Williams, and Gilbert J. Botvin. 2002. "How Universal Are Social Influences to Drink and Problem Behaviors for Alcohol Use? A Test Comparing Urban African-American and Caribbean-American Adolescents." *Addictive Behaviors* 27(1): 75–86.

Erikson, Erik. 1968. *Childhood and Society.* New York: Norton.

Fleming, Jan E., and David R. Offord. 1990. "Epidemiology of Childhood Depressive Disorders: A Critical Review." *Journal of the American Academy of Child and Adolescent Psychiatry* 29(4): 571–80.

French, Sabine Elizabeth, Edward Seidman, LaRue Allen, and J. Lawrence Aber. 2000. "Racial/Ethnic Identity, Congruence with the Social Context, and the Transition to High School." *Journal of Adolescent Research* 15: 587–602.

Gershoff, Elizabeth T., and J. Lawrence Aber. 2005. "Neighborhoods and Schools: Contexts and Consequences for the Mental Health and Risk Behaviors of Children and Youth." In *Child Psychology: A Handbook of Contemporary Issues,* 2nd ed., edited by L. Balter and C. Tamis-LeMonda. New York: Psychology Press/Taylor & Francis.

Gurin, Patricia, and Edgar Epps. 1975. *Black Consciousness, Identity, and Achievement: A Study of Students in Historically Black Colleges.* New York: Wiley.

Hamm, Jill V. 2000. "Do Birds of a Feather Flock Together? The Variable Bases for African American, Asian American, and European American Adolescents' Selection of Similar Friends." *Developmental Psychology* 36(2): 209–19.

Helms, Janet E. 1989. "Eurocentrism Strikes in Strange Ways and in Unusual Places." *The Counseling Psychologist* 17(4): 643–47.

Hinkle, Steve, Laurie A. Taylor, and D. Lee Fox-Cardamone. 1989. "Intragroup Identification and Intergroup Differentiation: A Multicomponent Approach." *British Journal of Social Psychology* 28(4): 305–17.

Hunt, Janet G., and Larry L. Hunt. 1977. "Racial Inequality and Self-Image: Identity Maintenance as Identity Diffusion." *Sociology and Social Research* 61:539–59.

Jencks, Christopher, and Susan Mayer. 1990. "The Social Consequences of Growing Up in a Poor Neighborhood." In *Inner-City Poverty in the United States,* edited by Lawrence Lynn Jr. and Michael McGeary. Washington, D.C.: National Academy Press.

Kim-ju, Greg M., and Ramsay Liem. 2003. "Ethnic Self-Awareness as a Function of Ethnic Group Status, Group Composition, and Ethnic Identity Orientation." *Cultural Diversity and Ethnic Minority Psychology* 9(3): 289–302.

Kinket, Barbara, and Maykel Verkuyten. 1997. "Levels of Ethnic Self-Identification and Social Context." *Social Psychology Quarterly* 60(4): 338–54.

Leventhal, Tama, and Jeanne Brooks-Gunn. 2000. "The Neighborhoods They Live In: The Effects of Neighborhood Residence on Child and Adolescent Outcomes." *Psychological Bulletin* 126(2): 309–37.

Marcia, James E. 1966. "Development and Validation of Ego-Identity Status." *Journal of Personality and Social Psychology* 3(5): 551–58.

Martinez, Ruben O., and Richard L. Dukes. 1997. "The Effects of Ethnic Identity, Ethnicity, and Gender on Adolescent Well-Being." *Journal of Youth and Adolescence* 26(5): 503–16.

Massey, Douglas S., and Nancy A. Denton. 1993. *American Apartheid: Segregation and the Making of the Underclass.* Cambridge, Mass.: Harvard University Press.

McCreary, Micah L., Lesley A. Slavin, and Eloise J. Berry. 1996. "Predicting Problem Behavior and Self-Esteem Among African American Adolescents." *Journal of Adolescent Research* 11(2): 216–34.

McGuire, William J., Claire V. McGuire, Pamela Child, and Terry Fujioka. 1978. "Salience of Ethnicity in the Spontaneous Self-Concept as a Function of One's Ethnic Distinctiveness in the Social Environment." *Journal of Personality and Social Psychology* 36(5): 511–20.

Miller, David B., and Randall MacIntosh. 1999. "Promoting Resilience in Urban African American Adolescents: Racial Socialization and Identity as Protective Factors." *Social Work Research* 23(3): 159–69.

Ocampo, Katheryn A., Martha E. Bernal, and George P. Knight. 1993. "Gender, Race, and Ethnicity: The Sequencing of Social Constancies." In *Ethnic identity: Formation and Transmission Among Hispanics and Other Minorities,* edited by Martha E. Bernal and George P. Knight. Albany: State University of New York Press.

Parham, Thomas A. 1989. "Cycles of Psychological Nigrescence." *The Counseling Psychologist* 17(2): 187–226.

Phinney, Jean S. 1989. "Stages of Ethnic Development in Minority Group Adolescents." *Journal of Early Adolescence* 9(1): 34–49.

————. 1990. "Ethnic Identity in Adolescents and Adults: Review of Research." *Psychological Bulletin* 108(3): 499–514.

————. 1992. "The Multigroup Ethnic Identity Measure: A New Scale for Use with Diverse Groups." *Journal of Adolescent Research* 7(2): 156–76.

————. 1996. "When We Talk About American Ethnic Groups, What Do We Mean?" *American Psychologist* 51(9): 918–27.

Phinney, Jean S., Cindy Lou Cantu, and Dawn A. Kurtz. 1997. "Ethnic and American Identity as Predictors of Self-Esteem Among African American, Latino, and White Adolescents." *Journal of Youth and Adolescence* 26(2): 165–85.

Phinney, Jean S., and Eric L. Kohatsu. 1997. "Ethnic and Racial Identity Development and Mental Health." In *Health Risks and Developmental Transitions During Adolescence*, edited by John Schulenberg, Jennifer L. Maggs, and Klaus Hurrelmann. New York: Cambridge University Press.

Rice, Audreys S., Rene A. Ruiz, and Amado M. Padilla. 1974. "Person Perception, Self-Identity, and Ethnic Group Preference in Anglo, Black, and Chicano Preschool and Third-Grade Children." *Journal of Cross-Cultural Psychology* 5(1): 100–8.

Roberts, Robert E., Jean S. Phinney, Louise C. Masse, Y. Richard Chen, Catherine R. Roberts, and Andrea Romero. 1999. "The Structure of Ethnic Identity of Young Adolescents from Diverse Ethnocultural Groups." *Journal of Early Adolescence* 19(3): 301–22.

Rosenberg, Morris. 1979. *Conceiving the Self*. New York: Basic Books.

Rosenberg, Morris, and Roberta G. Simmons. 1972. *Black and White Esteem: The Urban School Child*. Washington, D.C.: American Sociological Association.

Ross Leadbeater, Bonnie J., and Niobe Way, eds. 1996. *Urban Girls: Resisting Stereotypes, Creating Identities*. New York: New York University Press.

Scheier, Lawrence M., Gilbert J. Botvin, Tracy Diaz, and Michelle Ifill-Williams. 1997. "Ethnic Identity as a Moderator of Psychosocial Risk and Adolescent Alcohol and Marijuana Use: Concurrent and Longitudinal Analyses." *Journal of Child and Adolescent Substance Abuse* 6(1): 21–47.

Seidman, Edward. 1991. "Growing Up the Hard Way: Pathways of Urban Adolescents." *American Journal of Community Psychology* 19(2): 173–205.

Sellers, Robert M., Mia Smith, J. Nicole Shelton, Stephanie A. J. Rowley, and Tabbye M. Chavous. 1998. "Multidimensional Model of Racial Identity: A Reconceptualization of African American Racial Identity." *Personality and Social Psychology Review* 2(1): 18–39.

Semaj, Leahcim. 1980. "The Development of Racial Evaluation and Preference: A Cognitive Approach." *Journal of Black Psychology* 6(1): 59–79.

Shelton, J. Nicole, and Robert M. Sellers. 2000. "Situational Stability and Variability in African American Racial Identity." *Journal of Black Psychology* 26(1): 27–50.

Smith, Emilie Phillips, and Craig C. Brookins. 1997. "Toward the Development of an Ethnic Identity Measure for African American Youth." *Journal of Black Psychology* 23(4): 358–77.

Smucker, Mervin R., W. Edward Craighead, Linda W. Craighead, and Barbara J. Green. 1986. "Normative and Reliability Data for the Children's Depression Inventory." *Journal of Abnormal Child Psychology* 14(1): 25–39.

Spencer, Margaret B., and Carol Markstrom-Adams. 1990. "Identity Processes Among Racial and Ethnic Minority Children in America." *Child Development* 61(2): 290–310.

Steele, Claude M., and Joshua Aronson. 1995. "Stereotype Threat and the Intellectual Test Performance of African Americans." *Journal of Personality and Social Psychology* 69(5): 797–811.

Steinberg, Lawrence, and Elizabeth Cauffman. 1995. "The Impact of Employment on Adolescent Development." In *Annals of Child Development: A Research Annual,* edited by Ross Vasta. Volume 11. London: Jessica Kingsley.

Szapocznik, José, William M. Kurtines, and Tatjana Fernandez. 1980. "Bicultural Involvement and Adjustment in Hispanic-American Youths." *International Journal of Intercultural Relation* 4(3/4): 353–65.

Tajfel, Henry, and John C. Turner. 1986. "The Social Identity Theory of Inter-Group Behavior." In *Psychology of Intergroup Relations,* edited by Stephan Worchel and William G. Austin. Chicago: Nelson-Hall.

Thomas, Charles. 1970. "Different Strokes for Different Folks." *Psychology Today* 4(September): 48–53.

Trent, William T., and James M. McPartland. 1982. "The Sense of Well-Being and Opportunity of America's Youth: Some Sources of Race and Sex Differences in Early Adolescence." High School and Beyond. Washington, D.C.: National Center for Education Statistics.

Tweed, Dan L., Harold F. Goldsmith, Debra J. Jackson, Diane Stiles, Donald S. Rae, and Marlene Kramer. 1990. "Racial Congruity as a Contextual Correlate of Mental Disorder." *American Journal of Orthopsychiatry* 60(3): 392–403.

United Nations Children's Fund (UNICEF). 2002. "At a Glance: United States of America." Available at: http://www.unicef.org/infobycountry/usa.html (accessed October 13, 2004).

Vandiver, Beverly J., William E. Cross Jr., Frank C. Worrell, and Peony E. Fhagen-Smith. 2002. "Validating the Cross Racial Identity Scale." *Journal of Counseling Psychology* 49(1): 71–85.

Vandiver, Beverly J., Peony E. Fhagen-Smith, Kevin O. Cokley, William E. Cross Jr., and Frank C. Worrell. 2001. "Cross's Nigrescence Model: From Theory to Scale to Theory." *Journal of Multicultural Counseling and Development* 29(3): 174–99.

Waters, Mary C. 1990. *Ethnic Options: Choosing Identities in America.* Berkeley and Los Angeles: University of California Press.

———. 1996. "The Intersection of Gender, Race, and Ethnicity in Identity Development of Caribbean American Teens." In *Urban Girls: Resisting Stereotypes, Creating Identities,* edited by Bonnie J. Ross Leadbeater and Niobe Way. New York: New York University Press.

Wilson, William Julius. 1987. *The Truly Disadvantaged: The Inner City, the Underclass, and Public Policy.* Chicago: University of Chicago Press.

Yancey, Antronette K., Carol S. Aneshensel, and Anne K. Driscoll, 2001. "The Assessment of Ethnic Identity in a Diverse Urban Youth Population." *Journal of Black Psychology* 27(2): 190–208.

Yinger, J. Milton. 1994. *Ethnicity: Source of Strength? Source of Conflict?* Albany: State University of New York Press.

CHAPTER 8

SOCIALIZATION TO THE ACADEMY: COPING WITH COMPETING SOCIAL IDENTITIES

Abigail J. Stewart and Andrea L. Dottolo

Let us then begin by looking at the outside of things, the general aspect. . . . There they go, our brothers who have been educated at public schools and universities . . . a procession. . . . Great-grandfathers, grandfathers, uncles—they all went that way. . . . [M]ost of them kept in step, according to rule, and by hook or by crook made enough to keep the family house. . . . It is a solemn sight, this procession, a sight that has often caused us, . . . looking at it sidelong from an upper window, to ask ourselves certain questions. [I]t is no longer a sight merely, a photograph, or fresco scrawled upon the walls of time, at which we can look with merely an esthetic appreciation. For there, trapesing along at the tail end of the procession, we go ourselves. And that makes a difference. . . .

For we have to ask ourselves, here and now, do we wish to join that procession or don't we? On what terms shall we join that procession? Above all, where is it leading us, the procession of educated men? . . .

Let us never cease from thinking—what is this "civilization" in which we find ourselves? What are these ceremonies and why should we take part in them? What are these professions and why should we make money out of them? Where in short is it leading us, the procession of the sons of educated men?

—Virginia Woolf (1938/1966, 60–63)

In *Three Guineas,* Virginia Woolf (1938/1966) asked hard questions about war. As we can see from the quotation above, she also asked hard questions about the exclusion of women from education. Woolf noted that at that moment—1938—women were now "trapesing along at the tail end of the procession" of educated people. She urged them not merely to join the procession, but also to ask themselves and others tough questions about whether to join, or on what terms to join. In short, she counseled women to use their outsider status to raise important questions about education, the professions, and indeed about civilization and its ceremonies more generally.

More than half a century later, we still see women, along with students of color and sexual minorities, struggling with outsider status in graduate school. Too often these groups are seen only as struggling to get in, rather than as raising larger questions about educational institutions and the knowledge they generate and exclude. Because educational institutions are more inclusive now than they were in 1938, the hard questions are not so often asked by those seeking any education at all. They are asked, instead, by those who bring subordinate social identities to the context of training for professional standing in the university—standing in the professoriate. That training, or socialization to the academy, is socialization to the generation and transmission of valued knowledge. Everyone who enters the academy for socialization— that is, attends graduate school—comes with a history and social identities. But some of those who enter—perhaps most notably, white heterosexual sons of educated parents—bring identities that are deeply compatible with those of the institution. Others—children of poverty, daughters of all classes, and people with racial-ethnic and sexual-minority backgrounds and identities—bring with them identities that compete or conflict with the identity under construction. For these students, socialization to the academy carries with it pressures for substantial personal change, and the risk of losses of the self. And, as Woolf reminds us, it also carries with it the potential to ask profound questions about the values served by the institution.

SOCIALIZATION AND IDENTITY

Education for a doctoral or other professional degree is similar to earlier kinds of education in many ways, but it is crucially different as well. At earlier levels, students may encounter situations in which their own social identities (in terms of gender, race, or ethnicity, for example) may differ from the ones that dominate the school, either in terms of numbers or of perceived values and culture. Many chapters in this volume focus on a variety of ways that young adolescent and young adult students cope with bringing a subordinate social identity into a context defined by the majority (see, for example, chapter 9, by McLaughlin-Volpe et al.; chapter 2, by Lawrence, Crocker, and Dweck; chapter 3, by London et al.; chapter 4, by Strauss and Cross; and chapter 5, by Shelton et al.).

Unlike earlier educational contexts, doctoral education involves creating a new social identity, and doing so in the context of preexisting adult identities. That new identity includes elements of identification with a role as a scholar or knowledge producer; with a discipline or field, and possibly a subdiscipline within that field; and with a method or epistemology. This new identity (for instance, as a positivist biopsychologist, or a postmodern literary critic, or a constructivist anthropologist) must be taken on in the context of other social identities not normally directly addressed by graduate education, identities including gender, race or ethnicity, class, and sexuality.

Experience shows that because the disciplines have deep roots in the same cultural institutions that produce all of the other institutions of dominance in the culture, upper-class European American heterosexual males are most likely to find their social identities unchallenged by the process of academic socialization (Laden and Hagedorn 2000). For example, the U.S. Department of Education (2001) reports that in 1999 to 2000, 56 percent of the recipients of doctoral degrees were men, and 61 percent were white and born in the United States. In comparison, African American students earned 5 percent, Latinos earned 3 percent, Asians earned 5 percent, and Native Americans students earned .4 percent (includes Ph.D., Ed.D., and comparable degrees at doctoral level but excludes first-professional degrees such as M.D., D.D.S., and law degrees.) Upper-class white heterosexual men are likely to feel "at home" in situations that seem strange and unfamiliar to students from different backgrounds, and to see people "like them" in positions of authority. For example, of full professors in 1998, 76 percent were men, and 90 percent were white. If we see becoming a professor as the goal and endpoint for academic degrees, then that endpoint defines the social script in some important ways. Thus, privileged students are likely to feel like and to be perceived as relatively close to the "goal" of socialization in their general demeanor and habits of mind and behavior, whereas other students are likely to feel like and be perceived as quite distant from that goal. And white men's past life experiences—of educational institutions, of cultural exposure, and of work—are likely to seem quite relevant to the experiences they have in graduate school. In contrast, students with other backgrounds may feel that their past experiences are both irrelevant and actively devalued in the new context. Generally, socialization pressures emphasize "sameness (for example, conformity to dominant cultural norms)," and that emphasis—however unintentional the effect—"marginalizes and alienates those who feel different or are perceived as dif-. ferent" (Turner, Myers, and Creswell 1999, 54; see also Thompson and Dey 1998). Bonita London, Geraldine Downey, Niall Bolger, and Elizabeth Velilla (chapter 3, this volume), in their exploration of some of the effects of such pressures at the undergraduate level, highlight some important overlap in the experiences of marginalization in the academy. For example, the researchers found that negative race-related events minimized students' sense of belonging. However, there are also some important differences between undergraduate and graduate socialization, especially regarding academic professionalization.

Socialization to the academy for all students involves a wide range of dynamic processes that includes learning norms and performing roles on a variety of social and institutional levels. These processes are accessed in formal and informal contexts and through university, disciplinary, and departmental bureaucracies; classroom dynamics; and relationships with faculty and advisers, and peer groups. Messages conveyed about success and "appropriateness" in graduate school are explicit and implicit in nature; for example, they are communicated through policies, requirements, and verbal instruction on one hand, and through silence, innuendo, and casual conversation on the other (see Turner and Myers 1999, for a discussion of this phenomenon with faculty of color and tenure). William G. Tierney and Robert A. Rhoads (1994) describe the processes of investiture and divestiture as integral and necessarily present in socialization. "Investiture (more affirming) concerns the welcoming of the recruit's anticipatory socialization experiences and individual characteristics, whereas divestiture (more transforming) involves stripping away those personal characteristics seen as incompatible with the organizational ethos" (29). Investiture comes more easily to graduate students—especially white, middle-class, heterosexual men—who have experiences and characteristics that are congruent with the traditional academic script. Conversely, divestiture—which may involve expunging certain patterns of speech, behavior, and interests from one's repertoire—is more central to the experience of those who deviate from the norm. John C. Weidman, Darla J. Twale, and Elizabeth Leahy Stein (2001) explain that "the socialization process ultimately requires investiture for the student's transformation into the new professional role to be completed with an internalization of appropriate values, attitudes, and beliefs associated with their intended professions and professionalism" (8). In other words, accepting and internalizing academic norms is a key component of graduate enculturation. At the "suture" (Hall 1996, 5) of the graduate student identity with (usually) preexisting identities marked by race, class, gender, and sexuality, students who bring subordinate identities to graduate school encounter an academy that must "strip" them of their otherness (though of course socializers are often unaware of the ways in which their demands result in divestiture). We are interested in what happens in this encounter when the role of graduate student is given to those who historically have not had access to the part. How do graduate students respond to the socialization pressures they experience? How can they use their outsider status to challenge the institution that is simultaneously transforming them?

COPING WITH ACADEMIC SOCIALIZATION

One perspective that might help us think about the encounter between the academy and graduate students with subordinate social identities (women, people of color, sexual minorities, those from working-class backgrounds) is the psychological literature on coping with stress. Surely this encounter is one likely to engender "stress," or demands for adaptation that tax the individual's capacity and therefore elicit coping responses. In this case, the stressor is enduring and difficult to locate, and the coping responses must therefore be appropriately tailored to the kind of pervasive, diffuse, and long-lasting nature of the stress. Conventional accounts of responses to discrete stressors (Folkman and Lazarus 1980; Lazarus and Folkman 1991) emphasize the value to the individual's mental health of coping strategies that directly address the problem at hand over those that are either indirect or palliative.

Some psychologists have attempted to reframe the field of coping research by introducing alternative terminology and theory to encompass more adequately the experiences of members of marginalized groups, who can sometimes ill afford to engage in direct, instrumental coping. For example, Kay Deaux and K. A. Ethier (1998) noted that students may adopt strategies that enhance their identities (such as reaffirmation, remooring, intensified group contact, and social change) or negate them (such as elimination, denial, or decreasing importance of identity). Celina Chatman, Jacquelynne Eccles, and Oksana Malanchuk (chapter 6, this volume) find that minority adolescents when faced with discrimination experiences are much more likely to report using identity-enhancement strategies (strategies that allow them to retain valued social identities). London et al. (chapter 3, this volume) examine three strategies for coping with discriminatory experiences among minority college students in a predominantly white institution: confrontation, self-silencing, and transformation. They find that students in these contexts frequently self-silence, despite the fact that they pay a price in well-being for doing so.

In related work with older adults, M. Brinton Lykes (1983) found that "black women who worked in predominantly white institutions successfully confronted experiences of personal prejudice by electing purposively to ignore it" (97); those in predominantly black institutions used more direct confrontational methods of coping. Ella Bell, L. J. Edmonson, and Stella M. Nkomo (1998) use the term "armoring" to explain African American women's coping strategies, pointing out that racism, sexism, and classism place many African American women in a "perilous social position" where they "must be taught how to survive" (285). J. Faulkner (1983) describes armoring as "specific behavioral and cognitive skills used by Black and other people of color to promote self-caring during encounters with racist experiences and/or racist ideologies" (196). Beverly Greene (1990) discusses armoring as a mechanism of adaptation in coping with racial oppression, including recognizing and labeling racism, identifying positive role models, and "understanding the experience, which may be fraught with feelings of difference, rejection, and confusion" (23). According to this perspective, racial socialization often includes acquisition of specific strategies and resources for coping with pressure for divestiture—strategies that recognize the unequal power relations central to the situation. Linda Strauss and William E. Cross (chapter 4, this volume) suggest that different coping strategies may serve different functions: buffering against the negative impact of pressure for divestiture, bonding with other members of the out-group, bridging to the in-group, or expression of one's own individualism. In their study of young adolescents coping with discrimination, Chatman, Eccles, and Malanchuk (chapter 6, this volume) found that many students' coping strategies accomplish buffering or confirmation of their individualism.

Glynis M. Breakwell (1986) explored "passing" as another coping strategy employed by members of oppressed groups. She defined it as "the process of gaining access to a group or social category (sexual, racial, political, economic or religious) by camouflaging one's group origins" (116). Passing requires renouncing or hiding part of an individual's identity—a form of self-censorship; most often a person from a marginalized group will try to pass as a member of a privileged one. Mary Bucholtz (1995) explains that successful passing is accomplished by sufficiently learning and following the social rules of the desired group, which legitimizes group membership. "Authenticity—that is, the legitimacy of one's claim to ethnicity [or any social identity]—underlies the traditional definition of passing, . . . which posits a recategorization of the passing individual from her 'own' . . . group to another that is not her 'own' " (352). This is usually easiest when group membership is least visible, as in the case of sexuality or religion, although Bucholtz also examines the passing of biracial individuals and the social construction of race (see also Piper 1992). Actively constructing an identity inside a group other than one's own is also a dangerous task. Breakwell explains, "As a coping strategy for threat, passing requires strong resolve and is the option chosen only when the consequences of socially acknowledging the threatening position [or social identity] are more severe than those concomitant upon the fraud itself" (Breakwell 1986, 118). For example, passing as a heterosexual permits the lesbian access to the privileged group, and protects her from the punishment and derision of mainstream heterosexist, homophobic culture.

We began, then, with two key issues that are raised by studying an educational set-ting that is aiming at creating a new social identity: (1) the fact that socialization to the academy is a process that is designed to include investiture (or affirmation of a new identity) for all participants, but divestiture (particularly of valued aspects of the self associated with a devalued social identity) only for some (in this study, women, people of color, and sexual minorities); (2) the fact that groups coping with divestiture, or strip-ping of valued aspects of preexisting social identities, need to draw upon coping strate-gies that go well beyond directly instrumental responses. These might include strategies such as armoring, seeking social support, and collective action that build on positive associations to devalued social identities and strategies such as passing and purposive inaction that involve concealment and strategic withdrawal. These strategies—direct and less direct—may in turn offer members of subordinate groups opportunities for negotiating the terms on which they join the procession of "educated men."

THE SOCIALIZATION TO
THE ACADEMY PROJECT

This study is part of a larger, collaborative project involving interviews with both fac-ulty and graduate students. The sample for this study included eighty-three gradu-ate students who had completed at least two years of doctoral training in humanities and social science fields at a large midwestern research university. A stratified ran-dom sample of all graduate students eligible by that criterion was selected to produce roughly equal numbers of males and females, students of color and white students, and students in the humanities and social sciences. Data indicating field of study, race-ethnicity, year of initial registration, and gender of student were obtained directly from the graduate school. (Doctoral students in the natural sciences were excluded from this study because there were too few women and students of color in those fields.) In the analyses that follow we examine the relevance of students' social identities one at a time, without reference to other such identities (in other words, race regardless of gender, sexuality regardless of race, and so forth). We recognize the importance of the intersections of these social identities in creating unique pressures and responses, so we have examined them, despite the small numbers this sometimes produces. However, for the results reported here the only reliable differences emerged as main effects of race, gender, and sexuality. Analyses of other phenomena would likely require exploration of differences unique to particular intersections of these identities; and larger samples might permit subtle differences to emerge that could not be identified in this study.

Students were guaranteed confidentiality of their responses (and identifying infor-mation has been deleted from all quotations throughout this paper). They were, how-ever, interviewed by graduate students from the same institution; to increase their sense of privacy in the interviews, interviewers were assigned from different disci-plines than interviewees. On the basis of the data supplied by the graduate school, stu-dents and interviewers were roughly matched on race-ethnicity: European American interviewees were interviewed by European American interviewers; African American interviewees by African American interviewers; Latinos by Latinos; and Asian and

Asian Americans by Asian and Asian Americans. It was not, however, possible to match within race-ethnicity on country of origin or immigrant status, or on gender.

Interviews averaged over an hour in length, and the interview protocol consisted of open-ended questions about general demographics, background questions about student interests and aspirations in graduate school, and extensive questions about experiences in graduate school. Verbatim transcripts were analyzed with NVIVO, a qualitative software package that enabled examination of particular portions of the interviews as well as creation of a numerical file usable for statistical analyses. Coding categories were generated from the literature review outlined above. Occurrences of particular codes in a respondent's interview were transformed into presence-absence codes (1 for presence, 0 for absence) and frequency counts.

A file containing respondent demographic information (discipline, year in program, gender, race-ethnicity) was merged with these data. In addition, any references to participants' own sexuality in the interview were also coded. Ten of the eighty-three respondents identified themselves in the interview as other-than-heterosexual (gay, lesbian, bisexual, or simply "not heterosexual"). It should be noted, though, that participants were not directly asked to name their sexual identity. Similarly, students who mentioned another social identity in the course of the interview that was important to them were coded as concerned about "other" social identities. These included social class, disability, nontraditional age, family status (being married or a parent), and immigrant status. A total of twenty-seven students (32.5 percent) identified themselves in terms of one of these other identity statuses.

The focus of this study is on two key sets of questions: the first set appears midway in the interview protocol: "Can you think over your entire graduate school experience so far and identify some problem you have had—a pretty important problem that really worried you? Can you describe for me both what the problem was and how you handled it?" Students responded to these questions with descriptions of general problems in graduate school; some examples include issues around funding, passing preliminary examinations, and teaching obligations. The second set of questions was asked toward the end of the interview, and addressed issues of social identities: "How are issues of race and ethnicity, gender, or sexuality visible in your program?" Generally interviewers asked about each of these areas in turn. In addition, after the respondent answered this general question on each topic, he or she was asked, "How do you think your experiences have been affected by your race or ethnicity, gender, or sexuality?" Some students mentioned other social identities in responding to this question, such as social class, immigration status, or family status. Discussions of problems in these areas were also coded as relevant to "other social identities." A total of seventy-six students (91.6 percent) mentioned at least one social identity–related stressor in response to this second set of questions. Responses to all of these questions were coded (without reference to other information about the interviewee) for direct references to censorship, as well as for particular coping responses to problems identified in these areas. Both authors coded problem and identity-related issues from seven of the respondents (fourteen instances); interrater agreement was .96; since agreement was so high, one author (Dottolo) coded the remaining interview responses.

Censorship

Censorship is one critical indicator of divestiture. It was coded if the student reported having experienced censorship personally, or perceived censorship to be present for other students. For example, if a white student commented on ways in which students of color are ignored or pressured to be silent, this was coded for censorship. In other words, this category aimed to capture firsthand experiences of censorship, similar to those covered in London et al.'s (chapter 3, this volume) measure of "self-silencing," in addition to instances of witnessing others' censorship. There were three coding alternatives for this category: *explicit censorship, implicit censorship,* and *passing*. Statements that were coded for explicit and implicit censorship were very similar. A statement was coded for explicit censorship if a student described overt pressures not to discuss aspects of her or his identity, usually with reference to direct negative sanctions. For example, if a student said, "It has become very clear to me that I cannot discuss my partner in this environment, as being a lesbian is not okay," or "I have learned that it is not acceptable to discuss the ways that women in my department are treated differently than men," then this was coded as explicit censorship. Implicit censorship was coded when students said that they do not refer to aspects of themselves in the academy but did not indicate that they had been overtly pressured to avoid these references. These students typically reported that they chose not to engage in open conversations that reveal parts of their identity. For example, "It seems that issues of race are a touchy subject, so I don't talk about my experiences here. It's just not worth it." In discussing issues of gender, another student explained, "These monthly seminars—there's only one woman in our program right now, so if we're sitting in a room, and all of the three professors are male, so there will be five or six students, three professors, so there's like ten men and one woman . . . that obviously makes a huge difference in terms of this one student, her sort of comfort and ability to participate in the same way as the other students is definitely a factor."

Although no one explicitly informed the woman in this department that she could not participate, the interviewee perceives implicit censorship that silences her. The boundary between explicit and implicit censorship was relatively easy to draw in terms of the language of the descriptions, but the experiences being described may not have been very different at all. In both cases, the environment was experienced as incompatible with certain features of the individual's identities.

Passing

Passing was coded as a form of censorship if students discussed how they had either intentionally or unintentionally passed as a member of a group different from their own. For example, "I can easily pass as a heterosexual, and I try to keep it that way because of the way gays and lesbians are treated around here." Another student explained, "I'm half Hispanic, but I don't look Hispanic, so mostly no one notices except when they say, 'Is that your husband's last name?' You know, and I don't have an accent or anything, but my father is Mexican American. So, sometimes it feels lonely." In this case the fact that she was not recognized as a person of color was coded for passing. Passing was included as a form of censorship because of the ways in which silencing, concealing, and disguising function as integral to passing.

The identity questions were separately coded for four coping responses to perceived difficulties in any of the identity areas. Of the eighty-three interviewees, seventy-six discussed at least one of these areas as posing problems or difficulties. (The remaining seven cases were distributed across the different groups of interviewees; in some cases questions were not asked fully, or the interviewee had discussed identity-relevant issues earlier in the interview, so the interviewer did not ask these questions directly.) The four forms of coping were not mutually exclusive; thus, a student might engage in one or more coping strategies in response to any of these questions.

Direct Action

Direct action was coded if respondents described an instrumental, problem-related action in response to the problem or issue. In general, overt efforts to approach the source of the problem were coded as direct action. For example, in managing a difficult adviser, one student described how she "learned to set boundaries with him." This coding category coincides with more traditional psychological notions of coping.

Social Coping

Social coping is one alternative form of "problem" negotiation, including efforts to incorporate others in coping activity as collaborators or as providers of social support. J. Nicole Shelton, Tiffany Yip, Jacquelynne Eccles, Celina Chatman, Andrew Fuligni, and Carol Wong (chapter 5, this volume) found that by endorsing what we are calling social coping strategies, African Americans were able to minimize some of the negative effects of racial discrimination. Similarly, practices encompassed by Strauss and Cross's (chapter 4, this volume) notion of "bonding" would include most social coping. Reliance on others is the defining component of social coping. Social coping includes two more specific coping strategies: collective action and indirect action.

Collective Action

The use of collective action indicated that the student planned to respond to the "problem" actively, but in concert with other individuals. This plan might or might not have been enacted yet. The category aimed to capture the intent of the student both to take an active step, and to collaborate in making a response. In discussing her response to her adviser who sexually harassed her, one woman stated,

> There were like four women in the department, and it like happened to all of us, and what we did was that we sort of took a step back and said, "We need this guy for our prelim committees and our dissertation committees." . . . And so what we decided to do was ignore it and just warn any other woman who is coming to the department. . . . We always make sure that we are at recruitment things, and, if they're interested in doing race, then we pull them aside and say, "If you are here to work with this professor, don't, because as soon as we are all done, we're going to report him."

This description illustrates a variety of ways that this group of students collectively planned certain actions (and inactions) in response to the problem.

Indirect Action

Coping responses that were not directly focused at the source of the problem but were more intended to preserve the self were coded as indirect action. This most often included maintaining or developing social relationships with others (usually people in less "powerful" positions) for support or advice, sometimes about the problem. For example, one student explained, "The way that I saw the problem was I talked to a lot of people about it." Some students described their responses to various problems through conversations with friends and family members. Although these conversations were typically not with people who had institutional power to remedy the problem, the student attempted to find support and indirectly address the issues at hand. Another student explained, "I think I wouldn't have had to go and seek out Women's Studies as much if I [had] felt that those issues were adequately addressed, as well as having a feminist perspective, as well as theoretical issues." In this case, she addresses the problems in her department indirectly by seeking support from a Women's Studies community.

Instrumental Inaction

Instrumental inaction included apparent nonactions that had the purpose of preserving the self, or negotiating the circumstances of the "problem." This category was coded if the student mentioned making decisions or creating states of mind that were instrumental in coping with difficult experiences of graduate school, but did not take any action. The most important component here was an explicit acknowledgment of intentionality by the student, sometimes in the form of resistance, or a refusal to give in. For example, "I'm not going to let them get me down. I'm not going to let them kick me out of this place; so . . . you know, push me out of this place." This statement illustrates a stance toward the problem that was intentional and conscious on the part of the student, and was used to manage the problematic situation and her place within it. As another student described, "I know about the off-color remarks that they make and this kind of stuff. I would never trust them with my academic future. So that's a huge. . . . It's definitely a race thing." Again, the student did not directly confront the problematic behavior, but made a clear intentional choice not to trust these individuals with his academic future.

Noninstrumental Coping

In contrast, noninstrumental coping included no problem-solving activity at all, and no apparent recognition by students that their own thoughts or actions could in any way be a form of "coping." These actions could include engaging in distracting activities that are not described as connected to addressing their "problem." For example, watching TV for hours would be coded as noninstrumental coping, unless it was explicitly discussed as providing a break from work, or as a way of stepping away from a problem in order to gain perspective. Similarly, some students described increased drinking as a response to their problems, which also was coded as noninstrumental coping. Other examples included ignoring the problem or actively blaming oneself for it.

Table 8.1   Censorship and Social Identities

Type of Censorship	Percentage Describing
Any	47
Sexuality	30
Race-ethnicity	21
Gender	11
Other	5.3

Source: Authors' compilation.

QUANTITATIVE ANALYSIS OF CENSORSHIP AND COPING WITH COMPETING IDENTITIES

We focused on the seventy-six students who discussed at least one of the social identities (race, gender, sexuality, or "other social identities") as being problematic in some way in their graduate program. Of these seventy-six students, nearly half reported experiencing or observing censorship of some social identity. As may be seen in table 8.1, censorship was more commonly reported about sexuality than any other identity, though race-ethnicity was also a relatively common object of censorship. Gender and "other" social identities (class, disability, age, or family status) were rarely viewed as censored.

Interestingly, students of color were no more likely to report censorship than other students, nor were women more likely than men to do so; however, there was a significant relationship between sexual identity and reporting censorship ($\chi^2 = 8.40$, p < .004). Ninety percent of the ten students who identified themselves as "other than heterosexual" during the interview also reported experiencing or observing censorship of social identities, while twenty-seven of the sixty-six, or 41 percent, who explicitly or implicitly defined themselves as heterosexual did. Five of the ten reported it in the area of race, one in the area of gender, eight in the area of sexuality, and two in "other" identities.

The forms of coping varied as a function of both whether the issue under discussion was a *graduate school problem* (the first set of problems described earlier) or an *identity-related* problem (the second set of problems). They also varied as a function of students' own competing social identities. Graduate school problems were most often addressed directly (67.1 percent of the students reported direct actions in response to them), though a substantial minority of students reported taking indirect actions (44.7 percent), instrumental inaction (40.8 percent), and noninstrumental actions (31.6 percent). Very few reported collective actions (9.2 percent). When discussing social identity–related issues in graduate school, very few students described direct actions (9.2 percent), and even fewer mentioned noninstrumental actions (5.3 percent). The most frequent responses were indirect actions (21.1 percent) and instrumental inaction (22.4 percent), with collective action less common (11.8 percent). The high level of direct action in response to graduate school problems suggests that the students

Table 8.2   Strategies for Coping with Identity-Related Problems in Graduate School

Strategy and Groups	Percentage Using Strategy	χ^2	p
Instrumental inaction			
Students of color (N = 37)	38		
White students (N = 38)	5	9.99	.001
Instrumental inaction			
Sexual-minority students (N = 10)	60		
Heterosexual students (N = 66)	17	7.06	.007
Social coping			
Women students (N = 46)	39		
Men students (N = 30)	13	5.88	.015
Indirect action			
Women students (N = 46)	28		
Men students (N = 30)	10	3.64	.056
Collective action			
Women students (N = 46)	17		
Men students (N = 30)	3	3.44	.064

Source: Authors' compilation.
Note: χ^2 values corrected for continuity as necessary.

were generally quite instrumental and were able to "work the system" when they faced difficulties not presented as pertinent to social identities. On the other hand, the substantial rate of noninstrumental actions in response to graduate school problems (29 percent) also suggests that there was a relatively high level of students experiencing problems they could not address with any active strategy.

It was interesting that social identity–related problems were rarely described as being approached with direct actions, but they were also rarely simply internalized or avoided. This suggests both that the graduate school context did not readily permit identity-related challenges, and that those who felt their social identities were threatened in the course of graduate school actively, if indirectly, resisted those threats.

Students' own social identities were not associated with their description of particular coping strategies in response to graduate school problems. Thus, students with and without subordinate identities responded similarly to pressures they perceived as part of normative academic socialization, unmarked by relevance to other social identities. In contrast, students' own social identities were related to their descriptions of how they addressed social identity–related issues in their programs. This differential pattern may indicate that students with subordinate identities have difficulty recognizing how some normative socialization pressures may also carry demands for divestiture. As may be seen in table 8.2, in addressing identity-relevant issues in their programs, students of color and students who identified themselves as other than heterosexual were more likely than the contrasting groups to report using instrumental inaction as a coping strategy. Women were more likely than men to report social coping, including both taking indirect actions and collective actions. Only by looking in detail at the qualitative data can we understand precisely what these results mean about the difficulties students face in handling social identity–relevant issues in graduate school.

QUALITATIVE ANALYSIS OF CENSORSHIP AND COPING WITH COMPETING IDENTITIES

In this section we explore the precise language and content used in material coded under particular categories. Here we aimed to use the qualitative material we earlier subjected to systematic content analysis to enrich our understanding of what the categories really mean or imply about students' reported experiences.

Students' discussions of censorship experiences included discussions of their personal identities, of the visibility of these issues in the curriculum, and of the impact of graduate socialization on the work they were doing. Students' feelings in response to all of these experiences ranged from resignation and loneliness through frustration to rage. Virtually none of the students felt that it was possible for students to change the silences they encountered.

Censorship: Personal Identities

Students sometimes felt that aspects of themselves and of their own experience were viewed as irrelevant by the authority structure and other students. For example, one student said, "I don't think the system has the time to deal with that. . . . You are imposing your problem on them—on the system—if you talk about it." Another student felt that to correct inaccurate perceptions of her group in class would have negative repercussions: "It's just like you just feel like people eventually look at you, like, 'You're so petty, just shut up.' " Other students commented on the lack of support for certain groups of students. For example, one said, "There have been a few African American women who were in the program before I started, and they ended up not finishing. One of them I talked to felt that this program had no kind of support—moral support—for minority students." Another student commented that in her (male-dominated) program it was difficult for women students to "be given equal authority to speak."

Sexual identity was most often described as not visible in graduate programs. Students pointed out, "It's noteworthy in its rarity; I definitely don't think it's an open kind of environment" and "The people who are homosexual aren't really visible. . . . They are kind of keeping their sexuality to themselves." Another student said, "My sense on the campus as a whole is that there are particular departments where it's just like—you better keep your mouth shut, you know, because people just don't want to deal with it." More personally, one student reported, "I don't really have opportunity to talk about my personal life with mostly anybody." Sometimes the accounts were somewhat contradictory, but the overall impression was not of openness:

> Interviewer: What about issues of sexuality and sexual orientation; are they visible in your program?

Respondent: I don't know if they're visible. As far as discrimination or even as far as talking about it. I haven't noticed anything. It is just kind of interesting. I mean in a negative way.

Interviewer: Are there students and faculty who are openly gay in your department?

Respondent: Oh, yeah. But there is no—no one talks about it.

Censorship of Social Identities in the Curriculum

Students commented frequently on the relative silence surrounding certain issues in the classroom. For example, one student said, "I think they really feel uncomfortable talking about anything related to race, cause they don't want to offend anybody." Another said of gender issues, "In my department it's kind of just ignored by the men." One frustrated student said of his department, "It's just not a place where they will integrate social theories and identities into the actual practice of being an academic. . . . They're really afraid of identity politics." Students were sometimes shocked that identities that seemed to them critical to areas of their training were ignored. For example, one said, "On a substantive level, it should be a big part of what we do, because communities of color are heavily impacted by poverty and social problems that most of us are trying to address."

Censorship of Identity-Related Scholarship

Quite a few students commented on the impact of the environment on their own developing intellectual work. One said, "If I'm taking a class, I wouldn't write a paper about racial consciousness and hand it in for a grade. I would try to find something more suitable. So there is some self-censoring, you know, some anticipated reaction going on for me. I do know that I have changed my direction in some things."

Another student commented, "There's a bunch of us who have suspected that people would look down on people who do identity work, but that's not talked about. . . . We've intellectualized it enough that, you know, we're not talking about—they know we're not talking about our people."

Other students mentioned that they wait until they think they can afford to reveal certain interests. One Latino student said, "I do believe you have to be better in order to get the same treatment. I waited until I was at the top before I started expressing my interest in [Latino cultural production]."

Students were not asked directly about censorship, though they clearly encountered it and described it vividly. Since there was no direct questioning about it, of course they were not asked whether they could change or influence it. However, they rarely expressed any notion that the censorship they observed could be challenged or changed; in fact, there was an association between reporting censorship in one's graduate program and describing instrumental inaction as a strategy for coping with identity-relevant difficulties (32 percent of those reporting censorship vs. 11 percent of those not; $\chi^2 = 5.85$, p = .02). This coping strategy—rarely recognized at all in the literature on coping—was important not only in responding to censorship but more generally in students' responses to identity-related problems in graduate school.

Instrumental Inaction in Response to Identity-Related Problems

Why do people frequently respond to censorship with instrumental inaction? Why do people of color and sexual minorities in particular respond to identity-related problems in this way? We believe that students use intentional inaction as a strategy because it provides three distinct advantages: armoring, strategic placement of self, and perseverance.

ARMORING   Margie Kitano (1998) described armoring as a narrative strategy that includes acknowledging the existence of hardships, and stressing the need to persevere by "ignoring, reframing, affirming oneself, finding alternative paths, seeking support from others, or some combination of these" (262). Students who engaged in instrumental inaction as a coping strategy made "armoring" statements that reaffirmed their marginalized identities as a source of strength or protection. Many drew upon the way they understand their social location within oppressive structures as an advantage instead of a disadvantage. Similarly, Shelton et al. (chapter 5, this volume) explore some of the ways in which ethnic identity can be utilized as a buffer permitting psychological adjustment to stress. One woman stated, "Being a black woman makes you stronger and able to survive in the face of all adversity."

Some students responded to their situation with an explicitly oppositional stance— a form of direct resistance to the institution's attempts at divestiture. These students often used retaliatory language in their descriptions of anger and defensiveness against the system. One woman talked about how her competence as an academic in her field was repeatedly questioned because of her gender. She explained, "When I first took the job, I took it as a great challenge to dazzle them with my skills, but now I feel like, fuck you. How dare you ask me that, you know?" Another woman discussed how her working-class background was very salient for her in the community, where she feels others "spend a lot of time trying to get me into the culture" and her "directness" is seen as "tactlessness." She said, "I am constantly watching people and trying to figure out what it is I am trying to do and figuring out how I am different from that. I am not interested in changing, of course. There is always that element: 'This is me and fuck you.' " Because these students felt they could not change the way they were perceived, or control the structures that devalued them, they resisted conforming and presented their identities almost as an act of defiance. In this way they exercised a form of agency within a position of relative powerlessness. One woman explained, "I think that all of my experiences have been colored by the fact that, you know, I am a black woman. And that's just who I am, and that's what I bring with me to the table, and that's who I want people to see when they look at me. So if they can't deal with that, then they'll have to go on to someone else." She was unapologetic about her identities and was unwilling to hide or diminish who she is.

In cases where concealing an identity may be more feasible, for example, around sexuality, this type of armoring can be more obvious because the choice to use an "invisible" identity as "armor" is apparent. As a lesbian student described, "I think I was the second or third student to be very, very out with my partner and brought her to all the functions and was very open. That's who I am, so I'm not going to . . . too bad, you know, you're just going to have to deal." This student took a conscious emotional and psychological stance about how she managed her sense of self in a homophobic environment.

Another aspect of armoring students described involved protection and the management of identity-related losses that they encountered, often as a result of divestiture. For example, one student of color described his position on racial tensions in his department: "I guess I have a bit of a tough skin; it doesn't bother me." This is slightly different from finding strength in his identity, but is still a conscious choice in trying to remain unperturbed. A working-class black student talked about her interactions and lack of connection with some upper-class blacks in academia:

> [Some get] together, hanging out, talking, and it's always about food and what we eat. And I eat chitlins, not regularly, but I eat them. And it's like, "What!" You know . . . and I'm like, "What, you don't eat chitlins? You don't know about chitlins? How could you not know about chitlins? You're black, aren't you?" You know, one could argue that the orientation about chitlins is a kind of class thing, or even though there's some people who may have come from a working-class, lower-class environment, you know, go on up, become upper-class, or you know, middle-class still know about chitlins. There's some kind of, to me, I always interpret it as a kind of cultural loss as you move up.

Interestingly, this student was careful to tell the interviewer that she did not eat chitlins "regularly." She explained how her conceptions of an authentic black identity focused on particular cultural practices, including eating chitlins, and that upward social mobility resulted in "cultural loss." This illustrates instrumental inaction (in particular, armoring), because of the way she acknowledged this loss, attributed it to an upper-class script, and managed to maintain the practice for herself.

STRATEGIC PLACEMENT OF SELF   Another aspect of instrumental inaction involves the conscious presentation of self in a way that will maximize the positive conditions or outcomes of a difficult or hostile atmosphere, often in the form of protection against negative consequences. This is usually not a position of defiance toward the system around identities (as in armoring), perhaps because the normative sanctions would be too great. Instead, strategic placement of self can involve working within the system to minimize visibility. Strauss and Cross's (chapter 4, this volume) notion of code switching might be included in the repertoire of strategic placement of self. For example, when one lesbian student was asked, "How has your sexuality affected your experience?" she responded, "It makes me stand back a little bit more from people than I would otherwise, because every time you meet somebody new, it's like, oh, oh, should I tell them, when do I tell them? You get so used to worrying about a bad reaction . . . you spend a lot of time building up barriers to defend yourself against it. So you are friends with fewer people." This student engaged in instrumental inaction as a strategy to negotiate her position in a homophobic context, as she calculated the ways she might be perceived and responded by "standing back."

An Asian American student described the ways in which she had tried to become involved in student groups and conversations about race in her program, but was explicitly excluded because "racial issues" translated to "African American issues."

After repeated efforts to join the activities, she said, "I think I'm at a point where I just think, 'Well, if they don't want me to be part of the issue, then I won't be part of the issue.' It is frustrating because I have made an effort." In order to cope with a racially unwelcoming department, she attempted to take action by engaging with others in a collective way, but then coped with her exclusion through instrumental inaction, strategically placing herself outside of harm's way in both cases. She, too, "stands back." Another variation of strategic placement of self—with obvious costs to the generation of certain kinds of knowledge in the academy—concerns avoidance of certain scholarly work and concealment of academic interests, as outlined earlier, in the section on censorship.

PERSEVERANCE   The final function of instrumental inaction that students drew upon was perseverance. In the face of hostile climates, they consciously took a position of insistence, resolve, and determination to make it through the university and earn a degree. One student considered how she managed to stay: "I don't know if I started thinking that it didn't matter how you got here, just do it." Another student explained, "They had just tried to kick me any way they could, and I'm just not going to go for that. But still, I tried to remain professional in life, which is why they can't just get rid of me." These students might or might not hide their identities, or use them as "armor." They rooted themselves in the situation, determined to obtain what they want from the academic process. Although they "bit the bullet," they were aware of discrimination, and might choose to fight it directly or not. However, there was usually an emphasis on working within the system, or at least remaining inside it. Even when a social support network advised the student to escape, some refused, as an act of resistance. When one student talked with previous advisers about the prevalence of racism on campus and its negative effects on her experience in graduate school, they suggested that she leave the program, she responded with instrumental inaction: "When I tell my teachers and staff [about my experiences] . . . they kept telling me, 'Get the hell out of there. What are you doing there?' I'm like, 'No, I'm not going to let them get me down. I'm not going to let them kick me out of this place, you know, push me out of this place.' " There is a clear recognition that there are pressures to eliminate these individuals from the academy, but their perseverance is a form of coping and opposition.

Indirect and Collective Actions

Indirect actions and collective actions—employed more often by women than men in responding to identity-related problems in graduate school—share an important characteristic: they involve other people in the response to a problem. Both direct action and instrumental inaction are centered in a single individual's agency, but both indirect actions and collective actions—though also agentic—are profoundly social responses. Indirect actions usually are not aimed directly at the perceived problem, but instead address the individual's loneliness or alienation in graduate school. They are "indirect" if we take the problem they address to be the racism, sexism, or homophobia encountered; they are absolutely direct if instead we notice that they provide good solutions to the loneliness and alienation. "I needed to grow up outside the academy and I needed to form those relationships that really meant something to me, that would last."

Collective actions often have some element of social support or indirect action in them, but they include some element as well of working jointly with others to take "direct action" to address the problem at hand. Some students reported joining or belonging to formal identity-related groups, and they clearly drew strength from these groups. Others created smaller ad hoc groups to serve particular purposes. For example, one described addressing a funding problem this way: "There's a small group of students who are under the same [funding package] as me; so it began with a student conversation. And then we took it to the people that we thought were adviser-ish, in terms of administering that package . . ."

Another student described the function of a dissertation group: "I think what finally changed was getting some distance from that whole experience of having to churn out the papers and getting back to a place where I could feel more safe with my writing. And what I'm in now is like a dissertation group with, um, two of my closest friends . . . and it started out as this group of six women, but it was a very safe space."

Another student pointed out that it is often necessary to "piss people off," but "We find where we can that we have a lot more . . . we share resources a lot more. Like, you know, the five black women in the department will all share their resources." As was mentioned earlier, a group of four women in one department made a mutual pact to warn prospective students about a sexually harassing faculty member, and to bring charges against him when they graduated and were no longer vulnerable to his retaliation.

Choice of Strategies

We do not have any clear evidence indicating why women (both white women and women of color) were more likely to use social strategies such as indirect action and collective action, whereas students of color and nonheterosexual students of both sexes were more likely to use instrumental inaction as a strategy. We suspect that numbers—demography—play an important role; women are a substantial subgroup of nearly every academic program in the humanities and social sciences, while students of color and nonheterosexual students generally are not. Where numbers are substantial, social strategies are much more feasible. Where numbers are low, the dangers of visible action, even if it is collective, may be much greater, resulting in much greater reliance on strategic inaction and perseverance. We note, though, that some of the examples of women's indirect and collective action come from programs in which women were vastly outnumbered. We wonder whether even in these environments women are more likely than men to draw on the group-based strategies associated with the women's movement. Our findings suggest to us that it may be valuable for concerned faculty and students to facilitate more group-based coping for students of color and sexual minority students.

SOCIALIZATION TO THE ACADEMY WITHOUT DIVESTITURE

The accounts we have examined are limited: they are drawn from a single institution, and only include students who survived for at least two years. They do not include students in the science disciplines. We were unable to examine subgroups that may be important, including groups varying by their group identity as are discussed in so many chapters in this volume (see chapters 3, 4, 5, and 6). We explicitly explored only a few social identities.

Nevertheless, the accounts confirm that the process of socialization to the academy was not the same for students who entered the academy with and for those who entered without subordinate social identities. We found that many students with and without those identities noticed that the academy censors certain social identities both explicitly and implicitly, within and outside the curriculum. These observations suggest that the demands for divestiture are obvious and pervasive; they also suggest that there are losses not only for the individuals subject to those demands, but also to the disciplines represented in the academy.

We found, too, that there were few direct challenges to these exclusions. However, threats to identity did elicit resistance. All of the modes of resistance were aimed at persistence and survival in the academy, but they entailed costs, both for the individual and for the academy. Instrumental inaction—associated more with students of color and sexual-minority students—involves strategically withdrawing from confrontation while preserving a place within the institution. Many of the students who engaged in instrumental inaction planned—later—to challenge the divestiture required of them; we can only hope that their survival is whole, and that they do indeed eventually use their positions inside the academy to create more open space for others. Indirect and collective actions were attempted most often by women; these approaches strengthened individuals through mutual support, but risked dilution and diminution in the search for collaborators, and required the demographic possibility of finding safety in numbers.

Most of all, these strategies—though they clearly preserve critical aspects of the self that are threatened by socialization to the academy—are costly in psychic energy used to respond and often result in painful compromise. They make it more difficult for students to answer the question that Virginia Woolf enjoined them to ask (1938/1966, p. 62): "Do we wish to join that procession or don't we? On what terms shall we join that procession? Above all, where is it leading us . . . ?"

Although this study was not designed to provide clear directions for creating better terms for students who bring marginalized identities into the academy, the results suggest a few steps that might make the engagement more productive and less costly. Altering the demographics—that is, increasing the numbers of students with a given marginal identity—seems to enable students to draw on active social strategies rather than resorting to inactive, isolating, and self-censoring ones. Equally, the power of "role models" lies in part in the evidence they offer that it is possible to emerge intact and powerful from this potentially costly set of transactions; of course, that power in turn depends on the real presence of intact, powerful role models, not "tokens" whose past losses are all too visible. Best of all, though, lessening the demands for divestiture—that is, opening up academic practices and discourses to a wider range of possibilities—allows individuals with valued social identities to bring them into the academy, thereby enriching the institution and avoiding both the personal and the social cost.

We are grateful to our colleagues on the Socialization to the Academy Project (Laurie Morgan, Carla O'Connor, and Alford Young); to Domna Stanton and the larger program, Redefining Censorship, at the Institute for Research on Women and Gender; and to Dean Earl Lewis and the Horace Rackham School of Graduate Studies, all at the University of Michigan, for support for this project. We are also grateful to our graduate-student interviewers and interviewees for their generous participation in the project, and to Jennifer Churchwell, Julie Konik, David G. Winter and two anonymous reviewers for providing feedback on an earlier draft of this manuscript.

Many thanks to Laurie Morgan, Carla O'Connor, and Alford Young for their collaboration on this larger project, as well as to the Redefining Censorship Project at the Institute for Research on Women and Gender.

Many thanks to Mark Akiyama, Jennifer Churchwell, Julie Garcia, Kareem Johnson, Julie Konik, Tiffany Murray, Osmara Reyes, Joel Rodriguez, Allison Smith, and Daryl Wout for interviewing and transcribing they did on the project. Thanks, too, to Julie Konik for establishing and maintaining the database, and to Jennifer Churchwell for her assistance with NVIVO.

REFERENCES

Bell, Ella, L. J. Edmonson, and Stella M. Nkomo. 1998. "Armoring: Learning to Withstand Racial Oppression." *Journal of Comparative Family Studies* 29(2): 285–95.

Breakwell, Glynis M. 1986. *Coping with Threaded Identities*. New York: Methuen.

Bucholtz, Mary. 1995. "From Mulatta to Mestiza: Passing and the Linguistic Reshaping of Ethnic Identity." In *Gender Articulated: Language and the Socially Constructed Self*, edited by Kira Hall and Mary Bucholtz. New York: Routledge.

Deaux, Kay, and K. A. Ethier. 1998. "Negotiating Social Identity." In *Prejudice: The Target's Perspective*, edited by Janet K. Swim and Charles Stangor. San Diego: Academic Press.

Faulkner, Janette. 1983. "Women in Interracial Relationships." *Women and Therapy* 2: 193–203.

Folkman, Susan, and Richard Lazarus. 1980. "An Analysis of Coping in a Middle-aged Community Sample." *Journal of Health and Social Behavior* 21(3): 219–39

Greene, Beverly. 1990. "What Has Gone Before: The Legacy of Racism and Sexism in the Lives of Black Mothers and Daughters." *Women and Therapy* 9: 207–230.

Hall, Stuart. 1996. "Introduction: Who Needs Identity?" In *Questions of Cultural Identity*, edited by Stuart Hall and Paul du Gay. London: Sage.

Kitano, Margie. 1998. "Gifted African American Women." *Journal for the Education of the Gifted* 21(3): 254–87.

Laden, Berta Vigil, and Linda Serra Hagedorn. 2000. "Job Satisfaction Among Faculty of Color in Academe: Individual Survivors or Institutional Transformers?" *New Directions for Institutional Research* 105: 57–66.

Lazarus, Richard S., and Susan Folkman. 1991. "The Concept of Coping." In *Stress and Coping: An Anthology*, edited by Alan Monat and Richard S. Lazarus. 3rd edition. New York: Columbia University Press.

Lykes, M. Brinton. 1983. "Discrimination and Coping in the Lives of Black Women: Analyses of Oral History Data." *Journal of Social Issues* 39(3): 79–100.

Piper, Adrienne. 1992. "Passing for White, Passing for Black." *Transitions* 58: 4–32.

Thompson, Carolyn J., and Eric L. Dey. 1998. "Pushed to the Margins: Sources of Stress for African American College and University Faculty." *Journal of Higher Education* 69: 324–45.

Tierney, William G., and Robert A. Rhoads. 1994. "Faculty Socialization as Cultural Process: A Mirror of Institutional Commitment." ASHE-ERIC Higher Education Report no. 93–6. Washington, D.C.: George Washington University, School of Education and Human Development.

Turner, Caroline Sotelo Viernes, and Samuel L. Myers Jr. 1999. *Faculty of Color in Academe: Bittersweet Success.* Needham Heights, Mass.: Allyn & Bacon.

Turner, Caroline Sotelo Viernes, Samuel L. Myers Jr., and John W. Creswell. 1999. Exploring Underrepresentation: The Case of Faculty of Color in the Midwest. *Journal of Higher Education* 70(1): 27–59.

U.S. Department of Education, National Center for Education Statistics. 2001. Integrated Postsecondary Education Day System (IPEDS). "Completions" survey. Table 25.

Weidman John C., Darla J. Twale, and Elizabeth Leahy Stein. 2001. "Socialization of Graduate and Professional Students in Higher Education: A Perilous Passage?" ASHE-ERIC Higher Education Report no. 28-3. Washington, D.C.: George Washington University, School of Education and Human Development.

Woolf, Virginia. 1938/1966. *Three Guineas.* San Diego: Harcourt Brace Jovanovich.

PART IV

BRIDGING WORLDS:
INTERPLAY BETWEEN SOCIAL IDENTITIES
AND SOCIAL RELATIONSHIPS

CHAPTER 9

THE EXPERIENCE OF MINORITY STUDENTS AT PREDOMINANTLY WHITE UNIVERSITIES: THE ROLE OF INTERGROUP FRIENDSHIPS

Tracy McLaughlin-Volpe, Rodolfo Mendoza-Denton,
and J. Nicole Shelton

Ever since the publication of Gordon Allport's (1954) *The Nature of Prejudice*, much research has been devoted to understanding the conditions under which positive intergroup contact will thrive (see Cook 1986; Pettigrew and Tropp 2000). The impact of Allport's seminal writings cannot be underestimated: to this day, the conditions he outlined fifty years ago continue to inspire and set the agenda for research on intergroup contact. In his original writings, Allport outlined five different types of contact: casual contact, acquaintance, residential contact, occupational contact, and goodwill contact. Interestingly, one of the categories that Allport did not include in his analysis of intergroup contact was that of friendship. Over half a century later, a dearth of attention to intergroup friendship continues to characterize the field. In a recent review, for example, Thomas F. Pettigrew and Linda R. Tropp (2000) found that out of 746 tests examining the effect of intergroup contact, only 64 explicitly used cross-group friendships as the contact measure.

Despite the paucity of research on intergroup friendships, there is good reason to believe that such friendships—over and above mere contact—may be beneficial, albeit in different ways, for both members of a cross-group friendship. Though sparse, research on intergroup friendships is beginning to grow, and suggests that such relationships can reduce intergroup bias and prejudice (Levin, van Laar, and Sidanius 2003; McLaughlin-Volpe 2001; Paolini et al. 2004; Pettigrew 1997). Intergroup friendships seem to have a stronger effect on the reduction of prejudice than other types of intergroup contact (Pettigrew and Tropp 2000), and may even have vicarious benefits such that the mere knowledge of others' cross-group friendships reduces bias (Wright et al. 1997). Nevertheless, research on cross-group friendships to date has been limited by an overwhelming focus on the attitudes and outcomes of majority-group members (Oyserman and Swim 2001), and a lack of research designs that allow for a causal link between cross-race friendships and positive outcomes to be established (Levin, van Laar, and Sidanius 2003; Pettigrew 1997).

Although our focus in this chapter is on the potential benefits of cross-group friendships for minority students, we do not suggest that white students do not benefit from such relationships. Similarly, we do not minimize the importance and benefits of same-race friendships. To the contrary, evidence for such benefits abounds, some of which we briefly describe here. Similarly, although our arguments are applicable to a wide range of groups, our focus in this chapter is on interracial friendships between African American and Latino students on the one hand and white students on the other.

CROSS-RACE FRIENDSHIPS: OVERCOMING ODDS

Psychologically oriented theory and research on friendship is relatively recent (Newcomb and Bagwell 1995), and arguably began with Harry Sullivan's (1953) interpersonally oriented theory of friendship. Sullivan argued that close friendships begin to emerge in preadolescence and coincide developmentally with an increasing need for interpersonal intimacy and acceptance. Consistent with this functionalist view, friendship is often characterized today as a reciprocal relationship that provides a safe context for each member of the dyad to learn and practice important interpersonal skills. These skills include perspective taking (Buhrmester and Furman 1987), empathic accuracy (Stinson and Ickes 1992), and social-norm adoption (Hartup and Stevens 1997). When friendships reach across racial divides, these interpersonal skills may directly lead to enhanced cultural competence, a type of social competence that helps a person navigate or understand the world of the "other" (Mendoza-Denton et al. 1999). If true, then cross-race friendships may be a key element in moving beyond numerical diversity toward relational diversity, as Michelle Fine, Lois Weiss, and Linda C. Powell (1997) put it.

Although friendship is an almost ubiquitous aspect of human experience (Hartup 1996), cross-race friendships are nevertheless quite rare in the United States (Crandall, Schiffhauer, and Harvey 1997; Hamm 2000). Using data from 16,000 American high school seniors over a two-decade span Steven A. Tuch et al. (1999) found that although there has been a trend toward more diverse friendships, 70 percent of white respondents and 50 percent of black respondents reported that all or almost all of their friends were of the same race.

Various factors are likely to play a role in the paucity of cross-race friendships. Several researchers have pointed to organizational and structural factors, noting that there is relatively little opportunity for cross-race contact in many of today's organizational settings (Cohen 1975; Hallinan and Smith 1985; Hallinan and Teixeira 1987; Khmelkov and Hallinan 1999; Slavin 1979). Even in integrated institutional settings, however, cross-race friendships seem to be the exception rather than the rule (Moody 2001). Research suggests that the path to stable cross-race friendship needs to overcome certain barriers. Members of different cultural groups often do not share the same socialization and learning histories, which can lead to differences in the inter-pretation of social events (Mendoza-Denton et al. 1997) as well as an inability to relate to certain types of problems such as racism (Gaines 2001). Along similar lines, when interracial contact situations make race salient, people are likely to engage in top-down processing, in which a person's words and actions are perceived and interpreted in light of his or her group membership (Rothbart and John 1985). Consistent with this research, cross-race dyads often report increased discomfort and self-consciousness during social interaction (Frable, Blackstone, and Scherbaum 1990; Ickes 1984), with majority or high-status group members worrying about appearing prejudiced and minority or low-status group members worrying about being able to trust their part-ners (Crocker, Major, and Steele 1998; Shelton 2003). As James M. Jones (1972/1997) has noted, "Mutual anxiety escalates miscommunication and has a tendency to create a self-fulfilling prophecy whereby each confirms his or her own negative expectation" (320). Moreover, as a result of prior experiences of discrimination, some members of minority groups may be especially wary of forming friendships with members of the out-group (Mendoza-Denton et al. 2002; Shelton and Richeson 2003).

Pressures against cross-race friendships and toward in-group friendship may be especially pronounced among minority college students entering predominantly white institutions (Hamm 2000). Christian Crandall, Kristin L. Schiffhauer, and Richard Harvey (1997), for example, found that African American students in such institutions tend to choose friends who are like them in their level of ethnic identity, whereas stu-dents in predominantly black colleges choose friends on the basis of other similarity characteristics, such as achievement orientation or personal values (see also Fordham 1988; Fordham and Ogbu 1986). These findings suggest that when a particular social identity is threatened, students may cope by affiliating with those who share the threat-ened identity (Spencer 1995). Taken together, then, the evidence suggests that success-ful stable friendships across race, more often than not, must traverse an uphill road.

BENEFITS OF CROSS-RACE FRIENDSHIPS

Although establishing cross-group friendships may be difficult, research suggests that the benefits of these friendships may be substantial. Arguably, the most extensively studied outcome surrounding intergroup contact has been the reduction of prejudice. Allport (1954) listed four conditions that were necessary for positive intergroup con-tact to reduce prejudice: equal status, common goals, interdependence or lack of com-petition, and sanction by authority. These four conditions have enjoyed most of the research attention, despite additions to these criteria as well as criticisms of them (Amir 1976; Pettigrew 1997; Sherif 1966). A recent meta-analysis (Pettigrew and Tropp 2000) shows that mere contact seems to be effective in reducing intergroup prejudice, and that the satisfaction of Allport's conditions helps strengthen this relationship. Notably for our analysis, however, the relationship between contact and prejudice was strongest, with an effect size of −.57, among those studies in which intergroup friend-ship was measured. The strength of the benefits of intergroup friendships is perhaps most apparent in a study by Stephen C. Wright et al. (1997), which found that the mere *knowledge* of a cross-race friendship was enough to foster positive intergroup affect. Wright et al. (1997) refer to this finding as the extended-contact effect. Similarly,

J. Nicole Shelton and Jennifer Richeson (forthcoming) demonstrated that the mere knowledge of a cross-group friendship reduced white students' fears of being rejected with respect to approaching a cross-group contact situation.

There is also evidence that intimate cross-race interactions have benefits beyond the reduction of prejudice. Among a large sample of college graduates, 70 percent of white students with the most extensive interactions across racial lines reported that they were "very satisfied" with their education, compared with 62 percent of those having some interactions and 55 percent of those with no substantial interactions with individuals of other races (Bowen and Bok 1998). Other research indicates that informal cross-group interactions are related to a variety of positive learning outcomes, including both the ability and the motivation to understand a perspective other than one's own (Gurin et al. 2002). Research also shows that whites who have had greater intergroup contact in the past show fewer signs of physiological threat during an interaction with a black person (Blascovich et al. 2001). Similarly, recent research suggests that having prejudiced beliefs is linked to cognitive impairments for whites during interracial contact (Richeson and Shelton 2003). More specifically, Jennifer Richeson and Nicole Shelton (2003) found that in comparison to white individuals low in prejudice, high-prejudiced whites who engaged in an interracial interaction revealed impaired performance on a subsequent task requiring executive control.

In sum, close personal friendships with members of another group reduce prejudiced beliefs, provide useful skills and experiences that are necessary for success in college and beyond, and may increase general well-being.

BENEFITS OF CROSS-RACE FRIENDSHIPS FOR MINORITY-GROUP MEMBERS

As Jason S. Lawrence, Jennifer Crocker, and Carol S. Dweck (chapter 2, this volume) point out, the coping mechanisms and protective resources that allow individuals to cope with prejudice and alienation are likely to be multidimensional, operating not only at the individual level but also at the interpersonal and institutional levels (Mendoza-Denton, Page-Gould, and Pietrzak, forthcoming). Although coping strategies such as self-silencing (London et al., chapter 3, this volume) and ethnic identity (Shelton et al., chapter 5, this volume) can be seen as operating at the intrapersonal level, adjustment is also determined in part by the interpersonal relationships that individuals can draw on as a source of strength (Lawrence, Crocker, and Dweck, chapter 2, this volume; Andersen, Downey, and Tyler, chapter 10, this volume).

As noted earlier, the weight of the research conducted on the benefits of cross-race friendships has assessed their benefits to majority-group members (Pettigrew 1997). Is there any evidence that intergroup friendships are also beneficial for the minority-group member of the dyad? In asking this question, we begin by noting some of the unique challenges faced by minority-group members, and students in particular, as they navigate majority-dominated environments.

Although feelings of alienation and rejection may adversely affect any student (Cantor et al. 1987), feeling alienated from the majority culture on campus has been found to play a particularly significant role in minority students' adjustment at predominantly white colleges (Bowen and Bok 1998). Research suggests that many ethnic minorities at predominantly white universities feel they are encountering a sub-culture that is distinctively different from their own (Loo and Rolison 1986). Moreover, some ethnic minorities at these universities experience discrimination, which predicts their feelings of alienation from white students and the university (Willie 1981). Alienated students are more likely than those who do not feel alienated to drop out of school, have fewer friends, and participate less in extra-curricular activities (Pounds 1987; Suen 1983). Additional research shows that alienation is a significant predictor of depression, stress, and low self-esteem among African American students at pre-dominantly white universities (Millet 1995). Similar findings exist for other ethnic minorities. Feeling detached from the majority group and loneliness are positively cor-related among Hispanic students (Suarez et al. 1997). Among Hispanic and Asian stu-dents, the most alienated students are most likely to drop out of school (Bennett and Okinaka 1990).

Taken together, these findings suggest that intergroup alienation has adverse implications for the psychological well-being and development of interpersonal rela-tionships for ethnic minorities in a predominantly majority context. Implicit in these findings is the idea that positive interpersonal experiences with members of the dom-inant campus community may contribute positively to minority students' adjustment and well-being.

The Role of Prior Intergroup Contact

Calvin Graham, Robert W. Baker, and Seymour Wapner (1985) were interested in the effects of pre-college interracial contact on the adjustment and contentment of minor-ity students at a predominantly white college. A sample of incoming African American first-year students were asked to characterize the amount and nature of interracial contact they had in high school. The researchers asked participants to characterize the ethnic makeup of their neighborhood, their high school, and their friendship net-work. The researchers found that greater amounts of interracial contact prior to col-lege were positively linked to academic, social, and personal adjustment in college, as well as to institutional attachment. The strength of this relationship, however, was considerably stronger among students who reported a greater number of cross-race friends. Although the researchers did not take into account important variables such as socio-economic status and did not address the mechanisms underlying the rela-tionship between cross-race friendship and later adjustment, their finding is consis-tent with Pettigrew and Tropp's (2000) research showing that intergroup contact is especially effective if it occurs in the context of an intergroup friendship.

Contact—or Closeness?

Although the research discussed above has found positive outcomes from friendship to be more pronounced than those deriving from mere contact, it also shows that casual contact can also have positive outcomes (Cook 1978, 1986; Pettigrew and Tropp 2000). We suggest, however, that positive effects from mere contact may not be a given for members of minority groups, considering the unequal power and status of the groups to which interaction partners belong (Allport 1954). When one is a member of a devalued or low-status group, superficial interactions with majority-group members may only serve to enhance perceived intergroup differences and may even reinforce students' concerns about rejection and belonging. Tracy McLaughlin-Volpe and colleagues (2002) found that superficial interactions with large numbers of out-group acquaintances was unrelated to attitude change (in one study they found that students with more contact had more negative feelings toward the out-group). Thus, we would expect the predicted positive consequences of cross-group contact to be limited to minority students who develop a close and supportive relationship with a white friend.

This prediction was supported by Shelton's (2002) finding that the quality of intergroup contact played an important role in ethnic minorities' experiences in college settings. She asked African American students to rate how they would characterize the majority of their contact experiences with white students on campus—as very superficial–very intimate; not at all pleasant–very pleasant; and very competitive–very cooperative. For African American students who did not have positive, meaningful intergroup contact experiences, there was no relationship between the number of activities in which they participated with whites and their satisfaction with the university. However, for African American students who had more positive, meaningful intergroup contact experiences, participation in activities with whites was associated with greater satisfaction with the university. Similarly, McLaughlin-Volpe (2001) found that the quality, rather than the quantity, of cross-race contact that African American and Latino or Latina students at a predominantly white university reported was related positively to institutional identification and negatively to alienation. In this study, quality of cross-race contact was assessed with relationship indicators that included being able to talk about what it means to be a minority student on campus, feeling accepted, and feeling satisfied with one's friendships. Important, these findings held when student's overall sociability was held constant.

In support of the idea that having close out-group friendships may have benefits beyond increased feelings of belonging, McLaughlin-Volpe also found that relationship closeness predicted self-reported academic self-efficacy on the part of the minority students. Specifically, respondents who felt close to and accepted by their white friends were significantly more likely to affirm that they were willing to take initiative, complete projects, and persist in the face of adversity. Finally, minority students' level of social self-efficacy was also predicted by the quality of minority students' cross-group friendships, indicating that establishing and maintaining such friendships raises these students' interpersonal competence and their confidence in social situations.

Do Some Students Benefit More than Others?

Not all minority students experience concern about their belonging and inclusion within majority-dominated social institutions to the same extent. Recent research suggests that some individuals are prone to expect rejection and to feel alienated because of their ethnicity. Rodolfo Mendoza-Denton et al. (2002) have proposed that direct or vicarious experiences of exclusion, discrimination, and prejudice lead ethnic minorities to develop anxious expectations of rejection because of their race. These expectations, activated in situations where race-based rejection is a possibility, such as being an ethnic minority student at a predominantly white college, place the individual in a state of anticipatory threat, which lowers the threshold for perceiving the expected negative outcome.

Mendoza-Denton et al. (2002) developed and validated a questionnaire to assess anxious expectations of race-based rejection in situations where such rejection is both applicable and personally salient (for example, when an African American encounters a roadblock where police are randomly pulling people over). Such race-based rejection sensitivity (RS-race) was assessed prior to the beginning of classes in two cohorts of incoming African American students at the university. Participants then completed a structured daily diary for the first three weeks of classes. Controlling for rejection sensitivity in personal relationships (RS-personal), African American students identified as anxiously expecting race-based rejection in fact experienced a heightened sense of alienation over the first three weeks of college. They also felt less welcome at their university, had greater difficulties with their roommates, and formed a less positive view of their professors than did students low in RS-race.

Consistent with the model's predictions, high–RS-race students, who anxiously expected race-based rejection, reported less intergroup contact at the end of their first year in college than their low–RS-race counterparts. Specifically, they had fewer outgroup friends, interacted with professors less, and did not seek out teaching assistants as much as students low in RS-race. These results also held when controlling for number of black friends and level of RS-personal. Further, RS-race was unrelated to the number of black friends participants reported having, demonstrating the specificity of the RS-race construct as a dynamic that motivates people to avoid only those who are more likely to reject them on the basis of race. This is important because it distinguishes RS-race from a more generalized social anxiety or tendency to avoid social contact (see also Major, Quinton, and McCoy 2002).

In a similar study, Shelton (2002) administered to African American students Elizabeth Pinel's (1999) measure of stigma consciousness, which contained questions and statements such as "Being a member of my ethnic group does not influence how others act with me" and "I never worry that my behaviors will be viewed as stereotypical of my ethnic group." They also administered a measure of how rejected and alienated from the university students felt, containing questions and statements such as "To what extent do you feel a part of the student community?" and "Other students at this university do not want to get to know me because of my ethnicity." Similar to Mendoza-Denton et al., Shelton found that the more African Americans expected to be negatively stereotyped or discriminated against in general, the more they felt alienated from others at the predominantly white university. Taken together, these findings suggest that individual differences in expectations of race-based rejection influence ethnic minorities' feelings of connection to predominantly white institutions.

Role of Intergroup Friendships

To the degree that white peers are viewed as representatives of the dominant culture or value system within the university, friendships with such peers may uniquely signal acceptance and belonging to students who have been historically excluded from the university's doors. Shelton (2002) found that having white friends serves a positive function for African American students who felt rejected and alienated from the university. She asked students how often they participated in various activities with white students on campus, asking, for example, how often black and white students ate meals together, watched TV or movies, or participated in study groups. Finally, she asked students how satisfied they were with being a student at the university, asking, for example, how satisfied they were with their classes and with the students in their residential colleges. Shelton found that for African Americans who did not feel alienated or rejected, how often they participated in activities with white students was unrelated to their satisfaction with the university. In contrast, for African Americans who felt alienated and rejected from the university, the more they participated in activities with white students, the more satisfied they were with the university.

Establishing Cause and Effect

One of the biggest challenges for research on the benefits of cross-race friendship has been the establishment of a cause-and-effect relationship between cross-group friendships and positive outcomes (Levin, van Laar, and Sidanius 2003; Pettigrew 1997). When the data reveal a positive association between cross-race friendship and positive outcomes, it is important to ask whether reduced prejudice or better institutional adjustment are the result of friendship, or whether well-adjusted or less-prejudiced individuals are the ones who are able to establish and maintain cross-race friendships in the first place. Although both pathways are likely to be influential, our focus here is on the effects of cross-race friendship on positive outcomes. Longitudinal research designs have proved particularly helpful in allowing causal conclusions to be drawn from naturalistic data and in providing support for the causal pathway we focus on here. As one example, Levin, van Laar, and Sidanius (2003) employed a longitudinal design to examine the effects of in-group and out-group friendship choices during the first years of college on ethnic attitudes at the end of college. By statistically controlling for students' ethnic attitudes at the beginning of college in their longitudinal analyses, the researchers were able to examine the change over time in the students' attitudes and to see whether that change was related to the development of a cross-race friendship. Patricia Gurin et al. (2002) employed a similar strategy when they looked at the effects of diverse learning environments on subsequent perspective-taking ability.

Mendoza-Denton and Elizabeth Page-Gould (2002), also using a longitudinal design, examined the moderating effect of white friends on the relationship between RS-race and anxiety about speaking with peers about academic problems, and between RS-race and satisfaction with the university, both over a three-to-four-year period. The patterns were consistent with those found by Shelton (2002). Specifically, controlling for students' initial scores on the dependent variables, students high in RS-race who had greater numbers of outgroup friends reported the least anxiety about sharing academic problems, as well as the greatest satisfaction with the university. Given the longitudinal nature of the design—and the fact that the analyses controlled for students' initial levels of anxiety and satisfaction, these findings are supportive of a causal link between intergroup friendship and subsequent feelings of satisfaction within the institution.

Summary

Findings from independent research programs provide evidence for the claim that positive intergroup friendships can be beneficial for minority students. These benefits appear to be magnified for students who arrive on college campuses with the highest levels of race-based anxiety and mistrust, and they appear to be especially strong when the intergroup relationship is experienced as close. It should be noted that although McLaughlin-Volpe and colleagues (2002) emphasize the importance of relationship closeness over the number of white friends in predicting positive outcomes, Mendoza-Denton and Page-Gould (2002) as well as Shelton (2002) found that the number of white friends predicted positive outcomes among students who most strongly experienced doubts about belonging. We suggest that the methodology used to assess the number of white friends may account for these seemingly contradictory findings. In the latter two studies, participants were asked to name a finite number of their closest friends, thereby increasing the likelihood that the white friends participants listed were above a minimum threshold in terms of closeness.

Although the contact literature suggests that mere contact does have an effect on prejudice reduction (Pettigrew and Tropp 2000), our findings also suggest that unequal power relationships in such contact may make the mere contact experience—and related outcomes—different for low- and high-status groups. Our findings (McLaughlin-Volpe et al. 2002) suggest that simply providing opportunities for increased intergroup contact without regard for how that contact is experienced by the parties involved is at best ineffective and possibly detrimental to minority students (see also Fine et al. 1997; Moody 2001). Instead, students have to be allowed and encouraged to come together not just in passing, but in a way that allows for the development of true intimacy between partners.

MECHANISMS OF INTERGROUP FRIENDSHIPS

Why are close relationships successful in achieving the positive affective and academic outcomes we have observed in our studies? The potential mechanisms explored here as yet await empirical scrutiny and examination.

Disconfirmation of Negative Expectations

Close friendships, unlike mere acquaintanceships, are characterized by positive affect, mutual respect and support, and above all, trust (Hartup 1996; Hartup and Stevens 1997; Sullivan 1953). Feeling accepted and cared for by any person at the university has positive effects (Cross and Strauss 1998; Hodges et al. 1999) but for minority students at predominantly white universities, relationships with white friends may be perceived as a particularly strong sign of acceptance and inclusion, because white friends represent the majority group. Students from groups who come to campus expecting to be rejected on the basis of their group-membership have reason to be mistrustful of representatives of the institution and avoid contact with members of the majority group. When these students develop a close relationship with a white student, their expectation of rejection may be directly undermined. Feeling accepted and supported by a member of the dominant group may be a powerful indicator of broader acceptance and belonging at the university. The positive affect felt toward one's friend may generalize, if not to the institution as a whole, then to members of the campus community that are seen as similar to one's friend (see also Andersen, Downey, and Tyler, chapter 10, this volume; Wright et al. 1997).

If Mary McPerson (in Bowen and Bok 1998) is correct in suggesting that minority students' capacity to deal with concerns over belonging and relationships is limited and that such concerns undermine these students' ability to focus on academic pursuits, then freeing minority students (even if only partially) from these worries should allow them to become more effective students. In this light, friendships with members of the dominant group may serve to normalize concerns over belonging, allow these students to reduce their constant vigilance, and thus free up cognitive and emotional resources that can now be employed in the pursuit of academic goals.

Resource Transmission

Another way in which friendships with majority- or high-status group members may benefit minority-group members is through resource transmission. Students from the majority group tend to bring experiences and identities to the college campus that are easily compatible with the demands of college life and this puts them at a considerable advantage in dealing with their professors and other representatives of the institution (Dana 2002; Robinson 1999; Stewart and Dottolo, chapter 8, this volume). These students' pre-college experiences have taught them how to relate effectively to members of the faculty and how to access needed resources. In these terms, minority-group students are at a disadvantage: their ethnic identity can conflict with their institutional identity when the expression of ethnic identity is not valued by the institution (see Stewart and Dottolo, chapter 8, this volume). In addition, because of anticipated prejudice and discrimination minority students may prefer not to interact with their white peers, professors, and other institutional representatives (Mendoza-Denton et al. 2002), and consequently may be less likely to learn the subtle types of procedures and practices that ensure success in college—knowledge about the "inner workings" of the university that their white peers might possess.

A friendship with a member of the high-status group may help provide minority or low-status group members access to the "invisible knapsack of assets that an entitled group can refer to on a regular basis to more effectively negotiate their daily lives" (Robinson 1999, 76). A similar point was recently made by Robert Crosnoe, Shannon Cavanagh, and Glen H. Elder Jr. (2003), who argue that academically oriented friendships may well translate into social capital for minority students. Interacting with a high-status friend may allow a minority-group student to become familiar with the cultural norms and preferences of the institution and its representatives.

Inclusion of Other in the Self (IOS)

A third way in which cross-group friendships may benefit the relationship partners is through the inclusion of the other in one's concept of self. Arthur Aron and Elaine Aron (1986, 1996) proposed that in close relationships, the members of that relationship grow to feel and think as if the other were a part of the self and vice versa. A partner's points of view become one's own; the successes and failures of one partner become those of the other. In the IOS model, including a close other in the self is not a process of losing one's identity or sense of self in a relationship, but rather a process of self-expansion whereby each partner gains access to the other's resources, knowledge, and experience without compromising his or her own. This idea of self-expansion in relationships is captured in the Inclusion of Other in the Self Scale (Aron, Aron, and Smollan 1992), a self-report measure consisting of a series of overlapping circles that grow both closer and larger to signify increasing interdependence.

Consistent with a growing body of research that examines intergroup processes through models developed to understand close relationships (Mendoza-Denton et al. 2002; Smith, Murphy, and Coats 1999), McLaughlin-Volpe and colleagues (Aron and McLaughlin-Volpe 2001; McLaughlin-Volpe 2001; McLaughlin-Volpe et al. 2002) have extended their model to the domain of intergroup relationships. These researchers have proposed that when two people belonging to different groups become friends they each will include the other person's group into their own self-concept. To the extent that particular social identities, such as a person's ethnicity, are salient characteristics of an out-group friend, the process of inclusion of other in the self will increase one's ability to adopt the perspectives and identities of the out-group as one's own (McLaughlin-Volpe et al. 2002).

The study by McLaughlin-Volpe (2001) described earlier provides indirect evidence for some of these ideas. Minority-group students in that study also filled out the Inclusion of Other in the Self Scale (Aron, Aron, and Smollan 1992) concerning their relationships with their three closest white friends. Consistent with predictions, minority students who indicated high levels of overlap between self and a white friend on the IOS scale also reported high levels of identification with the institution, low levels of alienation, and a general sense of academic self-efficacy.

In sum, we suggest three mechanisms that may explain how cross-group friendship benefits the partners involved in these relationships:

1. Having a positive relationship with a member of the dominant group may undermine minority students' negative expectations about the dominant group, thereby fostering feelings of belonging and trust that may generalize to the group as a whole and the institution.

2. Cross-group friendships may also serve to transmit important resources and skills, and are a way to build social capital.

3. Finally, the IOS model proposes that in a close cross-group relationship, both partners come to include the other in their self-concept, a process that leads to an expanded sense of self in which each person gains access to the other's resources, perspectives, and identities.

FUTURE RESEARCH

What are the issues for future research relevant to the issue of interracial friendships and, more generally, to the role of interpersonal relationships in coping with alienation and rejection from the out-group? We suggest three areas for further study.

Examination and Comparison of the Proposed Mechanisms

Future research should identify the mechanisms that are responsible for the effect of close cross-group contact on minority students' college adjustment. In the previous section we discussed three plausible mechanisms whereby minority-group members profit from cross-group friendships, each apparently consistent with the findings of our research programs. Since an important goal of this research is to collect information that will allow us to design effective intervention programs, it is imperative that we understand exactly how minority students' friendships help them develop a sense of belonging at academic institutions.

Motivations Behind Intergroup Friendship Development

One of the principal questions that arises from the research reviewed here concerns the precursors and predictors of cross-race friendships. What motivates an individual to reach across the boundary of his or her in-group to develop a friendship with a member of the out-group? Although Aron and Aron (1996, 1997) cite a fundamental human motive for self-expansion to explain why people seek close relationships, we suggest that such a motive cannot by itself account for the development of friendships across the racial divide. Among members of stigmatized groups, such a motive is likely to be at odds with the apprehension and negative expectations that precede and coincide with interactions with out-group members. This is particularly true among people who anxiously expect race-based rejection and who may therefore be particularly unlikely to choose out-group members as targets for self-expansion. Research also shows that members of nonstigmatized groups are equally apprehensive about interactions with stigmatized people (Goffman 1963; Jones 1972/1997). Thus, a basic motivation for self-expansion seems unlikely to assure an interracial friendship in the absence of other contextual or dispositional factors. We can only speculate on the nature of such factors, as the data reviewed here do not allow us to speak directly to this issue. One contextual factor may be the availability of a strong superordinate identification, such as both parties being members of an athletic team (Gaertner, Dovidio, and Bachman 1996; Sherif 1966). Another likely factor is the explicit cultural support for and modeling of close cross-group relationships in a given environment. Dispositional factors may range from empathy (Davis 1983a, 1983b) to openness to experience (John 1990) to a belief in the malleability of human relationships (Dweck 1999). Future research in this area should address these factors (and potential others) empirically.

Benefits of Same-Race Friendships

Given the negative treatment of ethnic minorities on college campuses, we opted to focus on the benefits of cross-group friendships in this chapter. A small but growing body of research suggests that intragroup contact experiences can also play a major role in the social and personal experiences of college students. Research suggests that because of differences in backgrounds and experiences, some ethnic minorities do not feel a part of and close to members of their own ethnic group in this same context (Davis and Shelton 2002; Smith and Moore 2000). Furthermore, some ethnic-minority students feel pressured by their in-group to conform to certain behaviors that result in negative emotions, depressive symptoms, and negative physical symptoms (Contrada et al. 2001). Perhaps close same-group friendships would reduce these deleterious consequences. Thus, additional work is needed not only on the benefits of cross-group friendships but also on the benefits of same-race friendships for ethnic-minority students at predominantly white institutions.

IMPLICATIONS FOR POLICY AND INTERVENTION

In light of the presented evidence on the benefits of cross-race friendships, how can institutions of higher education foster these friendships? In this section we discuss avenues for intervention that have been informed by our research programs.

Before considering how to foster cross-group friendship we briefly summarize the potential barriers to the development of these friendships. One must consider whether members of minority groups are treated with warmth and respect (see also Andersen, Downey, and Tyler in this volume) at the level of the institution, or whether they are simply tolerated. Does the local culture make all groups feel equally welcome or are there status differences among the groups that make it difficult for members from different groups to come together as equals? When the environment is experienced as threatening, members of minority groups may be more likely to turn to each other for support, resulting in self-segregation and tense intergroup relationships. Intergroup factors that are likely to influence cross-group contact include whether or not prevailing in-group norms encourage or discourage the development of cross-group relationships. These norms do not have to be explicitly expressed, but are often inferred from observing the behavior of other in-group members. To the extent that others in one's group interact exclusively with in-group members, a person may infer that cross-group relationships are not accepted or encouraged by the group. Intrapersonal factors one would have to address include negative past experiences that may have resulted in race-based rejection sensitivity. Also, a lack of cross-cultural experiences can result in apprehension with respect to cross-cultural interactions.

ASPECTS OF THE INSTITUTION

Institutions that seek to foster cross-group relationships must first reduce the potential identity threat a minority-group member is likely to encounter when entering a predominantly white environment. Ultimately, this goal can only be accomplished if minority students can be made to feel at home in the institution. Unequal status between groups has been linked to prejudice and discrimination and this undermines minority students' trust in the institutions and its members (Tropp 2003). Here we list just a few strategies that are expected to help equalize status relationships between groups.

One way to communicate that minority-group members are valued by the institution is to foster equality within the institution, including in positions of authority and power. Further, institutions should try to find ways to publicly communicate to minority-group members that they are welcome, respected, and appreciated. This can be achieved by, for example, including members of the minority group in important committees, ensuring that they have a voice in decisions that directly or indirectly affect them, treating them with fairness, and, most important, making sure that their voices are heard. An institution can also communicate that it values minority groups by showing pride in the multicultural nature of the institution, by publicly signaling acceptance and diversity, and by instituting a public policy that explicitly encourages and supports cross-cultural activities and relationships. Part of such a policy should be a commitment to treat members of all groups with fairness, dignity, and respect. When what minority-group members have to offer is valued by the institution, and when they experience their interactions with representatives of the institution as warm and caring, they may be able to feel comfortable which in turn results in the development of institutional trust (Purdie et al. 2001; see also Andersen, Downey, and Tyler, chapter 10, this volume).

Intergroup Factors

To improve intergroup relations, institutions should encourage cross-group exchanges that allow participants to recognize their common humanity. One avenue for fostering racial trust that seems particularly promising is the inclusion of minority students in integrated "living and learning" communities on campus (Steele 1999). In addition to offering opportunities for academic growth, these communities offer regular opportunities (rap sessions) during which students simply get together and discuss the personal side of college life in an informal setting. Claude M. Steele suggests that during these rap sessions participants are likely to learn that their personal concerns overlap with those of other students and as a result they develop the social trust needed to feel comfortable and confident that they will not be prejudged because of the color of their skin.

Interpersonal Factors

As Susan M. Andersen, Geraldine Downey, and Tom R. Tyler (chapter 10, this volume) point out, a positive relationship may well result in changed expectations regarding new partners who seem to be similar to the person with whom one has developed a good relationship. To ensure a positive experience, this relationship should initially involve a person who is highly skilled in the navigation of cross-cultural interactions, such as a counselor, a faculty mentor, or an experienced older student. Perhaps this person could also be a white roommate, carefully selected on the basis of having certain interests in common with the minority student. Considering the worry with which many students approach cross-group interactions, they might also benefit from receiving training in relationship-building skills and from access to a wider network of interested peers who support diversity in their close relationships.

In sum, there are many potential avenues for intervention that an institution interested in furthering the development of cross-group friendships could consider. Some of these interventions have already been implemented at selected institutions and initial reports regarding their effectiveness are encouraging (Steele 1999). Others are more speculative. We hope that future research will put all of these ideas to the test.

SUMMARY

In this chapter we examined whether close cross-group relationships with members of the dominant group can ameliorate the stress and alienation felt by minority-group students at predominantly white institutions of higher education. The results of three independent programs of research provide support for these predictions by indicating that minority students who engage in close cross-group friendships feel less alienated from their institutions, are better able and more willing to take advantage of institutional resources, and feel more confident of their ability to succeed at their predominantly white institutions. Taken together these data suggest that engaging in close cross-group friendships may be a useful coping strategy whereby minority students manage to navigate a potentially hostile environment. Finally, engaging in cross-group friendships is a potentially powerful antidote to the negative expectations and fear of rejection that many students have regarding cross-group contact.

REFERENCES

Allport, Gordon W. 1954. *The Nature of Prejudice.* Reading, Mass.: Addison-Wesley.

Amir, Yehuda. 1976. "The Role of Intergroup Contact in Change of Prejudice in Race Relations." In *Towards the Elimination of Racism,* edited by Phyllis A. Katz. New York: Pergamon.

Aron, Arthur, and Elaine N. Aron. 1986. *Love as the Expansion of Self: Understanding Attraction and Satisfaction.* New York: Hemisphere.

———. 1996. "Self and Self-Expansion in Relationships." In *Knowledge Structures in Close Relationships: A Social Psychological Approach,* edited by Garth J. O. Fletcher and Julie Fitness. Mahwah, N.J.: Erlbaum.

———. 1997. "Self-Expansion Motivation and Including Other in the Self." In *Handbook of Personal Relationships,* edited by Steve Duck. Volume 1. 2nd edition. London: Wiley.

Aron, Arthur, Elaine N. Aron, and Danny Smollan. 1992. "Inclusion of Other in the Self Scale and the Structure of Interpersonal Closeness." *Journal of Personality and Social Psychology* 63(4): 596–612.

Aron, Arthur, and Tracy McLaughlin-Volpe. 2001. "Including Others in the Self: Extensions to Own and Partner's Group Memberships." In *Individual Self, Relational Self, and Collective Self: Partners, Opponents, or Strangers,* edited by Marilyn Brewer and Constantine Sedikides. Mahwah, N.J.: Erlbaum.

Bennett, Christina, and Alton M. Okinaka. 1990. "Factors Related to Persistence Among Asian, African American, Hispanic, and White Undergraduates at a Predominantly White University: Comparison Between First and Fourth Year Cohorts." *Urban Review* 22(1): 33–60.

Blascovich, Jim, Wendy B. Mendes, Sarah B. Hunter, Brian Lickel, and Neneh Kowai–Bell. 2001. "Perceiver Threat in Social Interactions with Stigmatized Others." *Journal of Personality and Social Psychology* 80(2): 253–67.

Bowen, William G., and Derek Bok. 1998. *The Shape of the River: Long-Term Consequences of Considering Race in College and University Admissions.* Princeton, N.J.: Princeton University Press.

Buhrmester, Duane, and Wyndol Furman. 1987. "The Development of Companionship and Intimacy." *Child Development* 58(4): 1101–13.

Cantor, Nancy, Julie K. Norem, Paula M. Niedenthal, and Christopher A. Langston. 1987. "Life Tasks, Self-Concept Ideals, and Cognitive Strategies in a Life Transition." *Journal of Personality and Social Psychology* 53(6): 1178–91.

Cohen, Elizabeth. 1975. "The Effects of Desegregation on Race Relations." *Law and Contemporary Problems* 39(2): 271–99.

Contrada, Richard J., Richard D. Ashmore, Melvin L. Gary, Elliot Coups, Jill D. Egeth, Andrea Sewell, Kevin Ewell, Tanya M. Goyal, and Valerie Chasse. 2001. "Measures of Ethnicity-Related Stress: Psychometric Properties, Ethnic Group Differences, and Associations with Well-Being." *Journal of Applied Social Psychology* 31(9): 1775–1820.

Cook, Stuart. 1978. "Interpersonal and Attitudinal Outcomes in Cooperating Interracial Groups." *Journal of Research and Development in Education* 12(1): 97–113.

———. 1986. "Experimenting on Social Issues: The Case of School Desegregation." *American Psychologist* 40(4): 452–60.

Crandall, Christian S., Kristin L. Schiffhauer, and Richard Harvey. 1997. "Friendship Pair Similarity as a Measure of Group Value." *Group Dynamics: Theory, Research, and Practice* 1(2): 133–43.

Crocker, Jennifer, Brenda Major, and Claude M. Steele. 1998. "Social Stigma." In *The Handbook of Social Psychology*, edited by Daniel T. Gilbert and Susan T. Fiske. Volume 2. 4th edition. New York: McGraw-Hill.

Crosnoe, Robert, Shannon Cavanagh, and Glen H. Elder Jr. 2003. "Adolescent Friendships as Academic Resources: The Intersection of Friendship, Race, and School Disadvantage." *Sociological Perspectives* 46(3): 331–52.

Cross, William E., Jr., and Linda Strauss. 1998. "The Everyday Functions of African American Identity." In *Prejudice: The Target's Perspective*, edited by Janet K. Swim and Charles Stangor. San Diego: Academic Press.

Dana, Richard H. 2002. "Mental Health Services for African Americans: A Cultural/Racial Perspective." *Cultural Diversity and Ethnic Minority Psychology* 8(1): 3–18.

Davis, Audrey, and J. Nicole Shelton. 2002. *Intragroup Alienation and Ethnic Identity*. Unpublished data. Princeton University.

Davis, Mark H. 1983a. "Measuring Individual Differences in Empathy: Evidence for a Multidimensional Approach." *Journal of Personality and Social Psychology* 44(1): 113–26.

———. 1983b. "The Effects of Dispositional Empathy on Emotional Reactions and Helping: A Multidimensional Approach." *Journal of Personality* 51(1): 167–84.

Dweck, Carol. 1999. *Self-Theories: Their Role in Motivation, Personality, and Development*. Philadelphia: Psychology Press/Taylor & Francis.

Fine, Michelle, Lois Weiss, and Linda C. Powell. 1997. "Communities of Difference: A Critical Look at Desegregated Spaces Created for and by Youth." *Harvard Educational Review* 67(2): 247–84.

Fordham, Signithia. 1988. "Racelessness as a Factor in Black Students' School Success: Pragmatic Strategy or Pyrrhic Victory?" *Harvard Educational Review* 58(1): 54–84.

Fordham, Signithia, and John Ogbu. 1986. "Black Students' School Success: Coping with the Burden of 'Acting White.'" *The Urban Review* 18(3): 176–206.

Frable, Deborah E., Tamela Blackstone, and Carol Scherbaum. 1990. "Marginal and Mindful: Deviants in Social Interactions." *Journal of Personality and Social Psychology* 59(1): 140–49.

Gaertner, Samuel L., John F. Dovidio, and Betty A. Bachman. 1996. "Revisiting the Contact Hypothesis: The Induction of a Common Ingroup Identity." *International Journal of Intercultural Relations* 20(3–4): 271–90.

Gaines, Stanley O. J. 2001. "Coping with Prejudice: Personal Relationship Partners as Sources of Socioemotional Support for Stigmatized Individuals." *Journal of Social Issues* (special issue: *Stigma: An Insider's Perspective*) 57(1): 113–28.

Goffman, Erving. 1963. *Stigma: Notes on the Management of Spoiled Identity.* New York: Touchstone.

Graham, Calvin, Robert W. Baker, and Seymour Wapner. 1985. "Prior Interracial Experience and Black Student Transition into Predominantly White Colleges." *Journal of Personality and Social Psychology* 47(5): 1146–54.

Gurin, Patricia, Eric Dey, Sylvia Hurtado, and Gerald Gurin. 2002. "Diversity and Higher Education: Theory and Impact on Educational Outcomes." *Harvard Educational Review* 72(3): 330–66.

Hallinan, Maureen T., and Stevens S. Smith. 1985. "The Effects of Classroom Racial Composition on Students' Interracial Friendliness." *Social Psychology Quarterly* 48(1): 3–16.

Hallinan, Maureen T., and Roy A. Teixeira. 1987. "Opportunities and Constraints: Black-White Differences in the Formation of Interracial Friendships." *Child Development* (special issue: *Schools and Development*) 58(5): 1358–71.

Hamm, Jill V. 2000. "Do Birds of a Feather Flock Together? The Variable Bases for African American, Asian American, and European American Adolescents' Selection of Similar Friends." *Developmental Psychology* 36(2): 209–19.

Hartup, Willard W. 1996. "The Company They Keep: Friendships and Their Developmental Significance." *Child Development* 67(1): 1–13.

Hartup, Willard W., and Nan Stevens. 1997. "Friendships and Adaptation in the Life Course." *Psychological Bulletin* 121(3): 355–70.

Hodges, Ernest V. E., Michel Boivin, Frank Vitaro, and William M. Bukowski. 1999. "The Power of Friendship: Protection Against an Escalating Cycle of Peer Victimization." *Developmental Psychology* 35(1): 94–101.

Ickes, William. 1984. "Compositions in Black and White: Determinants of Interaction in Interracial Dyads." *Journal of Personality and Social Psychology* 47(2): 330–41.

John, Oliver P. 1990. "The 'Big Five' Factor Taxonomy: Dimensions of Personality in the Natural Language and in Questionnaires." In *Handbook of Personality: Theory and Research,* edited by Lawrence Pervin. New York: Guilford.

Jones, James M. 1972/1997. *Prejudice and Racism.* Reading, Mass.: Addison-Wesley.

Khmelkov, Vladimir T., and Maureen T. Hallinan. 1999. "Organizational Effects on Race Relations in Schools." *Journal of Social Issues* 55(4): 627–45.

Levin, Shana, Colette van Laar, and Jim Sidanius. 2003. "The Effects of Ingroup and Outgroup Friendship on Ethnic Attitudes in College: A Longitudinal Study." *Group Processes and Intergroup Relations* 6(1): 76–92.

Loo, Chalsa M., and Garry Rolison. 1986. "Alienation of Ethnic Minority Students at a Predominantly White University." *Journal of Higher Education* 57(1): 58–77.

Major, Brenda, Wendy Quinton, and Shannon K. McCoy. 2002. "Antecedents and Consequences of Attributions to Discrimination: Theoretical and Empirical Advances." In *Advances in Experimental Social Psychology,* edited by Mark Zanna. Volume 34. San Diego: Academic Press.

McLaughlin-Volpe, Tracy. 2001. "The Self-Expansion Model: Extensions to Ingroup Identification." Paper presented at the Society for Personality and Social Psychology (SPSP) Conference. San Antonio (February 2001).

McLaughlin-Volpe, Tracy, Arthur Aron, Harry T. Reis, and Stephen C. Wright. 2002. "Intergroup Social Interactions and Intergroup Prejudice: Quantity Versus Quality." Unpublished paper. State University of New York, Stony Brook.

Mendoza-Denton, Rodolfo, Ozlem N. Ayduk, Yuchi Shoda, and Walter Mischel. 1997. "Cognitive-Affective Processing System Analysis of Reactions to the O. J. Simpson Criminal Trial Verdict." *Journal of Social Issues* (special issue: *The O. J. Simpson Trial: Research and Theory on the Dynamics of Ethnicity*) 53(3): 563–81.

Mendoza-Denton, Rodolfo, and Elizabeth Page-Gould. 2002. *Cross-Race Friendships and Academic Performance.* Unpublished data. University of California, Berkeley.

Mendoza-Denton, Rodolfo, Elizabeth Page-Gould, and Janina Pietrzak. Forthcoming. "Mechanisms for Coping with Status-Based Rejection Expectations." In *Stigma and Group Inequality: Social Psychological Perspectives,* edited by Shana Levin and Colette van Laar. Mahwah, N.J.: Erlbaum.

Mendoza-Denton, Rodolfo, Geraldine Downey, Valerie J. Purdie, Angelina Davis, and Janina Pietrzak. 2002. "Sensitivity to Status-Based Rejection: Implications for African American Students' College Experience." *Journal of Personality and Social Psychology* 83(4): 896–918.

Mendoza-Denton, Rodolfo, Yuchi Shoda, Ozlem Ayduk, and Walter Mischel. 1999. "Applying Cognitive-Affective Processing System Theory to Cultural Differences in Social Behavior." In *Merging Past, Present, and Future in Cross-Cultural Psychology,* edited by Walter L. Lonner, Dale L. Dinnel, Deborah K. Forgays, and Susanna A. Hayes. Lisse, Netherlands: Swets & Zeitlinger.

Millet, Peter E. 1995. "Predicting Depression, Stress, and Self-Esteem in Black and White Students at a Predominantly White University." Ph.D. diss., Ohio State University.

Moody, James. 2001. "Race, School Integration, and Friendship Segregation in America." *American Journal of Sociology* 107(3): 679–716.

Newcomb, Andrew F., and Catherine L. Bagwell. 1995. "Children's Friendship Relations: A Meta-Analytic Review." *Psychological Bulletin* 117(2): 306–47.

Oyserman, Daphne, and Janet K. Swim. 2001. "Stigma: An Insider's View." *Journal of Social Issues* (special issue: *Stigma: An Insider's Perspective*) 57(1): 113–28.

Paolini, Stefania, Miles Hewstone, Ed Cairns, and Alberto Voci. 2004. "Effects of Direct and Indirect Cross-Group Friendships on Judgments of Catholics and Protestants in Northern Ireland: The Mediating Role of an Anxiety-Reduction Mechanism." *Personality Social Psychology Bulletin* 30(6): 770–77.

Pettigrew, Thomas F. 1997. "Generalized Intergroup Effects on Prejudice." *Personality and Social Psychology Bulletin,* 23(2): 173–85.

Pettigrew, Thomas F., and Linda R. Tropp. 2000. "Does Intergroup Contact Reduce Prejudice? Recent Meta-Analytic Findings." In *Reducing Prejudice and Discrimination: The Claremont Symposium on Applied Social Psychology,* edited by Stuart Oskamp. Mahwah, N.J.: Erlbaum.

Pinel, Elizabeth C. 1999. "Stigma Consciousness: The Psychological Legacy of Social Stereotypes." *Journal of Personality and Social Psychology* 76(1): 114–28.

Pounds, Augustine W. 1987. "Black Students' Needs on Predominantly White Campuses." In *Responding to the Needs of Today's Minority Students: New Directions for Student Services,* no. 38, edited by Doris J. Wright. San Francisco: Jossey-Bass/Pfeiffer.

Purdie, Valerie J., Claude M. Steele, P. G. Davies, and Jennifer R. Crosby. 2001. "The Business of Diversity: Minority Trust Within Organizational Cultures." Paper presented at the annual meeting of the American Psychological Association. San Francisco (August 22–26).

Richeson, Jennifer A., and J. Nicole Shelton. 2003. "When Prejudice Does Not Pay: Effects of Interracial Contact on Executive Function." *Psychological Science* 14(3): 287–90.

Robinson, Tracy L. 1999. "The Intersections of Dominant Discourses Across Race, Gender, and Other Identities." *Journal of Counseling and Development* 77(1): 73–79.

Rothbart, Myron, and Oliver John. 1985. "Social Categorization and Behavioral Episodes: A Cognitive Analysis of the Effects of Intergroup Contact." *Journal of Social Issues* 41(3): 81–104.

Shelton, J. Nicole. 2002. "Minority Students' Experiences at Predominantly White Colleges." Unpublished data. Princeton University.

———. 2003. "Interpersonal Concerns in Social Encounters Between Majority and Minority Group Members." *Group Processes and Intergroup Relations* 6(2): 171–86.

Shelton, J. Nicole, and Jennifer A. Richeson. 2003. "Ethnic Minorities' Racial Attitudes and Contact Experiences with Whites." Unpublished paper. Princeton University.

———. Forthcoming. "Intergroup Contact and Pluralistic Ignorance." *Journal of Personality and Social Psychology.*

Sherif, Muzafer. 1966. *The Psychology of Social Norms.* Oxford: Harper Torchbooks.

Slavin, Robert. 1979. *Cooperative Learning.* Baltimore: Johns Hopkins University Center for Social Organization in Schools.

Smith, Eliot R., Julie Murphy, and Susan Coats. 1999. "Attachment to Groups: Theory and Measurement." *Journal of Personality and Social Psychology* 77(1): 94–110.

Smith, Sandra, and Mignon Moore. 2000. "Intraracial Diversity and Relations Among African-Americans: Closeness Among Black Students at a Predominantly White University." *American Journal of Sociology* 106(1): 1–39.

Spencer, Margaret B. 1995. "Old Issues and New Theorizing About African-American Youth: A Phenomenological Variant of Ecological Systems Theory." In *African-American Youth: Their Social and Economic Status in the United States,* edited by Ronald L. Taylor. Westport, Conn.: Praeger.

Steele, Claude M. 1999. "Thin Ice: 'Stereotype Threat' and Black College Students." *The Atlantic Monthly* (August).

Stinson, Linda, and William Ickes. 1992. "Empathic Accuracy in the Interactions of Male Friends Versus Male Strangers." *Journal of Personality and Social Psychology* 62(5): 787–97.

Suarez, Shirley A., Blaine J. Fowers, Carolyn S. Garwood, and Jose Szapocznik. 1997. "Biculturalism, Differentness, Loneliness, and Alienation in Hispanic College Students." *Hispanic Journal of Behavioral Sciences* 19(4): 489–505.

Suen, Hoi K. 1983. "Alienation and Attrition of Black College Students on a Predominantly White Campus." *Journal of College Student Personnel* 24(2): 117–21.

Sullivan, Harry S. 1953. *The Interpersonal Theory of Psychiatry.* New York: Norton.

Tropp, Linda R. 2003. "The Psychological Impact of Prejudice: Implications for Intergroup Contact." *Group Processes and Intergroup Relation* 6(2): 131–49.

Tuch, Steven A., Lee Sigelman, and Jason A. MacDonald. 1999. "The Polls—Trends: Race Relations and American Youth, 1976–1995." *Public Opinion Quarterly* 63(1): 109–48.

Willie, Charles V. 1981. *The Ivory and Ebony Towers: Race Relations and Higher Education.* Lexington, Mass.: Lexington Books.

Wright, Stephen C., Arthur Aron, Tracy McLaughlin-Volpe, and Stacy A. Ropp. 1997. "The Extended Contact Effect: Knowledge of Cross-Group Friendships and Prejudice." *Journal of Personality and Social Psychology* 73(1): 73–90.

CHAPTER 10

BECOMING ENGAGED IN THE COMMUNITY: A RELATIONAL PERSPECTIVE ON SOCIAL IDENTITY AND COMMUNITY ENGAGEMENT

Susan M. Andersen, Geraldine Downey, and Tom R. Tyler

All else being equal, it is valuable for people to be engaged in social institutions and in society. People benefit because engagement helps them cope more effectively with their problems, maintain feelings of self-worth and positivity, and experience a favorable identity (Tyler, Degoey, and Smith 1996). A sense of social integration is clearly of value for mental and physical health (House, Landis, and Umberson 1988). For example, among adolescents, having strong ties to school and family helps prevent emotional distress, violence, and substance abuse and promotes school achievement (Blum and Rinehart 1997; Connell, Aber, and Walker 1995; Elliott et al. 1996; Hoyle and Crawford 1994; National Research Council 1993; Resnick et al. 1997; Sampson, Raudenbush, and Earls 1997). Connectedness with still broader communities, such as one's neighborhood or other social groups beyond family and kin, is also likely to be beneficial. Although there may be limits to the benefits of being well connected with a poorly functioning or otherwise problematic community or family, the overall effect of social integration is undoubtedly positive.

Of course, when people are engaged in institutions, the institutions function more effectively. Engaged people are willing to cooperate voluntarily with institutional norms and rules. Work organizations depend on their members' doing things for the good of the group and not just when required to do so (Tyler and Blader 2000). Voluntary "extra-role behaviors" such as, in most universities, faculty service on university or departmental committees, are necessary for the functioning of the group. Likewise, legal and political authorities rely on voluntary cooperation from the public at large in obeying the law (Tyler 1990a; Tyler and Huo 2002). Neighborhoods and communities are characterized as cohesive when members go beyond their role requirements to monitor and regulate the antisocial behavior of their own youths for the sake of the broader group and for the sake of the youths themselves.

Why are people willing to voluntarily make a behavioral commitment to a group, rather than simply pursue their own personal, individual self-interest? Our purpose in this chapter is to examine this question, and also to consider how dyadic relationships may be relevant, thereby enabling a multilayered approach to social identity that includes the relational level of analysis. It is well established that people tend to go along with group decisions that do not necessarily serve their immediate self-interest to the extent that they identify strongly and positively with the group and experience a sense of merging of self with the group (Tyler and Huo 2002). Thus, understanding the process by which such social identification with groups and institutions may arise is critical for understanding how people engage in their communities. Our overarching goal is to elucidate the role of personal or dyadic relations in social identification and group engagement.

SOCIAL IDENTIFICATION

Like other authors in this volume, we define social identification fairly broadly and assume that it is multifaceted (for example, chapters 7 and 8, this volume; see Ashmore, Deaux, and McLaughlin-Volpe 2004). One view of social identity is that it involves an overlap between a person's concept of the self and his or her concept of a group (Aron and McLaughlin-Volpe 2001; Smith and Henry 1996). Still more simply, social identity presupposes self-categorization, labeling oneself as an x or a y. The minimal intergroup paradigm makes it clear that merely categorizing oneself as a member of a group is sufficient to produce a variety of biases associated with identification with a group, such as in-group bias and out-group derogation (Hogg and Abrams 1988; Tajfel and Turner 1979). A more stringent set of criteria for determining whether or not one holds a particular social identity can be considered as well, such as the centrality of group membership to the self (Sellers and Shelton 2003). On another level, group identification is considerably more likely to matter when the group is in the minority than when it is in the majority, and under such circumstances group membership becomes salient (for example Brewer and Roccas 2001).

Although we acknowledge that social identity is multiply determined and multidimensional (see Ashmore, Deaux, and McLaughlin-Volpe 2004), we emphasize in particular two facets of social identity that reflect our interest in the construct of community engagement. These are voluntary cooperation with a group and the sense of belonging. Other researchers have argued, on the basis of existing evidence, that an important motivation for people's identification with and behavioral commitment to a group is the fundamental human need to belong (Baumeister and Leary 1995; see also Andersen and Chen 2002; Andersen, Reznik, and Chen 1997). People can meet this need by virtue of shared group memberships (the "collective self") or by virtue of dyadic links to specific others (the "relational self"; see Sedikides and Brewer 2001; see also Andersen and Chen 2002).

RELEVANCE OF DYADIC RELATIONSHIPS
FOR SOCIAL IDENTITY AND
GROUP ENGAGEMENT

Much work on understanding how people develop a sense of belonging or a comparable feeling points to the role of dyadic relationships or interactions in conveying a sense of acceptance (Levy, Ayduk, and Downey 2001). The evidence involves the relational level of analysis, and suggests that dyadic relationships may be the core glue that binds people together in social groups. Dyadic relationships have long been assumed to be represented in memory through mental models of attachment, and the evidence for this is quite compelling (Reis and Patrick 1996). Indeed, attachment to groups appears to proceed in much the same way as does attachment in close relationships (see Aron and McLaughlin-Volpe 2001; Smith, Coats, and Murphy 2001; Smith and Henry 1996). In our view of the human need for connection, we define connectedness as kindness, compassion, warmth, and bondedness, and suggest that it exists alongside needs for group affiliation rather than simply as an aspect of needs for group affiliation.

This working assumption guides our efforts to elucidate the role of personal or dyadic relationships in the process of social identification and hence in enhancing social engagement. Social identification concerns the degree to which one sees oneself as part of a group and regards this as important; such groups are formal and informal, large and small communities and institutions. Perhaps the most fundamental group identifications are those that arise first, involving gender and ethnic background (see Brewer 1988). Religion, extended family, neighborhood or village, school, and tribe or clan can also be relevant. Whereas much scholarly work has been devoted to social or collective identity in recent years, far less has focused on relational identity (see Sedikides and Brewer 2001), and still less has explicitly linked the two. Relational identity is the sense of self in relation to a specific other in one's life, that is, the way the self is experienced and manifested by means of a particular relationship (Andersen, Reznik, and Chen 1997). A comprehensive model of social identity needs to take into account that multiple levels of identity exist in considering the self, and that these different levels of identity may be differentially active in differing situations, depending on the contextual cues to which the individual is exposed (Brewer and Roccas 2001). For example, a person may choose to do something like "code switching" not only between competing social identities (Strauss and Cross, chapter 4, this volume) but perhaps between social, relational, and personal levels of identity.

FOCUS OF THIS CHAPTER

We focus in this chapter on the links between relational and social identity and concern ourselves with the following questions: How can positive dyadic relationships promote a strong and positive social identity? How can we best understand the processes involved in relational identities and the ways these processes function in social identity? In pursuing these questions, we seek to develop a framework that integrates three highly relevant but quite distinct theoretical models and empirical literatures, each of which sheds light on the relational aspects of social identity and engagement. We begin by reviewing these theories and their respective empirical literatures. We then present an integrative framework for thinking about social and relational identity and a set of broad hypotheses deriving from the framework. Finally, we describe evidence from a series of studies that offers some support for these hypotheses and discuss the evidence in a way that suggests a number of conclusions as well as questions for future research. We also consider the implications of these findings for effective coping and engagement within communities, institutions, and even nations.

OVERVIEW OF THREE
THEORETICAL MODELS

A core assumption of the three models is that interpersonal interactions convey information that can affect a perceiver. Notably, the group value model highlights the fact that trust and respect can signify (and matter for) social identity (Tyler and Blader 2000). Likewise, the relational self and rejection sensitivity models highlight the role of acceptance and bonding, communicated either directly or indirectly in social encounters, in shaping people's subsequent interpersonal relations (Andersen, Reznik, and Manzella 1996; Downey and Feldman 1996). Of course, there are also differences in the questions the models were developed to study (social identity versus interpersonal relationships) and the theoretical tradition from which they emerge. Our goal is to highlight both the common and distinctive features of each model, as well as the ways they complement each other as we use them to construct an integrative framework for understanding both relational and social identity.

GROUP-VALUE MODEL   Of the three theories we consider, the group-value theory and its extension to group engagement (for example, Tyler and Lind 1992) is most directly concerned with the question of what fosters positive behavioral engagement in communities. The model is rooted in social-justice accounts of social identification and organizational engagement, and it assumes that voluntary cooperation with groups cannot be explained entirely by rational self-interest. Instead, relational aspects of how one is treated by group authorities are crucial for eliciting willing cooperation with the group—that is, if one identifies with the group.

The group-value model and research supporting it provides both the rationale and the evidence that interactions matter in identification. On the other hand, it provides few insights into the processes whereby relational treatment might influence behavioral engagement, regardless of initial level of identification. To unpack these processes we draw on thinking about the relational self (Andersen and Chen 2002) and also rejection sensitivity (Downey and Feldman 1996).

RELATIONAL-SELF MODEL   The relational-self model offers a social-cognitive account of how prior relationships shape what one expects, wants, thinks, and feels, and even how one behaves in later relationships (Andersen and Chen 2002). The model emphasizes how specific relationships with significant others give rise to specific relational identities, how these are evoked in new situations when cues in a new person remind one of a given significant other, activating the representation of this other and the process of transference in everyday perception (Andersen and Glassman 1996; Chen and Andersen 1999). This is an if-then model focused on shifts in responses across situations.[1] The process includes becoming the version of the self one typically is with this significant other in an encounter with a different person. With respect to social identity, it is likely that, when a significant other is activated by contextual cues, so are various categorical aspects of the other that are likely to be relevant to one's own social identity, such as gender and ethnicity. Thus, any social identity one shares with a significant other should be activated when the mental representation of that other is activated (see Baum and Andersen 1999; see also Karylowski, Konarzewski, and Motes 2000). Being treated in a way that is similar to the way one is (or was) treated by a significant other promotes transference and, in a positive transference, leads to positive responses to this new person. Moreover, the fact that the categories to which the significant other belongs are activated along with the representation suggests that under some circumstances, the positive responses that one has in transference are applied to the groups the individual belongs to as well.

REJECTION-SENSITIVITY MODEL   The rejection-sensitivity model provides a different kind of social-cognitive account of how interactional experiences shape how people perceive their relations with others and with social groups. The basic contention is that experiences of rejection with important people in one's life will foster expectancies of rejection, under the right conditions. A distinctive sensitivity to rejection may arise with caretakers or with others in important role relations with the individual, and comes to influence current expectancies in new contexts when triggered by interpersonal cues, especially under conditions similar to initial contexts of rejection. Being rejection-sensitive can lead one to anxiously expect rejection and to respond with hostility or withdrawal to ambiguous interpersonal cues. The rejection-sensitivity model distinguishes between rejection based on personal characteristics and that based on status characteristics. It also addresses, through a qualitatively based inductive approach, how people's concerns about lack of support in times of vulnerability arise. The potential for support (or lack of support) in times of vulnerability is central in understanding close relationships. This is not usually considered especially relevant to collective identity because the respect (or lack of respect) from the group is what has been emphasized (Tyler and Lind 1992). Our argument here is that both factors are relevant in collective identity. The model of the relational self suggests that being treated with warmth and care may evoke not only relational identity but also collective identity under some conditions, whereas the rejection-sensitivity model emphasizes the distinctness of the relational and the collective. The latter model assumes that both processes are likely to be operational, and assumes that which level of identification is most prominent at any moment is likely to depend on environmental cues.

   We now examine each model in greater detail.

The Group-Value Model

The basic premise of the group-value model is that people care about the nature of their social connection with groups and are thus influenced by relational indicators of the quality of that connection (Tyler and Lind 1992). In general, people's reactions to groups are shaped by procedural-fairness judgments that reflect relational assessments and that are relatively unrelated to the favorability of the outcomes of the interactions. This becomes even more the case when the nature of people's social connection to the group is more identity-relevant, as when their sense of self is more strongly merged with the group. Yet relational indicators are also a critical determinant of whether people identify with a group. When people experience a group as having fair procedures, their sense of status and feelings of self-worth is affirmed and they are more likely to identify with the group, and incorporate it into their sense of self.

Whereas groups can usually enact decision-making procedures that their members will experience as fair, it is not always possible to give people exactly what they want or what they feel they deserve. For example, a group may have too little of a desired resource (such as funds for salary increases), or regulatory authorities such as the police and the courts may have to deliver outcomes that people do not like. In such cases, there is evidence that authorities benefit from being judged against criteria of how fairly they exercise their authority. Whether they use fair and just procedures matters a great deal because the use of such procedures is associated with people's cooperation with decisions emanating from the group even when they receive outcomes that do not favor them. That is, even when self-interest is not satisfied, people will tend to go along with the group decision when the decision-making process is fair.

Studies of procedural justice have identified neutrality, trust, and respect as especially important relational predictors of people's identities and level of cooperation in groups. Allowing people opportunities for participation in decisions that influence the group is also an important relational influence because it recognizes people's status as members of their group who are entitled to be involved in determinations of group action (Tyler and Lind 1992; Tyler and Smith 1999). Neutrality communicates to people that their status within the group is defended via unbiased and factual decision making that protects them from being undermined by the exercise of prejudice or unfair preference. Trust is linked to the person's assessment that authorities are concerned about their needs and will consider them. Finally, respectful, dignified, and polite treatment communicates inclusion and standing within the group.

There is considerable evidence from correlational studies to support the central tenets of the group-value model and its extension to the group-engagement model (see Tyler and Blader 2000). First, relational aspects of treatment have been consistently found to predict behavioral engagement, especially when people identify with groups. Second, these aspects of treatment are strong predictors of whether people do, in fact, come to identify with groups.

IMPORTANCE OF RELATIONAL TREATMENT   There is much evidence from a variety of studies by Tom R. Tyler and colleagues that when people identify with a group or institution, they are more willing to undertake "extra-role" behavior that is useful to the group but not required by it. In addition, when people identify with a group or institution, they are more willing to accept the decisions handed down by authorities within the group or institution. In fact, a central finding is that when one identifies with a group, the exact outcomes one receives and their favorability matter much less than how one is treated. If one does not identify with the group, what matters most is whether the outcome itself is good or bad. For example, a study (Tyler and Huo 2002) of the relationship between legal authorities and those living within two urban communities suggests that if people identify with a group, in this case their community, they evaluate the decisions of its authorities by judging the fairness of the procedures by which those decisions were made. If they do not identify with the group, they evaluate decisions by their favorability.

Further evidence that the impact of relational aspects of treatment depends on whether or not one is identified with the group comes from studies showing that people are more strongly influenced by how they are treated by in-group than out-group members when social membership information is salient to them and central to their self-definitions. First, studies of naturally occurring disputes suggest that people care more strongly about how they are treated by an authority when they share a common group membership with that authority than when they do not (Tyler and Smith 1999), and they care more about their treatment by in-group than out-group peers (Tyler et al. 1998). Second, when people are primed to think of an authority as a member of their group, as opposed to an outsider, they are more strongly influenced by how that person treats them. Of particular importance is the finding that people's sense of self-esteem is shaped by quality of treatment when that treatment is from an in-group member, but not when it is from an outsider (Smith et al. 1998).

Third, studies focusing on the strength of people's psychological identification with groups also suggest that when people have merged their sense of self more completely into a group, they are more strongly influenced by the quality of the treatment they experience from others in the group. For example, research exploring the psychology underlying people's willingness to cooperate with water-use restrictions during a drought has shown that people were more cooperative with group rules when they thought those rules were enacted and implemented via fair procedures (Tyler and Degoey 1995). In addition, those who identified more strongly with the group were more strongly influenced by their own perceptions of how procedurally just the group decisions are. Similarly, research conducted in a work setting has shown that whether employees accepted decisions made by their supervisor was shaped by their perception of the fairness of the decision-making procedure (Huo et al. 1996). In addition, those who identified more strongly with the work organization were more strongly influenced by their perception of whether or not procedures were fair.

WHAT PROMOTES SOCIAL IDENTIFICATION   When people identify with a group, their acceptance of decisions by group authorities and their self-esteem depend on whether or not group authorities treat them in relationally appropriate ways. What influences whether people identify with groups? Once again the relational aspects of their treatment by the group, including decision-making procedures and socio-emotional aspects of interactions with group members, appear to be a particularly influential determinant of the strength of identification. In fact, how people are treated has a stronger effect on their identification with a group than either the resources that they obtain from group membership or the fairness of the resource-distribution process (Tyler et al. 1997; Tyler and Lind 1988; Tyler and Smith 1997).

Four data sets support the claim not only that the relational aspects of authorities' treatment are salient when individuals have become identified with a group but also that these same behaviors shape the strength of identification and mediate the link between procedural-justice judgments and cooperative behaviors (Tyler, Degoey, and Smith 1996). The data are from parents dealing with children; managers dealing with employees; teachers dealing with students; and political leaders dealing with citizens. The data show that the quality of treatment that people experience from authorities changes their assessments of their social relationship to the group, specifically their sense of belonging within the group and having status that is linked to membership in a group. Changes in these aspects of identity helped mediate the impact of procedural justice on people's cooperation with groups and their self-esteem, supporting the argument that social identification matters for the well-being of both the individual and the group.

SUMMARY   Converging evidence shows that social identification matters for group engagement and that understanding its relational underpinnings is of profound significance. This issue is of particular interest with regard to those entering the group from a disadvantaged position or with doubts about whether they should commit to the group or will be accepted by the group.

The Relational-Self Model

Whereas the group-value model posits that people's sense of identity with groups is shaped by relational aspects of the treatment they receive from group members, the central question of the relational-self model is how relational experiences with significant others impact interpersonal relations more generally, and by extension, social identity (Andersen and Chen 2002).

The basic assumption of the theory of the relational self is that individuals form relational identities in relation to other people who are significant to the self. They are emotionally and motivationally important. Hence, people have a distinctive mental representation of the self linked to each significant other in their lives. These relational self-representations encompass varying aspects of the self and are indirectly triggered when the significant-other representation is triggered, such as in the social-cognitive process of transference. Triggering cues may include a few similar habits, preferences, styles of interacting, thoughts, feelings, or physical appearance. When such contextual cues emanating from a new person activate a significant-other representation, this indirectly activates the version of the self associated with that other. Through cue-triggered activation of the transference process, variability in how the self perceives, remembers, and responds arises across interpersonal contexts. The model is thus in the class of if-then personality models that emphasize contemporary (if momentary) situational cues and changes in the self that result from them (Chen and Andersen 1999).

This social-cognitive account of the process of transference delineates how prior relational experiences with significant others, as represented in memory, are activated with new people in the present. The result is very "hot" cognition (Metcalfe and Mischel 1999) slanted by emotion and motivation—rejection expectations that are affectively amplified because they reflect appraisals of threat (Lazarus 1993), as well as the motives, emotions, interpersonal roles, expectations, and behavior that characterized one's experiences with the significant other, as well as the concept of self one typically experienced in this context, are evoked in response to a new person.

The relational self consists of those aspects of the self and identity that are bound up (or entangled) with specific significant others and that tend to manifest themselves in these relationships. The model proposes that transference underlies both stability in the self over time and context-dependency in the present time frame (shifts across differing interpersonal contexts). Because the relational self involves the representation of a close other and relationship with this other, multiplied by all the significant persons in one's life, it encompasses various properties of close relationships. These include the familiarity of the other (for example, Andersen, Reznik, and Glassman 2005; Prentice 1990); the emotional and motivational relevance of the other to the self; and the interdependencies between self and other that exist in the relationship (see, for example, Rusbult and Van Lange 1996). In this sense, a kind of unit relation exists with the other irrespective of the valence of the relationship or whether the other person is accepting or rejecting (for example, Chen and Andersen 1999). In other words, someone you detest may nonetheless have been of deep significance in your life, and the mental representation of such a person may still be triggered and brought to bear in present encounters. The relational-self model thus highlights the long-standing influences on the self and social relations that people bring to situations as "baggage." One is familiar with these selves, and experiences them with new people within a contemporaneous context, when the significant other is not physically present.

THE EVIDENCE   Experiments intended to activate a significant-other representation use trigger cues presented as features of a new person, for example, apparent attitudes, preferences, traits, habits and activities, and styles of relating. If these cues "map onto" (see also Markman and Gentner 2005) those of a significant other, the representation will be activated and used, influencing interpersonal perception and relations as well as the self. In this way, past relationships arise in the present. Experimental studies using this logic have provided considerable support for the relational-self model. Weeks in advance of the experiment participants describe features of a few significant others. Later, in an allegedly unrelated study, they are exposed to information about a new person whom they expect to meet and who shares (or does not) a small number of a significant other's qualities.

The results show that the significant-other representation drives inferences about and memory of a new person when his or her features resemble (versus do not resemble) those of the significant other (Andersen and Cole 1990), even when such features are presented completely outside of awareness (Glassman and Andersen 1999). This process appears to be the result of both the chronic accessibility of significant-other representations and transient contextual cueing (Andersen et al. 1995; Chen, Andersen, and Hinkley 1999). The quality and content of the features of the significant other that are used as triggering cues have been ruled out as an alternative explanation for the effect, as have other mnemonic effects and biases.

Activation of a significant-other representation also elicits the evaluative responses, expectations, motivations, goal states, and self-regulatory patterns associated with the significant other (Andersen and Baum 1994; Andersen, Reznik, and Manzella

1996; Berenson and Andersen 2004; Berk and Andersen 2000; Shah 2003a, 2003b), as in the process of schema-triggered affect (Fiske and Pavelchak 1986). In terms of affective and motivational evidence, when transference occurs, a relatively immediate automatic positive or negative response is shown in the participant's facial expressions of emotion (Andersen, Reznik, and Manzella 1996; Andersen, Reznik, and Glassman 2005). Once these responses are evoked, they may help shape the subsequent course of the initial interaction, even triggering the self-fulfilling prophecy (Berk and Andersen 2000). In this way, the new person who is the object of the transference may inadvertently end up confirming, through his or her actions, the very expectations perceivers formed at the outset.

When a new person activates a significant-other representation, this also leads the self typically experienced with the significant other to influence the content of the working self-concept at the moment (Hinkley and Andersen 1996; Reznik and Andersen 2002). One's evaluation of these relational aspects of the self-concept also change in transference in a way that mirrors the valence of the relationship. That is, the features of the working self-concept reflecting the self typically experienced around a significant other come to be evaluated more positively in the context of a positive transference, and more negatively in the context of a negative transference, with the latter also presenting a threat to overall self-evaluation.

Self-regulation arises in transference in at least two ways. First, in a negative or threatening transference, one becomes motivated to protect the self by bolstering self-regard, perhaps to distance oneself from the other, and to highlight distinctions (Hinkley and Andersen 1996; Reznik and Andersen 2002). Second, one may become motivated to protect the relationship with the significant other in a positive transference when the positive view of this other is somehow threatened, as when negative aspects of a positive significant other are encountered in a new person. That is, such negative features of a new person end up evoking especially positive facial affect (Andersen, Reznik, and Manzella 1996), presumably in compensation for encountering a negative aspect of the other that one is used to discounting (see, for example, Murray and Holmes 1994). These forms of self-regulation have implications for how people cope with threatened identities—when the individual self or significant other is threatened, or when the notion of falling short of parental standards is activated, leading to differential approach versus avoidance.

IMPLICATIONS FOR SOCIAL IDENTITY AND ENGAGEMENT   The relevance of relational selves to social identities relies on how exemplars of specific persons (Smith and Zàrate 1992) are linked to generic knowledge, such as that of social categories and group memberships, in memory. Activating a significant-other representation thus activates generic concepts like gender (Karylowski, Konarzewski, and Motes 2000), interpersonal role (Baum and Andersen 1999), and normative self-standards, or self-discrepancies (Reznik and Andersen 2002), demonstrating that such generic knowledge is clearly linked with these representations.[2] Likewise such social categories as ethnicity and kinship should also be linked to significant-other representations and be activated in transference. Whether or not a social category linked to a significant-other representation is one that the participant shares—in other words, is part of his or her own social identity—should matter in terms of whether one's own social identity is transiently activated (see Andersen and Chen 2002; Chen and Andersen 1999). Whereas little evidence exists that directly tests this argument thus far, the general notion that a new person experienced as friend not foe may contribute to social identification has been examined using a different paradigm in studies described in a later section.

Overall, the notion that a positive transference evokes a positive relational self may help elucidate a basis from which social identity and community engagement may be fostered. When transference involves a liked or loved significant other, one gives a new person more benefit of the doubt, heightened comfort arises, and an easier interaction ensues. Because transference sets in motion not only what is unique about the significant-other relationship but also what is more generic and normative—for example, role (Baum and Andersen 1999)—social categories and social identities should arise in transference as well. Thus, if one is led to relate to a new person as to an intimate because somehow the inner circle of one's own identity (and of one's assumptions about intimate relations) has been triggered, one may bond with the new person for nonrational reasons, and this may have implications for social identity.

For example, if features of a new person activate a significant other who happens to share some social-category membership with the self, this new person may be assumed to belong to the social category as well, and thus may be conceived as an in-group member even if he or she is not. Likewise, if the bonding experienced in the moment is sufficiently pronounced that it carries through over time, one may become more likely to incorporate the new other into one's own array of important personal relationships. This can have social-identity implications in its own right down the road, expanding the repertoire of relational selves one has available and the social categories with which one is relatively close. Put simply, a European American married to an African American may be likely over time to acquire a nearly comparable level of social identification with African Americans, and vice versa.

Familiar and warm relations may even lead people to come to describe themselves with reference to the dyad or the larger set of people involved by use of the personal pronoun "we" (see assessments of Brewer and Gardner 1996), and this alone may set in motion a new way of thinking about the self. Either way, a kind of "projection"[3] of the familiar should occur, along with displacement, the process in transference in which the significant-other representation is applied to the new person. Relational identities thus provide a kind of "glue" connecting individuals to each other on a daily basis and should be relevant to whether or not a shared social identity is formed, refined, or reactivated.

In short, how might personal relationships influence social identification? First, they may do so by defining some of the first and most primordial social identities one comes to hold (for example, gender, age, ethnicity), those that are shared and not shared with early significant others. Second, they may do so by highlighting the contextual triggering process through which interpersonal cues emanating from a new person can activate transference and relational selves, which may also activate social identities. For example, if the ethnicity of my significant other is one I happen to share, when the mental representation of this significant other is triggered, my own ethnicity will also be activated and the social identity I have associated with this ethnic background might also be activated. Although research is needed to verify predictions such as this, the conceptualization is provocative.

Rejection-Sensitivity Model

Like the relational-self model, the rejection-sensitivity (RS) model was developed to account for the psychological processes linking experiences in important relationships with behavior in subsequent relationships (Downey and Feldman 1996; Downey et al. 1998; Feldman and Downey 1994). Rather than focusing on unique aspects of specific relationships, however, the RS model seeks to explain how specific relational experiences are coded as acceptance or rejection and in the aggregate generate expectations of either acceptance or rejection in subsequent social encounters where rejection is possible. This focus on the abstraction of information about how others view you from whether their behavior communicates acceptance or rejection is highly compatible with the group-value model's focus on how people use the extent to which group members' behavior toward them is respectful, fair, and unbiased to determine their status vis-à-vis the group, the trustworthiness of the group, and ultimately to determine whether or not they identify with the group.

The basic assumption of the rejection-sensitivity model is that anxious rejection expectations develop when people's expressed needs for acceptance in ongoing relationships or their bids for acceptance in new relationships are repeatedly met with rejection. The model was initially developed to explain the consequences of rejection in people's formative close relationships for the development of their subsequent close relationships. Reasoning that relationships with a single individual and with a group of individuals are similar in that they both can provide or deny acceptance, Sheri Levy, Ozlem Ayduk, and Geraldine Downey (2001) have also proposed that rejection should have the same basic cognitive, affective, and behavioral influences on people's relationships with groups as on relationships with individual others. Support for this proposal has been found in research on the implications of sensitivity to rejection because of status characteristics such as race and gender for intergroup relations (London et al. 2005; Mendoza-Denton et al. 2002) and on the implications of sensitivity to rejection for personal reasons for people's identification with and engagement with new social groups (Levy, Ayduk, and Downey 2001; Romero-Canyas and Downey, forthcoming).

REJECTION-SENSITIVITY DYNAMIC   The model proposes that in situations where rejection is a possibility, anxious expectations of rejection get activated in rejection-sensitive individuals, for example, at a party full of strangers (Mischel and Shoda 1995). As explained earlier, rejection expectations can be viewed as affectively amplified, or "hot" cognitions (Metcalfe and Mischel 1999) that reflect appraisals of threat (Lazarus 1993). When in a state of being threatened, people's threshold for perceiving the expected negative outcome is lower and they are prepared physiologically to react intensely when such an outcome is perceived. Thus, in the presence of rejection cues, even innocuous or ambiguous ones, people high in anxious expectations of rejection should more readily perceive rejection and react with intense hurt, anger, and blame of the self or the other. These intense cognitive-affective reactions may trigger the enactment of behavioral scripts that can unintentionally sabotage important relationships and personal goals and bring about a self-fulfilling prophecy (for example, Merton 1948) in which actual rejection is elicited. The particular behavioral consequences, however, should depend on the typical ways in which rejection-sensitive people cope with their sensitivity in regulating their interactions with others. Some rejection-sensitive people may try to avoid rejection by investing in securing social connections. They may blindly do things to please others and overreact when their efforts are rejected. Alternatively, some rejection-sensitive individuals may attempt to shield themselves from rejection through reduced involvement in important relationships. Whereas this strategy may reduce the risk of interpersonal negativity, it may also increase the likelihood of chronic loneliness and alienation and lack of access to opportunities for attaining important personal goals. Although it is not clear why rejection-sensitive individuals behave in one way instead of another, both paths have the potential to undermine relationships and well-being, resulting in actual rejection and exclusion, which reinforce rejection expectations.

Findings from experimental and correlational studies support the various links of the rejection-sensitivity model as applied to close relationships. First, rejection by parents and peers predicts heightened levels of anxious expectations of rejection (London et al. 2005; Downey, Khouri, and Feldman 1997; Feldman and Downey 1994). Second, anxious rejection expectations predict a readiness to perceive rejection in the ambiguous behavior of others (Downey and Feldman 1996, studies 2 and 3; Downey et al. 1998). Third, anxious rejection expectations predict a heightened physiological state of threat in the presence of ambiguous cues of rejection (Downey et al. 2004). Fourth, anxious expectations of rejection lead to cognitive, affective, and behavioral reactions that undermine significant relationships and personal well-being (Ayduk, Downey, and Kim 2001; Downey and Feldman 1996; Downey et al. 1998). Finally, these relationship-undermining behaviors occur specifically in response to perceived rejection (Ayduk et al. 1999). Whereas rejection-sensitive individuals who are connection-avoidant show heightened risk of social anxiety, rejection-sensitive individuals who are connection-seeking are also at heightened risk for troubled relationships and for self-undermining ingratiation (Purdie and Downey 2000). Taken together, these studies demonstrate the applicability of the rejection-sensitivity model to personal relationships.

APPLYING THE REJECTION SENSITIVITY MODEL TO RELATIONS WITH SOCIAL GROUPS
Support for the generalizablity of the rejection-sensitivity model to intergroup relations has come mainly from research on the implications of race-based rejection sensitivity (RS-race) among African Americans for their relations with majority-group members of predominantly nonminority institutions (Mendoza-Denton et al. 2002; see also McLaughlin-Volpe, Mendoza-Denton and Shelton, chapter 9, this volume). Consistent with predictions, the research has shown that high–RS-race African American college students report having experienced more race-based discrimination in the past than low–RS-race students. In addition, they are more likely to attribute negative outcomes to their race in situations where race-based rejection is a possibility and to feel more negative following the occurrence of such events. Moreover, African American students entering college with high RS-race experienced greater personal and interpersonal discomfort during the college transition than did students low in RS-race expectations, with some of these differences increasing over

the initial three-week period of college. Annual follow-ups indicated that higher RS-race was associated with less diverse friendships, less trust in and sense of obligation to the university, greater anxiety about seeking academic help, and a decline in grade-point average. Recent research has also shown the applicability of the rejection-sensitivity model to rejection anxiety based on gender (London et al. 2005).

These findings confirm that the basic structure of this processing dynamic generalizes readily from rejection of the self by significant others to rejection based on membership in a social group. However, the trigger features and consequences differ across the personal and status-group domains to reflect the different ways and contexts in which personal rejection and status-based rejection are communicated. Whereas sensitivity to rejection for personal reasons is viewed as primarily developing from rejection experienced directly from significant and typically close others, sensitivity to status-based rejection can primarily involve mistreatment by representative members of other social groups and can be communicated vicariously by others who share membership in a stigmatized group.

SUMMARY   Rejection expectations influence people's perceptions of and relationships with social groups. Rejection expectations seem to negatively color individuals' impressions of an unfamiliar group whose intentions may appear ambiguous. In field and lab studies, rejection sensitivity can prompt negative affect, dissatisfaction, and both preoccupation with what others think and avoidance coping strategies. Thus, rejection expectations, shaped by experience, map onto how people think, feel, and respond to social groups.

INTEGRATIVE FRAMEWORK LINKING SOCIAL AND RELATIONAL IDENTITIES

Social identification is of profound relevance in predicting willingness to engage. Thus, understanding the processes that promote social identification is of considerable importance. We now lay out a framework for conceptualizing social identity in terms of social relationships through an approach that integrates our three theories and empirical research trajectories. We propose that dyadic relationships are central to the process of how individuals form their important social identities with specific groups of people—in neighborhoods, communities, institutions, organizations, and nations. Overall, our purpose is to better understand how relationships may or may not translate into positive social identities and the framework is constructed in light of this aim.

Our integrative framework begins with some key assumptions from the group-value and group-engagement model, and highlights how consideration of the two relational models, the relational-self and the rejection-sensitivity models, can extend a group-value model. A central assumption of the group-value model is that social identity is particularly powerful because it provides a lens through which the individual perceives, evaluates, and responds to how he or she is being treated by others in the group. A second assumption is that treatment by the group matters also for identity formation. Consideration of the relational models extends the group-value model.

Relevance of Warmth

According to the group-value model, the most salient dimensions of the individual's treatment by group members are respect, neutrality, and trustworthiness. A dyadic, relational perspective would suggest that these dimensions do not fully capture what is fundamental in human relations. Studies of close relationships ranging from parent-child interactions (for example, Thompson 1998) to close friendships and marriage (Gottman 1979; Hazan and Shaver 1994) highlight the importance of warmth and responsiveness on the part of the other. In research on interactions in workplaces and other institutions, this component of human relations—the warmth or nurturing, supportive component, broadly speaking—is often overlooked. Nonetheless, we have every reason to believe that this component is important to individual members of institutions in their dyadic interactions, even if perhaps moderated by a variety of factors.

We view warmth as fundamental to smooth and edifying social interactions. Hence, factors that typically co-occur with being treated warmly by others—including expectancies for acceptance rather than rejection, the motive to be close and disclosing rather than distancing, and positive evaluation and positive affect—should all play some role in interactions with a group. Perceptions of warmth and caring in an interaction also tend to increase when a positive mental representation of a significant other is activated, suggesting that a positive transference in which one perceives a new person as friend not foe may be one mechanism by which the formation of a new social identity begins. In the same vein, individual differences in rejection sensitivity should, when triggered, predict a wide range of negative responses within dyads that may also extend to the relevant group.

Our integrative framework extends the group-value model by placing special emphasis on the dimension of warmth in social encounters. We argue that warmth should play a profound role in addition to the other relational factors that are highlighted in the group-value model, and will predict how encounters are perceived, with implications for social identity. Hence, while social identification increases the relevance of being treated warmly by others within the group, social identification can also be provoked and, over time, formed, by warmth in interactions with people identified with the group.

"Baggage" from the Past in the Present

The rejection-sensitivity and relational-self models assume that new encounters and new relations are often perceived in terms of the past, and studies confirm this (see, for example, Chen, Fitzsimons, and Andersen, forthcoming; Pietrzak, Downey, and Ayduk 2005). Thus, an important way of thinking about how people relate to groups is also in terms of the "baggage" they bring from the past to the new situations relevant to the group. Whether in a work environment, at school, or in a neighborhood, an encounter is likely to be colored by prior relationship experience in combination with various cues in the situation.

For instance, when a positive significant-other representation is triggered in transference, one is considerably more likely to quite automatically see a new person as "friend" not "foe" (Andersen and Chen 2002). Likewise, a rejection-sensitive person, who is hypervigilant to cues of rejection, will be more likely to perceive rejection than those who are not rejection-sensitive (Downey and Feldman 1996). In either case, people should readily generalize their positive feelings for a group member to the group to which he or she belongs, especially if they are already reasonably positively inclined toward the group and are themselves potential members. In turn, as people come to feel more connected with the group member, they may become more connected to and engaged in the group.

Context-Specificity: If-Then Responses to Contextual Cues

Both the rejection-sensitivity and relational-self models emphasize that contextual triggering cues causally influence subsequent responses by activating prior knowledge. Thus, our integrative perspective also brings to the group-value model the notion that contextual triggering is important, and that examining triggering cues in a particular situation may increase understanding of how interpersonal qualities may contribute to social identification. The integrative model assumes that the if–then shifts in people's perceptions across situations, triggered by relevant cues in the setting, can be especially revealing about the texture of people's responses. Thus, contextual cues can heighten or dampen the use of various bits of preexisting interpersonal knowledge for interpreting and relating to the others.

Hierarchical Versus Lateral Relations

Authority figures in a social system control resources and thus may be seen to represent the group by those in it. At the same time, group members in lateral positions or roles can control relational, if not material, resources, and so may also symbolize the group. Hence, how one is treated both by authorities and by peers in lateral relations (for example, colleagues, team members, fellow students) should influence social identification and cooperation. Indeed, research examining communitarian principles in sociology, politics, and economics (see Etzioni 1988, 1993) has emphasized lateral associations, as has work on social capital (Putnam 1995, 2000; Wilson 1991), and such work strongly suggests that lateral relations will be central in voluntary cooperation and perceptions of bias.

Until recently, the group-value model focused on authority figures and relational treatment by authorities. As a result, relatively little is known about how treatment by others within a group, who are peers and thus at a parallel level within the group, may function in terms of cooperation with group aims (for a somewhat different view, see Blader and Tyler 2002). The relational-self model, by contrast, has emphasized relations with both authority figures (such as parents) and peers (such as siblings or friends). Likewise, the rejection-sensitivity model has focused on how rejection expectancies develop with parents and are evoked with other authorities, as well as in peer and romantic relationships. Both hierarchical and lateral relationships capture important interpersonal encounters one is likely to have within any given group. It is thus probable that both types of relations offer signals or cues that may have an impact on the degree to which one is willing to cooperate and identify with the group.

Specific and Generic Qualities of Relationships and Relational Identity

Beliefs about a relationship with a specific individual can be contrasted with generalized expectancies about others. Both types of knowledge exist, and generic concepts and inferences derive in part from autobiographical knowledge (for example, "He treats me with respect" → "He respects me" → "People in this group may respect me" → "I am respected"). The rejection-sensitivity model focuses on generalized expectancies whereas the relational-self model focuses on specific relationships, and both forms of knowledge representation can play a role in interpersonal relations and are likely to promote or work against social identification.

Processes Linking Specific Treatment by Others with Social Identification and Group Engagement

Although the group-value model links fair, respectful and trustworthy treatment by group members with the individual's identification with the group, the model does not specify the mediating processes. Consideration of the relational models reviewed suggests a number of possible processes. For example, encounters with out-group members, perhaps as colleagues or friends or neighbors—when these involve fairness, respect, and warmth—could potentially facilitate a positive transference. Indeed, treatment that is familiar and similar in some manner to one's typical treatment by valued intimates should also facilitate a positive transference. When a positive transference does arise, it should lead one to see the out-group member as friend, not foe, and this mechanism may facilitate social identification with the group and willingness to cooperate with group decisions. Beyond this, the motive to be socially connected combined with acceptance expectations may generalize to the group under some circumstances. Work on rejection sensitivity (Downey and Feldman 1996) shows that chronic expectancies for acceptance or rejection developed from prior relational experiences are brought to bear on new experiences as "baggage" and thus shape how one perceives and responds to other people. We argue in constructing this framework that re-experiencing the past in the present in the form of generalized expectancies has an important effect in shaping how an encounter goes with someone who is a member of a given group. Moreover, the personal reaction one has to the individual may well end up influencing how one feels about the group he or she represents and thus one's likelihood of identifying with it.

Bidirectional Link Between Relational Concerns and Social Identities

A guiding assumption of the integrative framework is therefore that relational concerns and social identification have a bidirectional influence on one another. Social identification shapes relational interest, and particular relational experiences with specific others are key antecedents of social identification. This assumption is grounded in the group-value model, which, as indicated, shows that quality of treatment by the authorities that represent a group will mold the degree to which one is willing to go along with group decisions, to cooperate, especially if one is already identified with the group (for example, Tyler 1999, 2001). The assumption is also consistent with the relational-self model's focus on personal relationships in how the self develops. Activation of mental representations of significant others spreads to other associated knowledge in memory such as possibly the groups to which the significant other belongs and thereby influences current perceptions and social identities (Andersen and Chen 2002). Moreover, because social identities and feelings of belonging that they create are part of significant-other relationships, they should also be activated when the significant-other representation is activated. Likewise, activating a specific social identity or a feeling of belonging might call to mind the significant others, or other people in general whom one knows, who share this identity. The rejection-sensitivity model and evidence based on it suggest bidirectional influence as well, because the anxious expectations derived from rejection in past relationships can generalize to encounters with a new individual, group, or institution in which rejection is possible (see Levy, Ayduk, and Downey 2001), with implications for social identification.

Summary

Our integrative model reflects both common assumptions of the three theoretical models and also the distinctions between them that complement one another. Our model can encompass both hierarchical and lateral relationships, both specific relationships and generalized expectancies, both relationships from the past and the present, and both perceptions triggered by contextual cues in particular situations and stable perceptions. Moreover, our integrative model suggests mutual and bidirectional pathways by which relational identity and social identity may influence each other.

RECENT FINDINGS BASED ON THE INTEGRATIVE FRAMEWORK

Although we do not test all the assumptions of this model or the predictions derived from it in the studies we present, we offer a preliminary set of findings relating to some of the specific hypotheses that arise from this conceptualization, primarily concerning identity formation. The central hypothesis for which we provide evidence is that people's interpersonal experiences with others in dyadic relationships carry identity-relevant messages. Communications that signal a meaningful dyadic connection—that signal potential "friendship"—should be pivotal, not only for dampening rejection expectancies but for encouraging a positive transference, and this should be relevant to one's willingness to engage with the group to whom the person giving the "friendship" signals belongs. In the next section we present research that tests this hypothesis, focusing on hierarchical and lateral relations, on specific relationships and generic expectancies (for example, expectancies for rejection), and on past relationships brought to a new encounter as baggage and current interpersonal cues in a given context.

Our integrative framework predicts that being treated with a level of warmth or kindness—as friend, not foe—should matter in increasing social identification and cooperation within the group, and should go beyond respect, trustworthiness, and neutrality in effecting this outcome. This central hypothesis should hold for both hierarchical and peer types of relationships, although perhaps taking a different form in the former than in the latter. We examine the "warmth" assumption in five different studies, all conducted from different perspectives and in different settings but converging on similar themes.

The first two studies examined the prediction that personal relationships may promote voluntary cooperation as an index of behavioral engagement within a community or institution. The third study examined these predictions in a real-world context: the relationships that developed among public school teachers who voluntarily took part in a youth development program promoting voluntary cooperation; it was assessed in terms of their effective implementation of the program. The three studies largely supported the argument that the warmth of relationships mattered for both hierarchical and peer relationships.

The final two studies examined how prior baggage influenced the perception of current relationships. The fourth study focused on whether polite treatment by an authority could overcome expectations of negative outcomes based on baggage concerning aspects of personal and social identity. The experimental procedure arranged that a new authority figure reminded participants of a prior figure who treated them fairly or did not, and when unfairly, presumably because of their category membership (for example, their gender) or personal qualities. The research shows that polite treatment matters differentially as a function of whether or not one is reminded of a positive and fair near-significant other. The fifth study examined the immediate and long-term effects of expectations of acceptance or rejection for voluntarily cooperation and identification with a new institution. Expectations shaped the quality of initial relations with institutional authority figures and peers and long-term voluntary cooperation and identification with the institution.

AUTHORITY AND PEER RELATIONS IN VOLUNTARY COOPERATION IN TWO CONTEXTS

In the first two studies we focused both on hierarchical relationships with authority figures (a police officer, a professor) and on lateral relations among equals in the same group (neighbors, fellow students).

Hierarchical or Vertical Relations

The group-value approach has tended to focus on how authority figures within a system are perceived, that is, on how hierarchical (vertical) relations within the system are perceived.

COMMUNITY SAMPLE   With this same focus, a large sample of ethnic minorities, African Americans and Latinos, was contacted for a telephone survey, using stratified random sampling, in two urban areas of Los Angeles and Oakland, California (Davis, Tyler, and Andersen 2003; see also Tyler and Huo 2002). A prerequisite for inclusion in the sample was having experienced at least one contact with a legal authority in the past year. For example, the subject might have been stopped or contacted by or sought assistance from a police officer. The focus on ethnic minorities enabled examination of responses among participants who might not identify strongly with the broader (superordinate) community.

Voluntary cooperation with authorities was assessed as a behavioral index of social identity. Fairness of the outcome and process were also measured (to index distributive and procedural justice respectively), as was favorability of the outcome. Respondents were also asked whether they felt a sense of connection with this authority figure (for example, the police officer) such that they could, under other circumstances, imagine being friends with this person.

Consistent with prior research, willingness to cooperate with the authority was predicted by being fairly treated by the authority figure (Tyler and Huo 2002). Both receiving a fair outcome and perceiving that the process of arriving at the outcome was fair independently predicted voluntary cooperation, whereas the favorability of the actual outcome did not matter. Of central relevance to the integrative framework was the finding that feeling a sense of connection and ease with the authority—as if he or she was a potentially friend, not foe—promoted cooperation over and above procedural and distributive justice. A sense of connection with the authority also interacted with procedural fairness in predicting cooperation. When the authority figure acted in good faith and in accord with rules of fair play and was respectful in so doing, the relevance of feeling a sense of connection with him or her mattered more. If the experience of connection is applied to the larger group that contains both the police officer and the respondent, then a shift in the individual's sense of belonging in the group (that is, the community) might occur.

COLLEGE SAMPLE   The same hypotheses as those just described were tested in sample of African American or Latino undergraduates entering a large university in an urban setting (Davis, Tyler, and Andersen 2003, study 2). Respondents were surveyed before their first semester began and again at the end of the semester. With this longitudinal design, it was possible to assess how relationships with professors predicted voluntary cooperation and engagement, indexed by help seeking, while controlling for preexisting differences in help seeking and expectancies. Help seeking was conceptualized as voluntary cooperation because the educational effectiveness of universities depends on students' willingness to engage in discretionary educational activities such as going to a professor during his or her office hours to get advice or clarification of course material.

Consistent with evidence from the community study and much prior work on the group-value model, both distributive and procedural fairness mattered for voluntary cooperation and engagement. When students believed that they had been fairly treated by the professor both in terms of the grade they received at the end of the semester and the process of grade assignment, they were more willing to seek help from the professor, controlling for initial levels of help seeking and other relevant measures.

In addition, the "warmth" hypothesis was again supported, although only when the professor was using a fair process. There was a significant interaction between perceptions of procedural justice and feeling comfortable with the professor in predicting whether or not students would seek out the professor for feedback and help. When students were treated fairly by their professors, it also mattered for help seeking whether they felt a sense of comfort with the professor. When treated fairly, it also mattered to students if they felt respected, but feeling personally comfortable was a significant predictor even holding this factor constant (as well as other factors).

Lateral or Horizontal Relations

In both the community and college samples, it was also possible to assess the links between warmth and dignified treatment by peers and participants' voluntary cooperation with them in the group.

COMMUNITY SAMPLE   Respondents in the community sample were also asked about various aspects of their engagement with their neighbors (Davis, Tyler, and Andersen 2003, study 1). Of interest were answers to the question, Why do people affiliate with their neighbors? Consistent with rational-choice economic models (for example, Etzioni 1988), having instrumental motives in relation to neighbors was a good predictor of affiliation. This is presumably because it is valuable to know that neighbors might help out in an emergency. However, the best predictor of affiliation was the degree to which the respondents reported having relational motives. When people reported caring about belonging in their community and thus caring about their neighbors (for example, wanting to affiliate with them and trusting that they are fundamentally good people), they were more likely to be engaged with them. These findings are not consistent with rational-choice goals.

COLLEGE SAMPLE   Students' level of engagement or voluntary cooperation with their peers was assessed (as it was with authority figures) in terms of help seeking. Once again, the best predictor of respondents' willingness to seek out peers at school with whom to study or obtain whatever assistance or support might be needed was having strong relational motives—wanting to feel connected. On the other hand, just having friends or feeling respected by peers did not independently predict seeking help from peers (just as simply feeling respected by professors did not predict seeking help from professors). Instead, having friends within the school or feeling respected by fellow students predicted higher levels of voluntary cooperation in the context of strong relational motives.

Relationships and Teachers' Implementation of a Youth Program in Urban Public Schools

This study again assessed the prediction that bonding and connection between people promotes voluntary cooperation, but with appropriate implementation of a youth development program as the index of cooperation. The study involved a public school system and teachers in K-to-12 education who took part in a youth service program over the course of a semester. Survey data were obtained from teachers at the beginning and end of the semester (Andersen and Zeldin 2003). The evaluation focused on the potential relevance of relationships between teachers and their students, fellow teachers, and program personnel for the fidelity of program implementation and for program effectiveness. It was expected that fidelity of program implementation would mediate the link between teacher relationships and program effectiveness, indexed by teachers' ratings of student educational engagement and academic improvement and by benefits of the program to the community.

The Penny Harvest Program is designed to promote school engagement through community service. Participating students spend the fall semester collecting pennies from family, kin, friends, and neighbors and bringing them to school to be counted and bagged. In the winter and spring, supervised by their teachers, the most effective student leaders participate in a youth philanthropy roundtable of ten to twenty students. One roundtable group and one Penny Harvest teacher per school participates; students working as a team and using an organized curriculum are viewed as factors reflecting proper implementation. Students' task is to identify problems in the community and community organizations that deal with these problems. Students also determine how these organizations spend their money and whether they are effective. They also decide whether any student service projects might also be useful. They then decide how to allocate the pot of $1,000 in their school (which students themselves collected, qualifying them for a roundtable).

The program is pursued in elementary, middle, and high schools in the New York City school system, comparable to the school system of a small state. The study was conducted during the academic year that began with September 11, 2001. The program for that year was named the Twin Towers Penny Harvest and focused on the relief effort after the World Trade Center attacks. Almost nine hundred New York City public schools participated and students collected nearly three quarters of a million dollars, every penny of which they distributed to the relief effort, including $36,000 to women and children in Afghanistan.

The sample was drawn from teachers in New York City public schools who were responsible for implementing a roundtable. These teachers were of varying ethnicities and had students from widely diverse backgrounds. Data were teachers' responses to questionnaires obtained at the beginning and end of the spring semester.

HIERARCHICAL RELATIONS BETWEEN TEACHERS AND PROGRAM PERSONNEL   As indicated, one way program implementation was assessed was through teachers' reports of providing an integrated, organized curriculum for the youth philanthropy roundtable. Such curriculum integration, as well as student outcomes (engagement in school and academic improvement), assessed at the end of the semester, were found to be predicted by strong, positive relationships between teachers and the personnel involved in promoting the program and training teachers to use it (a hierarchical relation, which had been assessed early in the semester). Curriculum integration also helped account for the link between teacher-program personnel relationships and student outcomes.

HIERARCHICAL RELATIONS BETWEEN TEACHERS AND STUDENTS   Teachers' sense of being able to work with students as a team was also expected to be critical to program implementation. Teamwork was expected to be predicted by the initial quality of teacher-student relationships and to help mediate the association between the quality of these relations and students' academic engagement and improvement. Again, these predictions were supported, extending previous findings into the realm of downward hierarchical relations and providing additional support for the integrative framework by showing that affectively positive hierarchical relations predict more effective program implementation.

LATERAL RELATIONS BETWEEN TEACHERS   Teachers' rating of their sense of bonding with other Penny Harvest teachers at the beginning and end of the semester provided an index of lateral relationships within the program. Although lateral feelings of bonding with other Penny Harvest teachers did not translate into better program implementation or better student outcomes per se, they did predict perceptions that the program benefited the community, and thus may have motivational significance. Perhaps this bonding between the Penny Harvest teachers reflected their initial excitement about the program, which then predicted their later perceptions of community impact. In this respect, the bonding experienced between teachers may have indicated a kind of social identification with the aims of the program and its having achieved these aims. A sense of being bonded with peers may thus promote identification in terms of positive view of group outcomes. Work on social identity suggests that a sense of belonging in the group (Baumeister and Leary 1995) and also the perceived centrality of the group for the self (Sellers and Shelton 2003) reflect ways of defining and assessing social identity. In this research, teachers' perceptions of their relations with other participating teachers predicted their perception of the program's impact on the community and this might reflect a shift in positive social identification.

In sum, the research suggests that hierarchical relations matter for program outcomes and that this effect is partially mediated by the effect of such relationships on program implementation. However, it must be remembered that the data all came from teacher ratings and were correlational in nature. Nonetheless, the evidence suggests that teachers' relationships with program staff and with students in the program predicted cooperation with the policies and procedures of the program, in terms of implementing the program properly, and also led teachers to view participating students as having become more academically engaged and improved. In short, program implementation and outcomes were predicted by two kinds of hierarchical relationships. Finally, lateral relations also appear to promote program engagement, in terms of viewing the impact of the program on the community as positive. This evidence is important because it conceptually replicates other evidence and extends our framework into the policy arena. Overall, this research offers some added support for our conceptualization of relationships, voluntary cooperation, and social identity. It also has applied implications for how to put youth development programs in place that promote school engagement.

THE ROLE OF "BAGGAGE" FROM PRIOR RELATIONSHIPS   The three studies just discussed established an important role for warm, humane treatment for social identification and group engagement. The next two studies test another important assumption from our integrative framework: that the quality of one's initial social interactions with group representatives can be influenced by the baggage from past experiences and relationships. These include preexisting beliefs and expectations that one employs to interpret new social cues. If one expects rudeness or unfairness from representatives of a new social group, one is probably more likely to perceive that one has received such treatment and to respond with distress and a diminished institutional identification and engagement.

Experimental Investigations

In an experimental investigation of these predictions, Janina Pietrzak, Rodolfo Mendoza-Denton, and Downey (2003) made use of an "explicit transference paradigm" in which the individual with whom a university student would be interacting reminded the student of a professor from his or her past. Participants were randomly assigned to have had either a positive, helpful, comfortable relationship with that earlier professor or a relationship that was negative, unhelpful, and uncomfortable.[4] In the case of the negative relationship, students were further randomly assigned to imagine the professor's negativity as having been due either to something about the student as a person or to the student as a member of an identifiable status group (gender). The research therefore manipulated the expectations with which participants approached the interpersonal situation by inducing participants to experience a positive or negative transference that encompassed expectations of either helpfulness or unhelpfulness, based either on personal characteristics or on a group characteristic. According to group-value theory (Lind and Tyler 1988), this manipulation should affect whether the encounter was perceived as procedurally just. According to the rejection-sensitivity model, it should induce expectations of rejection that lead to ready perceptions of rejection, whereas expectations specifically based on group membership should lead to ready perceptions of group-based rejection. According to the relational-self model, prior relationships should be especially meaningful as a way of inducing interpersonal expectancies about a new encounter.

Combining these insights, the hypothesis was that affective and cognitive responses to new interactions should differ depending on the type of bias that people expected. Attributions that prior rejection was due to a particular cause (one's personal characteristics or one's group-membership status) should lead to similar attributions for the new person's treatment. Insofar as these inferred causes underlying a negative outcome, the predicted rejection, are assumed, perceptions of procedural justice should be dampened. After a rejecting interaction, expectations of bias should thus predict diminished perceptions of procedural justice and also a lack of belonging.

Participants in the research read a scenario about an interaction with a rude or polite professor, the outcome of which was either favorable or unfavorable. The scenario set up expectations either of polite, helpful treatment or unhelpful, rejecting treatment, with the rejection based either on group characteristics (in this case, gender) or on personal characteristics. The design was thus a 3 by 2 by 2 between-subjects factorial: 3 (expectations: helpfulness and acceptance, or rejection and unhelpfulness based on either the participants' personal or status characteristics); 2 (outcome: positive or negative); 2 (treatment: polite or impolite). The scenario involved the student asking the professor for an important class handout. In the negative-outcome condition, the student did not receive the handout. In the helpful version of this negative outcome the professor searches through some papers and says, "I'm sorry, I don't have any more copies. I'll bring a copy to the next class, or you can find it on-line." In the unhelpful, rejecting version, the professor looks at the student, shuffles through some papers, snaps, "Make an appointment!" and turns away. After reading the scenario, participants reported on their affect, their perceptions of and attributions for this treatment, and their perceptions of the professor.

As hypothesized, attributions for treatment were driven by expectations. Expectations of unhelpfulness and discomfort based on personal qualities and group-based status led to greater distress, greater perceptions of bias in the new professor's behavior, and more devaluation of the professor than expectations of comfort and helpfulness. In addition, expectations of group-based bias were readily overcome by polite, helpful treatment, whereas expectations of personal bias were not. This suggests an intriguing discontinuity between group- and individual-based evaluations of oneself by others. Students expecting bias based on personal qualities who were treated politely still devalued the professor and reported feeling uncomfortable and irritable after the imagined interaction. They were also just as likely to complain about the professor and to feel badly about their major as were students who were treated impolitely. For expectations of group-based rejection, polite, helpful treatment mattered more.

In a follow-up study, using a similar procedure and design, the hypothesis was tested that polite treatment of an in-group member and hence vicariously experienced rather than personally experienced might overcome group-based rejection expectations, and the results showed that it in fact did so, and just about as easily as did direct individual experience (Pietrzak, Mendoza-Denton, and Downey 2003). That is, the study showed that vicarious disconfirmation of rejection expectations based on group memberships was as effective as were personal experiences of disconfirmation of such expectations based on group membership. In addition, although polite treatment was enough to overcome expectations of group bias in this study, it again was not enough to overcome expectations of personal bias. Moreover, similar findings emerged when a more explicitly warm and immediately helpful version of the politeness manipulation was used. Together, the findings show that humane treatment, above and beyond "lack of bias," is crucial in subsequently shaping expectations about authority figures' treatment of devalued groups. However, the baggage resulting from ill treatment based on personal characteristics appears to be more difficult to overcome than that based on membership of a devalued group. It will be important in future experimental research to establish whether these findings extend to lateral relationships such as between fellow students.

Longitudinal Study

Do the experimental results on the effects of baggage described extend to the baggage from earlier close relationships that people bring to new groups? We attempted to answer this question in a study of students we followed from just before they began college classes through the end of their first year (Levy, Ayduk, and Downey 2001). The objective was to establish whether sensitivity to rejection in close relationships can influence an individual's identification and engagement with the university.

Because the transition to a new social institution such as college is stressful for both newcomers and for existing members of the institution, the behavior of individuals who are viewed as representatives of the university, whether peers or authority figures, is particularly important. Authority figures such as residence advisers, professors, financial aid advisers, and other authorities may be unavailable or unhelpful, and may unintentionally communicate rejection to newcomers, which may trigger negative experiences from prior relational experiences. Fellow incoming students may also give mixed social messages reflecting their own adjustment stress. Difficulties in becoming an engaged and committed member of the new community seem likely to be accentuated for people entering college who are high in rejection sensitivity.

This prediction was supported in a study that combined a three week daily-diary approach with a year-end follow-up of the transition to college. Students who entered college high in rejection sensitivity, which is thought to be based on treatment in prior relationships, felt less belonging at the college and less comfort with and liking for peers and professors than did students who were low in rejection sensitivity (Mendoza-Denton et al. 2002). This initial difference widened over the first three weeks of college and persisted through the end of the academic year. Students high in rejection sensitivity also felt significantly less satisfied with the university, had less respect for the university, and reported less trust in the university to make decisions that are good for everyone when they reported their views at the end of the year. They showed less willingness to recommend the university to a friend who was accepted for admission, suggesting that they might be willing to act on their more negative evaluations of the university. In short, the more students were rejection-sensitive, the less they identified with and became engaged in the university community over their first academic year. Analyses of the same data set focusing on sensitivity to rejection based on one's race rather than on rejection from close others yielded similar results.

Summary of Findings and Agenda for Future Research

This evidence leads us to some clear conclusions and implications for further research.

THE WARMTH HYPOTHESIS   Despite differences in the measures of warmth and of cooperation and in the context and population, the findings from these studies are remarkably consistent in showing that bonded, warm relations matter in both hierarchical and lateral relationships for the promotion of social engagement, at least given basic fairness and desire to feel connected with others. The studies were correlational, which limited the ability to make causal inferences. Nonetheless, the evidence provides promising support for the view that warmth by others and by feeling a sense of connection with an authority or with someone in a lateral position fosters collective engagement.

THE PRIOR-BAGGAGE HYPOTHESIS   The baggage one brings to an institutional context also predicts (and can interfere with) engagement. The experimental evidence shows that when a new person (in this case, a professor) reminds a student of an earlier teacher or professor who was accepting or one who was rejecting, this baggage influenced how biased participants expected the new professor to be. Moreover, the impact of these expectations varied according to whether the previous bias appeared to be against one's group or against one's personal characteristics. When the potential bias was interpreted as being against the participant's group, the new professor's actual warmth and actual politeness diminished expectations of bias. This evidence also offers support for distinguishing social identity and relational identity, and at the same time shows that current experiences are influenced by the psychological legacy of past experiences. The daily-diary study also showed the impact of prior baggage in that expectations of rejection led to more negative perceptions of interactions with peers and professors during the initial transition and to reduced identification and engagement with the university over time.

ISSUES FOR FUTURE RESEARCH   All in all, this evidence makes clear, in three distinct settings, that relationships matter in social identification, voluntary cooperation, and engagement. More work is needed to identify and assess specific triggering cues in specific contexts, the ways these cues are subjectively perceived by the individual, and the ways perceived cues lead to transient shifts and cross-situational variability in relational identity and also social identity. Our integrative model assumes contextual specificity in what baggage is likely to be activated, making room for shifts based on transient priming. Thus far, little evidence we know of has used such methods to examine the dual relevance of relational and social identity. Work is especially needed on how prior relationship knowledge (or a lack thereof) may circumscribe cooperation and engagement and do so as a result of contextual cues. In addition, although this integrative framework assumes that both specific individuals one knows well and highly familiar generalized expectancies are likely to play a role in interpersonal relations and thus in both relational and social identity, the research described does not exactly focus on the representation of a specific person in memory and its relevance to social engagement.

Overall, future research would do well to examine the triggering cues in particular group, community, or institutional contexts that evoke differing relational and social identities. It would also do well to acknowledge and measure the relevance of particular, specific human beings in the lives of each respondent whose responses to the respondent have created that respondent's baggage and of particular individuals within a group whose responses to newcomers facilitate a sense of identification with the group. Although these are gaps in the data for now, the current evidence lends credence to our overall approach, and to the likely fruitfulness of future research exploring further aspects of this framework.

IMPLICATIONS FOR
POSITIVE ENGAGEMENT

In a society and world as diverse as ours, the imperative to understand how some semblance of social cohesion, integration, and tolerance can be fostered is increasingly pressing. Given the diversity of specific people's social identifications and of local cultures and subcultures, customs, and norms, the question of how cultures and traditions may function cooperatively is of global as well as national significance. The increasing interdependence across the globe in terms of culture and economics and the sheer scope of travel makes this even more true. Both macro-level world concerns and internecine conflicts within countries, social institutions, and social groups may be coming to define our time and suggest an urgency in the social sciences to identify tools for building and sustaining pluralistic societies and democracies. These tools include focusing on both micro-level factors at the level of dyads and relational bonds and macro-level factors such as public trust or engagement.

Helping to promote relationships that foster cooperative engagement of the kind that reflects social identification is much needed. Relations based on mutual respect and warmth can communicate a sense of common bonds and, more broadly, of shared humanity and potentially globally common aims, and this should promote cooperation. If groups, communities, and institutions create conditions under which relational bonds can grow and thrive, cooperation should be fostered.

Implications of Our Main Evidence

Although the data are largely correlational, they offer compelling support for the relevance of relational warmth to social identities. A caveat is in order, however. Warmth in the absence of respect for competence may be a factor in how prejudice arises. Evidence on ambivalent prejudice has shown that when an out-group member was perceived as warm but incompetent, he or she elicited paternalistic prejudice, whereas those who were not warm but were competent elicited envious prejudice (Fiske et al. 1999). This finding implies that warmth may not always promote cooperation and positive responses to others. Nonetheless, extending this kind of research on prejudice into the realm of dyadic relationships and social identities, we have evidence suggesting the importance of warmth in dyadic relations for voluntary cooperation and belonging for social identity within an in-group.

Broader Scholarly, Societal, and Cultural Implications

Finding that lateral relationships matter for social identity is of interest because prior evidence was largely limited to relations with authorities (see, for example, Tyler and Lind 1992). Our data thus extend prior work and provide support for the emphasis of communitarian thought in sociology, politics, and economics (Etzioni 1988, 1993) on lateral associations within communities; similarly, research on social capital and on concentrated poverty in given locales has emphasized lateral bonds (nonhierarchical interpersonal relations within a community) in individual and societal functioning (see, for example, Wilson 1991). Of course, public discourse on "bowling alone" in contemporary America (Putnam 1995, 2000) also focuses largely on the lack of lateral bonds as a characteristic of social *dis*engagement.[5]

In addition, social-network analysis shows that informal, often relatively weak social ties are crucial in the diffusion of innovation (see Watts 1999, 2002; Watts, Dodds, and Newman 2002). Research on social networks extends from evolutionary psychology (Kenrick, Li, and Butner 2003) to institutional (Powell, Koput, and Smith-Doerr 1996), political (Keck and Sikkink 1998), and economic (Fafchamps and Minten

1999; Foster and Rosenzweig 1995) analyses. In this vein, our integrative framework and research is in provocative company in emphasizing lateral as well as hierarchical relationships, and in focusing on dyadic relationships. Until recently, however, little research on social identity measured dyadic relations.

Our work can also be considered in the context of evidence suggesting that the norm of self-interest is less influential in political attitudes (Sears and Funk 1991) and economic decisions (Tyler 1990b) than courses on microeconomics might lead one to believe (Larrick, Nisbett, and Morgan 1993; Miller 1999; see also Etzioni 1988; Wright 2000). From this vantage point, the present work shows that the micro-level of analysis of interpersonal relations yields evidence that self-interest may not necessarily hold sway in voluntary cooperation, because relational motives and nonrational considerations may carry considerable weight. The baggage one brings to an interpersonal and group context will influence perceptions of treatment and thus the consequences of that treatment for relational and social identity. Under some circumstances, warmth and politeness become quite important when there is a tendency to see bias. We would argue, then, that it is imperative that this be better understood if the building blocks of group, community, national, and transnational identities are to be fully understood.

On yet another level, it has in fact been argued that relationships may be natural categories in social perception (Fiske 1992; Sedikides, Olsen, and Reis 1993). Research on social roles in interpersonal relationships has identified four fundamental relational types, two of which are authority-ranking and equality-matching relations, respectively, which both involve exchange, whereas those that are more communal do not (Fiske 1992; for roles involving sharing, see also Mills and Clark 1994). The importance of these types of relational types, or roles, is that they offer further support for the relevance of the hierarchical versus lateral distinction in social life. This is also on point for our present purposes because it focuses on social roles. Some researchers have in fact gone so far as to define social identity as synonymous with social role (Stryker 1987; Stryker and Serpe 1982; see also Sarbin and Allen 1968). Although we assume there is more to social identity than relational roles, we concur that roles are integral to relationships (see Baum and Andersen 1999) and are associated with social identities.

Potential Cultural Influences on These Phenomena

Are relational processes more influential in social identification and behavioral engagement in some cultures than in others? It is difficult to speculate about this, as we have no evidence that directly bears on the question. Existing literature is not particularly helpful because the contemporary study of culture in psychology is largely focused on the global distinction between collectivist and individualist cultures (Markus and Kitayama 1991; Nisbett et al. 2001; Triandis 1989) and tends not to assess dyadic relationships. The assumption that Eastern cultures are more interdependent, collectivist, and holistic than are Western cultures is reasonably well supported (although, see Oyserman, Coon, and Kemmelmeier 2002), with data showing meaningful differences between such cultures and subcultures in terms of cognitive processes, self-evaluations, and behaviors. But predictions at the relational level are far less commonly

examined. It is nonetheless clear from our evidence that even in the highly individualist culture of the United States, relational issues in the self, in rejection expectancies,
and in how one responds to being treated fairly and with warmth and dignity by
authorities and other group members all matter a great deal, even though cultural
influences in a sense work against this.

The fact that differing contexts trigger different self-with-other knowledge
(Brewer and Gardner 1996; Higgins 1989a; Higgins and May 2001; Reid and Deaux
1996; Trafimow et al. 1997) also suggests that it is important to focus on cultural differences in contextual cueing. There are a number of reasons to do so. For example,
there are objective differences in the prevalence of evocative situations across cultures. For example, more contexts evoke shame in Japan and pride in the United
States. Beyond objective differences in the prevalence of evocative situations across
cultures, there are also cultural differences in how people subjectively perceive the
same objective events in a given culture, like when feeling ashamed feels especially
called for (see Kitayama et al. 1997). Both the actual context and the subjective interpretation contribute to how previously stored knowledge is evoked, and this dove-
tails nicely with our integrative model, and thus warrants research in terms of its
implications for relational and social identity.

There are multiple relational selves that any person is capable of manifesting
across situations that can be brought to bear in navigating the different contexts of
life (Andersen and Chen 2002). Cultures vary in the kinds of situations people encounter, the kinds of relationships they have, and thus the kinds of relational selves
they are likely to develop. When triggered, these culturally located relational selves
are likely to result in various expectancies and affective vulnerabilities. Examining
multiple relational selves in conjunction with overall tendencies to expect and experience rejection and also with differing contextual cues encountered in situations is
likely to be valuable in predicting subjectively perceived realities—expectancies,
emotions, and social identifications.

Coping with Threatened Identities

What implications does our evidence have for how people cope with threatened
social identities or with threatened relationships? Put differently, what are the implications of this evidence for stigmatization, stereotyping, and prejudice? Taking the
inverse of our primary conclusions, one implication is that humiliating people is not
likely to build relationships and shared social identities. If humiliation can be construed as an extreme form of rejection and we can extrapolate from what is known
about rejection, it can lead to anger and rage, lashing out at others, and disidentification (for example, Levy, Ayduk, and Downey 2001; Steele 1997; for more on lashing
out, see Andersen 1995). Such responses, it would seem, could be all the more likely
on the basis of humiliating treatment.

A lack of warmth also impedes the fulfillment of fundamental human needs, and
from this point of view, may interfere with the "glue" of connectedness in everyday
social relations with strangers. A strong, positive, and warm relationship with at least
one human being may thus be able to offer an opportunity to add a new significant-
other relationship to one's inner circle of relational identities (Andersen, Reznik, and

Chen 1997) and in turn enable the same feelings and responses to be experienced with another new person. Under the right circumstances, this might also generalize to the overarching group to which both individuals belong, as suggested by the current evidence. By contrast, when individuals experience a lack of connectedness to others or to groups, they may bring this to new others and new groups. On the other hand, because it leaves fundamental needs unsatisfied, a lack of connectedness may also make people vulnerable and thus more open to individuals from different groups or communities who might treat them positively. These issues warrant research attention.

Again, humiliating treatment by others is the opposite of the warmth that is the focus here. It also threatens the self and people often respond defensively to threats to the self with compensatory inflation of the assets of their own in-group (Gaertner, Sedikides, and Graetz 1999; Simon, Pantaleo, and Mummendey 1995; see also Chen, Brockner, and Katz 1998; Greenberg et al. 1992). This appears to be a robust phenomenon. There is also provocative research showing the propensity of cultures of honor—and more focused than other cultures on humiliation and defending one's honor—are grounded in a code of honor to perceive threat and to respond violently, even though they are otherwise regarded as friendly and hospitable (Cohen and Nisbett 1994; Nisbett 1993; see also Horowitz 1983). In these cultures, humiliation may be particularly likely to accentuate in-group favoritism and out-group derogation.

At the very least, even for cultures less grounded in a code of honor, being treated by others as though they care about your views, respect you, and accept the legitimacy of your right to voice an opinion is likely to enhance motivation to cooperate, and perhaps even to let potential slights pass that might otherwise be viewed as confirming chronic expectancies of disrespect or disregard. If some shred of openness to dialogue remains between otherwise warring cultural, political, or ethnic factions (Pettigrew 2003; Rouhana and Fiske 1995), as ideally can be the case within diverse deliberative democracies, an atmosphere of mutual respect, inclusion, and even embrace may still be able to prevail. Shared bonds can provide an instrument, then, for coping with a threatened identity.

The take-home message is that when individuals experience their own identities as threatened, as stigmatized minorities often might, there are conditions that enable difficult feelings and perceptions to be overcome—depending in part on actual circumstances and the behavior of majority-group members. Being treated with procedural justice and also with the warmth and geniality of a friend—and the sense of inclusion that goes along with that—reliably predicts voluntary cooperation. The simple kindness and connection expressed and experienced in such interactions, as well as the respect and fairness, matters in human relations and very likely in intergroup relations as well.

CONCLUSION

As prior research has suggested, if people are placed in a situation in which they must work together toward aims they genuinely share—in the context of mutual respect, believing they are on equal footing, with each person having a role to play and different talents to contribute—this kind of contact itself may break down barriers between people and between groups (Pettigrew 1998). Indeed, when interdependence is present, people are more likely to individuate rather than stereotype others (Erber and Fiske 1984; Fiske 2000; Neuberg and Fiske 1987). Individuating is a precondition for forming an individual-person representation in memory as opposed to merely assimilating the person into a category and stereotyping (Brewer 1988). When interdependence continues over an extended period, it can also lead to the formation of significant-other representations (Higgins 1989b; Holmes 2002; see also Andersen, Reznik, and Chen 1997; Andersen and Chen 2002). Indeed, when such representations are formed outside kin networks, outside one's ethnicity, religion, or nation, the positive expectations accruing to these individuals should become transferable to others (especially within that group) as a result of the social-cognitive process of transference and the relational self (Andersen, Reznik, and Chen 1997; Andersen and Chen 2002). This could possibly break down barriers all the more between groups, although this remains speculative (see relevant work by Dovidio, Gaertner, and Validzic 1998; Wright et al. 1997). It is also an important prediction of the integrative framework and warrants research.

In short, relationships matter in social identification, defined in terms of voluntary cooperation beyond barriers of difference. More speculatively, relationships may also matter in community building and in the implementation of social policy. Humane, respectful interactions are the "glue" that allows societies to function effectively when they must rely on voluntary cooperation, that is, when they are not totalitarian or fascist in nature. Facilitating these kinds of interactions among a population, not to mention among authorities such as government officials, bosses, or teachers, is no small matter, of course, since humane interactions cannot fully be legislated, mandated, or enforced, but rather must ultimately be internalized and performed voluntarily in light of intrinsic motives and needs (Deci and Ryan 1985). Nonetheless, our work, combined with what is known in the wide literature on conflict resolution (for example, Pruitt and Carnevale 1993; Ury 1991), suggests some simple actions that one might, as an authority figure or as a peer, take to draw on what is humane in the other. One can always . . .

. . . listen

. . . treat other people fairly and with dignity

. . . convey mutual respect

. . . express warmth, kindness, and relatedness

. . . have a bidirectional dialogue rather than a unidirectional monologue

. . . allow role structures to become more permeable

. . . foster the development of shared purpose based on common human experience

. . . allow common ground to be revealed

If you can contact a person as a human being, getting beneath whatever personal defenses may be there, and engage with him or her humanely, it will matter in whether or not the person is likely to cooperate with your purposes and sees them as shared purposes. Of course, having some preexisting knowledge of shared purpose and common ground is a way of describing people who have a social identity—membership in a group and investment in it—and we know that social identification facilitates voluntary cooperation. Furthermore, to the degree that there is a capacity to interact in an organization, community, or institution as human beings rather than merely on the basis of roles or functions, common ground has a chance to arise and the power of human connection has a chance to do its work in easing tensions, reducing perceptions of bias, and promoting feelings of inclusion, participation, and mutual commitment to finding solutions.

NOTES

1. Two other if-then models described in this volume are the model of contingencies of self-worth, focusing on the domains or contexts most threatening to self-worth (that is, involving most vulnerability), and the model of rejection sensitivity, highlighted in this chapter, focusing on contextual cues that signal the possibility of rejection to people who are rejection-sensitive.
2. It may also be possible, of course, to activate a significant-other representation by activating the generic concept linked to this representation (a father by activating an authority role, a mother by activating her ethnicity and so on). But such generic concepts also may not be linked uniquely enough with any specific significant other to uniquely trigger that significant-other representation (to the exclusion of others). Nonetheless, the link should be stored together in memory.
3. Of course, projection of one's own qualities onto another is classically projection in psychodynamic theories, whereas transference relies on the classical mechanism of displacement—feelings toward one person applied to another.
4. Although a former professor is not necessarily a significant other in terms of intimacy or mutuality, a professor can become a kind of significant other if important enough that he or she influences the student's interests, experiences, life decisions, or life course. Even a public figure, a film star, or a religious leader that one has not met may presumably become someone in whom one is emotionally invested, and who is thus significant, with comparable cognitive and affective consequences in transference and the relational self.
5. Of course, it may be questionable to assume "bowling alone" reflects social disengagement in America, especially in the post-9/11 context, which brought many together in common cause, at least for a period of time. Beyond 9/11, modernity and mobility can indeed enable social dislocations, and yet it also enables different kinds of interpersonal and social connections that are relatively nontraditional, such as by means of website postings and internet chat room groups (for example, Bargh, McKenna, and Fitzsimons 2002), or spontaneous groupings of strangers arranged by instant messaging—for a specific purpose or no purpose at all. There has also been a considerable increase in organized community service activity that belies the "bowling alone" metaphor, not to mention poetry jams and other kinds of gatherings. The point is that these may have little resemblance to traditional affiliations like the Lions club, Little League baseball, or bowling leagues of yore.

REFERENCES

Andersen, Susan M. 1995. "On Lashing Out in Rage: Thoughts on the Anger-Aggression Syndrome." *Contemporary Psychology* 40(1): 43–44.

Andersen, Susan M., and Alana Baum. 1994. "Transference in Interpersonal Relations: Inferences and Affect Based on Significant-Other Representations." *Journal of Personality* 62(4): 460–97.

Andersen, Susan M., and Serena Chen. 2002. "The Relational Self: An Interpersonal Social-Cognitive Theory." *Psychological Review* 109(4): 619–45.

Andersen, Susan M., and Steve Cole. 1990. "'Do I Know You?': The Role of Significant Others in General Social Perception." *Journal of Personality and Social Psychology* 59(3): 384–99.

Andersen, Susan M., and Noah Glassman. 1996. "Responding to Significant Others When They Are Not There: Effects on Interpersonal Inference, Motivation, and Affect." In *Handbook of Motivation and Cognition,* edited by Richard Sorrentino and E. Tory Higgins. Volume 3. New York: Guilford Press.

Andersen, Susan M., Noah Glassman, Serena Chen, and Steve Cole. 1995. "Transference in Social Perception: The Role of Chronic Accessibility in Significant-Other Representations." *Journal of Personality and Social Psychology* 69: 41–57.

Andersen, Susan M., Inga Reznik, and Serena Chen. 1997. "Self in Relation to Others: Cognitive and Motivational Underpinnings." In *The Self Across Psychology: Self-Recognition, Self-Awareness, and the Self-Concept,* edited by Joan Gay Snodgrass and Robert Thompson. New York: New York Academy of Science.

Andersen, Susan M., Inga Reznik, and Noah Glassman. 2005. "The Unconscious Relational Self." In *The New Unconscious,* edited by Ran R. Hassin, James S. Uleman, and John Bargh. New York: Oxford University Press.

Andersen, Susan M., Inga Reznik, and Lenora Manzella. 1996. "Eliciting Transient Affect, Motivation, and Expectancies in Transference: Significant-Other Representations and the Self in Social Relations." *Journal of Personality and Social Psychology* 71(6): 1108–29.

Andersen, Susan M., and Shepherd Zeldin. 2003. "Relationships and Engagement: Program Implementation in the Penny Harvest Program." Unpublished manuscript. New York University.

Aron, Arthur, and Tracy McLaughlin-Volpe. 2001. "Including Others in the Self: Extensions to Own and Partner's group Membership." In *Individual Self, Relational Self, Collective Self,* edited by Constantine Sedikides and Marilynn Brewer. Philadelphia: Psychology Press/Taylor & Francis.

Ashmore, Richard, Kay Deaux, and Tracy McLaughlin-Volpe. 2004. "An Organizing Framework for Collective Identity: Articulation and Significance of Multidimensionality." *Psychological Bulletin* 130: 80–114.

Ayduk, Ozlem, Geraldine Downey, and Minji Kim. 2001. "Rejection Sensitivity and Depressive Symptoms in Women." *Personality and Social Psychology Bulletin* 27: 868–77.

Ayduk, Ozlem, Geraldine Downey, Alessandra Testa, Ying Yen, and Yuchi Shoda. 1999. "Does Rejection Elicit Hostility in Rejection Sensitive Women?" *Social Cognition* 17: 245–71.

Bargh, John A., Katelyn Y. A. McKenna, Grainne M. Fitzsimons. 2002. "Can You See the Real Me? Activation and Expression of the 'True Self' on the Internet." *Journal of Social Issues. Special Consequences of the Internet for Self and Society: Is Social Life Being Transformed?* 58(1): 33–48.

Baum, Alana, and Susan M. Andersen. 1999. "Interpersonal Roles in Transference: Transient Mood States Under the Condition of Significant-Other Activation." *Social Cognition* 17: 161–85.

Baumeister, Roy, and Mark Leary. 1995. "The Need to Belong: Desire for Interpersonal Attachments as a Fundamental Human Motivation." *Psychological Bulletin* 117: 497–29.

Berenson, Kathy, and Susan M. Andersen. 2004. "Childhood Physical and Emotional Abuse by a Parent: Transference-Based Manifestations in Adult Interpersonal Relations." Unpublished manuscript. New York University.

Berk, Michelle, and Susan M. Andersen. 2000. "The Impact of Past Relationships on Interpersonal Behavior: Behavioral Confirmation in the Social-Cognitive Process of Transference." *Journal of Personality and Social Psychology* 79(4): 546–62.

Blader, Steven, and Tom R. Tyler. 2002. "Justice and Empathy: What Motivates People to Help Others?" In *The Justice Motive in Everyday Life,* edited by Michael Ross and Dale T. Miller. New York: Cambridge University Press.

Blum, Robert, and Peggy Mann Rinehart. 1997. *Reducing the Risk: Connections That Make a Difference in the Lives of Youth.* Reprint. Handbook. Minneapolis: University of Minnesota, General Division of Pediatrics and Adolescent Health.

Brewer, Marilynn. 1988. "A Dual Process Model of Impression Formation." In *Advances in Social Cognition,* edited by Thomas Srull and Robert Wyer. Volume 1. Hillsdale, N.J.: Erlbaum.

Brewer, Marilynn, and Wendi Gardner. 1996. "Who Is This 'We'? Levels of Collective Identity and Self Representations." *Journal of Personality and Social Psychology* 71: 83–93.

Brewer, Marilynn, and Soma Roccas. 2001. "Individual Values, Social Identity, and Optimal Distinctiveness." In *Individual Self, Relational Self, Collective Self,* edited by Constantine Sedikides and Marilynn Brewer. Philadelphia: Psychology Press/Taylor & Francis.

Chen, Serena, and Susan M. Andersen. 1999. "Relationships from the Past in the Present: Significant-Other Representations and Transference in Interpersonal Life." In *Advances in Experimental Social Psychology,* edited by Mark Zanna. Volume 31. San Diego: Academic Press.

Chen, Serena, Susan M. Andersen, and Katrina Hinkley. 1999. "Triggering Transference: Examining the Role of Applicability and Use of Significant-Other Representations in Social Perception." *Social Cognition* 17: 332–65.

Chen, Serena, Grainne Fitzsimons, and Susan M. Andersen. Forthcoming. "Automaticity in Close Relationships." In *Automatic Processes in Social Thinking and Behavior,* edited by John A. Bargh. New York: Psychology Press.

Chen, Ya-Ru, Joel Brockner, and Tal Katz. 1998. "Toward an Explanation of Cultural Differences in In-Group Favoritism: The Role of Individual Versus Collective Primacy." *Journal of Personality and Social Psychology* 75: 1490–1502.

Cohen, Dov, and Richard Nisbett. 1994. "Self-Protection and the Culture of Honor: Explaining Southern Violence." *Personality and Social Psychology Bulletin* 20: 551–67.

Connell, James P., J. Lawrence Aber, and Gary Walker. 1995. "How Do Urban Communities Affect Youth? Social Science Research to Inform the Design and Evaluation of Comprehensive Community Initiatives." In *New Approaches to Evaluating Community Initiatives,* edited by James P. Connell, Anne Kubisch, Lisbeth B. Schorr, and Carol H. Weiss. Washington, D.C.: Aspen Institute.

Davis, Angelina, Tom R. Tyler, and Susan M. Andersen. 2003. "The Impact of Dyadic Relationships on Helping Behaviors." Unpublished manuscript. New York University.

Deci, Edward, and Richard Ryan. 1985. *Intrinsic Motivation and Self-Determination in Human Behavior.* New York: Plenum Press.

Dovidio, John F., Samuel L. Gaertner, and Ana Validzic. 1998. "Intergroup Bias: Status, Differentiation, and a Common In-Group Identity." *Journal of Personality and Social Psychology* 75(1): 109–20.

Downey, Geraldine, and Scott Feldman. 1996. "Implications of Rejection Sensitivity for Intimate Relationships." *Journal of Personality and Social Psychology* 70: 1327–43.

Downey, Geraldine, Antonio A. Freitas, Benjamin Michaelis, and Hala Khouri. 1998. "The Self-Fulfilling Prophecy in Close Relationships: Do Rejection Sensitive Women get Rejected by Their Partners?" *Journal of Personality and Social Psychology* 75: 545–60.

Downey, Geraldine, Hala Khouri, and Scott Feldman. 1997. "Early Interpersonal Trauma and Adult Adjustment: The Mediational Role of Rejection Sensitivity." In *The Effects of Trauma on the Developmental Process,* edited by Dante Cicchetti, Sheree Toth, and Jacob Burack. Rochester Symposium in Developmental Psychopathology, volume 8. Rochester, N.Y.: University of Rochester Press.

Downey, Geraldine, Amy Lebolt, Claudia Rincon, and Antonio Freitas. 1998. "Rejection Sensitivity and Adolescent Interpersonal Difficulties." *Child Development* 69: 1072–89.

Downey, Geraldine, Vivian Mougios, Ozlem Ayduk, Bonita London, and Yuchi Shoda. 2004. "Rejection Sensitivity and the Startle Response to Rejection Cues: A Defense Motivational System Approach." *Psychological Science* 15: 668–73.

Elliott, Delbert, William Julius Wilson, David Huizinga, Robert Sampson, Amanda Elliott, and Bruce Rankin. 1996. "The Effects of Neighborhood Disadvantage on Adolescent Delinquency." *Journal of Research in Crime and Delinquency* 33(4): 389–426.

Erber, Ralph, and Susan Fiske. 1984. "Outcome Dependency and Attention to Inconsistent Information." *Journal of Personality and Social Psychology* 47: 709–26.

Etzioni, Amitai. 1988. *The Moral Dimension: Toward a New Economics.* New York: Free Press.

———. 1993. *The Spirit of Community: Rights, Responsibility, and the Communitarian Agenda.* New York: Crown.

Fafchamps, Marcel, and Bart Minten. 1998. "Relationships and Traders in Madagascar." *Journal of Development Studies* 35: 1–35.

Feldman, Scott, and Geraldine Downey. 1994. "Rejection Sensitivity as a Mediator of the Impact of Childhood Exposure to Family Violence on Adult Attachment Behavior." *Development and Psychopathology* 6: 231–47.

Fiske, Alan. 1992. "The Four Elementary Forms of Sociality: Framework for a Unified Theory of Social Relations." *Psychological Review* 99: 689–723.

Fiske, Susan. 2000. "Interdependence and the Reduction of Prejudice." In *Reducing Prejudice and Discrimination,* edited by Stuart Oskamp. Mahwah, N.J.: Lawrence Erlbaum Associates.

Fiske, Susan, and Mark Pavelchak. 1986. "Category-Based Versus Piecemeal-Based Affective Responses: Developments in Schema-Triggered Affect." In *Handbook of Motivation and Cognition,* edited by Richard M. Sorrentino and E. Tory Higgins. New York: Guilford Press.

Fiske, Susan, Jun Xu, Amy Cuddy, and Peter Glick. 1999. "(Dis)respecting Versus (Dis)liking: Status and Interdependence Predict Ambivalent Stereotypes of Competence and Warmth." *Journal of Social Issues* 55: 473–89.

Foster, Andrew, and Mark Rosenzweig. 1995. "Learning by Doing and Learning from Others: Human Capital and Technical Change in Agriculture." *Journal of Political Economy* 103: 1176–1209.

Gaertner, Lowell, Constantine Sedikides, and Kenneth Graetz. 1999. "In Search of Self-Definition: Motivational Primacy of the Individual Self, Motivational Primacy of the Collective Self, or Other Contextual Primacy?" *Journal of Personality and Social Psychology* 76: 5–18.

Glassman, Noah, and Susan M. Andersen. 1999. "Activating Transference Without Consciousness: Using Significant-Other Representations to Go Beyond What Is Subliminally Given." *Journal of Personality and Social Psychology* 77(6): 1146–62.

Gottman, John. 1979. *Marital Interaction: Experimental Investigations.* New York: Academic Press.

Greenberg, Jeff, Tom Pyszczynski, Sheldon Solomon, and Daniel Chatel. 1992. "Terror Management and Tolerance: Does Mortality Salience Always Intensify Negative Reactions to Others Who Threaten One's World View?" *Journal of Personality and Social Psychology* 58: 308–19.

Hazan, Cindy, and Philip Shaver. 1994. "Attachment as an Organizational Framework for Research on Close Relationships." *Psychological Inquiry* 5: 1–22.

Higgins, E. Tory. 1989a. "Knowledge Accessibility and Activation: Subjectivity and Suffering from Unconscious Sources." In *Unintended Thought,* edited by James Uleman and John Bargh. New York: Guilford Press.

———. 1989b. "Continuities and Discontinuities in Self-Regulatory and Self-Evaluative Processes: A Developmental Theory Relating Self and Affect." *Journal of Personality* 57: 407–44.

Higgins, E. Tory, and Danielle May. 2001. "Individual Self-Regulatory Functions: It's Not 'We' Regulation, but It's Still Social." In *Individual Self, Relational Self, Collective Self,* edited by Constantine Sedikides and Marilynn Brewer. Philadelphia: Psychology Press/Taylor & Francis.

Hinkley, Katrina, and Susan M. Andersen. 1996. "The Working Self-Concept in Transference: Significant-Other Activation and Self-Change." *Journal of Personality and Social Psychology* 71(6): 1279–95.

Hogg, Michael, and Dominic Abrams. 1988. *Social Identifications: A Social Psychology of Intergroup Relations and Group Processes.* London: Routledge.

Holmes, John. 2002. "Interpersonal Expectations as the Building Blocks of Social Cognition: An Interdependence Theory Perspective." *Personal Relationships* 9: 1–26.

Horowitz, Ruth. 1983. *Honor and the American Dream: Culture and Identity in a Chicano Community.* New Brunswick, N.J.: Rutgers University Press.

House, James, Karl Landis, and Debra Umberson. 1988. "Social Relationships and Health." *Science* 241: 540–45.

Hoyle, Rich, and Anne Crawford. 1994. "Use of Individual-Level Data to Investigate Group Phenomena: Issues and Strategies." *Small Group Research* 25: 464–85.

Huo, Yuen J., Heather Smith, Tom R. Tyler, and E. Allen Lind. 1996. "Superordinate Identification, Subgroup Identification, and Justice Concerns: Is Separatism the Problem? Is Assimilation the Answer?" *Psychological Science* 7: 40–45.

Karylowski, Jerzy, Krzysztof Konarzewski, and Michael Motes. 2000. "Recruitment of Exemplars as Reference Points in Social Judgements." *Journal of Experimental Social Psychology* 36: 275–303.

Keck, Margaret, and Kathryn Sikkink. 1998. *Activists Beyond Borders: Advocacy Networks in International Politics.* New York: Cornell University Press.

Kenrick, Douglas, Norman Li, and Jonathan Butner. 2003. "Dynamical Evolutionary Psychology: Individual Decision Rules and Emergent Social Norms." *Psychological Review* 110: 3–28.

Kitayama, Shinobu, Hazel Markus, Hisaya Matsumoto, and Vinai Norasakkunkit. 1997. "Individual and Collective Processes in the Construction of Self: Self-Enhancement in the United States and Self-Criticism in Japan." *Journal of Personality and Social Psychology* 72: 1245–67.

Larrick, Richard, Richard Nisbett, and James Morgan. 1993. "Who Uses the Cost-Benefit Rules of Choice? Implications for the Normative Status of Microeconomic Theory." In *Rules for Reasoning*, edited by Richard E. Nisbett. Hillsdale, N.J.: Erlbaum.

Lazarus, Richard. 1993. "Coping Theory and Research: Past, Present, and Future." *Psychosomatic Medicine* 55: 234–47.

Levy, Sheri, Ozlem Ayduk, and Geraldine Downey. 2001. "The Role of Rejection Sensitivity in People's Relationships with Significant Others and Valued Social Groups." In *Interpersonal Rejection*, edited by Mark Leary. London: Oxford University Press.

Lind, E. Allen, and Tyler, Tom R. 1988. *The Social Psychology of Procedural Justice*. New York: Plenum Press.

London, Bonita, Geraldine Downey, Cheryl Bonica, and Iris Paltin. 2005. "Causes and Consequences of Rejection Sensitivity in Adolescents." Unpublished manuscript.

London, Bonita, Geraldine Downey, Aneeta Rattan, and Diana Tyson. 2005. "Sensitivity to Gender-Based Rejection: Theory, Validation and Implications for Engagement." Unpublished manuscript. Columbia University, New York City.

Markman, Arthur B., and Dedre Gentner. 2005. "Nonintentional Similarity Processing." In *The New Unconscious*, edited by Ran R. Hassin, Jim S. Uleman, and John Bargh. Oxford, England: Oxford University Press.

Markus, Hazel, and Shinobu Kitayama. 1991. "Culture and the Self: Implications for Cognition, Emotion, and Motivation." *Psychological Review* 98: 224–53.

Mendoza-Denton, Rodolfo, Geraldine Downey, Valerie Purdie, Angelina Davis, and Janina Pietrzak. 2002. "Sensitivity to Status-Based Rejection: Implications for African American Students' College Experience." *Journal of Personality and Social Psychology* 83: 896–918.

Merton, Robert. 1948. "The Self-Fulfilling Prophecy." *Antioch Review* 8: 193–210.

Metcalfe, Janet, and Walter Mischel. 1999. "A Hot/Cool-System Analysis of Delay of Gratification: Dynamics of Willpower." *Psychological Review* 106: 3–19.

Miller, Dale. 1999. "The Norm of Self-Interest." *American Psychologist* 54: 1053–60.

Mills, Judson, and Margaret Clark. 1994. "Communal and Exchange Relationships: Controversies and Research." In *Theoretical Frameworks for Personal Relationships*, edited by Ralph Erber and Robin Gilmour. Hillsdale, N.J.: Erlbaum.

Mischel, Walter, and Yuchi Shoda. 1995. "A Cognitive-Affective System Theory of Personality: Reconceptualizing Situations, Dispositions, Dynamics, and Invariance in Personality Structure." *Psychological Review* 102: 246–68.

Murray, Sandra, and John Holmes. 1994. "Storytelling in Close Relationships: The Construction of Confidence." *Personality and Social Psychology Bulletin* 20: 650–63.

National Research Council. 1993. *Losing Generations: Adolescents in High-Risk Settings*. Washington, D.C.: National Academy Press.

Neuberg, Steven, and Susan Fiske. 1987. "Motivational Influences on Impression Formation: Outcome Dependency, Accuracy-Driven Attention, and Individuating Processes." *Journal of Personality and Social Psychology* 53: 431–44.

Nisbett, Richard. 1993. "Violence in U.S. Regional Culture." *American Psychologist* 48: 441–49.

Nisbett, Richard, Kaiping Peng, Incheol Choi, and Ara Norenzayan. 2001. "Culture and Systems of Thought: Holistic Versus Analytic Cognition." *Psychological Review* 108: 291–310.

Oyserman, Daphna, Heather Coon, and Markus Kemmelmeier. 2002. "Rethinking Individualism and Collectivism: Evaluation of Theoretical Assumptions and Meta-Analyses." *Psychological Bulletin* 128: 3–72.

Pettigrew, Thomas. 1998. "Intergroup Contact Theory." *Annual Review of Psychology* 49: 65–85.

———. 2003. "Peoples Under Threat: Americans, Arabs, and Israelis." *Peace and Conflict: Journal of Peace Psychology* 9: 69–90.

Pietrzak, Janina, Geraldine Downey, and Ozlem Ayduk. 2005. "Rejection Sensitivity as an Interpersonal Vulnerability." In *Interpersonal Cognition,* edited by Mark Baldwin. New York: Guilford Press.

Pietrzak, Janina, Rodolfo Mendoza-Denton, and Geraldine Downey. 2003. "The Effects of Expecting Rejection Based on Personal Versus Group Characteristics." Paper presented at the annual meeting of the Society for Personality and Social Psychology. Los Angeles (February).

Powell, Walter, Kenneth Koput, and Laurel Smith-Doerr. 1996. "Interorganizational Collaboration and the Locus of Innovation: Networks of Learning in Biotechnology." *Administrative Science Quarterly* 41: 116–45.

Prentice, Deborah A. 1990. "Familiarity and Differences in Self- and Other-Representations." *Journal of Personality and Social Psychology* 59: 369–83.

Pruitt, Dean G., and Peter Carnevale. 1993. *Negotiation in Social Conflict.* Pacific Grove, Calif.: Brooks/Cole.

Purdie, Valerie, and Geraldine Downey. 2000. "Rejection Sensitivity and Adolescent Girls' Vulnerability to Relationship Centered Difficulties." *Child Maltreatment* 5: 338–49.

Putnam, Robert D. 1995. "Bowling Alone: America's Declining Social Capital." *Journal of Democracy* 6(January 1): 65–78.

———. 2000. *Bowling Alone: The Collapse and Revival of American Community.* New York: Simon & Schuster.

Reid, Anne, and Kay Deaux. 1996. "Relationship Between Social and Personal Identities: Segregation or Integration?" *Journal of Personality and Social Psychology* 71: 1084–91.

Reis, Harry, and Brian C. Patrick. 1996. "Attachment and Intimacy: Component Processes." In *Social Psychology: Handbook of Basic Principles,* edited by Arie Kruglanski and E. Tory Higgins. New York: Guilford Press.

Resnick, Michael, Peter Bearman, Robert W. Blum,, Karl E. Bauman,, Kathleen M. Harris, Jo Jones, Joyce Tabor, Trish Beuhring, Renee E. Sieving, Marcia Shew, Marjorie Ireland, Linda H. Bearinger, and J. Richard Udry. 1997. "Protecting Adolescents from Harm: Findings from the National Longitudinal Study on Adolescent Health." *Journal of the American Medical Association* 278(10): 823–32.

Reznik, Inga, and Susan M. Andersen. 2002. "Self-Discrepancy Theory and Significant-Other Representations: Eliciting Specific Negative Affects by Triggering Everyday Transference." Unpublished manuscript. New York University.

Romero-Canyas, Rainer, and Geraldine Downey. Forthcoming. "Rejection Sensitivity as a Predictor of Affective and Behavioral Responses to Interpersonal Stress: A Defensive Motivational System." In *The Social Outcast: Ostracism, Social Exclusion, and Bullying,* edited by Kip Williams, Joseph P. Forgas, and William Von Hippel. New York: Psychology Press.

Rouhana, Nadim, and Susan Fiske. 1995. "Perception of Power, Threat, and Conflict Intensity in Asymmetric Intergroup Conflict: Arab and Jewish Citizens of Israel." *Journal of Conflict Resolution* 39: 49–81.

Rusbult, Caryl E., and Paul A. M. Van Lange. 1996. "Interdependence Processes." In *Handbook of Social Psychology: Basic Principles,* edited by E. Tory Higgins and Arie W. Kruglanski. New York: Guilford Press.

Sampson, Robert J., Stephen Raudenbush, and Felton Earls. 1997. "Neighborhoods and Violent Crime: A Multi-Level Study of Collective Efficacy." *Science* 277: 918–24.

Sarbin, Theodore, and Vernon Allen. 1968. "Role Theory." In *The Handbook of Social Psychology,* edited by Gardner Lindzey and Elliot Aronson. Volume 1. Reading, Mass.: Addison-Wesley.

Sears, David, and Carolyn Funk. 1991. "The Role of Self-Interest in Social and Political Attitudes." In *Advances in Experimental Social Psychology,* edited by Mark P. Zanna. Volume 24. New York: Academic Press.

Sedikides, Constantine, and Marilynn Brewer. 2001. *Individual Self, Relational Self, Collective Self.* Philadelphia: Psychology Press/Taylor & Francis.

Sedikides, Constantine, Nils Olsen, and Harry Reis. 1993. "Relationships as Natural Categories." *Journal of Personality and Social Psychology* 64: 71–82.

Sellers, Robert, and J. Nicole Shelton. 2003. "The Role of Racial Identity in Perceived Racial Discrimination." *Journal of Personality and Social Psychology* 84: 1079–92.

Shah, James. 2003a. "Automatic for the People: How Representations of Significant Others Implicitly Affect Goal Pursuit." *Journal of Personality and Social Psychology* 84: 661–81.

———. 2003b. "The Motivational Looking Glass: How Significant Others Implicitly Affect Goal Appraisals." *Journal of Personality and Social Psychology* 85: 424–39.

Simon, Bernd, Giuseppe Pantaleo, and Amelie Mummendey. 1995. "Unique Individual or Interchangeable Group Member? The Accentuation of Intragroup Differences Versus Similarities as an Indicator of the Individual Self Versus the Collective Self." *Journal of Personality and Social Psychology* 69: 106–19.

Smith, Eliot R., Susan Coats, and Julie Murphy. 2001. "The Self and Attachment to Relationship Partners and to Groups: Theoretical Parallels and New Insights." In *Individual Self, Relational Self, Collective Self,* edited by Constantine Sedikides and Marilynn Brewer. Philadelphia: Psychology Press/Taylor & Francis.

Smith, Eliot R., and Susan Henry. 1996. "An In-Group Becomes Part of the Self: Response Time Evidence." *Personality and Social Psychology Bulletin* 22: 635–42.

Smith, Eliot R., and Michael A. Zàrate. 1992. "Exemplar-Based Model of Social Judgment." *Psychological Review* 99: 3–21.

Smith, Heather, Tom R. Tyler, Yuen J. Huo, Daniel J. Ortiz, and E. Allen Lind. 1998. "The Self-Relevant Implications of the Group-Value Model: Group Membership, Self-Worth, and Procedural Justice." *Journal of Experimental Social Psychology* 34: 470–93.

Steele, Claude. 1997. "A Threat in the Air: How Stereotypes Shape Intellectual Identity and Performance." *American Psychologist* 52: 613–29.

Stryker, Sheldon. 1987. "Identity Theory: Developments and Extensions." In *Self and Identity: Psychosocial Perspectives,* edited by Krysia Yardley, K. M. Yardley, and Terry Honess. Chichester, England: Wiley.

Stryker, Sheldon, and Richard T. Serpe. 1982. "Commitment, Identity Salience, and Role Behavior." In *Personality, Roles, and Social Behavior,* edited by William Ickes and Eric S. Knowles. New York: Springer Verlag.

Tajfel, Henri, and John C. Turner. 1979. "An Integrative Theory of Intergroup Conflict." In *The Social Psychology of Intergroup Relations,* edited by William Austin and Stephen Worchel. Monterey, Calif.: Brooks/Cole.

Thompson, Ross A. 1998. "Early Sociopersonality Development." In *Handbook of Child Psychology.* Volume 3, *Social, Emotional, and Personality Development,* edited by William Damon and Nancy Eisenberg. 5th edition. New York: Wiley.

Trafimow, David, Ellen Silverman, Ruth Mei-Tai Fan, and Josephine Shui Fun Law. 1997. "The effects of Language and Priming on the Relative Accessibility of the Private Self and the Collective Self." *Journal of Cross-Cultural Psychology* 28: 107–23.

Triandis, Harry C. 1989. "The Self and Social Behavior in Differing Cultural Contexts." *Psychological Review* 96: 506–20.

Tyler, Tom R. 1990a. *Why People Obey the Law: Procedural Justice, Legitimacy, and Compliance.* New Haven: Yale University Press.

———. 1990b. "Justice, Self-Interest, and the Legitimacy of Legal and Political Authority." In *Beyond Self-Interest,* edited by Jane J. Mansbridge. Chicago: University of Chicago Press.

———. 1999. "Why Do People Help Organizations? Social Identity and Pro-Organizational Behavior." In *Research on Organizational Behavior,* edited by Robert Sutton and Barry Staw. Volume 21. Greenwich, Conn.: JAI Press.

———. 2001. "Why Do People Rely on Others? Social Identity and Social Aspects of Trust." In *Trust in Society: Russell Sage Foundation Series on Trust,* edited by Karen S. Cook. Volume 2. New York: Russell Sage Foundation.

Tyler, Tom R., and Steven Blader. 2000. *Cooperation in Groups: Procedural Justice, Social Identity, and Behavioral Engagement.* Philadelphia: Psychology Press.

———. 2003. "Procedural Justice, Social Identity, and Cooperative Behavior." *Personality and Social Psychology Review* 7: 349–61.

Tyler, Tom R., Robert Boeckmann, Heather Smith, and Yuen J. Huo. 1997. *Social Justice in a Diverse Society.* Denver: Westview Press.

Tyler, Tom R., and Peter Degoey. 1995. "Collective Restraint in a Social Dilemma Situation: The Influence of Procedural Justice and Community Identification on the Empowerment and Legitimacy of Authority." *Journal of Personality and Social Psychology* 69: 482–97.

Tyler, Tom R., Peter Degoey, and Heather Smith. 1996. "Understanding Why the Justice of Group Procedures Matters: A Test of the Psychological Dynamics of the Group-Value Model." *Journal of Personality and Social Psychology* 70: 913–30.

Tyler, Tom R., and Yuen J. Huo. 2002. *Trust in the Law: Encouraging Public Cooperation with the Police and Courts.* New York: Russell Sage Foundation.

Tyler, Tom R., and E. Allen Lind. 1988. *The Social Psychology of Procedural Justice.* New York: Plenum Press.

———. 1992. "A Relational Model of Authority in Groups." *Advances in Experimental Social Psychology* 25: 115–91.

Tyler, Tom R., E. Allen Lind, Ken-Ichi Ohbuchi, Ikuo Sugawara, and Yuen J. Huo. 1998. "Conflict with Outsiders: Disputing Within and Across Cultural Boundaries." *Personality and Social Psychology Bulletin* 24: 137–46.

Tyler, Tom R., and Heather Smith. 1997. "Social Justice and Social Movements." In *Handbook of Social Psychology,* edited by Daniel Gilbert, Susan Fiske, and Gardner Lindzey. 4th edition. New York: McGraw-Hill.

———. 1999. "Sources of the Social Self." In *The Psychology of the Social Self,* edited by Tom R. Tyler, Roderick Kramer, and Oliver John. Hillsdale, N.J.: Erlbaum.

Ury, William. 1991. *Getting to Yes: Negotiating Agreement Without Giving In.* 2nd edition. New York: Penguin.

Watts, Duncan J. 1999. *Small Worlds: The Dynamics of Networks Between Order and Randomness.* Princeton: Princeton University Press.

———. 2002. *Six Degrees: The Science of a Connected Age.* New York: Norton.

Watts, Duncan J., Peter S. Dodds and M. E. J. Newman. 2002. "Identity and Search in Social Networks." *Science* 296: 1302–5.

Wilson, William Julius. 1991. "Studying Inner-City Dislocations: The Challenges of Public Agenda Research." *American Sociological Review* 45: 1–14.

Wright, Robert. 2000. *Non Zero: The Logic of Human Destiny.* New York: Pantheon Books.

Wright, Stephen C., Arthur Aron, Tracy McLaughlin-Volpe, Stacy A. Ropp. 1997. "The Extended Contact Effect: Knowledge of Cross-Group Friendships and Prejudice." *Journal of Personality and Social Psychology* 73(1): 73–90.

INDEX

Boldface numbers refer to figures or tables.